MGA Owners Workshop Manual

by J H Haynes
Member of the Guild of Motoring Writers
and Ian Coomber

Models covered:
MGA 1500, 1600, 1600 Mk II and Twin Cam in Tourer, Two-Seater and Coupe form with 1489 cc (90.88 cu in) ohv, 1588 cc (96.9 cu in) ohv, 1622 cc (99.5 cu in) ohv and 1588 cc (96.9 cu in) dohc engines

ISBN 978 0 85733 645 3

© J H Haynes & Co. Ltd. 1980, 1989

All rights reserved. No part of this book may be reproduced or transmitted in any form or by any means, electronic or mechanical, including photocopying, recording or by any information storage or retrieval system, without permission in writing from the copyright holder.

Printed in Malaysia   (475-9N1)

ABCDE
FGHIJ

2

J H Haynes & Co. Ltd.
Sparkford, Nr. Yeovil
Somerset BA22 7JJ England

Haynes North America, Inc
859 Lawrence Drive
Newbury Park
California 91320 USA

Printed using NORBRITE BOOK 48.8gsm (CODE: 40N6533) from NORPAC; procurement system certified under Sustainable Forestry Initiative standard. Paper produced is certified to the SFI Certified Fiber Sourcing Standard (CERT - 0094271)

Acknowledgements

Thanks are due to MG Cars, Austin Morris Limited and the MG Owners Club for the provision of technical information, to Castrol Limited who supplied lubrication data and to the Champion Sparking Plug Company who supplied the illustrations showing the various spark plug conditions. The bodywork repair photographs used in this manual were provided by Holt Lloyd Ltd who supply 'Turtle Wax', 'Dupli-Color Holts' and other Holts range products.

Thanks are also due to Mr Tony Breakspear from Oakhill, Shepton Mallet, Somerset for the loan of his MGA Twin Cam for photographic work. The Section in Chapter 10 dealing with the suppression of electrical interference was originated by Mr I.P. Davey, and was first published in *Motor* magazine.

Lastly thanks are due to all those people at Sparkford who helped in the production of this manual. Particularly Alan Jackson and Tony Stedman who carried out the mechanical work and took the photographs respectively, Annette Cutler who planned the layout of each page and David Neilson who edited the text.

About this manual

Its aims

The aim of this manual is to help you get the best value from your car. It can do so in several ways. It can help you decide what work must be done (even should you choose to get it done by a garage), provide information on routine maintenance and servicing, and give a logical course of action and diagnosis when random faults occur. However, it is hoped that you will use the manual by tackling the work yourself. On simpler jobs it may even be quicker than booking the car into a garage, and going there twice to leave and collect it. Perhaps most important, a lot of money can be saved by avoiding the costs the garage must charge to cover its labour and overheads.

The manual has drawings and descriptions to show the function of the various components so that their layout can be understood. Then the tasks are described and photographed in a step-by-step sequence so that even a novice can do the work.

Its arrangement

The manual is divided into twelve Chapters, each covering a logical sub-division of the vehicle. The Chapters are divided into Sections, numbered with single figures, eg 5; and the Sections into paragraphs (or sub sections), with decimal numbers following on from the Section they are in, eg 5.1, 5.2, 5.3 etc.

It is freely illustrated, especially in those parts where there is a detailed sequence of operations to be carried out. There are two forms of illustration: figures and photographs. The figures are numbered in sequence with decimal numbers, according to their position in the Chapter: eg Fig. 6.4 is the 4th drawing/illustration in Chapter 6. Photographs are numbered (either individually or in related groups) the same as the Section or sub-section of the text where the operation they show is described.

There is an alphabetical index at the back of the manual as well as a contents list at the front.

References to the 'left' or 'right' of the vehicle are in the sense of a person in the driver's seat facing forwards.

Unless otherwise stated, nuts and bolts are removed by turning anti-clockwise, and tightened by turning clockwise.

Whilst every care is taken to ensure that the information in this manual is correct no liability can be accepted by the authors or publishers for loss, damage or injury caused by any errors in, or omissions from, the information given.

Introduction to the MGA

First introduced in September 1955, the MGA was a new concept by the designers at Abingdon and was a distinct break from the traditional lines of its predecessors. Powered by the 1489 cc (90.8 cu in) 'B' Series Leyland engine, the MGA had smooth flowing lines, was well balanced in appearance and was generally attractive and distinctive.

Whilst the body was new, the basic mechanics of the car were similar to the then current MG Magnette Saloon. Initially just the two seater roadster model was available but after a year a fixed-head Coupe was introduced. As a compromise for somebody who wouldn't make their mind up which model to have, a works fibreglass hardtop became available for the roadster.

July 1958 saw the introduction of the Twin Cam MGA. The engine was of 1588 cc (96.9 cu in), had a crossflow design cylinder head with twin overhead camshafts. It was no mean performer giving 108 BHP at 6700 rpm and consequently the bottom end of the power unit had to be strengthened to take the extra stress.

The other main feature of the Twin Cam model was that it was equipped with Dunlop disc brakes all round to deal with the extra performance. The original MGA 1500 was fitted with Lockheed drum brakes all round but in 1960 this model was replaced by the 1588 cc (96.9 cu in) engine model and this was fitted with Lockheed disc brakes to the front wheels and drum brakes at the rear. The Twin Cam model finished production in 1960 and was the last ohc MG engine to be produced.

The MGA 1600 Mk II was introduced in 1961 and was fitted with a 1622 cc (99.5 cu in) engine. The model continued in this form until the end of production in September 1962 when the MGB made its appearance.

Over 100 000 MGAs were produced making it one of the most successful sports cars ever produced and many fine examples are still in daily use proving its reliability and timeless appeal.

Contents

	Page
Acknowledgements	2
About this manual	2
Introduction to the MGA	2
General dimensions	5
Use of English	6
Buying spare parts and vehicle identification numbers	7
Tools and working facilities	8
Jacking	10
Lubrication chart	11
Safety first!	13
Routine maintenance	14
Chapter 1 Engine	18
Chapter 2 Cooling system	60
Chapter 3 Fuel and exhaust systems	69
Chapter 4 Ignition system	81
Chapter 5 Clutch	89
Chapter 6 Gearbox	95
Chapter 7 Propeller shaft	106
Chapter 8 Rear axle	110
Chapter 9 Braking system	117
Chapter 10 Electrical system	134
Chapter 11 Suspension and steering	160
Chapter 12 Bodywork and fittings	173
General repair procedures	184
Conversion factors	185
Index	186

The MGA 1500 used as the project car for this manual

The MGA 1600 Coupe

General dimensions, weights and capacities

Dimensions
Overall length . . . . 156.0 in (3962 mm)
Overall width . . . . 58.0 in (1473 mm)
Overall height . . . . 50.0 in (1270 mm)
Wheelbase . . . . 94.0 in (2388 mm)
Ground clearance . . . . 6.0 in (152.4 mm)

Weights
Kerb weight
   1500 . . . . 1988 lb (901.81 kg)
   1600 . . . . 2016 lb (914 kg)
   Twin Cam . . . . 2185 lb (991 kg)

Capacities
Engine (oil capacity)
   1500 and 1600 . . . . 8 Imp pt (9.6 US pt, 4.56 litres)
   Twin Cam . . . . 13 Imp pt (15.6 US pt, 7.38 litres)
Gearbox (oil capacity)
   1500 and 1600 . . . . 4.5 Imp pt (5.4 US pt, 2.56 litres)
   Twin Cam . . . . 4.75 Imp pt (5.7 US pt, 2.69 litres)
Rear axle (oil capacity)
   1500 and 1600 . . . . 2.25 Imp pt (2.7 US pt, 1.28 litres)
   Twin Cam . . . . 2.75 Imp pt (3.25 US pt, 1.56 litres)
Cooling system (coolant capacity)
   1500 and 1600 . . . . 10.0 Imp pt (12.0 US pt, 5.67 litres)
   Twin Cam . . . . 13.5 Imp pt (16.2 US pt, 7.7 litres)
Fuel tank (capacity) . . . . 10 Imp gals (12 US gals, 45.4 litres)

Use of English

As this book has been written in England, it uses the appropriate English component names, phrases, and spelling. Some of these differ from those used in America. Normally, these cause no difficulty, but to make sure, a glossary is printed below. In ordering spare parts remember the parts list may use some of these words:

English	American	English	American
Accelerator	Gas pedal	Locks	Latches
Aerial	Antenna	Methylated spirit	Denatured alcohol
Anti-roll bar	Stabiliser or sway bar	Motorway	Freeway, turnpike etc
Big-end bearing	Rod bearing	Number plate	License plate
Bonnet (engine cover)	Hood	Paraffin	Kerosene
Boot (luggage compartment)	Trunk	Petrol	Gasoline (gas)
Bulkhead	Firewall	Petrol tank	Gas tank
Bush	Bushing	'Pinking'	'Pinging'
Cam follower or tappet	Valve lifter or tappet	Prise (force apart)	Pry
Carburettor	Carburetor	Propeller shaft	Driveshaft
Catch	Latch	Quarterlight	Quarter window
Choke/venturi	Barrel	Retread	Recap
Circlip	Snap-ring	Reverse	Back-up
Clearance	Lash	Rocker cover	Valve cover
Crownwheel	Ring gear (of differential)	Saloon	Sedan
Damper	Shock absorber, shock	Seized	Frozen
Disc (brake)	Rotor/disk	Sidelight	Parking light
Distance piece	Spacer	Silencer	Muffler
Drop arm	Pitman arm	Sill panel (beneath doors)	Rocker panel
Drop head coupe	Convertible	Small end, little end	Piston pin or wrist pin
Dynamo	Generator (DC)	Spanner	Wrench
Earth (electrical)	Ground	Split cotter (for valve spring cap)	Lock (for valve spring retainer)
Engineer's blue	Prussian blue	Split pin	Cotter pin
Estate car	Station wagon	Steering arm	Spindle arm
Exhaust manifold	Header	Sump	Oil pan
Fault finding/diagnosis	Troubleshooting	Swarf	Metal chips or debris
Float chamber	Float bowl	Tab washer	Tang or lock
Free-play	Lash	Tappet	Valve lifter
Freewheel	Coast	Thrust bearing	Throw-out bearing
Gearbox	Transmission	Top gear	High
Gearchange	Shift	Torch	Flashlight
Grub screw	Setscrew, Allen screw	Trackrod (of steering)	Tie-rod (or connecting rod)
Gudgeon pin	Piston pin or wrist pin	Trailing shoe (of brake)	Secondary shoe
Halfshaft	Axleshaft	Transmission	Whole drive line
Handbrake	Parking brake	Tyre	Tire
Hood	Soft top	Van	Panel wagon/van
Hot spot	Heat riser	Vice	Vise
Indicator	Turn signal	Wheel nut	Lug nut
Interior light	Dome lamp	Windscreen	Windshield
Layshaft (of gearbox)	Countershaft	Wing/mudguard	Fender
Leading shoe (of brake)	Primary shoe		

Miscellaneous points

An 'oil seal' is fitted to components lubricated by grease!

A 'damper' is a 'shock absorber', it damps out bouncing, and absorbs shocks of bump impact. Both names are correct, and both are used haphazardly.

Note that British drum brakes are different from the Bendix type that is common in America, so different descriptive names result. The shoe end furthest from the hydraulic wheel cylinder is on a pivot; interconnection between the shoes as on Bendix brakes is most uncommon. Therefore the phrase 'Primary' or 'Secondary' shoe does not apply. A shoe is said to be 'Leading' or 'Trailing'. A 'Leading' shoe is one on which a point on the drum, as it rotates forward, reaches the shoe at the end worked by the hydraulic cylinder before the anchor end. The opposite is a 'Trailing' shoe, and this one has no self servo from the wrapping effect of the rotating drum.

Buying spare parts and vehicle identification numbers

Buying spare parts

Spare parts are available from many sources, for example: Leyland garages, other garages and accessory shops, and motor factors. Our advice regarding spare parts is as follows:

Officially appointed Leyland garages: This is the best source of parts which are peculiar to your car and are otherwise generally not available (eg complete cylinder heads, internal gearbox components, badges, interior trim etc). To be sure of obtaining the correct parts it will always be necessary to give the storeman your car's engine and chassis number, and if possible to take the old part along for positive identification. Remember that many parts are available on a factory exchange scheme – any parts returned should always be clean! It obviously makes good sense to go to the specialists on your car for this type of part as they are best equipped to supply you.

Other garages and accessory shops – These are often very good places to buy material and components needed for the maintenance of your car (eg oil filters, spark plugs, bulbs, fan belts, oils and grease, touch-up paint, filler paste etc). They also sell general accessories, usually have convenient opening hours, charge lower prices and can often be found not far from home.

Motor factors – Good factors will stock all of the more important components which wear out relatively quickly (eg clutch components, pistons, valves, exhaust systems, brake cylinders/pipes/hoses/seals/ shoes and pads etc). Motor factors will often provide new or reconditioned components on a part exchange basis – this can save a considerable amount of money.

MG Owners Club – The MG Owners Club may be able to supply parts which are no longer generally available (eg body panels, some engine parts, door seals etc) and may be able to give good advice as to the interchangeability of parts from other similar cars.

Vehicle identification numbers

The MGA had a relatively long production run and was produced in differing types and versions during this period. Several improvements and modifications were also made during its production and therefore it is essential to supply accurate information when buying spare parts for your particular model or you may end up with the wrong part. The following identification numbers should always be at hand when ordering spares:

The chassis number is located on a stamped identification plate attached to the engine bulkhead on the top left-hand side. Always quote the full number including the prefix.

The engine number on the ohv series engines is on a plate attached to the cylinder block on the right-hand side below the cylinder head joint face. On the Twin Cam engine the number is stamped on a plate which is located on the rear of the cylinder block on the ledge of the clutch housing flange joint.

The gearbox number is stamped into the gearbox housing top face next to the dipstick.

The rear axle number can be found stamped into the front face of the left-hand tube.

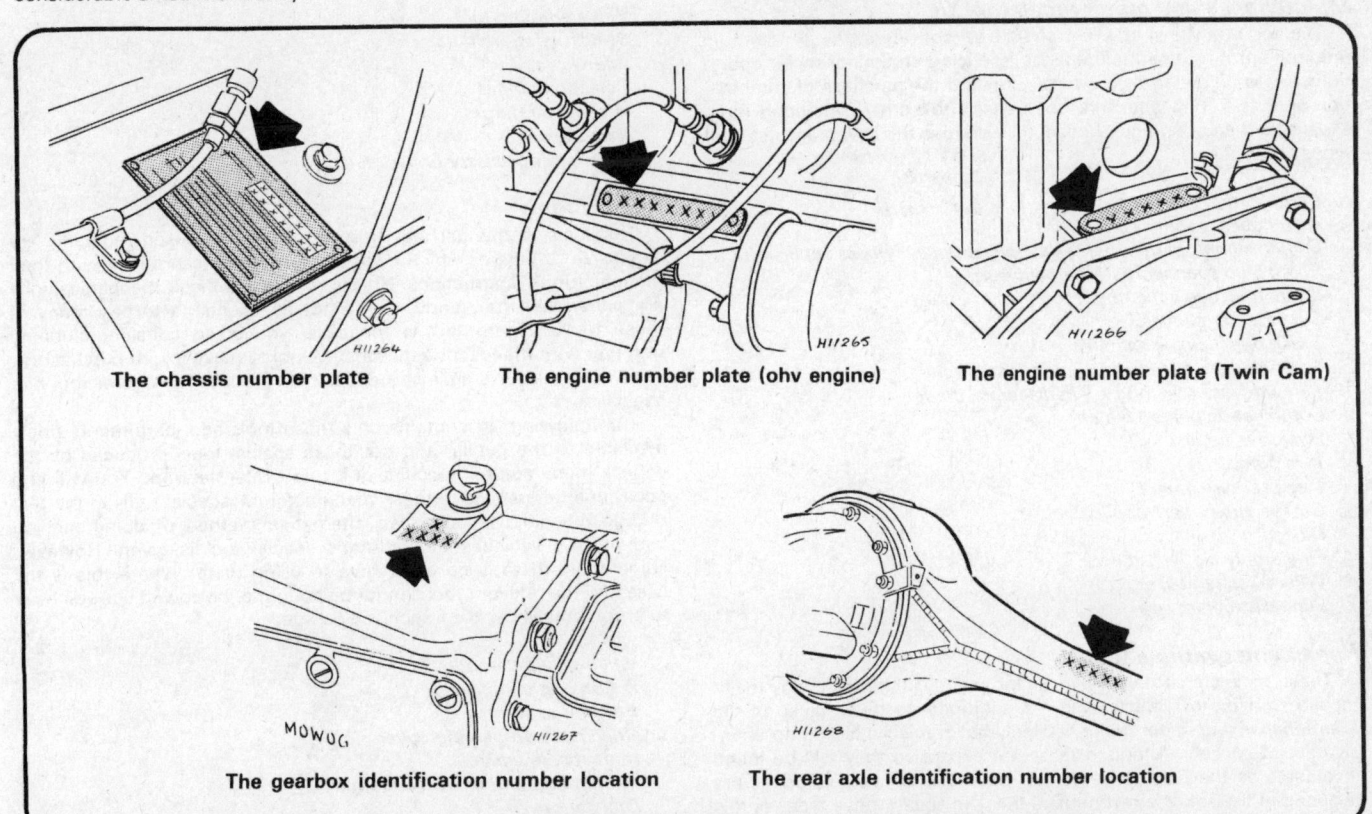

The chassis number plate

The engine number plate (ohv engine)

The engine number plate (Twin Cam)

The gearbox identification number location

The rear axle identification number location

Tools and working facilities

Introduction

A selection of good tools is a fundamental requirement for anyone contemplating the maintenance and repair of a motor vehicle. For the owner who does not possess any, their purchase will prove a considerable expense, offsetting some of the savings made by doing-it-yourself. However, provided that the tools purchased meet the relevant national safety standards and are of good quality, they will last for many years and prove an extremely worthwhile investment.

To help the average owner to decide which tools are needed to carry out the various tasks detailed in this manual, we have compiled three lists of tools under the following headings: *Maintenance and minor repair, Repair and overhaul,* and *Special.* The newcomer to practical mechanics should start off with the *Maintenance and minor repair* tool kit and confine himself to the simpler jobs around the vehicle. Then, as his confidence and experience grow, he can undertake more difficult tasks, buying extra tools as, and when, they are needed. In this way, a *Maintenance and minor repair* tool kit can be built-up into a *Repair and overhaul* tool kit over a considerable period of time without any major cash outlays. The experienced do-it-yourselfer will have a tool kit good enough for most repair and overhaul procedures and will add tools from the *Special* category when he feels the expense is justified by the amount of use to which these tools will be put.

It is obviously not possible to cover the subject of tools fully here. For those who wish to learn more about tools and their use there is a book entitled *How to Choose and Use Car Tools* available from the publishers of this manual.

Maintenance and minor repair tool kit

The tools given in this list should be considered as a minimum requirement if routine maintenance, servicing and minor repair operations are to be undertaken. We recommend the purchase of combination spanners (ring one end, open-ended the other); although more expensive than open-ended ones, they do give the advantages of both types of spanner.

Combination spanners - $\frac{1}{4}, \frac{5}{16}, \frac{3}{8}, \frac{7}{16}, \frac{1}{2}, \frac{9}{16}, \frac{5}{8},$ & $\frac{11}{16}$ AF
Adjustable spanner - 9 inch
Engine sump/gearbox/rear axle drain plug key (where applicable)
Spark plug spanner (with rubber insert)
Spark plug gap adjustment tool
Set of feeler gauges
Brake bleed nipple spanner
Screwdriver - 4 in long x $\frac{1}{4}$ in dia (flat blade)
Screwdriver - 4 in long x $\frac{1}{4}$ in dia (cross blade)
Combination pliers - 6 inch
Hacksaw, junior
Tyre pump
Tyre pressure gauge
Grease gun (where applicable)
Oil can
Fine emery cloth (1 sheet)
Wire brush (small)
Funnel (medium size)

Repair and overhaul tool kit

These tools are virtually essential for anyone undertaking any major repairs to a motor vehicle, and are additional to those given in the *Maintenance and minor repair* list. Included in this list is a comprehensive set of sockets. Although these are expensive they will be found invaluable as they are so versatile - particularly if various drives are included in the set. We recommend the $\frac{1}{2}$ in square-drive type, as this can be used with most proprietary torque wrenches. If you cannot afford a socket set, even bought piecemeal, then inexpensive tubular box spanners are a useful alternative.

The tools in this list will occasionally need to be supplemented by tools from the *Special* list.

Sockets (or box spanners) to cover range in previous list
Reversible ratchet drive (for use with sockets)
Extension piece, 10 inch (for use with sockets)
Universal joint (for use with sockets)
Torque wrench (for use with sockets)
'Mole' wrench - 8 inch
Ball pein hammer
Soft-faced hammer, plastic or rubber
Screwdriver - 6 in long x $\frac{5}{16}$ in dia (flat blade)
Screwdriver - 2 in long x $\frac{5}{16}$ in square (flat blade)
Screwdriver - 1$\frac{1}{2}$ in long x $\frac{1}{4}$ in dia (cross blade)
Screwdriver - 3 in long x $\frac{1}{8}$ in dia (electricians)
Pliers - electricians side cutters
Pliers - needle nosed
Pliers - circlip (internal and external)
Cold chisel - $\frac{1}{2}$ inch
Scriber (this can be made by grinding the end of a broken hacksaw blade)
Scraper (this can be made by flattening and sharpening one end of a piece of copper pipe)
Centre punch
Pin punch
Hacksaw
Valve grinding tool
Steel rule/straight edge
Allen keys
Selection of files
Wire brush (large)
Axle-stands
Jack (strong scissor or hydraulic type)

Special tools

The tools in this list are those which are not used regularly, are expensive to buy, or which need to be used in accordance with their manufacturers' instructions. Unless relatively difficult mechanical jobs are undertaken frequently, it will not be economic to buy many of these tools. Where this is the case, you could consider clubbing together with friends (or a motorists' club) to make a joint purchase, or borrowing the tools against a deposit from a local garage or tool hire specialist.

The following list contains only those tools and instruments freely available to the public, and not those special tools produced by the vehicle manufacturer specifically for its dealer network. You will find occasional references to these manufacturers' special tools in the text of this manual. Generally, an alternative method of doing the job without the vehicle manufacturer's special tool is given. However, sometimes, there is no alternative to using them. Where this is the case and the relevant tool cannot be bought or borrowed you will have to entrust the work to a franchised garage.

Valve spring compressor
Piston ring compressor
Balljoint separator
Universal hub/bearing puller
Impact screwdriver
Micrometer and/or vernier gauge
Dial gauge
Stroboscopic timing light

Tools and working facilities

Carburettor flow balancing device
Dwell angle meter/tachometer
Universal electrical multi-meter
Cylinder compression gauge
Lifting tackle (photo)
Trolley jack
Light with extension lead

Buying tools

For practically all tools, a tool factor is the best source since he will have a very comprehensive range compared with the average garage or accessory shop. Having said that, accessory shops often offer excellent quality tools at discount prices, so it pays to shop around.

There are plenty of good tools around at reasonable prices, but always aim to purchase items which meet the relevant national safety standards. If in doubt, ask the proprietor or manager of the shop for advice before making a purchase.

Care and maintenance of tools

Having purchased a reasonable tool kit, it is necessary to keep the tools in a clean serviceable condition. After use, always wipe off any dirt, grease and metal particles using a clean, dry cloth, before putting the tools away. Never leave them lying around after they have been used. A simple tool rack on the garage or workshop wall, for items such as screwdrivers and pliers is a good idea. Store all normal spanners and sockets in a metal box. Any measuring instruments, gauges, meters, etc, must be carefully stored where they cannot be damaged or become rusty.

Take a little care when tools are used. Hammer heads inevitably become marked and screwdrivers lose the keen edge on their blades from time to time. A little timely attention with emery cloth or a file will soon restore items like this to a good serviceable finish.

Working facilities

Not to be forgotten when discussing tools, is the workshop itself. If anything more than routine maintenance is to be carried out, some form of suitable working area becomes essential.

It is appreciated that many an owner mechanic is forced by circumstances to remove an engine or similar item, without the benefit of a garage or workshop. Having done this, any repairs should always be done under the cover of a roof.

Wherever possible, any dismantling should be done on a clean flat workbench or table at a suitable working height.

Any workbench needs a vice: one with a jaw opening of 4 in (100 mm) is suitable for most jobs. As mentioned previously, some clean dry storage space is also required for tools, as well as the lubricants, cleaning fluids, touch-up paints and so on which become necessary.

Another item which may be required, and which has a much more general usage, is an electric drill with a chuck capacity of at least $\frac{5}{16}$ in (8 mm). This, together with a good range of twist drills, is virtually essential for fitting accessories such as wing mirrors and reversing lights.

Last, but not least, always keep a supply of old newspapers and clean, lint-free rags available, and try to keep any working area as clean as possible.

Spanner jaw gap comparison table

Jaw gap (in)	Spanner size
0.250	$\frac{1}{4}$ in AF
0.276	7 mm
0.313	$\frac{5}{16}$ in AF
0.315	8 mm
0.344	$\frac{11}{32}$ in AF; $\frac{1}{8}$ in Whitworth
0.354	9 mm
0.375	$\frac{3}{8}$ in AF
0.394	10 mm
0.433	11 mm
0.438	$\frac{7}{16}$ in AF
0.445	$\frac{3}{16}$ in Whitworth; $\frac{1}{4}$ in BSF
0.472	12 mm
0.500	$\frac{1}{2}$ in AF
0.512	13 mm
0.525	$\frac{1}{4}$ in Whitworth; $\frac{5}{16}$ in BSF
0.551	14 mm
0.563	$\frac{9}{16}$ in AF
0.591	15 mm
0.600	$\frac{5}{16}$ in Whitworth; $\frac{3}{8}$ in BSF
0.625	$\frac{5}{8}$ in AF
0.630	16 mm
0.669	17 mm
0.686	$\frac{11}{16}$ in AF
0.709	18 mm
0.710	$\frac{3}{8}$ in Whitworth; $\frac{7}{16}$ in BSF
0.748	19 mm
0.750	$\frac{3}{4}$ in AF
0.813	$\frac{13}{16}$ in AF
0.820	$\frac{7}{16}$ in Whitworth; $\frac{1}{2}$ in BSF
0.866	22 mm
0.875	$\frac{7}{8}$ in AF
0.920	$\frac{1}{2}$ in Whitworth; $\frac{9}{16}$ in BSF
0.938	$\frac{15}{16}$ in AF
0.945	24 mm
1.000	1 in AF
1.010	$\frac{9}{16}$ in Whitworth; $\frac{5}{8}$ in BSF
1.024	26 mm
1.063	$1\frac{1}{16}$ in AF; 27 mm
1.100	$\frac{5}{8}$ in Whitworth; $\frac{11}{16}$ in BSF
1.125	$1\frac{1}{8}$ in AF
1.181	30 mm
1.200	$\frac{11}{16}$ in Whitworth; $\frac{3}{4}$ in BSF
1.250	$1\frac{1}{4}$ in AF
1.260	32 mm
1.300	$\frac{3}{4}$ in Whitworth; $\frac{7}{8}$ in BSF
1.313	$1\frac{5}{16}$ in AF
1.390	$\frac{13}{16}$ in Whitworth; $\frac{15}{16}$ in BSF
1.417	36 mm
1.438	$1\frac{7}{16}$ in AF
1.480	$\frac{7}{8}$ in Whitworth; 1 in BSF
1.500	$1\frac{1}{2}$ in AF
1.575	40 mm; $\frac{15}{16}$ in Whitworth
1.614	41 mm
1.625	$1\frac{5}{8}$ in AF
1.670	1 in Whitworth; $1\frac{1}{8}$ in BSF
1.688	$1\frac{11}{16}$ in AF
1.811	46 mm
1.813	$1\frac{13}{16}$ in AF
1.860	$1\frac{1}{8}$ in Whitworth; $1\frac{1}{4}$ in BSF
1.875	$1\frac{7}{8}$ in AF
1.969	50 mm
2.000	2 in AF
2.050	$1\frac{1}{4}$ in Whitworth; $1\frac{3}{8}$ in BSF
2.165	55 mm
2.362	60 mm

A Haltrac hoist and gantry in use during a typical engine removal sequence

Jacking

Use the jack supplied with the car when changing a roadwheel. Locate the jack pad in the depression between the front suspension spring seating and the lower link when jacking-up the front, or under the rear spring close to the rear axle when jacking-up the rear. Never position the jack beneath the chassis side members. As an added precaution always apply the handbrake and chock the wheels remaining on the ground. Before getting under the car, always supplement the jack with axle-stands.

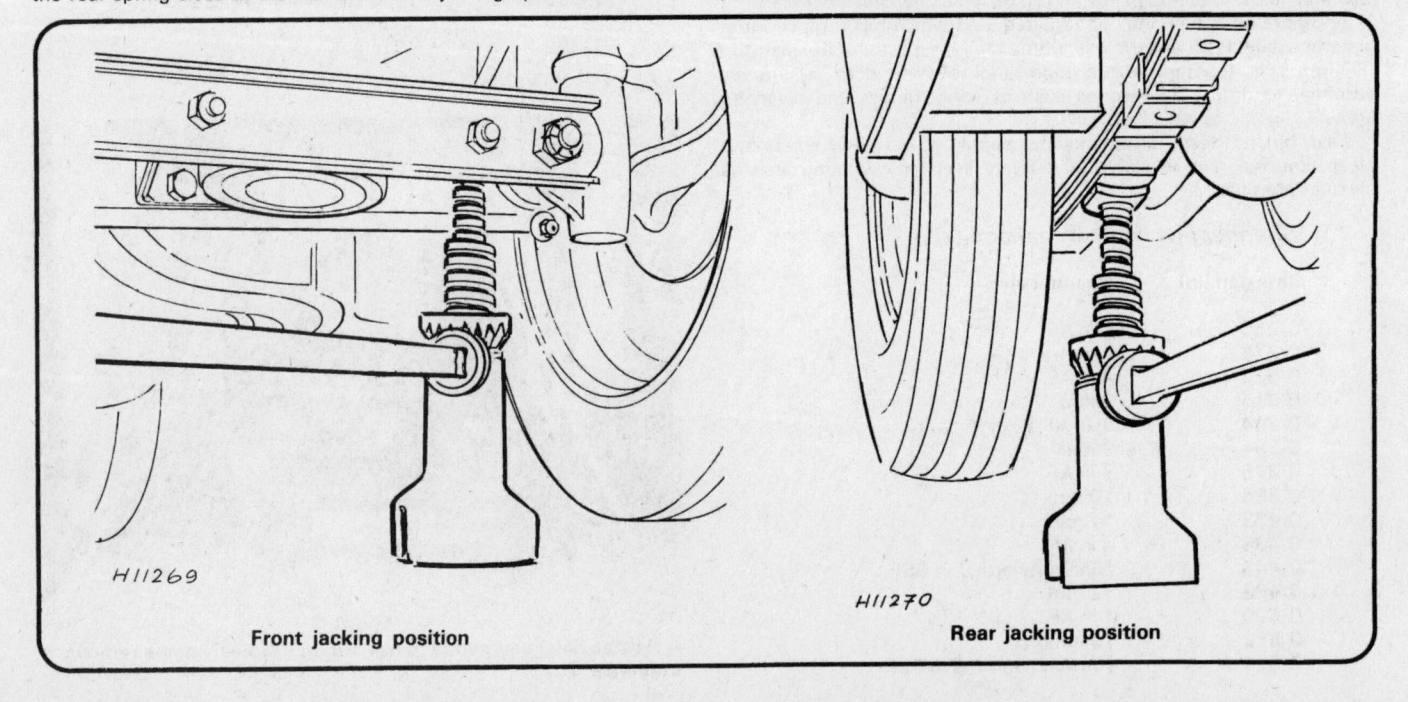

Front jacking position

Rear jacking position

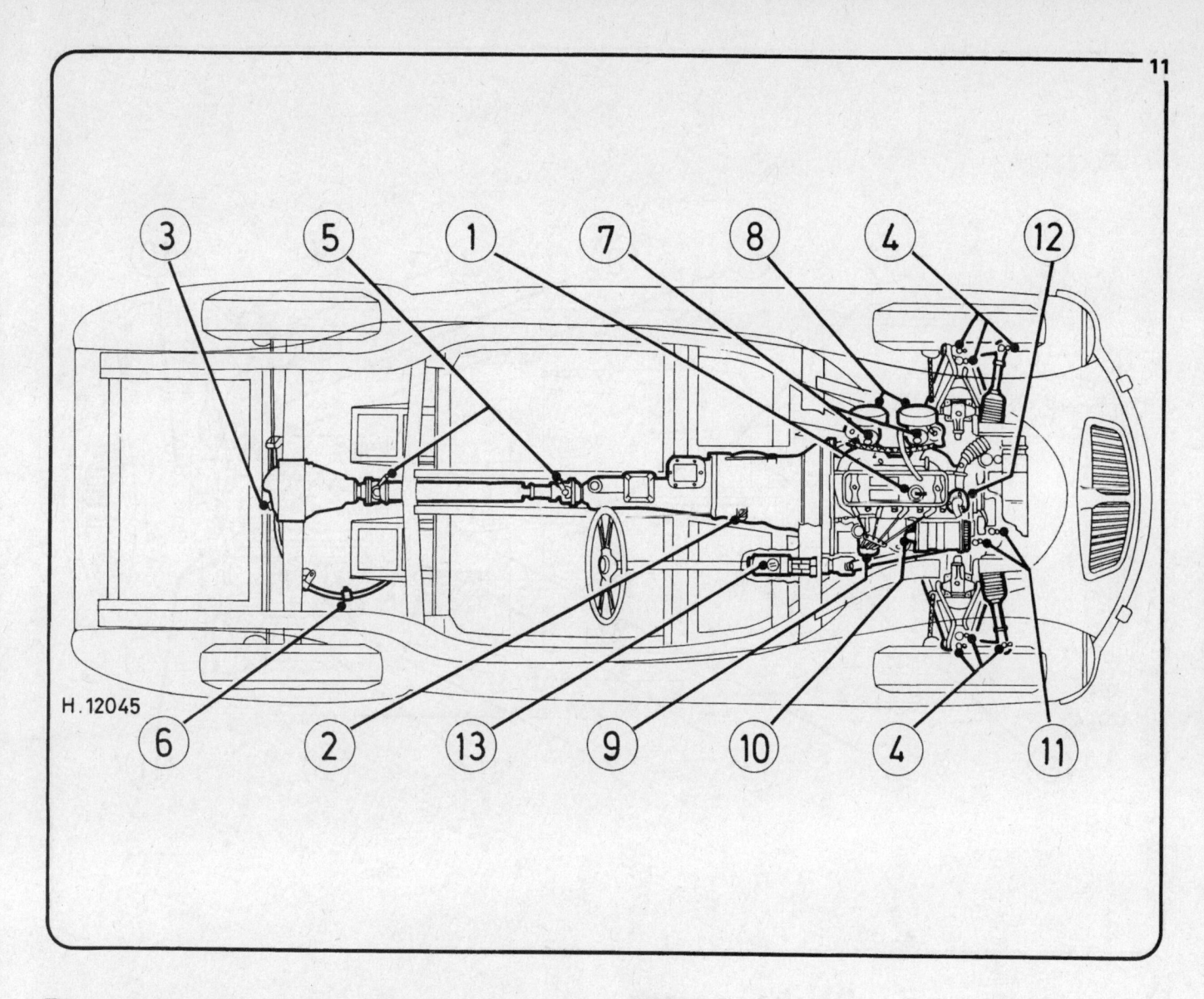

Recommended lubricants and fluids (MGA and MGA 1600)

Component or system	Lubricant type or specification
Engine (1) Gearbox (2) Air cleaner elements (8)	Castrol GTX (20W/50)
Rear axle (3) Steering gearbox (11)	Castrol Hypoy (SAE 90EP oil)
Steering joints (4) Propeller shaft (5) Handbrake (6)	Castrol LM grease (NGL1 No 2)
Carburettor dashpots (7) Distributor (9) Dynamo bearing (10)	Castrolite (10W/30)
Water pump (12)	Castrol D (SAE 140)
Brake and clutch fluid reservoir (13)	Castrol Girling Universal Brake and Clutch Fluid (SAE J1703c)

Note: *The above are general recommendationsss only. Lubrication requirements vary from territory to territory and depend on vehicle usage. If in doubt consult your nearest dealer or the operator's handbook supplied with the vehicle.*

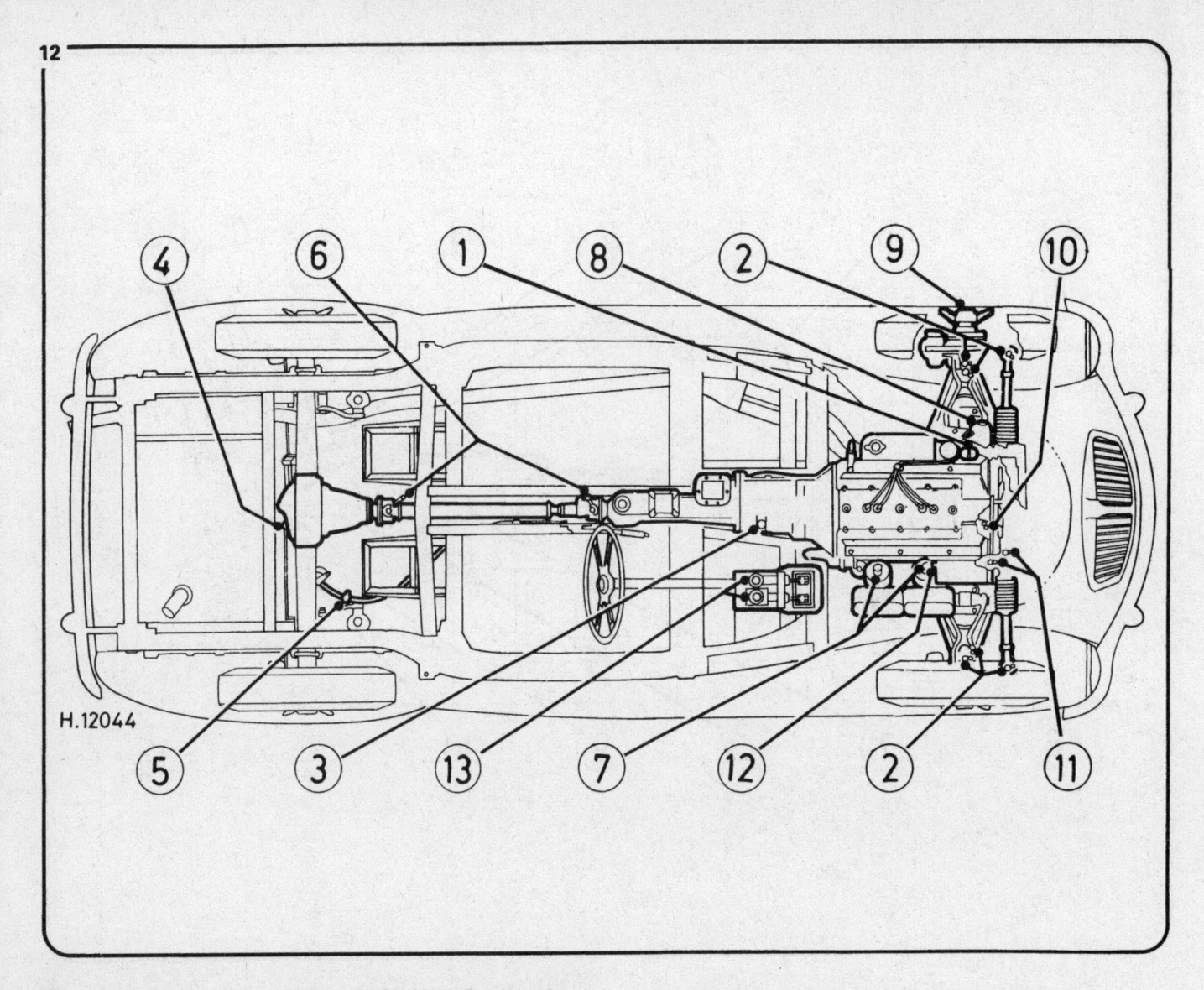

Recommended lubricants and fluids (MGA Twin Cam)

Component or system	Lubricant type or specification
Engine (1) **Gearbox (3)**	Castrol GTX (20W/50)
Rear axle (4) **Steering rack (11)**	Castrol Hypoy (SAE 90EP)
Steering joints (2) **Handbrake cable (5)** **Propeller shaft (6)** **Front hubs (9)**	Castrol LM grease (NGL1 No 2)
Carburettor dashpots (7) **Distributor (8)** **Dynamo (12)**	Castrolite (10W/30)
Water pump (10)	Castrol D (SAE 140)
Brake and clutch hydraulic reservoirs (13)	Castrol Girling Universal Brake and Clutch Fluid (SAE J1703c)

Note: *The above are general recommendations only. Lubrication requirements vary from territory to territory and depend on vehicle usage. If in doubt consult your nearest dealer or the operator's handbook supplied with the vehicle.*

Safety first!

Professional motor mechanics are trained in safe working procedures. However enthusiastic you may be about getting on with the job in hand, do take the time to ensure that your safety is not put at risk. A moment's lack of attention can result in an accident, as can failure to observe certain elementary precautions.

There will always be new ways of having accidents, and the following points do not pretend to be a comprehensive list of all dangers; they are intended rather to make you aware of the risks and to encourage a safety-conscious approach to all work you carry out on your vehicle.

Essential DOs and DON'Ts

DON'T rely on a single jack when working underneath the vehicle. Always use reliable additional means of support, such as axle stands, securely placed under a part of the vehicle that you know will not give way.

DON'T attempt to loosen or tighten high-torque nuts (e.g. wheel hub nuts) while the vehicle is on a jack; it may be pulled off.

DON'T start the engine without first ascertaining that the transmission is in neutral (or 'Park' where applicable) and the parking brake applied.

DON'T suddenly remove the filler cap from a hot cooling system – cover it with a cloth and release the pressure gradually first, or you may get scalded by escaping coolant.

DON'T attempt to drain oil until you are sure it has cooled sufficiently to avoid scalding you.

DON'T grasp any part of the engine, exhaust or catalytic converter without first ascertaining that it is sufficiently cool to avoid burning you.

DON'T allow brake fluid or antifreeze to contact vehicle paintwork.

DON'T syphon toxic liquids such as fuel, brake fluid or antifreeze by mouth, or allow them to remain on your skin.

DON'T inhale dust – it may be injurious to health (see *Asbestos* below).

DON'T allow any spilt oil or grease to remain on the floor – wipe it up straight away, before someone slips on it.

DON'T use ill-fitting spanners or other tools which may slip and cause injury.

DON'T attempt to lift a heavy component which may be beyond your capability – get assistance.

DON'T rush to finish a job, or take unverified short cuts.

DON'T allow children or animals in or around an unattended vehicle.

DO wear eye protection when using power tools such as drill, sander, bench grinder etc, and when working under the vehicle.

DO use a barrier cream on your hands prior to undertaking dirty jobs – it will protect your skin from infection as well as making the dirt easier to remove afterwards; but make sure your hands aren't left slippery. Note that long-term contact with used engine oil can be a health hazard.

DO keep loose clothing (cuffs, tie etc) and long hair well out of the way of moving mechanical parts.

DO remove rings, wristwatch etc, before working on the vehicle – especially the electrical system.

DO ensure that any lifting tackle used has a safe working load rating adequate for the job.

DO keep your work area tidy – it is only too easy to fall over articles left lying around.

DO get someone to check periodically that all is well, when working alone on the vehicle.

DO carry out work in a logical sequence and check that everything is correctly assembled and tightened afterwards.

DO remember that your vehicle's safety affects that of yourself and others. If in doubt on any point, get specialist advice.

IF, in spite of following these precautions, you are unfortunate enough to injure yourself, seek medical attention as soon as possible.

Asbestos

Certain friction, insulating, sealing, and other products – such as brake linings, brake bands, clutch linings, torque converters, gaskets, etc – contain asbestos. *Extreme care must be taken to avoid inhalation of dust from such products since it is hazardous to health.* If in doubt, assume that they *do* contain asbestos.

Fire

Remember at all times that petrol (gasoline) is highly flammable. Never smoke, or have any kind of naked flame around, when working on the vehicle. But the risk does not end there – a spark caused by an electrical short-circuit, by two metal surfaces contacting each other, by careless use of tools, or even by static electricity built up in your body under certain conditions, can ignite petrol vapour, which in a confined space is highly explosive.

Always disconnect the battery earth (ground) terminal before working on any part of the fuel or electrical system, and never risk spilling fuel on to a hot engine or exhaust.

It is recommended that a fire extinguisher of a type suitable for fuel and electrical fires is kept handy in the garage or workplace at all times. Never try to extinguish a fuel or electrical fire with water.

Note: *Any reference to a 'torch' appearing in this manual should always be taken to mean a hand-held battery-operated electric lamp or flashlight. It does NOT mean a welding/gas torch or blowlamp.*

Fumes

Certain fumes are highly toxic and can quickly cause unconsciousness and even death if inhaled to any extent. Petrol (gasoline) vapour comes into this category, as do the vapours from certain solvents such as trichloroethylene. Any draining or pouring of such volatile fluids should be done in a well ventilated area.

When using cleaning fluids and solvents, read the instructions carefully. Never use materials from unmarked containers – they may give off poisonous vapours.

Never run the engine of a motor vehicle in an enclosed space such as a garage. Exhaust fumes contain carbon monoxide which is extremely poisonous; if you need to run the engine, always do so in the open air or at least have the rear of the vehicle outside the workplace.

If you are fortunate enough to have the use of an inspection pit, never drain or pour petrol, and never run the engine, while the vehicle is standing over it; the fumes, being heavier than air, will concentrate in the pit with possibly lethal results.

The battery

Never cause a spark, or allow a naked light, near the vehicle's battery. It will normally be giving off a certain amount of hydrogen gas, which is highly explosive.

Always disconnect the battery earth (ground) terminal before working on the fuel or electrical systems.

If possible, loosen the filler plugs or cover when charging the battery from an external source. Do not charge at an excessive rate or the battery may burst.

Take care when topping up and when carrying the battery. The acid electrolyte, even when diluted, is very corrosive and should not be allowed to contact the eyes or skin.

If you ever need to prepare electrolyte yourself, always add the acid slowly to the water, and never the other way round. Protect against splashes by wearing rubber gloves and goggles.

When jump starting a car using a booster battery, for negative earth (ground) vehicles, connect the jump leads in the following sequence: First connect one jump lead between the positive (+) terminals of the two batteries. Then connect the other jump lead first to the negative (–) terminal of the booster battery, and then to a good earthing (ground) point on the vehicle to be started, at least 18 in (45 cm) from the battery if possible. Ensure that hands and jump leads are clear of any moving parts, and that the two vehicles do not touch. Disconnect the leads in the reverse order.

Mains electricity and electrical equipment

When using an electric power tool, inspection light etc, always ensure that the appliance is correctly connected to its plug and that, where necessary, it is properly earthed (grounded). Do not use such appliances in damp conditions and, again, beware of creating a spark or applying excessive heat in the vicinity of fuel or fuel vapour. Also ensure that the appliances meet the relevant national safety standards.

Ignition HT voltage

A severe electric shock can result from touching certain parts of the ignition system, such as the HT leads, when the engine is running or being cranked, particularly if components are damp or the insulation is defective. Where an electronic ignition system is fitted, the HT voltage is much higher and could prove fatal.

Routine maintenance

In the paragraphs that follow are detailed the routine servicing that should be done on the car. This work has two important functions. First is that of doing adjustments and lubrication to ensure the least wear and most efficient function. But the second gain from maintenance, could almost be more important. By looking your car over, on top and underneath, you have the opportunity to check that all is in order.

Every component should be checked. Dirt cracking near a nut or a flange can indicate something loose. Leaks will show. Electric cables rubbing, rust appearing through the paint underneath, will also be found before they bring on a failure on the road, or a more expensive repair if not tackled quickly.

When you are checking the car, if something looks wrong look it up in the appropriate Chapter. If something seems to be working badly look in the fault finding section.

Always road test after a repair, and inspect the work after it, and check nuts etc for tightness. Check again after about 150 miles (250 km).

All oil and coolant checks should be made with the car on level ground. The tyre pressures should be checked with the tyres cold.

Daily checks

Check the engine oil level on the dipstick and top-up if required to the correct level between the minimum and maximum marks on the dipstick. The oil filler cap is located on the top face of the rocker cover on the ohv engine types whilst on the Twin Cam variant it is situated on the left-hand cam cover (exhaust)
Check the coolant level in the radiator/header tank, and top-up if necessary to the required level (see Chapter 2)

Every 250 miles (400 km) or weekly – whichever is first

Check the tyre pressures including the spare and if necessary adjust the pressures to the specified amounts as given in Chapter 11
Check the lights, indicators and horns for satisfactory operation
Check the battery electrolyte levels and top-up if necessary as described in Chapter 10 (photo)

Every 3000 miles (5000 km) or 3 months – whichever is first

Unscrew the carburettor piston dashpot caps and top-up the oil level in the dashpots using a thin grade engine oil. Do not use a heavy grade oil and ensure that the caps are secure when completed (photo)
Lightly lubricate the carburettor control linkages
Drain and renew the engine oil. The drain plug is situated in the base of the sump on the right-hand side. Empty the oil when the engine is still warm and make sure that the container into which the oil is being emptied is correctly situated when the plug is removed. Refit and tighten the plug once drained, and top-up the oil level with the recommended quantity and grade of engine oil and check the level on dipstick when complete
The carburettor air cleaner elements must be removed (see Chapter 3) and washed in petrol, allowed to drain and then lubricated with engine oil. Allow the oil to drain and then refit the elements. The front element must be located with the corrugations clear of the breather spigot in the casing
Check the condition and tension of the fan belt and if necessary adjust or possibly renew as described in Chapter 2
Check the clutch hydraulic fluid level in the reservoir and if necessary top-up. The constant need to top-up indicates a leak in the system and this should be investigated and repaired as soon as possible
Check the brake hydraulic fluid level in the master cylinder reservoir and if necessary top-up. Again, where regular topping-up is required a fault exists in the brake circuits and must be located and repaired without delay.
Check the brake adjustments and if necessary adjust as described in Chapter 9. Inspect the various brake hydraulic lines and lubricate the handbrake cable nipple
Check the gearbox oil level via the combined level check/filler plug located on the right-hand side of the transmission housing and covered by a rubber plug under the carpet flap (photo). Do not overfill the gearbox oil level – if you do, drain off the excess amount, as it may enter the clutch case if left and cause clutch slip
Check the rear axle oil level by removing the filler/level plug (photo). The level of oil should be up to the base of the plug level. Use only hypoid oil of the recommended grade to top-up. Ensure that the plug is secure when refitted
Check the front and rear shock absorbers for signs of leakage and where this is apparent they must be renewed. Top-up the fluid level as described in Chapter 11 if necessary, the filler/level check plugs being on top of the units (photo)
Refer to the lubrication chart and lubricate all grease nipples with the exception of the steering rack and pinion
To even the tyre wear, interchange the wheel positions (including the spare). The recommended change sequence for crossply tyres is shown in the diagram on page 160. Make a periodic inspection of the tyres for signs of uneven wear and/or damage. Uneven wear is usually caused by incorrect tyre pressures and/or steering – suspension geometry misaligned (see Chapter 11)
Clean and polish the bodywork. Lubricate the door locks and hinges, the bonnet catch release and safety catch and boot lid release

Every 6000 miles (10 000 km) or 6 months – whichever is first

Attend to the 3000 mile service items plus the following:

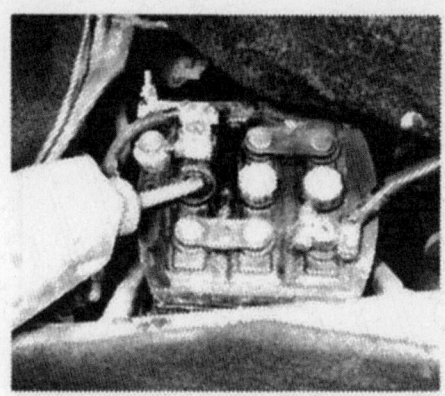

Check and top-up the battery electrolyte level, if necessary	 Topping-up the carburettor piston dashpot	 The engine oil drain plug (ohv engines)
 Check the fluid level in the Lockheed hydraulic clutch/brake master cylinder reservoir	 Check the gearbox oil level	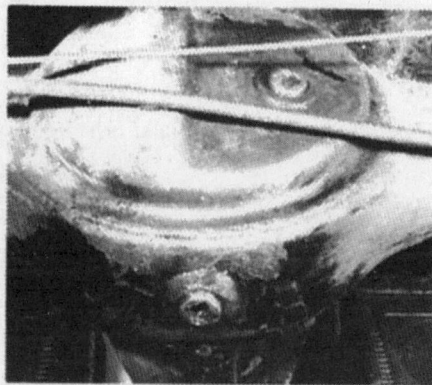 The rear axle oil level check plug and drain plug
 The front shock absorber fluid filler plug	 The gearbox drain plug	 Check the rear road spring clamp nuts for tightness
Lubricate the steering gear nipples – 10 strokes to gearbox nipple (A) and 2 strokes to pinion nipple (B)	Checking the engine oil level	Check the coolant level (ohv engine)

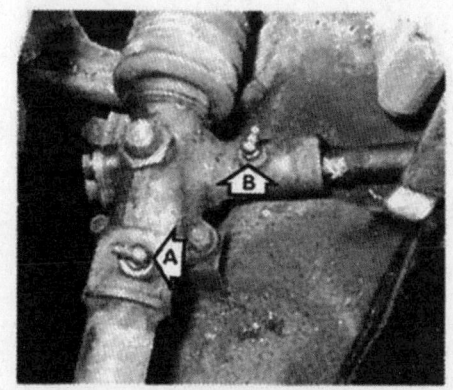

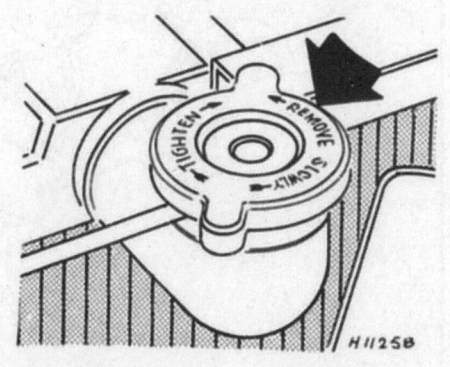

Check the coolant level in the header tank (Twin Cam)

The engine oil drain plug (Twin Cam engine)

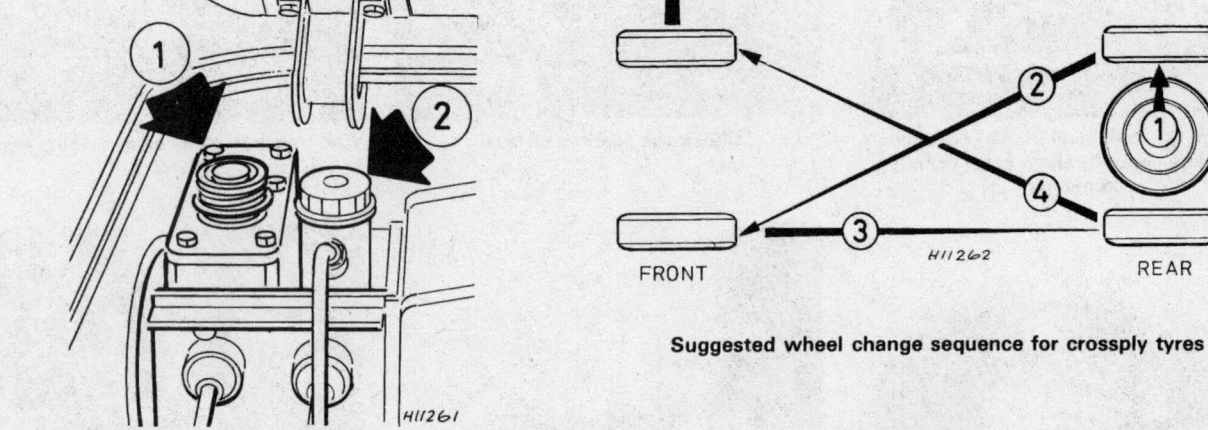

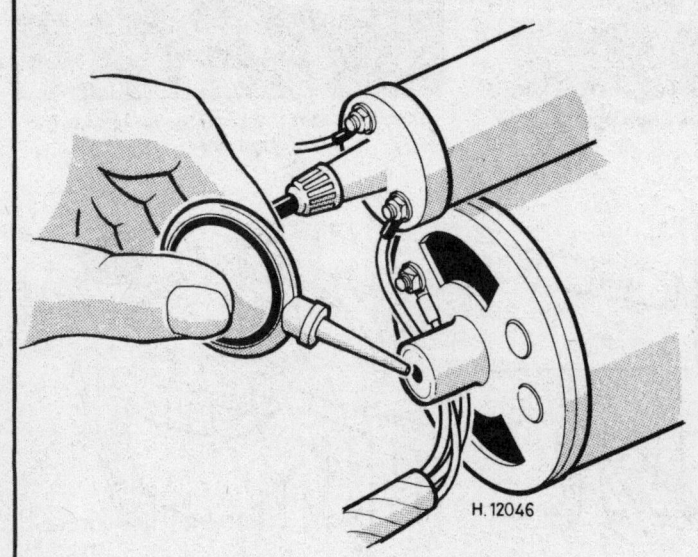

The brake hydraulic master cylinder (1) and clutch hydraulic master cylinder (2) on the Twin Cam model and 1600 de Luxe

Suggested wheel change sequence for crossply tyres

Lubricate the dynamo bearing

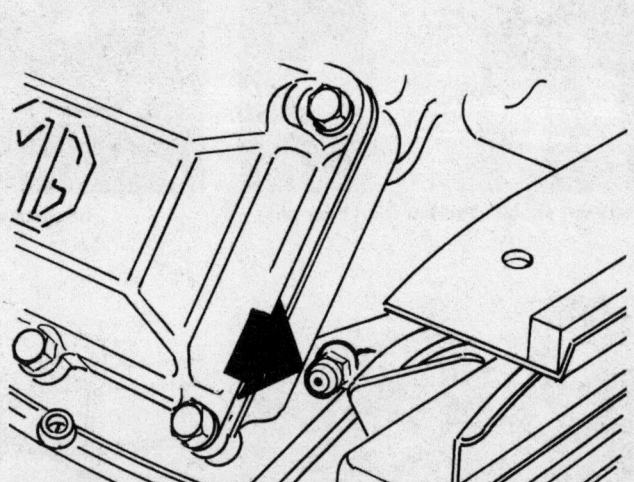

Lubricate the water pump (Twin Cam)

When draining the engine oil for renewal, unscrew and remove the oil filter unit case. Unscrew the central filter body bolt and lower to remove. Empty out the oil, extract the filter element and clean out the bowl

Insert the new element and locate the new seal washer into the groove in the upper body flange section. Fit the small felt washer between the pressure plate and washer above the pressure spring. Assemble the filter unit and secure with the central bolt. Check for signs of leaks on completion when the engine is running

Remove the distributor cap and lift the rotor arm clear

Check/clean and adjust as required the distributor contact breaker points (see Chapter 4). Lightly oil the cam bearing (do not remove the retaining screw). Smear the cam face lightly with grease. Lubricate the automatic timing control with a few drops of engine oil applied through the hole in the base plate. On no account let oil or grease touch the contact breaker point faces. Lightly oil the contact pivot pin

Remove, clean and adjust the spark plugs (see Chapter 4)

Drain the gearbox oil and refill to the specified level with the recommended oil (see Chapter 6)

Drain and refit the rear axle oil with oil of the specified type and quantity (see Chapter 8)

Remove and clean the fuel pump filters (see Chapter 3)

Lubricate (lightly) the dynamo bearing with engine oil and lightly oil the water pump

Inspect the steering and suspension components for signs of wear, damage and/or misalignment and repair as necessary (see Chapter 11)

Every 12 000 miles (20 000 km) or yearly – whichever is first

Refer to Chapter 1 and check the valve clearances. Adjust if necessary as required

Check that the advance/retard mechanism on the distributor is operational

Remove the spark plugs and replace them with new ones of the specified type. Check the condition of the old plugs against the types shown in Chapter 4 as an indication of the state of tune the engine is in

Check the brake and clutch for free play

Check the operation of the handbrake

Make an inspection of the brake linings/disc pads as applicable

Full details of brake inspection and overhaul procedures are given in Chapter 9. Renew the linings/pads if the old ones are worn down to the limit

Check that the rear road spring clamp bolts are secure (photo)

Lubricate the steering rack and pinion (photo)

Repack the front wheel hubs with grease

Every 24 000 miles (40 000 km) or 2 years – whichever is first

Overhead valve engines

Remove the engine sump (having drained the oil) and clean it out thoroughly. Also wash the oil pick up strainer. Refit the sump using a new gasket and refill with oil of the specified type and quantity

Check all electrical leads and connections for location and security

Twin Cam engines

Drain the oil and fill the engine with 6 Imp pt (7.2 US pt, 3.41 litres) of flushing oil. Run the engine at a fast tick-over for $2\frac{1}{2}$ to 3 minutes, then stop the engine, drain the flushing oil, and fill it with fresh oil. Renew the oil filter before starting the engine; do not renew the filter before flushing the engine otherwise the filter will retain a quantity of flushing oil

Check all electrical leads and connections for location and security

Chapter 1 Engine

Contents

Part A Overhead valve engines

Big-ends and main bearings – examination and renovation	27
Camshaft and camshaft bearings – examination and renovation	30
Camshaft – removal	16
Camshaft and engine front plate – refitting	45
Connecting rods, big-end bearings and pistons – removal	17
Connecting rods to crankshaft – refitting	44
Crankcase cylinder bores and engine mountings – examination and renovation	28
Crankshaft and main bearings – removal	21
Crankshaft and main bearings – examination and renovation	26
Crankshaft – refitting	41
Cylinder head and rocker assembly – removal	9
Cylinder head – decarbonising and servicing	35
Cylinder head – refitting	54
Distributor drive gear and distributor – refitting	56
Distributor drive gear – removal	14
Engine ancillary components – removal	8
Engine and gearbox – removal	5
Engine components – examination and renovation	25
Engine dismantling – general	7
Engine – final assembly prior to refitting	57
Engine – refitting	58
Engine reassembly – general	40
Engine – removal methods	4
Engine without gearbox – removal	6
Fault diagnosis – overhead valve engines	60
Flywheel and engine rear plate – removal	20
Flywheel and starter ring – examination and renovation	39
Flywheel – refitting	48
Gauze strainer/oil pump and rear end plate – refitting	47
General description	1
Initial start-up after major overhaul	59
Lubrication system – description	22
Major operations only possible with the engine removed	3
Major operations possible with the engine fitted	2
Oil filter – renewal	23
Oil pressure relief valve – removal and refitting	24
Oil pump – examination and renovation	38
Oil pump – reassembly and refitting	46
Pistons and connecting rods – refitting	43
Pistons and piston rings – examination and renovation	29
Pistons, connecting rods and gudgeon pins – dismantling	18
Pistons, piston rings, connecting rods and gudgeon – reassembly	42
Pistons rings – removal	19
Rocker arm shaft assembly – dismantling	12
Rocker arm shaft assembly – examination and renovation	33
Rocker arm shaft assembly – reassembly	52
Sump – examination and renovation	37
Sump – refitting	49
Sump, oil pump and strainer – removal	15
Tappets and tappet covers – refitting	53
Tappets – examination and renovation	34
Timing chain tensioner – examination and renovation	32
Timing cover, sprockets and chain assembly – removal	13
Timing gears and chain – examination and renovation	31
Timing sprockets, chain, tensioner and cover – refitting	50
Valve clearances – adjustment	55
Valve guides – renewal	11
Valves and springs – reassembly to cylinder head	51
Valves and valve seats – examination and renovation	36
Valves – removal	10

Part B Twin Cam engine

Camshafts and camshaft bearings – examination and renovation	89
Camshafts – refitting	105
Camshafts – removal	69
Connecting rods and big-ends bearings – examination and renovation	85
Crankcase and engine mountings – examination and renovation	87
Crankshaft and main bearings – examination and renovation	84
Crankshaft and main bearings – reassembly	97
Crankshaft and main bearings – removal	79
Cylinder bores – examination and renovation	86
Cylinder head, valves and valve seats – decarbonising and servicing	92
Cylinder head – refitting	104
Cylinder head – removal	68
Distributor drive gear – refitting	110
Engine ancillary components – removal	67
Engine and gearbox – removal	65
Engine dismantling – general	66
Engine components – examination and renovation	83
Engine – final assembly	111
Engine front plate and half speed shaft – refitting and adjustment	103
Engine front plate – removal	73
Engine – refitting	112
Engine lubrication system – description	80
Engine reassembly – general	96
Engine without gearbox – removal	64
Fault diagnosis – Twin Cam engine	114
Flywheel – refitting	102
Flywheel and starter ring – examination and renovation	95
Flywheel/starter ring – removal	78
General description	61
Gudgeon pins and connecting rod small-end bushes – removal	76
Half speed shaft – removal	77
Initial start-up after major overhaul	113
Major operations only possible with the engine removed	63
Major operations possible with the engine fitted	62
Oil filter – renewal	81
Oil pressure relief valve – removal, inspection and fitting	82
Oil pump and gauze strainer – refitting	101
Oilseals – renewal	94
Pistons and connecting rods – reassembly	98
Pistons and connecting rods – refitting	100
Pistons and connecting rods – removal	75
Pistons and piston rings – examination and renovation	88
Piston rings – refitting	99
Sump and oil pump assembly – examination and renovation	93
Sump, oil pump and strainer – removal	74
Tappet clearances – checking and adjusting	106
Timing chain – adjustment	108
Timing chain, sprockets and tensioner – examination and renovation	90
Timing cover, sprockets and chain – removal	72
Timing gears and half speed shaft – examination and renovation	91
Timing sprockets and chain – refitting	102
Valve guides – removal	71
Valves – removal	70
Valve timing – checking and adjustment	109

Chapter 1 Engine

Specifications

Part A Overhead valve engines

MGA 1500 (engine Type 15GB and Type 15GD (from Car No. 61504)

Engine general
Type	4 cylinders in line, ohv pushrod-operated
Bore	2·875 in (73·025 mm)
Stroke	3·5 in (89 mm)
Cubic capacity	1489 cc (90·88 cu in)
Compression ratio	8·3 : 1
Combustion chamber capacity (with valves fitted)	38·2 to 39·2 cc (2·3 to 2·4 cu in)
BMEP	130 lbf/in^2 at 3500 rpm
Torque	77·4 lbf ft at 3500 rpm
Firing order	1 – 3 – 4 – 2
Number 1 cylinder location	Radiator (front) end
Number of main bearings	3

Crankshaft
Diameter of main journal	2·0 in (50·8 mm)
Minimum main bearing regrind diameter	1·96 in (49·78 mm)
Crankpin journal diameter	1·875 to 1·876 in (47·65 to 47·66 mm)
Minimum crankpin regrind diameter	1·8359 in (46·64 mm)
Main bearing type/material	Shell type/steel backed white metal
Main bearing end clearance	0·002 to 0·003 in (0·051 to 0·076 mm)
End thrust adjustment method	Thrust washers at central main bearing
Running clearance	0·0005 to 0·002 in (0·0127 to 0·0508 mm)
Main bearing undersizes	–0·010 in (–0·254 mm), –0·020 in (–0·508 mm), –0·030 in (0·762 mm), –0·040 in (–1·016 mm)

Connecting rods
Length between centres	6·5 in (165·1 mm)
Big-end bearings material	Steel and lead-indium or lead tin
Big-end bearing side clearance	0·008 to 0·012 in (0·203 to 0·305 mm)
Big-end bearing diametrical clearance	0·0001 to 0·0016 in (0·002 to 0·04 mm)
Big-end bearing undersizes	–0·010 in (–0·254 mm), –0·020 in (–0·508 mm), –0·030 in (–0·762 mm), –0·040 in (–1·016 mm)

Pistons and piston rings
Type	Aluminium alloy with 3 compression and 1 oil ring
Piston clearance at bottom of skirt	0·0017 to 0·0023 in (0·043 to 0·051 mm)
Piston clearance at top of skirt	0·0035 to 0·0042 in (0·090 to 0·106 mm)
Piston oversizes	+0·010 in (+0·254 mm), +0·020 in (+0·508 mm), +0·030 in (+0·762 mm), +0·040 in (+1·016 mm)

Piston ring type:
Top	Plain (compression)
2nd	Tapered (compression)
3rd	Tapered (compression)
4th	Slotted scraper (oil control)

Piston ring width:
Top, 2nd and 3rd	0·0615 to 0·0625 in (1·56 to 1·58 mm)
4th	0·1552 to 0·1562 in (3·94 to 3·99 mm)

Piston ring depth:
Up to engine No 40824	0·111 to 0·118 in (2·81 to 3·0 mm)
From engine No 40825	0·119 to 0·126 in (3·02 to 3·2 mm)
Piston ring gap (fitted)	0·008 to 0·013 in (0·20 to 0·33 mm)

Piston ring groove clearance:
Top, 2nd and 3rd	0·0015 to 0·0035 in (0·038 to 0·089 mm)
4th	0·0016 to 0·0036 in (0·040 to 0·091 mm)

Gudgeon pins
Location	Rotates in piston – clamped to connecting rod
Fit in piston	Hand push at temperature of 20°C (68°F)
Fitting clearance in piston	0·0001 to 0·00035 in (0·0025 to 0·009 mm)
Diameter (outer)	0·6869 to 0·6871 in (17·447 to 17·4523 mm)

Crankcase cylinder bore oversizes
1st rebore	0·010 in (0·254 mm)
Maximum rebore	0·040 in (1·016 mm)

Valves
Seat angle	45°
Valve head diameter – inlet	1·500 in (38·1 mm)

Chapter 1 Engine

Valve head diameter – exhaust	1·281 in (32·54 mm)
Valve stem diameter (inlet and exhaust)	0·342 in (8·68 mm)
Valve lift	0·357 in (9·06 mm)
Valve stem to guide clearances:	
Inlet	0·00155 to 0·00255 in (0·0394 to 0·0635mm)
Exhaust (up to engine No. 4044)	0·00105 to 0·00205 in (0·027 to 0·052 mm)
Exhaust (from engine No. 4045)	0·002 to 0·003 in (0·051 to 0·076 mm)
Valve clearances (hot)	0·017 in (0·432 mm)
Valve timing:	
Inlet opens	16° BTDC
Inlet closes	56° ABDC
Exhaust opens	51° BBDC
Exhaust closes	21° ATDC
Valve timing marks	Dimples on timing sprockets
Timing chain: pitch/number of pitches	0·375 in (9·52 mm)/52

Valve guides

Diameter:	
Inlet outside	0·5635 in (14·31 mm)
Inlet inside	0·3438 in (8·73 mm)
Exhaust outside	0·5635 in (14·31 mm)
Exhaust inside	0·3438 in (8·73 mm)
Length:	
Inlet	1·875 in (47·63 mm)
Exhaust	2·281 in (57·94 mm)
Height above head (fitted)	0·625 in (15·87 mm)

Valve springs

Free length (inner)	1·97 in (50 mm)
Free length (outer)	2·05 in (51·99 mm)
Fitted length (inner)	1·44 in (36·51 mm)
Fitted length (outer)	1·56 in (39·69 mm)
Working coils (inner)	6·5
Working coils (outer)	4·5

Tappets

Diameter of body	0·812 in (20·64 mm)
Length	2·293 to 2·303 in (58·25 to 58·5 mm)

Camshaft

Number of journals	3
Diameter of journals	
Front	1·7887 to 1·7892 in (45·43 to 45·44 mm)
Centre	1·7287 to 1·7292 in (43·91 to 43·92 mm)
Rear	1·6227 to 1·6232 in (41·22 to 41·23 mm)
Camshaft endplay	0·003 to 0·007 in (0·076 to 0·178 mm)

Camshaft bearings

Type	Thinwall, steel back/white metal
Clearance	0·001 to 0·002 in (0·0254 to 0·0508 mm)
Bearing inside diameter (reamed in position)	
Front	1·790 in (45·47 mm)
Centre	1·730 in (43·94 mm)
Rear	1·624 in (41·25 mm)

Lubrication system

Type	Pressure and splash with wet sump
Oil pump type	Eccentric rotor
Oil pressure (normal running):	
Minimum	10 to 25 lbf/in^2 (0·7 to 1·7 kgf/cm^2)
Maximum	50 to 75 lbf/in^2 (3·5 to 5·2 kgf/cm^2)
Pressure relief valve operating pressure	75 to 80 lbf/in^2 (5·3 to 5·6 kgf/cm^2)
Relief valve spring free length	3·00 in (76·2 mm)
Relief valve spring fitted length	2·156 in (54·77 mm) @ 16 lbf (7·26 kgf) load
Colour identification	Red spot

Oil filter

Oil filter type	Tecalmit or Purolator element
Element number up to engine number 26932:	
Tecalmit	Pat No. 1H779
Puralator	Part No. 1H1054
Element number from engine number 26933:	
Tecalmit/Puralator	Part No. 8G683
Oil filter capacity	0·5 pint (0·28 litre)

Chapter 1 Engine

Torque wrench settings	lbf ft	kgf m
Cylinder head nuts	50	6.91
Main bearing nuts	70	9.7
Connecting rod big-end setscrews	35	4.83
Gudgeon pin clamp bolt	25	3.45
Oil filter bolt	15	2.07
Manifold stud nuts	25	3.45

MGA 1600 (Engine type 16GA). The specifications given are those items that differ from the details given previously for the 15GB and 15GD engine models

Engine general
Bore	2.968 in (75.39 mm)
Cubic capacity	1588 cc (96.9 cu in)
Combustion chamber capacity (valves fitted)	38.7 cc (2.36 cu in)
BMEP	135 lbf/in^2 (9.5 kgf/cm^2) at 4000 rpm
Maximum BHP	79.5 at 5600 rpm
Torque	87 lbf ft at 3800 rpm

Crankshaft
Main bearing material	Steel and lead-indium
Main bearing diametrical clearance	0.001 to 0.0025 in (0.025 to 0.063 mm)

Piston rings
Compression ring depths	0.141 to 0.148 in (3.57 to 3.76 mm)
Oil control ring depth	0.135 to 0.142 in (3.43 to 3.61 mm)
Piston ring gap (fitted)	0.009 to 0.014 in (0.229 to 0.356 mm)

Valves
Valve lift	0.350 in (8.89 mm)
Valve stem to guide clearance (exhaust)	0.002 to 0.003 in (0.051 to 0.076 mm)
Valve clearance (cold)	0.015 in (0.38 mm)

Valve guides
Exhaust guide length	2.203 (55.95 mm)

Lubrication system
Pressure relief valve operating pressure	50 lbf/in^2 (3.5 kgf/cm^2)
Oil filter capacity	1 pint (0.57 litre) (1.2 US pints)
Oil pressure at normal running:	
Minimum	15 lbf/in^2 (1.05 kgf/cm^2)
Maximum	50 lbf/in^2 (3.5 kgf/cm^2)

MGA 1600 Mk II (Engine type 16GC). The specifications given are those items that differ from those details given previously for the 15GB/15GD/16GA engine models

Engine general
Bore	3.0 in (76.2 mm)
Capacity	1622 cc (99.5 cu in)
Combustion chamber capacity (valves fitted)	43.0 cc (2.624 cu in)
Compression ratio:	
High compression	8.9 : 1
Low compression	8.3 : 1
Maximum BHP:	
High compression	90 at 5500 rpm
Low compression	85 at 5500 rpm
BMEP:	
High compression	148 lbf/in^2 (10.4 kgf/cm^2) at 4000 rpm
Low compression	140 lbf/in^2 (9.84 kgf/cm^2) at 3000 rpm
Torque:	
High compression	97 lbf ft (13.1 kgf m) at 4000 rpm
Low compression	92 lbf ft (12.72 kgf m) at 3000 rpm

Crankshaft
Journal length:	
Front	1.528 to 1.544 in (38.817 to 39.224 mm)
Centre	1.471 to 1.473 in (37.363 to 37.414 mm)
Rear	1.494 to 1.498 in (37.940 to 38.049 mm)
Main bearing length	1.25 in (31.75 mm)
Main bearing diametrical clearance	0.001 to 0.0027 in (0.0254 to 0.0685 mm)
Big-end diametrical clearance	0.001 to 0.0025 in (0.0254 to 0.063 mm)

Pistons and piston rings
Compression ring depths	0.125 to 0.132 in (3.175 to 3.35 mm)
Gudgeon pin outside diameter	0.749 to 0.750 in (19.04 to 19.05 mm)

Valves

Inlet	1·562 to 1·567 in (39.6 to 39.8 mm)
Exhaust	1·343 to 1·348 in (34.11 to 34.23 mm)
Valve lift	0·350 in (8·89mm)
Valve stem to guide clearance:	
Exhaust	0·002 to 0·003 in (0·051 to 0·076 mm)
Inlet valve guide length	1·625 in (41·275 mm)
Exhaust and inlet valve guide inside diameter	0·3442 to 0·3447 (8·744 to 8·757 mm)

Valve spring
Free length:

Outer	1·9 in (48·8 mm)

Lubrication system

Oil pressure at 30 mph	70 lbf/in^2 (4·9 kgf/cm^2)
Oil pressure idling (at 500 rpm)	15 lbf/in^2 (1·05 kgf/cm^2)

Part B Twin Cam engine

Engine general

Engine designation	BC16GB
Engine type	4 cylinders, double overhead camshaft, water cooled
Bore	2·969 in (75·41 mm)
Stroke	3·5 in (89 mm)
Capacity	1588 cc (96·906 cu in)
Firing order	1 – 3 – 4 – 2
Compression ratio:	
High compression (piston type AEH681)	9·9 : 1
Low compression (piston type AEH690)	8·3 : 1
Combustion chamber capacity (valves fitted)	86·6 cc (5·28 cu in)
BMEP	163 lbf/in^2 (11·46 kgf/cm^2) at 4500 rpm
Torque	105 (14·5) at 4500 rpm
Cylinder bore oversizes:	
1st	0·010 in (0·254 mm)
Maximum	0·040 in (1·016 mm)

Crankshaft

Main bearing diameter	2·00 in (50·8 mm)
Crankpin journal diameter	1·875 to 1·876 in (47·65 to 47·66 mm)
Number of main bearings	3
Main bearing type	Shell, steel back, lead indium or lead tin plated
End clearance (maximum)	0·006 in (0·152 mm)
Main bearing diametrical clearance	0·002 to 0·003 in (0·051 to 0·094 mm)

Connecting rods

Length of rods between centres	6·50 in (165·1 mm)
Big-end bearing material	Steel back lead indium or lead tin plated
Big-end bearing diametrical clearance	0·002 to 0·0037 in (0·051 to 0·094 mm)
Big-end bearing side clearance	0·008 to 0·012 in (0·203 to 0·305 mm)

Pistons and piston rings

Piston type	Aluminium alloy, flat top (high compression) or domed top (low compression) with 3 compression and 1 oil control ring
Piston skirt clearances:	
Bottom of skirt (HC)	0·0035 to 0·006 in (0·090 to 0·168 mm)
Bottom of skirt (LC)	0·0035 to 0·004 in (0·090 to 0·101 mm)
Top of skirt (HC)	0·0058 to 0·008 in (0·147 to 0·211 mm)
Topof skirt (LC)	0·0070 to 0·0076 in (0·177 to 0·192 mm)
Piston ring type:	
1st	Plain (compression)
2nd	Tapered (compression)
3rd	Tapered (compression)
4th	Microland scraper or from engine No 446 twin segment scraper (oil control)
Piston ring width:	
1st, 2nd and 3rd	0·054 to 0·055 in (1·37 to 1·39 mm)
4th	0·1552 to 0·1562 in (3·94 to 3·99 mm)
Piston ring depth	0·124 to 0·131 in (3·15 to 3·33 mm)
Piston ring gap (fitted)	0·008 to 0·013 in (0·20 to 0·33 mm)
Piston ring groove clearance	0·0015 to 0·0035 in (0·038 to 0·089 mm)

Gudgeon pin

	Fully floating, hand push fit at air temperature
Diameter	0·875 in (22·22 mm)

Valves

Valve seat angle (inlet and exhaust)	45°

Chapter 1 Engine 23

Valve head diameter:	
Inlet	1·59 in (40·38 mm)
Exhaust	1·44 in (36·58 mm)
Valve stem diameter	0·342 in (8·68 mm)
Valve lift	0·375 in (9·52 mm)
Valve stem to guide clearance	0·00155 to 0·00255 in (0·0394 to 0·0635 mm)
Valve clearance (cold)	0·014 to 0·015 in (0·356 to 0·381 mm)
Valve timing:	
Inlet opens	20° BTDC
Inlet closes	50° ABDC
Exhaust opens	50° BBDC
Exhaust closes	20° ATDC
Timing chain pitch/number of pitches	0·375 in (9·52 mm)/132

Valve guides

Length:	
Inlet	2·06 in (52·39 mm)
Exhaust	2·44 in (61·91 mm)
Valve guide diameters:	
Inside (inlet and exhaust)	0·3438 to 0·3443 in (8·73 to 8·74 mm)
Outside (inlet and exhaust)	0·5645 to 0·5655 in (14·33 to 14·36 mm)
Guide protrusion above head when fitted:	
Inlet	0·750 in (19·05 mm)
Exhaust	0·844 in (21·43 mm)
Valve spring free length (inner)	2·3 in (58·42 mm)
Valve spring free length (outer)	2·54 in (64·51 mm)
Valve spring length fitted (inner)	1·62 in (41·15 mm)
Valve spring length fitted (outer)	1·78 in (45·21 mm)
Working coils (inner)	7·8
Working coils (outer)	6

Tappets

Type	Inverted bucket
Body diameter	1·5 in (38·1 mm)
Work face diameter	1·5 in (38·1 mm)
Length (up to engine No 1086)	1·25 in (31·75 mm)
Length (from engine No 1087)	1·5 in (38·1 mm)

Camshafts

End float	0·001 to 0·005 in (0·025 to 0·127 mm)
Number of bearings	3
Camshaft journal diameters	1·250 to 1·2505 in (31·75 to 31·76 mm)
Bearing inside diameter	1·2515 to 1·2525 in (31·788 to 31·813 mm)
Bearing clearance	0·001 to 0·0025 in (0·0254 to 0·0635 mm)
Bearing type	D2 bi-metal

Half speed shaft

Number of bearings	3
Bearing type	Thin wall, steel backed white metal
Journal diameters:	
Front	1·7887 to 1·7892 in (45·43 to 45·44 mm)
Centre	1·7287 to 1·7295 in (43·91 to 43·92 mm)
Rear	1·6277 to 1·6232 in (41·22 to 41·23 mm)
Endplay	0·003 to 0·006 in (0·076 to 0·152 mm)
Bearing inside diameters (when reamed):	
Front	1·790 in (45·47 mm)
Centre	1·730 in (43·94 mm)
Rear	1·624 in (41·25 mm)
Clearance	0·001 to 0·002 in (0·025 to 0·051 mm)

Lubrication system

Oil pump type	Eccentric rotor
Pressure relief valve operating pressure	50 lbf/in^2 (3·52 kgf/cm^2)
Pressure relief valve spring free length	3 in (76·2 mm)
Pressure relief valve spring fitted length	2·2 in (54·77 mm) at 16 lb (7·26 kg) loading
Oil filter type	Full flow, external location, renewable element
Filter capacity	0·5 pint (0·28 litre, 0·6 US pint)
Oil pressure at idle	10 to 15 lbf/in^2 (0·7 to 1·05 kgf/cm^2)
Oil pressure at normal running	50 to 60 lbf/in^2 (3·52 to 4·22 kgf/cm^2)

Torque wrench settings

	lbf ft	kgf m
Cylinder head nuts	70	9·68
Main bearing cap nuts	70	9·68
Big-end bearing cap nuts	50	6·91
Camshaft bearing nut	33	4·56
Clutch assembly to flywheel	35 to 40	4·8 to 5·5

Part A OVERHEAD VALVE ENGINES

1 General description

The engine is a four cylinder, water cooled, overhead valve type. The engine is located and supported on each side by rubber mountings which assist in absorbing vibrations. The engine is bolted to the gearbox and this is located at the rear within a rubber mounting located between the transmission tunnel.

Two valves per cylinder are mounted vertically in the cast iron cylinder head and operate in pressed in valve guides. They are operated by rocker arms, pushrods and tappets from the camshaft which is located in line with the base of the cylinder bores on the left-hand side of the engine. The correct valve stem to rocker arm pad clearance can be obtained by the adjusting screws in the ends of the rocker arms.

The cylinder head has all inlet and exhaust ports on the left-hand side. Cylinders 1 and 2 share a siamised inlet port and also cylinders 3 and 4. Cylinders 1 and 4 have individual exhaust ports and cylinders 2 and 3 share a siamised exhaust port.

The cylinder block and the upper half of the crankcase are cast together. The bottom half of the crankcase consists of a pressed steel sump.

The pistons are made from anodised aluminium alloy with split or solid skirts. Three compression rings and a slotted oil control ring are fitted. The gudgeon pin is retained in the little-end of the connecting rod by a pinch bolt. Renewable lead-indium, or lead-tin big-end bearings are fitted. Replacement pistons may sometimes have an oil control ring below the gudgeon pin in the piston skirt.

At the front of the engine a duplex chain drives the camshaft via the camshaft and crankshaft chain wheels.

The chain is tensioned automatically on engines commencing at No 259 by a Reynolds spring operated, hydraulically assisted rubber slipper tensioner which presses against the duplex chain thus avoiding any lash or rattle.

The camshaft is supported by three steel-backed white metal bearings which can be renewed when worn. Endfloat is controlled by a bi-metal locating plate positioned between the rear of the camshaft chain wheel and the camshaft front bearing.

The statically and dynamically balanced forged steel crankshaft is supported by three renewable main bearings. Crankshaft endfloat is controlled by four semi-circular thrust washers, two of which are located on either side of the centre main bearing.

The centrifugal water pump and radiator cooling fan are driven together with the dynamo from the crankshaft pulley wheel by a rubber/fabric belt. The distributor is mounted towards the rear of the right-hand side of the cylinder block and advances and retards the ignition timing by mechanical and vacuum means. The distributor is driven at half crankshaft speed by a short shaft and skew gear from a skew gear on the camshaft.

The oil pump is located in the crankcase and is driven by a short shaft from the skew gear on the camshaft.

Attached to the end of the crankshaft by six bolts is the flywheel to which is bolted the 8 in diameter Borg and Beck clutch. Attached to the engine end plate is the gearbox bellhousing.

Crankcase ventilation is provided by a breather pipe attached to the front tappet chest cover. On later models a proportion of blow-by gases is driven into the air cleaner via a hose attached to the rocker cover.

2 Major operations possible with the engine fitted

1 The following work can be carried out with the engine still in position in the car.

 (a) Cylinder head – removal and refitting
 (b) Sump – removal and refitting
 (c) Big-end bearings – removal and refitting
 (d) Pistons and connecting rods – removal and refitting
 (e) Timing chain and sprockets – removal and refitting
 (f) Camshaft – removal and refitting
 (g) Oil pump – removal and refitting

3 Major operations only possible with the engine removed

1 The following operations can only be carried out with the engine removed from the car.

 (a) Main bearings – removal and refitting
 (b) Crankshaft – removal or refitting

4 Engine – removal methods

1 The engine can be removed in unison with the gearbox or as a separate unit. In both instances the engine/gearbox unit/s are withdrawn through the top of the engine compartment.

2 Before attempting to remove either or both units, thought must be given to the best approach to the job and also the lifting tackle and lift point. If the engine and gearbox are to be removed allow for the extra weight and also height requirement above the bonnet line which will be necessary to enable the tail end of the gearbox to clear it. If the lifting tackle is suspended from a fixed point, leave room at the rear of the car to allow it to be pushed back out of the way once the power unit is extracted, so that it can be lowered direct.

3 An assistant will be helpful from time to time particularly during the actual engine removal process.

5 Engine and gearbox – removal

1 Disconnect the battery positive lead from its terminal.
2 Raise the bonnet and mark the relative positions of the hinges using a pencil or felt tip pen. This will assist you on reassembly to align the bonnet correctly. Get an assistant to support the raised bonnet whilst you unscrew the hinge bolts, then lift the bonnet clear and store somewhere out of the way.
3 Locate a suitable container under the sump drain plug, remove the plug and drain the oil from the engine.
4 Repeat this procedure under the gearbox. When drained refit the respective drain plugs as applicable.
5 Drain the radiator and cylinder block as given in Chapter 2.
6 Detach the hoses from their radiator connections. Unscrew the radiator retaining bolts from each side and remove together with the spring and flat washers. Carefully lift out the radiator and place out of the way.
7 Refer to Chapter 3 and remove the carburettors and air cleaner units.
8 Make a note of their respective locations and disconnect the various electrical cables and wires. A simple way of doing this is to stick a masking tape tag onto each wire in turn and write the particular connecting point on the tag. This avoids any possible confusion during reassembly. Disconnect the following wires plus any other auxilliary connections:

 (a) Starter motor
 (b) Dynamo
 (c) Distributor cap and respective HT leads from the spark plugs and coil. The distributor LT lead

9 Detach the rev counter (tachometer) cable from its connection to the engine on the left-hand side at the rear (photo).
10 Disconnect the exhaust down pipe from the manifold and also the steady bracket.
11 Unscrew and detach the engine coolant temperature sender unit from the cylinder head. Free the conductor from the support clip.
12 Disconnect the oil pressure gauge pipe from its junction on the right-hand rear side of the crankcase.
13 Working underneath the car, remove the clutch slave cylinder but leave it attached to the flexible pipe.
14 Now working in the car, unscrew and remove the gear lever to gearbox cover rubber surround retaining screws and remove the surround.
15 Working through the aperture in the cover, unscrew and remove the gear lever turret bolts and remove the lever and turret unit. Although access to the bolts is somewhat restricted they can be removed using a small extension socket and ratchet. By removing this turret it eliminates the need to remove the floorboards/seats/centre cover and handbrake cable linkage as suggested by MG originally (photo).

5.9 Disconnect the tachometer drive cable

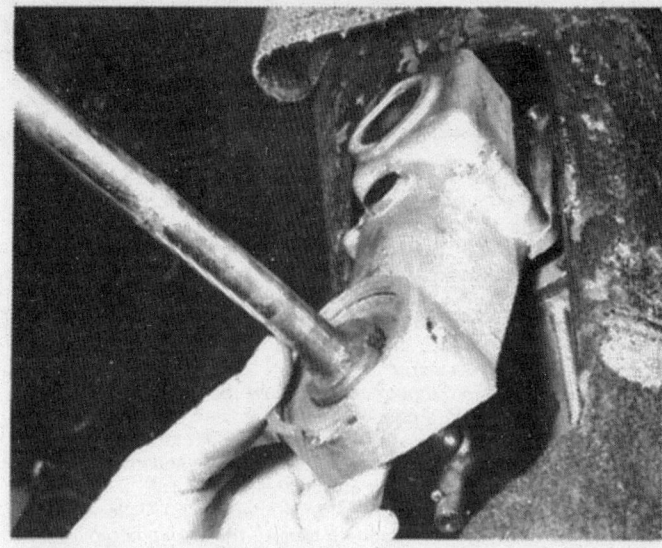

5.15 Withdraw the extension turret

5.17 Disconnect the speedometer drive cable

5.20 Detach the engine mountings and note earth strap

5.23a Removing the engine and transmission units ...

5.23b ... guide the transmission clear of the bulkhead

16 Mark the relative positions of the propeller shaft flange to rear axle flange and remove the propeller shaft (see Chapter 7).
17 Unscrew the speedometer drive cable connector to the gearbox (photo).
18 Arrange a lifting sling around the engine in such a manner that when lifted the engine will tilt downwards at the rear. Check that the sling is secure and connect it to the lifting tackle.
19 Raise the hoist so that the sling just supports the weight of the power unit without actually lifting it.
20 Disconnect the engine mountings at the front and remove the rubbers, noting the earth cable on the near side (photo).
21 Unscrew and remove the gearbox to mounting bracket retaining nut, bolt and spring washer.
22 The engine and gearbox should now be ready for removal. However make a check around the units to ensure that all fittings and connections are free and out of the way. On later models, particularly those exported an engine oil cooler was fitted as standard equipment. Detach the pipes at their connections to the engine.
23 Carefully raise the engine and simultaneously pull it forward and with the aid of an assistant guide it clear of the engine compartment. Tilt it downwards at the rear to enable the gearbox to clear the bulkhead housing and upwards at the front to enable the crankshaft pulley/starter dog nut to clear the steering rack housing (photos).
24 Remove the gearbox from the engine as follows.
25 Remove the starter motor.
26 Ensure that the engine and gearbox are well supported. Undo and remove the nuts and bolts securing the gearbox bellhousing to the engine. Do not allow the weight of the gearbox to rest on the input shaft.
27 Withdraw the gearbox from the engine keeping the gearbox flange parallel with the crankcase face until the input shaft is clear of the clutch.
28 Remove the clutch (Chapter 5).

6 Engine without gearbox – removal

1 Follow the instructions given in the previous Section in paragraphs 1 to 12 accordingly, then proceed as follows.
2 Unbolt and withdraw the starter motor.
3 Unscrew and remove the clutch housing to engine retaining bolts. Position a jack under the gearbox to support it.
4 Locate the engine lifting sling into position round the engine in such a manner that when raised the engine will tilt slightly up at the front. Engage the sling and hoist and raise the support the weight of but not lift the engine.
5 Unbolt and remove the engine mountings.
6 Make a check to ensure that all associate fittings and connections are detached and out of the way, then carefully pull the engine forwards to disengage it from the gearbox input shaft and then upwards to remove from the car. An assistant is most essential here to help steady and manoeuvre the unit during removal. Do not allow the weight of the engine to rest on the gearbox input shaft!
7 If the car is to be moved during or after engine removal loop some cord around the front gearbox housing and tie up to a suitable protrusion on the bulkhead to support the gearbox when the jack is removed.
8 Remove the clutch (Chapter 5).

7 Engine dismantling – general

1 It is best to mount the engine on a dismantling stand, but as this is frequently not available, then stand the engine on a strong bench so as to be at a comfortable working height. Failing this, it can be stripped down on the floor.
2 During the dismantling process the greatest care should be taken to keep the exposed parts free from dirt. As an aid to achieving this aim, it is a very sound scheme to thoroughly clean down the outside of the engine, removing all traces of oil and congealed dirt.
3 A good grease solvent will make the job much easier, as, after the solvent has been applied and allowed to stand for a time, a vigorous jet of water will wash off the solvent and all the grease and filth. If the dirt is thick and deeply embedded, work the solvent into it with a wire brush. Cover all the electrical equipment with oily rags to prevent the ingress of water.
4 Finally wipe down the exterior of the engine with a rag and only then, when it is quite clean, should the dismantling process begin. As the engine is stripped, clean each part in a bath of paraffin or petrol.
5 Never immerse parts with oilways in paraffin, ie the crankshaft, but to clean wipe down carefully with a petrol dampened rag. Oilways can be cleaned out with pipe cleaners. If an air line is present all parts can be blown dry and the oilways blown through as an added precaution.
6 Re-use of old gaskets is a false economy and can give rise to oil and water leaks, if nothing worse. To avoid the possibility of trouble after the engine has been reassembled always use new gaskets throughout.
7 Do not throw the old gaskets away as it sometimes happens that an immediate replacement cannot be found and the old gasket is then very useful as a template. Hang up the old gaskets as they are removed on a suitable hook or nail.
8 To strip the engine it is best to work from the the top down. The sump provides a firm base on which the engine can be supported in an upright position. When the stage where the sump must be removed is reached, the engine can be turned on its side and all other work carried out with it in this position.
9 Wherever possible, refit nuts, bolts and washers finger-tight from wherever they were removed. This helps avoid later loss and muddle. If they cannot be refitted then lay them out in such a fashion that it is clear from where they came.

8 Engine ancillary components – removal

1 Before basic engine dismantling begins it is necessary to strip it of ancillary components and these are as follows:

Dynamo
Distributor
Thermostat
Inlet manifold
Exhaust manifold

2 It is possible to strip all these items with the engine in the car if it is merely the individual items that require attention.
3 Presuming the engine to be out of the car on the bench, starting on the right-hand side of the unit, follow the procedure described below:-
4 Slacken off the dynamo retaining bolts and remove the unit with its support brackets.
5 To remove the distributor first disconnect the manifold vacuum advance/retard pipe which leads from the small securing clip on the cylinder head. Unscrew the retaining bolts at the base of the distributor and lift the distributor away from the drive shaft. Do not unscrew the clamp plate bolt as this will upset the distributor timing.
6 Remove the thermostat cover by releasing the three nuts and spring washers which hold it in position and then remove the gasket and thermostat unit.
7 Undo and remove the nuts holding the inlet and exhaust manifolds to the cylinder head. Remove the manifolds and gasket.
8 The engine is now stripped of its ancillary components and is ready for dismantling.

9 Cylinder head and rocker assembly – removal

Where the engine has been removed from the car, proceed from paragraph 5
1 Disconnect the battery positive lead from its terminal.
2 Drain the coolant as given in Chapter 2. An antifreeze solution can be saved and re-used if desired.
3 Unscrew the three thermostat housing nuts and washers, and carefully detach the housing. Extract the thermostat. Disconnect the HT leads from the spark plugs.
4 Refer to Chapter 3 and remove the air cleaner units, the carburettors and inlet/exhaust manifolds.
5 Disconnect the rocker cover front breather pipe.
6 Unscrew the two retaining nuts and remove the cover tapping or levering it upwards if stuck. Note the washers and seals under the retaining nuts.
7 Refer to Fig. 1.1 and progressively loosen off the respective cylinder head retaining nuts in the sequence shown. It will be observed that four of the cylinder head nuts also retain the rocker shaft brackets.

Chapter 1 Engine

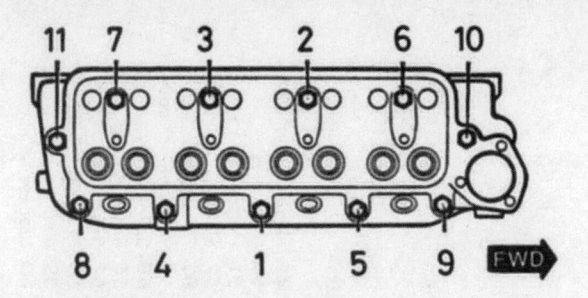

Fig. 1.1 The cylinder head retaining nuts must be loosened/tightened in the sequence shown (Sec 9)

If for any reason the rocker shaft only is being removed it will still be necessary to loosen off the other cylinder head retaining nuts in order not to cause distortion.

8 Remove the remaining rocker shaft bracket retaining nuts in a progressive manner and detach the rocker shaft assembly. Note the special lock washer in position under the nut retaining the rear rocker bracket in position.

9 Withdraw the respective pushrods and keep them in order of appearance by pushing them into a piece of suitable cardboard in numerical order.

10 Remove any cylinder head retaining nuts left in position and then carefully lift the head clear. If the cylinder head is reluctant to free from the block, refit the spark plugs if removed and then turn the engine over by hand using the starting handle or if out of the car the flywheel (whilst an assistant steady's the crankcase). Do *not* try to lever the cylinder head off by inserting a tool in the gasket joint as this may damage the mating faces of the block and cylinder head.

10 Valves – removal

1 The valves can be removed from the cylinder head by following method. With a pair of pliers remove the spring circlips holding the two halves of the split tapered collets together. Compress the springs in turn with a valve spring compressor until the two halves of the collets can be removed. Release the compressor and remove the springs, cap shroud, collar and valve.

2 If, when the valve spring compressor is screwed down, the valve spring retaining cap refuses to free and expose the split collet, do not continue to screw down on the compressor as there is a likelihood of damaging it.

3 Gently tap the top of the tool directly over the cap with a light hammer. This will free the cap. To avoid the compressor jumping off the valve spring retaining cap when it is tapped, hold the compressor firmly in position with one hand.

4 Slide the rubber oil control seal off the top of each valve stem and then drop out each valve through the combustion chamber.

5 It is essential that the valves are kept in their correct sequence unless they are so badly worn that they are to be renewed (photo). If they are going to be kept and used again, place them in a sheet of card having eight holes numbered 1 to 8 corresponding with the relative positions the valves were in when fitted. Also keep the valve springs, washers etc. in the correct order.

11 Valve guides – replacement

1 If it is wished to remove the valve guides they can be removed from the cylinder head in the following manner. Place the cylinder head with the gasket face on the bench and with a suitable hard steel punch drive the guides out of the cylinder head.

2 New guides should be fitted by your local Leyland dealer.

12 Rocker arm shaft assembly – dismantling

1 To dismantle the rocker assembly, release the rocker shaft locating screw, remove the split pins, flat washers, and spring washers from each end of the shaft and slide from the shaft the pedestals, rocker arms, and rocker spacing springs.

2 From the end of the shaft undo the plug which gives access to the inside which can now be cleaned of sludge etc. Ensure the rocker arm lubricating holes are clear.

3 When the parts are removed from the shaft ensure that they are kept in the same order so that they can be correctly refitted.

13 Timing cover, sprockets and chain assembly – removal

1 To remove the timing cover and sprocket assemblies with the engine in the car the following items must first be removed:

 (a) Radiator (see Chapter 2)
 (b) Dynamo (see Chapter 10)

The procedure for removing the timing cover, gears and chain is otherwise the same irrespective of whether the engine is in the car or on the bench, and is as follows.

2 Bend back the lock tab of the crankshaft pulley lock washer under the crankshaft pulley retaining bolt, and with a large spanner (wrench) remove the bolt and locking washer.

3 Placing two large screwdrivers behind the crankshaft pulley wheel at 180° to each other, carefully lever off the wheel. It is preferable to use a proper pulley extractor if this is available, but large screwdrivers or tyre levers are quite suitable, providing care is taken not to damage the pulley flange.

4 Unscrew the bolts holding the timing cover to the front plate and block. Note that three different sizes of bolts are used, and that each bolt has a large flat washer and a spring washer.

5 Pull off the timing cover and gasket.

6 Prise out the felt oil seal ring from the groove in the timing cover, and if necessary remove the Woodruff key from the crankshaft and store it in a safe place.

7 With the timing cover removed, take off the oil thrower. Note that

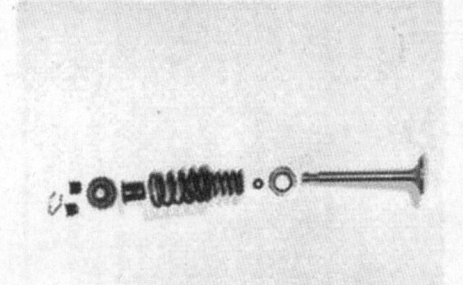

10.5 Keep the valves/springs/seals and collets in order of appearance ready for inspection and renovation

13.7 Remove the oil thrower washer from crankshaft

13.9 Use an Allen key to lock the tensioner in the retracted position

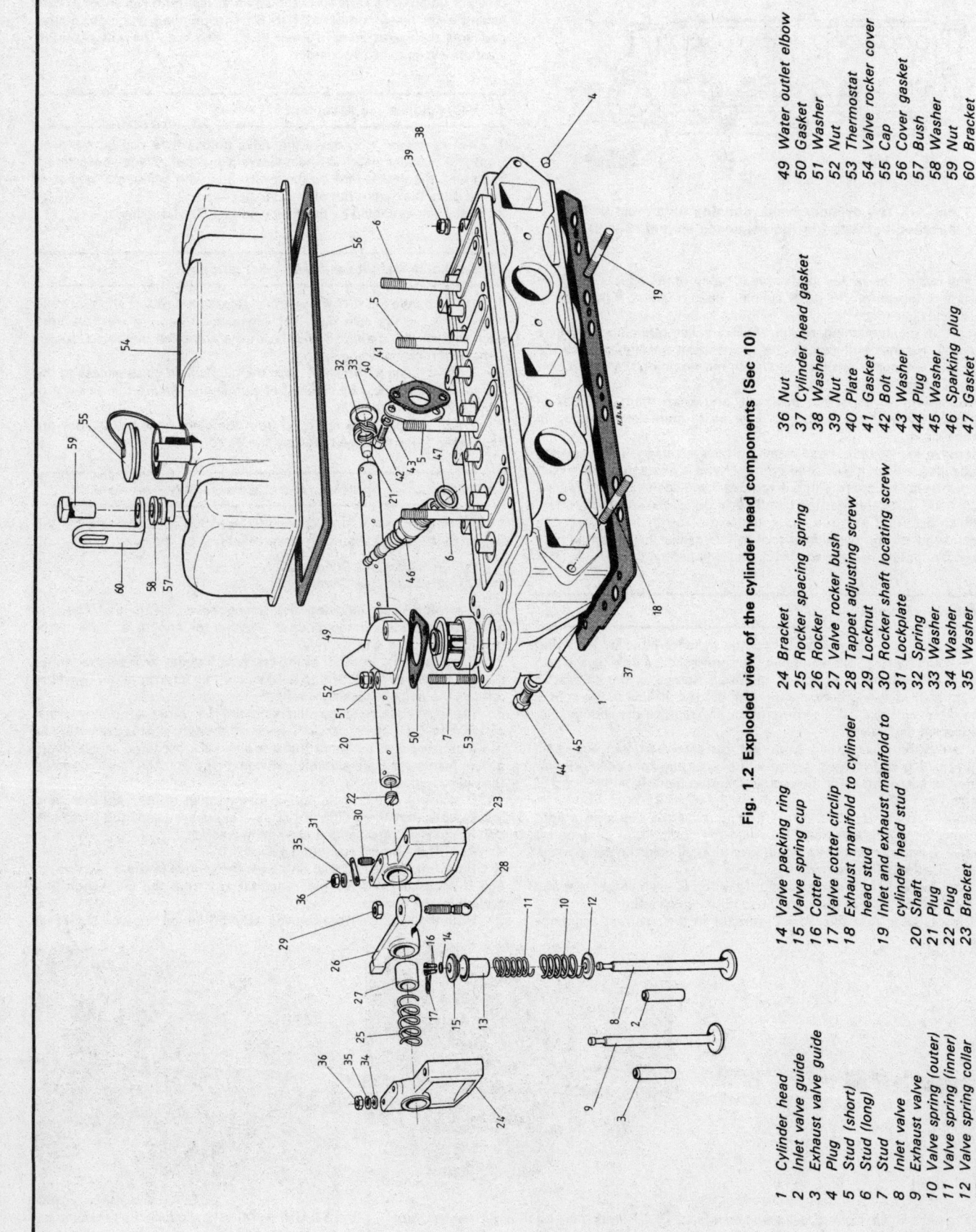

Fig. 1.2 Exploded view of the cylinder head components (Sec 10)

1 Cylinder head
2 Inlet valve guide
3 Exhaust valve guide
4 Plug
5 Stud (short)
6 Stud (long)
7 Stud
8 Inlet valve
9 Exhaust valve
10 Valve spring (outer)
11 Valve spring (inner)
12 Valve spring collar
13 Valve guide shroud
14 Valve packing ring
15 Valve spring cup
16 Cotter
17 Valve cotter circlip
18 Exhaust manifold to cylinder head stud
19 Inlet and exhaust manifold to cylinder head stud
20 Shaft
21 Plug
22 Plug
23 Bracket
24 Bracket
25 Rocker spacing spring
26 Rocker
27 Valve rocker bush
28 Tappet adjusting screw
29 Locknut
30 Rocker shaft locating screw
31 Lockplate
32 Spring
33 Washer
34 Washer
35 Washer
36 Nut
37 Cylinder head gasket
38 Washer
39 Nut
40 Plate
41 Gasket
42 Bolt
43 Washer
44 Plug
45 Washer
46 Sparking plug
47 Gasket
49 Water outlet elbow
50 Gasket
51 Washer
52 Nut
53 Thermostat
54 Valve rocker cover
55 Cap
56 Cover gasket
57 Bush
58 Washer
59 Nut
60 Bracket

Chapter 1 Engine

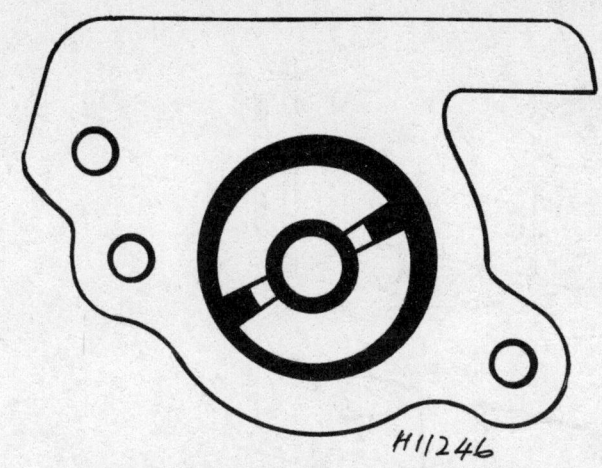

Fig. 1.3 Insert the distributor drive shaft with the slot positioned as shown (large section uppermost). When engaged the slot will be at the one o'clock position when the crankshaft is at 7° BTDC (Sec 14)

the concave side faces forward (photo).
8 From engine No. 259 a chain tensioner is fitted to the front mounting plate together with a redesigned camshaft location plate and timing gear, the original rubber tension ring being no longer used. This tensioner cannot be fitted to engines manufactured prior to this number. Lubrication to the chain on the later types is via the tensioner slipper, whilst on the earlier type lubrication was supplied by oil injection through the camshaft location plate.
9 To remove the tensioner, take out the bottom plug from the tensioner, engage an Allen key into the cylinder (photo) and turn the key clockwise to pull the slipper head back and locked behind the limit peg. Bend the lock tabs straight and remove the tensioner retaining bolts. Withdraw the tensioner unit and backplate.
10 Bend back the lock tab on the washer under the camshaft retaining nut and unscrew the nut noting how the locking washer locating tag fits in the camshaft gearwheel keyway.
11 To remove the camshaft and crankshaft timing wheels complete with chain, ease each wheel forward a little at a time levering behind each gearwheel in turn with two large screwdrivers at 180° to each other. If the gearwheels are locked solid then it will be necessary to use a proper gearwheel and pulley extractor, and if one is available this should be used anyway in preference to screwdrivers. With both gearwheels safely off, remove the woodruff keys from the crankshaft and camshaft with a pair of pliers and store them away safely until needed for reassembly. Note also the number of thin shim washers behind the crankshaft gearwheel. These are used to pack behind the gearwheel to enable it to be aligned with the camshaft gearwheel. These washers should also be stored away ready for refitting on assembly. Take care not to distort them during removal and assembly.

14 Distributor drive gear – removal

1 If dismantling the engine refer to paragraphs 4 and 5.
2 If the engine is in the car and the distributor drive gear only is to be removed, first turn the engine over to the TDC position (number 1 piston on compression stroke). The crankshaft pulley notch and pointer on the timing case must be in alignment.
3 Now use a suitable spanner and locate it onto the crankshaft pulley nut and turn it back to locate the pulley notch at 7° before the pointer on the timing case. As a guide to 7°, the short pointers on the timing case are 5° and 10° BTDC respectively.
4 Assuming that the distributor has been removed, unscrew the drive gear flange retaining screw.
5 To assist withdrawal of the drive gear, screw a suitable $\frac{5}{8}$ in (UNF) bolt into the threaded end of the drive gear and withdraw it from the aperture in the crankcase (photo).
6 Where the sump has been removed, the drivegear can simply be pushed out from within the underside of the crankcase.
7 If only the drive gear is being replaced, leave the engine set at the 7° BTDC position for correct refitting of the new shaft. Enter the drive gear in the position shown in Fig. 1.4 with the large offset uppermost;

as the gear engages the camshaft the slot will turn anti-clockwise to the one o'clock position.

15 Sump, oil pump and strainer – removal

1 If removing the sump with the engine in the car first drain the oil into a suitable container and then refit the drain plug. If possible position the car over an inspection pit or raise it at the front and support with chassis stands, but make sure that the handbrake is fully applied and place chocks against the rear wheels.
2 Unscrew and remove the respective sump retaining bolts. Lower and remove the sump.
3 Unscrew the two oil strainer retaining bolts and detach the strainer from the cover of the oil pump.
4 Unscrew the three retaining nuts and remove the oil pump unit. Clean and inspect the oil pump as given in Section 38.
5 To dismantle the strainer unit for cleaning and inspection unscrew the central nut and bolt and also the two oil delivery tube bolts. When separating the cover note the location tag. Use a stiff brush and paraffin (kerosene) to clean the strainer unit.

16 Camshaft – removal

1 If the camshaft is to be removed with the engine in the car the following items must first be removed.

(a) Inlet manifold (with carburettors) and exhaust manifold (Chapter 3)
(b) Radiator (Chapter 2)
(c) Rocker gear assembly, pushrods and tappets (Section 9)
(d) Timing cover sprockets and chain (Section 13)
(e) Distributor (Chapter 4) and drive gear (Section 14)
(f) Sump and oil pump unit (Section 16)
(g) Tachometer (revolution counter) drive gear

2 Unscrew and remove the camshaft location plate setscrews with their shakeproof washers. Carefully withdraw the camshaft.
3 If dismantling the engine unbolt and remove the front plate retaining bolts and detach the plate and gasket.

17 Connecting rods, big-end bearings and pistons – removal

1 The connecting rods and piston assemblies are withdrawn from the top of the cylinder block and therefore the cylinder head should be removed (see Section 9). If only the big-end bearings are being checked and/or renewed then only the sump need be removed (Section 16).
2 Bend the lock tabs straight and unscrew the big-end cap retaining bolts. Withdraw the bolts and tabs and disconnect the connecting rod cap.
3 As each cap is removed, check that it is marked numerically on its side face. The connecting rod should be correspondingly marked. Note also how the offset big-end caps of the connecting rods are located.
4 With the bearing caps removed the connecting rods and pistons can be pushed up and out of their respective cylinder bores using a hammer handle to push against the connecting rod from underneath.
5 If only the big-end bearings are to be removed then push the connecting rods up the cylinder just far enough to enable the rods and shaft to separate, enabling the bearings to be removed.
6 Once removed keep each connecting rod and cap together and also their bearings ready for inspection.

18 Pistons, connecting rods and gudgeon pins – dismantling

1 Before dismantling the pistons from their connecting rods check that the rods and pistons are numbered 1 to 4. The rods (and caps) will be marked on the side whilst the pistons should be marked on their crown. Scrape off the carbon build up on the crown of each piston taking care not to scratch or damage the piston surface which being aluminium will be soft.
2 If the pistons are not already marked numerically, this must now be done (unless the pistons are being renewed). Mark the top of the pistons accordingly using a centre punch or felt tip pen, on the same

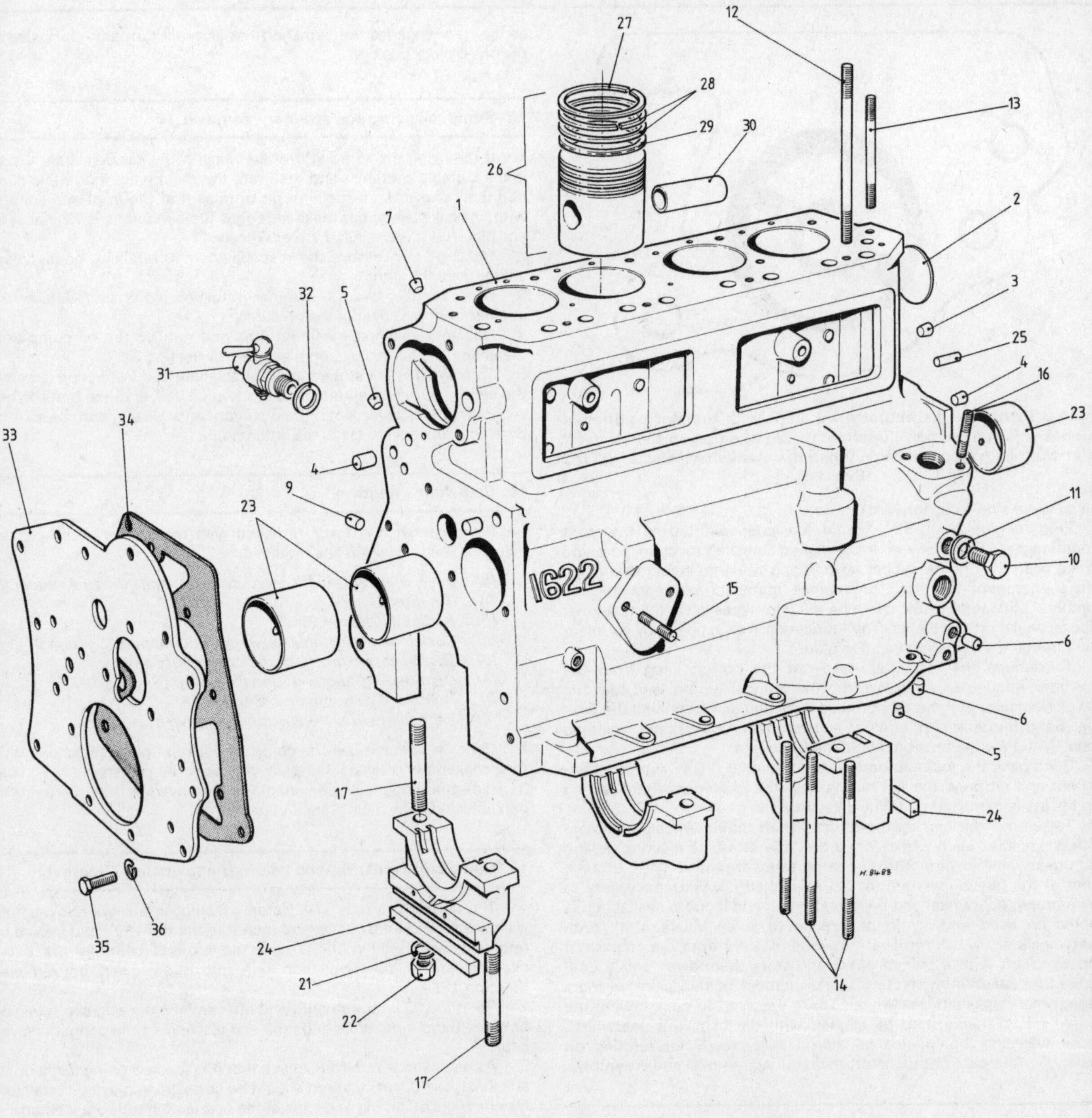

Fig. 1.4 The cylinder block and associated components (Sec 15)

1 Cylinder block
2 Welch plug
3 Oil gallery plug
4 Oil gallery plug
5 Plug (taper) crankcase oil hole
6 Oil relief valve vent hole plug
7 Plug
9 Chain tensioner oil feed plug
10 Plug for oil hole
11 Washer
12 Stud (long)
13 Stud (short)
14 Stud
15 Stud
16 Stud
17 Stud
21 Spring washer
22 Nut
23 Liner (camshaft bearing)
24 Front and rear bearing cap joint
25 Gearbox mounting plate dowel
26 Piston assembly (standard)
27 Ring – compression – top
 (standard)
28 Ring – compression – second and third (standard)
29 Ring – scraper (standard)
30 Gudgeon pin
31 Cylinder block drain tap
32 Drain tap washer
33 Engine mounting plate
34 Mounting plate gasket
35 Mounting plate to crankcase screw
36 Washer

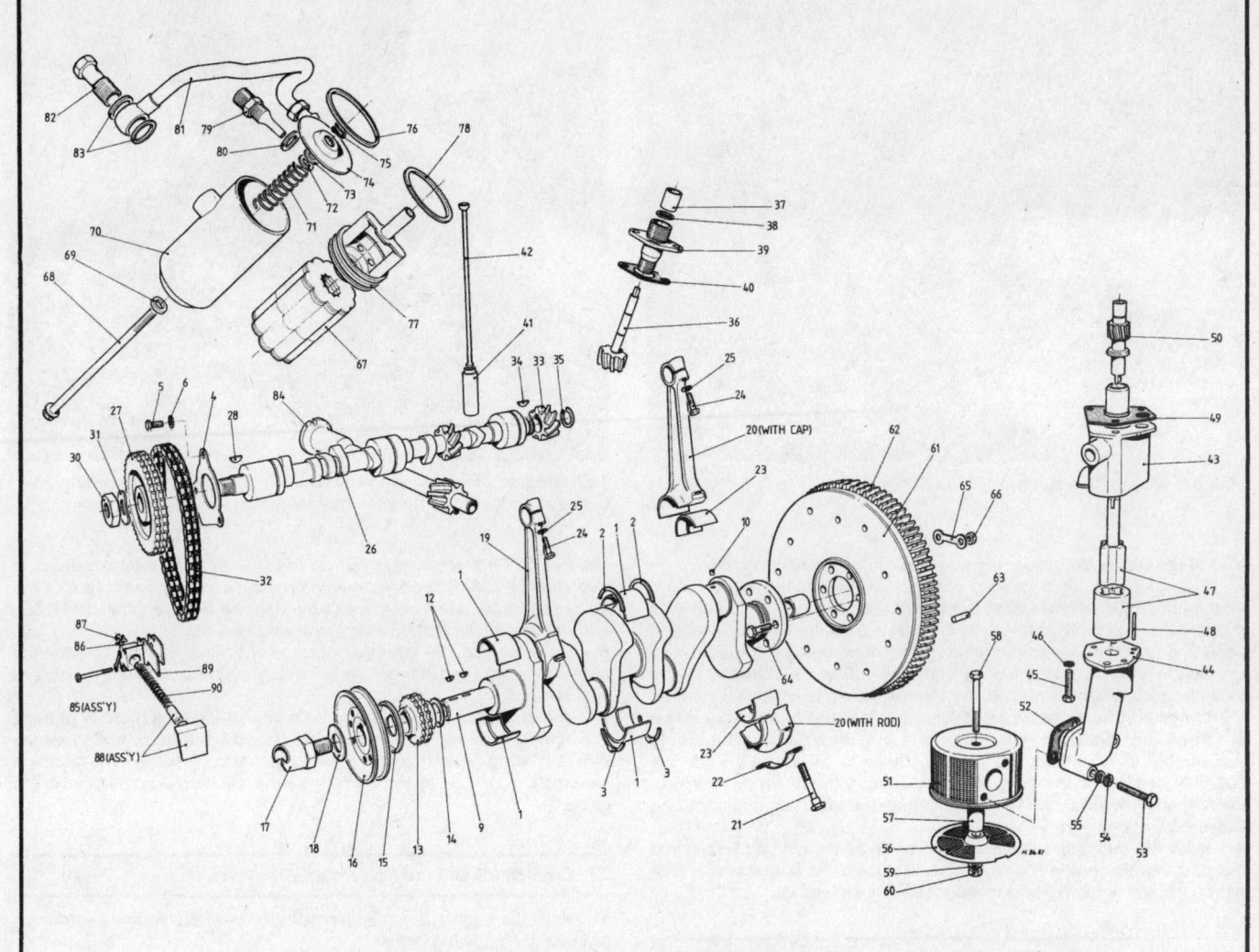

Fig. 1.5 The crankshaft, camshaft, oil pump and oil filter assembly components (Sec 15)

1 Main bearing	25 Spring washer	47 Shaft	69 Washer (seal)
2 Thrust washer	26 Camshaft	48 Dowels	70 Container
3 Thrust washer	27 Camshaft gear	49 Pump to block gasket	71 Spring
4 Camshaft locating plate	28 Key	50 Oil pump driving spindle	72 Washer
5 Screw	29 Tensioner ring	51 Oil strainer body	73 Washer (felt)
6 Spring washer	30 Nut	52 Strainer to pump gasket	74 Pressure plate
9 Crankshaft	31 Lockwasher	53 Strainer to pump setscrew	75 Circlip
10 Oil restrictor	32 Timing chain	54 Spring washer	76 O-ring
11 First motion shaft bush	33 Tachometer drive gear	55 Plain washer	77 Valve assembly
12 Key	34 Key	56 Cover	78 Washer
13 Gear	35 Spring ring	57 Distance piece	79 Adaptor
14 Washer	36 Pinion	58 Bolt	80 Joint washer
15 Oil thrower	37 Oil seal	59 Shakeproof washer	81 Pipe assembly
16 Pulley	38 Retaining ring	60 Nut	82 Screw
17 Nut	39 Housing pinion	61 Flywheel	83 Washer
18 Lockwasher	40 Joint washer	62 Starter ring	84 Spindle
19 Rod and cap	41 Tappet	63 Clutch dowel	85 Timing chain tensioner
20 Rod and cap	42 Pushrod	64 Bolt	86 Lockwasher
21 Set screw	43 Body and plug	65 Lockwasher	87 Plug
22 Lockwasher	44 Cover	66 Nut	88 Slipper head and cylinder
23 Bearings	45 Set screw	67 Oil filter element	89 Back plate
24 Screw	46 Spring washer	68 Bolt	90 Spring

14.5 Extracting the distributor drive spindle

18.3 Method of removing/fitting small end bolt – note protruding bolt heads in gudgeon pin holes to protect piston

side of the crown as the identity numbers on the connecting rods.
3 The gudgeon pin is located centrally to the connecting rod via a clamp bolt. When removing or tightening these bolts, it is advisable to support the assembly in a vice by locating a protective nut as a spacer each end of the gudgeon pin (photo). The nuts must protrude beyond the piston outside diameters so that when they are clamped in the vice, the piston isn't damaged. By clamping the pin in such a manner the connecting rod cannot be twisted or distorted in any way when unscrewing or tightening the clamp bolt. It is especially useful during reassembly as it allows the rod bolt hole to be aligned with the cutaway section of the gudgeon pin, easing the bolt fitting and preventing any possibility of it being damaged due to misalignment during assembly.
4 With the gudgeon pin clamp bolt removed the pin can be pushed out and the piston and rod separated. Relocate the gudgeon pin with its rod as the respective pins must not become mixed up.

19 Piston rings – removal

1 To remove the piston rings, slide them carefully over the top of the piston, taking care not to scratch the aluminium alloy. Never slide them off the bottom of the piston skirt. It is very easy to break the iron piston rings if they are pulled off roughly so this operation should be done with extreme caution. An old feeler gauge is ideal for this purpose.
2 Lift one end of the piston ring to be removed out of its groove and insert the end of the feeler gauge under it.
3 Turn the feeler gauge slowly round the piston and as the ring comes out of its groove apply slight upward pressure so that it rests on the land above. It can then be eased off the piston with the feeler gauge stopping it from slipping into any empty grooves.
4 As the rings are removed, keep them in the order that they were removed and the correct way up. This is only necessary if there is any possibility of them being refitted and this is normally only the case when both rings and piston are known to be in good condition and/or are relatively new.

20 Flywheel and engine rear plate – removal

1 This operation can only be achieved with the engine removed from the car. To remove the flywheel bolts, the sump and rear main bearing cap must also be removed.
2 Refer to Chapter 5 and remove the clutch unit.
3 The flywheel is located onto the rear flange of the crankshaft by six nuts and these are secured by three lock plates.
4 Straighten the lock plate tabs and unscrew the nuts. Remove the nuts and lock plates and withdraw the flywheel. **Note:** *Some difficulty may be experienced in removing the nuts by the rotation of the crank-*

shaft every time pressure is put on the spanner. The only answer is to lock the crankshaft in position while the nuts are removed. To lock the crankshaft a wooden wedge can be inserted between the crankshaft and the side of the block inside the crankcase.
5 On removing the flywheel observe that it is marked for location onto the crankshaft flange, each having a similar marking (1 and 4) (see photo).
6 The engine rear end plate is held in position by a number of bolts and spring washers of varying size. Release the bolts noting where different sizes fit and place them together to ensure none of them become lost. Lift away the end plate from the block complete with the gasket.

21 Crankshaft and main bearings – removal

1 With the engine removed from the car and the engine oil drained, remove the following items:

   (a) *Sump (Section 37)*
   (b) *Timing case, sprockets and chain (Section 31)*
   (c) *Clutch and flywheel (Section 20)*
   (d) *The oil pump strainer unit from the pump (Section 38)*
   (e) *The engine rear end plate*

2 Wipe clean the big-end and main bearing caps and check to see if they are marked for their relative positions, if not file mark them accordingly (ends and caps).
3 Disconnect the connecting rod big-ends and remove the caps.
4 Disconnect the main bearing caps in a similar manner and lift the crankshaft out of the crankcase.
5 The main bearing shells can be removed for renewal but if for any reason they are to be refitted, keep them in order. Note the location of the thrust washers each side of the centre main bearing.

22 Lubrication system – description

1 A forced feed lubrication system is employed, the oil from the sump being distributed around the engine to the various components via an eccentric rotor pump.
2 The oil level in the sump must obviously be kept at a certain level for this system to operate and a dipstick located on the right-hand side of the engine is provided as a means of checking the oil level, maximum and minimum oil level markings being provided.
3 The pump is mounted within the crankcase and draws oil from the sump through a gauge strainer to prevent oil sludge and unwanted dirt particles entering the oil circuit.
4 From the pump the oil is transferred through the crankcase oilways to the relief valve unit situated in the rear of the block on the left side. The oil then passes on across the rear face of the block into

Chapter 1 Engine 33

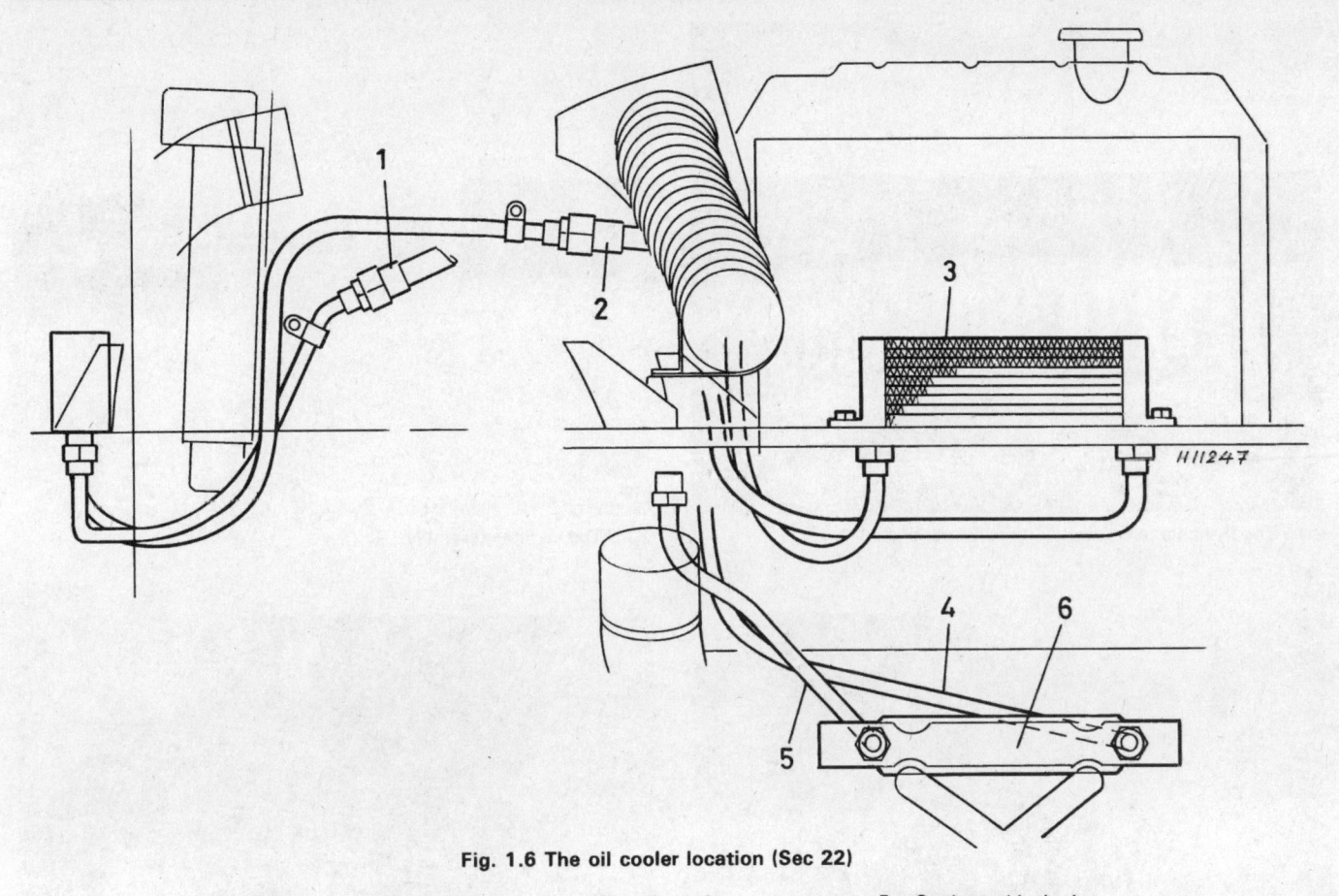

Fig. 1.6 The oil cooler location (Sec 22)

1 Cooler to filter flexible pipe	3 Oil cooler unit	5 Cooler to block pipe
2 Cooler to block flexible pipe	4 Cooler to filter pipe	6 Cooler packing

an external oil pipe where it is passed into the oil filter unit, (also externally situated).
5 The oil filter element is renewable and must be replaced at the specified mileage/time intervals along with the engine oil (see Routine Maintenance Section at beginning of this manual).
6 The filtered oil then passes on to the main oil galleries which directs it to the main and big-end bearings of the crankshaft and up to the respective camshaft bearings.
7 Each connecting rod has an oil hole in it and oil is fed up under pressure to exit from the rods and lubricate the cylinder walls.
8 At the rear camshaft bearing the oil is directed up to the rocker shaft assembly. From here the oil passes back down through the pushrod holes in the block to the sump.
9 The timing chain and sprocket assemblies are lubricated with oil supplied through the camshaft thrust plate up to engine No 259. From the engine the oil is delivered to the chain and sprockets via the chain tensioner slipper.
10 A drain hole at the bottom of the crankcase front face allows the oil to return to the sump.
11 The oil pressure relief valve is of a non-adjustable type and comprises of a plunger and spring which are retained in position by a domed head nut. The recommended oil pressures are given in the Specifications.
12 The oil filter also has two relief valves incorporated into its upper main body section and these are fitted to allow the oil to by-pass the filter in the event of it becoming blocked.
13 From car No 102737, all export models were equipped with an engine oil cooler, whilst this became an optional fitting for home market models (Fig. 1.6).

23 Oil filter – renewal

1 The full flow filter fitted to all engines is located three quarters of the way down the right-hand side of the engine towards the front.
2 It is removed by unscrewing the long centre bolt which holds the filter bowl in place. With the bolt released carefully lift away the filter bowl which contains the filter and will also be full of oil. It is helpful to have a large basin under the filter body to catch the amount which is bound to spill.
3 Throw the old filter element away and thoroughly clean down the filter bowl, the bolts and associated parts with petrol and when perfectly clean wipe dry with a non-fluffy rag (photo).
4 A rubber sealing ring is located in a groove round the head of the oil filter and forms an effective leak-proof joint between the filter head and the filter bowl. A new rubber sealing ring is supplied with each new filter element.
5 Carefully prise out the oil sealing ring from the locating groove. If the ring has become hard and is difficult to move take great care not to damage the sides of the sealing ring groove.
6 With the old ring removed, fit the new ring in the groove at four equidistant points and press it home a segment at a time as shown (photo). Do not insert the ring at just one point and work round the groove pressing it home as, using this method, it is easy to stretch the ring and be left with a small loop of rubber which will not fit into the locating groove.
7 Reassemble the oil filter assembly by first passing up the bolt through the hole in the bottom of the bowl, and with a steel washer under the bolts head and a rubber or felt washer on top of the steel washer and next to the filter bowl.
8 Slip the spring over the bolt inside the bowl.
9 Then fit the other steel washer and the remaining rubber or felt washer to the centre bolt.
10 Fit the sealing plate over the centre bolt with the concave side facing the bottom of the bowl, and push on the spring clip.
11 Then slide the new element into the oil filter bowl.
12 With the bolt pressed hard up against the filter bowl body (to avoid leakage) three quarter fill the bowl with engine oil.
13 Offer up the bowl to the rubber sealing ring and before finally tightening down the centre bolt, check that the lip of the filter bowl is

20.5 The flywheel to crankshaft location marking

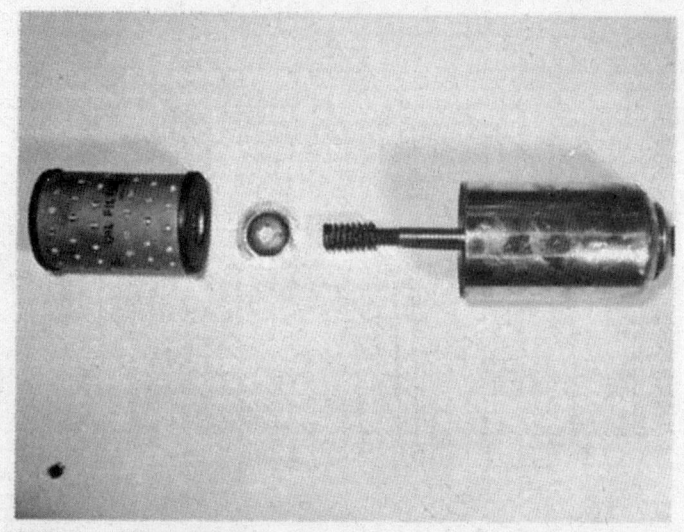

23.3 The oil filter assembly

23.6 Locate the new seal into its groove (arrowed) – filter head to block seal shown

26.2 Measure the crankshaft journals for ovality and wear

resting squarely on the rubber sealing ring and is not offset and off the ring. If the bowl is not seating properly, rotate it until it is. Run the engine and check the bowl for leaks. **Note:** *Prior to engine No 15GB/U/H26661 and between H26700 to H26933 the oil supply pipe can also be disconnected when replacing the filter and/or element.*

24 Oil pressure relief valve – removal and refitting

1 To prevent excessive oil pressure – for example when the engine is cold – an oil pressure relief valve is built into the left-hand side of the engine at the rear just below the rev counter drive take-off point.
2 The relief valve is identified externally by a large domed hexagon nut. To dismantle the unit unscrew the nut and remove it, complete with the two fibre or copper sealing washers. The relief spring and the relief spring cup can be easily extracted.
3 In position, the metal cup fits over the opposite end of the relief valve spring resting in the dome of the hexagon nut, and bears against a machining in the block. When the oil pressure exceeds the specified pressure the cup is forced off its seat and the oil by-passes it and returns via a drilling directly to the sump.
4 Check the tension of the spring by measuring its length. If it is shorter than 3 in it should be replaced by a new spring. Reassembly of the relief valve unit is a reversal of the above procedure.

25 Engine components – examination and renovation

1 Having dismantled the engine (or parts of it), the various assemblies and components can be cleaned and carefully examined for wear and possible damage.
2 Ideally the parts should be cleaned using an oil and grease solvent, hosed down and dried off. Gummed up oilways can be cleaned out using suitable twist drills or wire and blown through with a compressed air line or foot pump.
3 With all the parts cleaned they can be individually examined for wear and defectiveness and a list made of the new items needed.
4 Apart from normal visual checking, items such as bearing journals and the cylinders can only be inspected for wear using suitable internal and external micrometers. If such tools are not at your disposal have the components concerned measured for wear by a qualified auto mechanic who will be able to advise you accordingly on your requirements.
5 The following sections give details on the examination and renovation of the various engine components.

26 Crankshaft and main bearings – examination and renovation

1 Examine the crankpin and main journal surfaces for signs of

Chapter 1 Engine

scoring or scratches. Check the ovality of the crankpins at different positions with a micrometer. If more than 0.001 in out of round, the crankpins will have to be reground. It will also have to be reground if there are any scores or scratches present.

2 Also check the journals in the same fashion (photo). On highly tuned engines the centre main bearing has been known to break up. This is not always immediately apparent, but slight vibration in an otherwise normally smooth engine and a very slight drop in oil pressure under normal conditions are clues. If the centre main bearing is suspected of failure it should be immediately investigated by dropping the sump and removing the centre main bearing cap. Failure to do this will result in a badly scored centre main journal.

3 If it is necessary to regrind the crankshaft and fit new bearings your local Leyland garage or engineering works will be able to decide how much metal to grind off and the correct undersize shells to fit.

4 Where a major overhaul of the engine is being undertaken, it is a good idea to have the crankshaft checked for balance. The crankshaft balance check is made with the flywheel, clutch and connecting rods assembled to it so that any inbalance of the associate components can be taken into account. This is a specialist job and as such must be entrusted to somebody with the necessary test rig and knowledge of its useage.

5 Check the gearbox input shaft spigot bush for wear and renew it if necessary. To remove it either tap a thread in it, or use a close fitting dowel rod (after packing the cavity with water pump grease) to force it out.

27 Big-ends and main bearings – examination and renovation

1 Big-end bearing failure is accompanied by a noisy knocking from the crankcase, and a slight drop in oil pressure. Main bearing failure is accompanied by vibration which can be quite severe as the engine speed rises and falls and a drop in oil pressure.

2 Bearings which have not broken up, but are badly worn will give rise to low oil pressure and some vibration. Inspect the big-ends, main bearings, and thrust washers for signs of general wear, scoring, pitting and scratches. The bearings should be matt grey in colour. With lead-indium bearings, should a trace of copper colour be noticed, the bearings are badly worn as the lead bearing material has worn away to expose the indium underlay. Renew the bearings if they are in this condition or if there is any sign of scoring or pitting.

3 The undersizes available are designed to correspond with the regrind sizes, ie – 0.010 bearings for correct for a crankshaft reground – 0.010 undersize. The bearings are in fact, slightly more than the stated undersize as running clearances have been allowed for in their manufacture.

28 Crankcase cylinder bores and engine mountings – examination and renovation

1 Make a general inspection of the crankcase to ensure that it is thoroughly cleaned out. Sludge and metal particles can easily get lodged in the internal castings ledges and up between the cylinders.

2 Check that the internal oilways are clear.

3 Check that the core plugs are in good condition and show no signs of leaking. To renew a defective plug, drive a screwdriver blade or nail through the old one and lever it out. Clean around the plug housing and then smear some sealant around the aperture. Carefully drive the new plug into position. It should be squarely and securely located.

4 The cylinder bores must be examined for taper, ovality, scoring and scratches. Start by carefully examining the top of the cylinder bores. If they are at all worn a very slight ridge will be found on the thrust side. This marks the top of the piston ring travel. There will be a good indication of the bore wear prior to dismantling the engine, or on removing the cylinder head. Excessive oil consumption accompanied by blue smoke from the exhaust is a sure sign of worn cylinder bores and piston rings.

5 Measure the bore diameter just under the ridge with a micrometer and compare it with the diameter at the bottom of the bore, which is not subject to wear. If the difference between the two measurements is more than 0.006 in (0.15 mm) then it will be necessary to fit special piston rings or to have the cylinders rebored and fit oversize pistons and rings. If no micrometer is available remove the rings from a piston and place the piston in each bore in turn about 0.75 in (19 mm) below the top of the bore. If an 0.010 in (0.25 mm) feeler gauge can be slid between the piston and the cylinder wall on the thrust side of the bore then remedial action must be taken. Oversize pistons are available in the following sizes:- + 0.010 in (0.254 mm), + 0.020 in (0.508 mm), + 0.030 in (0.762 mm), + 0.040 in (1.016 mm).

6 These are accurately machined to just below these measurements so as to provide correct running clearances in bores bored out to the exact oversize dimensions.

7 If the bores are slightly worn but not so badly worn as to justify reboring them, then special oil control rings can be fitted to the existing pistons which will restore compression and stop the engine burning oil. Several different types are available and the manufacturers instructions concerning their fitting must be followed closely.

8 Where one or more cylinder bores have worn beyond the maximum permissible oversize, cylinder liners can be fitted to take the bore back to standard or an alternative acceptable oversize.

9 Renew the engine mounting rubbers where the old ones show signs of perishing or oil impregnation.

29 Pistons and piston rings – examination and renovation

1 If the old pistons are to be refitted, carefully remove the piston rings and then thoroughly clean them. Take particular care to clean out the piston ring grooves. At the same time do not scratch the aluminium in any way. If new rings are to be fitted to the old pistons then the top ring should be stepped so as to clear the ridge left above the previous top ring. If a normal but oversize new ring is fitted, it will hit the ridge and break, because the new ring will not have worn in the same way as the old, which will have worn in unison with the bore.

2 Before fitting the rings on the pistons each should be inserted approximately 3 in (76 mm) down the cylinder bore and the gap measured with a feeler gauge. It is essential that the gap should be measured at the bottom of the ring travel, as if it is measured at the top of a worn bore and gives a perfect fit, it could easily seize at the bottom. If the ring gap is too small rub down the ends of the ring with a very fine file until the gap, when fitted, is correct. To keep the rings square in the bore for measurement line each up in turn by inserting an old piston in the bore upside down, and use the piston to push the ring down. Remove the piston and measure the piston ring gap.

3 When fitting new pistons and rings to a rebored engine the piston ring gap can be measured at the top of the bore as the bore will not show taper. It is not necessary to measure the side clearance in the piston ring grooves with the rings fitted as the groove dimensions are accurately machined during manufacture. When fitting new oil control rings to old pistons it may be necessary to have the grooves widened by machining to accept the new wider rings. In this instance the manufacturers representative will make this quite clear and will supply the address to which the pistons must be sent for machining.

4 When new pistons are fitted, take great care to fit the exact size best suited to the particular bores in your engine. Leyland go one stage further than merely specifying one size of piston for all standard bores. Because of very slight differences in cylinder machining during production it is necessary to select just the right size piston for the bore. Five different sizes are available for the standard bore as well as the four oversize dimensions already shown.

5 Examination of the cylinder block face will show adjacent to each bore a small diamond shaped box with a number stamped in the metal. Careful examination of the piston crown will show a matching diamond and number. These are the standard piston sizes and will be the same for all four bores. If standard pistons are to be refitted or standard low compression pistons changed to standard high compression pistons, then it is essential that only pistons with the same number in the diamond are used. With larger pistons, the amount oversize is stamped in an ellipse in the piston crown.

6 On engines with tapered second and third compression rings, the top arrow side of the ring is marked with a 'T'. Always fit this side uppermost and carefully examine all rings for this mark before fitting.

30 Camshaft and camshaft bearings – examination and renovation

1 Carefully examine the camshaft bearings for wear. If the bearings are obviously worn or pitted or the metal underlay is showing through, then they must be renewed. This is an operation for your local Leyland

32.1 The timing chain tensioner components. The Allen key at the top is needed to release the assembly and for locking in position when refitting

33.1a The rocker shaft assembly retaining pin and washers with location screw removed from bracket

33.1b The bracket plug in position – note the location indent in the shaft (arrowed)

dealer or the local engineering works as it demands the use of specialised equipment. The bearings are removed with a special drift after which new bearings are pressed in, care being taken to ensure the oil holes in the bearings line up with those in the block. With a special tool the bearings are then reamed in position to give 0.001 to 0.002 in (0.025 to 0.051 mm) clearance (diametrical).

2   The camshaft itself should show no signs of wear, but, if very slight scoring of the cams is noticed, the score marks can be removed by very gentle rubbing down with a very fine emery cloth. The greatest care should be taken to keep the cam profiles smooth.

3   Fit the retaining plate and then the chainwheel to the end of the camshaft while it is out on the bench, and measure the endfloat between the thrust face of the camshaft front journal and the retaining plate. If more than 0.007 in (0.18 mm) the retaining plate must be renewed.

31 Timing gears and chain – examination and renovation

1   Examine the teeth on both the crankshaft gear wheel and the camshaft gearwheel for wear. Each tooth forms an inverted 'V' with the gearwheel periphery, and if worn the side of each tooth under tension will be slightly concave in shape when compared with the other side of the tooth ie one side of the inverted 'V' will be concave when compared with the other. If any sign of wear is present the gearwheels must be renewed.

2   Examine the links of the chain for side slackness and renew the chain if any slackness is noticeable when compared with a new chain. It is a sensible precaution to renew the chain at about 30 000 miles (48 000 km) and at a lesser mileage if the engine is stripped down for a major overhaul. The actual rollers on a very badly worn chain may be slightly grooved.

32 Timing chain tensioner – examination and renovation

1   Thoroughly clean the component parts in petrol and clean out the oil holes in the slipper and spigot. If either of these holes become blocked slipper wear will increase considerably. After high mileages the slipper head is bound to be worn and must be renewed together with the cylinder assembly (photo).

2   Check the bore of the adjuster body for ovality. If the diameter is more than 0.003 in (0.076 mm) out of round at the bore mouth, then a new adjuster unit must be fitted.

3   Before reassembly check to ensure that the inlet and outlet oil feed holes are clear. Blow through with compressed air to clean and dry.

4   On engines not fitted with a timing chain tensioner, examine the rubber tensioner ring in the camshaft gearwheel for deterioration. Renew the ring unless it is in very good condition.

33 Rocker shaft assembly – examination and renovation

1   Remove the threaded plug with a screwdriver from the end of the rocker shaft and thoroughly clean out the shaft. As it acts as the oil passage for the valve gear also ensure the oil holes in it are quite clear after having cleaned them out (photos).

2   Check the shaft for straightness by rolling it on the bench. It is most unlikely that it will deviate from normal, but, if it does, then a judicious attempt must be made to straighten it. If this is not successful purchase a new shaft. The surface of the shaft should be free from any worn ridges caused by the rocker arms. If any wear is present, renew the shaft.

3   Wear is only likely to have occurred if the rocker shaft oil holes have become blocked.

4   Check the rocker arms for wear of the rocker bushes, for wear at the rocker arm face which bears on the valve stem, and for wear of the adjusting ball ended screws. Wear in the rocker arm bush can be checked by gripping the rocker arm tip and holding the rocker arm in place on the shaft, noting if there is any lateral rocker arm shake. If shake is present, and the arm is very loose on the shaft, remedial action must be taken. Forged rocker arms which have worn bushes may be taken to your local Leyland agent or engineering works to have the old bush drawn out and a new bush fitted.

5   Check the top of the rocker arm where it bears on the valve stem for cracking or serious wear on the case hardening. If none is present reuse the rocker arm. Check the lower half of the ball on the end of the rocker arm adjusting screw. On high performance engines, wear on the ball and top of the pushrod is easily noted by the unworn 'pip' which fits in the small central oil hole on the ball. The larger this 'pip' the more wear has taken place to both the ball and the pushrod.

6   Check the pushrods for straightness by rolling them on the bench. Renew any that are bent.

34 Tappets – examination and renovation

1   Examine the bearing surface of the tappets which lie on the camshaft. Any indentation in this surface or any cracks indicate serious wear and the tappets should be renewed. Thoroughly clean them out, removing all traces of sludge.

2   It is most unlikely that the sides of the tappets will prove worn, but, if they are a very loose fit in their bores and can readily be rocked, they should be exchanged for new units. It is very unusual to find any wear in the tappets, and any wear present is likely to occur only at very high mileages.

3   Later pushrods and tappets had a larger spherical diameter and if removing older types they must be as a set.

35 Cylinder head – decarbonising and servicing

1   This can be carried out with the engine either in or out of the car. With the cylinder on the bench carefully remove with a wire brush and blunt scraper all traces of carbon deposits from the combustion spaces and the ports. The valve head stems and valve guides should also be freed from any carbon deposits. Wash the combustion spaces and ports down with petrol and scrape the cylinder head surface free of any foreign matter with the side of a steel rule, or a similar article.

2   Clean the pistons and top of the cylinder bores. If the pistons are still in the block then it is essential that great care is taken to ensure

Chapter 1 Engine

38.2 Measure the oil pump rotor endfloat

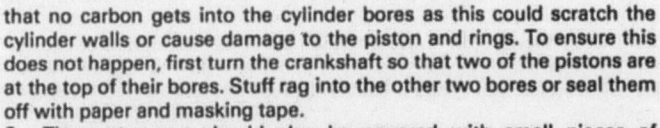

38.4 Measure the oil pump lobe peak clearance

that no carbon gets into the cylinder bores as this could scratch the cylinder walls or cause damage to the piston and rings. To ensure this does not happen, first turn the crankshaft so that two of the pistons are at the top of their bores. Stuff rag into the other two bores or seal them off with paper and masking tape.

3 The waterways should also be covered with small pieces of masking tape to prevent particles of carbon entering the cooling system and damaging the water pump.

4 There are two schools of thought as to how much carbon should be removed from the piston crown. One school recommends that a ring of carbon should be left round the edge of the piston and on the cylinder bore wall as an aid to low oil consumption. Although this is probably true for early engines with worn bores, on later engines the thought of the second school can be applied; which is that for effective decarbonisation all traces of carbon should be removed.

5 If all traces of carbon are to be removed, press a little grease into the gap between the cylinder walls and the two pistons which are to be worked on. With a blunt scraper carefully scrape away the carbon from the piston crown, taking great care not to scratch the aluminium. Also scrape away the carbon from the surrounding lip of the cylinder wall. When all carbon has been removed, scrape away the grease which will now be contaminated with carbon particles, taking care not to press any into the bores. To assist prevention of carbon build-up the piston crown can be polished with a metal polish. Remove the rags or masking tape from the other two cylinders and turn the crankshaft so that the two pistons which were at the bottom are now at the top. Place rag or masking tape in the cylinders which have been decarbonised and proceed as just described.

6 If a ring of carbon is going to be left round the piston then this can be helped by inserting an old piston ring into the top of the bore to rest on the piston and ensure that carbon is not accidentally removed. Check that there are no particles of carbon in the cylinder bores. Decarbonising is now complete.

7 Examine the valve guides internally for wear. If the valves are a very loose fit in the guides and there is the slightest suspicion of lateral rocking, then new guides will have to be fitted. If the valve guides have been removed compare them internally by visual inspection with a new guide as well as testing them for rocking with the valves. Valve guide replacement is best left to your Leyland agent or local automotive workshop.

36 Valves and valve seats – examination and renovation

1 Examine the heads of the valves for pitting and burning, especially the heads of the exhaust valves.

2 The valve seatings should be examined at the same time. If the pitting on valve and seat is very slight the marks can be removed by grinding the seats and valves together with coarse, and then fine, valve grinding paste.

3 Where bad pitting has occurred to the valve seats it will be necessary to recut them and fit new valves. If the valve seats are so worn that they cannot be recut, then it will be necessary to fit new valve seat inserts. These latter two jobs should be entrusted to the local Leyland agent or engineering works.

4 In practice it is very seldom that the seats are so badly worn that they require renewal. Normally, it is the valve that is too badly worn, and the owner can easily purchase a new set of valves and match them to the seats by valve grinding.

37 Sump – examination and renovation

1 The sump must be thoroughly washed out with petrol and wiped dry. Ensure that all traces of sump gasket have cleaned off the flange faces.

2 Inspect the cork packings in the crankshaft seal housings. Unless they are known to be fairly new and are obviously in good condition, they must always be renewed. Prise out the old seals and carefully insert the new ones. Cut off any seal protruding from the seal face by more than about 0.06 in (1.6 mm).

3 If the sump to crankcase flange face is distorted or damaged, the sump must be renewed.

38 Oil pump – examination and renovation

1 Unscrew the two bolts and detach the oil pump cover, rotors and shaft. Thoroughly clean all the component parts in petrol and then check the rotor endfloat and lobe clearances in the following manner.

2 Position the rotors in the pump and place the straight edge of a steel ruler across the joint face of the pump. Measure the gap between the bottom of the straight edge and the top of the rotors with a feeler gauge (photo). If the measurement exceeds 0.005 in (0.127 mm) then check the lobe clearances as described in paragraph 4.

3 If the lobe clearances are correct then remove the dowels from the joint face of the pump body and lap the joint face on a sheet of plate glass.

4 Measure the gap between the lobe peaks and lobes within the pump using a feeler gauge (photo). Should the gap exceed 0.010 in (0.254 mm) renew the pump unit.

5 Where a new pump is to be fitted to engines previous to engine No 15GB/U/H46045 and between 46100 to 46342, the later type pump can be fitted. The later pump was modified so that its suction pipe pointed to the front of the engine thus preventing oil starvation when cornering or braking hard. The only modification needed to fit the later type pump is to replace the location studs for longer ones as the oil pump bottom cover is thicker. The part number of the studs is 51K267.

39 Flywheel and starter ring – examination and renovation

1 If the teeth on the flywheel starter ring are badly worn, or if some are missing, then it will be necessary to remove the ring. This is achieved by splitting the ring with a cold chisel. The greatest care should be taken not to damage the flywheel during this process.

2 To fit a new ring heat it gently and evenly with an oxy-acetylene flame until a temperature of approximately 350°C (660°F) is reached. This is indicated by a light metallic blue surface colour.

3 With the ring at this temperature, fit it to the flywheel with the teeth taper on the clutch side of the flywheel. The ring should be tapped gently down onto its register and left to cool naturally when the shrinkage of the metal on cooling will ensure that it is a secure and permanent fit. Great care must be taken not to overheat the ring, as if this happens the temper of the ring will be lost.

4 Alternatively, your local Leyland agent or local engineering works may have a suitable oven in which the flywheel can be heated. The normal domestic oven will only give a temperature of about 250°C (480°F) at the very most and, although it may be possible to fit the ring with it at this temperature, it is unlikely and no great force should have to be used.

40 Engine reassembly – general

To ensure maximum life with minimum trouble from a rebuilt engine, not only must everything be correctly assembled, but everything must be spotlessly clean, all the oilways must be clear, lock washers and spring washers must always be fitted where indicated and all bearing and other working surfaces must be thoroughly lubricated during assembly. Before assembly begins renew any bolts or studs the threads of which are in any way damaged, and whenever possible use new spring washers. Apart from your normal tools, a supply of clean rag, an oil can filled with engine oil (an empty plastic detergent bottle thoroughly cleaned and washed out, will invariably do just as well), a new supply of assorted spring washers, a set of new gaskets, and a torque wrench, should be collected together.

41 Crankshaft – refitting

1 The crankshaft must be thoroughly clean before fitting, and the internal oilways must be clear. Blow them through with compressed air to remove any particles of dirt or metal, and inject with clean engine oil. The crankcase should be similarly treated. If machining work has been undertaken on the engine then it is most essential that all swarf and metal particles are removed prior to assembly.

2 Wipe clean the upper bearing shell locations in the crankcase. Note that the back of each bearing shell has a tab which engages in corresponding location grooves in the crankcase and main bearing cap housings.

3 Where new bearings are being fitted carefully clean all traces of protective grease coatings from the shells.

4 Locate the upper bearing shells into position in the crankcase and the remaining shells into the bearing caps. Check that the shells are fully located (photo).

5 Wipe clean the recesses each side of the centre main bearing which locates the thrust washers.

6 Generously lubricate each crankshaft journal and the respective bearing shells with clean engine oil. Carefully lower the crankshaft into position (photo).

7 Before fitting the bearing caps, slide the thrust washers into position each side of the centre main bearing. The upper thrust washer half sections are those not having the location tag. As the bearings are fitted rotate the crankshaft in the same direction but do not allow the bearing shells to slide out. The thrust washers must be fitted with their oil grooves outwards away from the bearing (photo).

8 Fit the main bearing shells to the caps ensuring that the mating surfaces are perfectly clean or they will not seat correctly (photo).

9 As the centre main bearing cap is fitted the thrust washer must be in position (photo) on each side. The washers can be retained in position whilst fitting the cap by greasing the mating surfaces. The location tab of each washer must be in the bearing cap slot. Before fitting the rear main bearing cap coat its horizontal surface with a sealing compound.

10 Use new washers and locate them over the bearing caps, and refit the main bearing cap retaining nuts. Tighten the nuts finger tight and then rotate the crankshaft to test it for freedom of rotation. Use a feeler gauge and check that the crankshaft endfloat is as specified (photo). If the crankshaft is binding or possibly too loose when rotated then a further careful inspection must be made, preferably by a qualified mechanic to find the cause of the problem.

11 Having checked that the crankshaft is a good fit, tighten the retaining nuts up to the specified torque wrench setting (photo).

42 Pistons, rings and connecting rods – reassembly

1 Check that the piston ring grooves and oilways are thoroughly clean and unblocked. Piston rings must always be fitted over the head of the piston and never from the bottom.

2 The easiest method to use when fitting rings is to wrap a 0.020 in (0.5 mm) feeler gauge round the top of the piston and place the rings one at a time, starting with the bottom oil control ring, over the feeler gauge.

3 The feeler gauge, complete with ring, can then be slid down the piston over the other piston ring grooves until the correct groove is reached. The piston ring is then slid gently off the feeler gauge into the groove.

4 An alternative method is to fit the rings by holding them slightly open with the thumbs and both of your index fingers. This method requires a steady hand and great care as it is easy to open the ring too much and break it.

5 When each piston ring is fitted into its groove compress and rotate it to ensure that there are no tight spots possibly caused by carbon deposits left in the groove. Finally arrange the ring gaps at 180° to each other.

6 If the same pistons are being used, then they must be mated to the same connecting rod with the same gudgeon pin. If new pistons are being fitted it does not manner which connecting rod they are used with, but, the gudgeon pins should be fitted on the basis of selective assembly.

7 This involves trying each of the pins in each of the pistons in turn and fitting them to the ones they fit best as is detailed below.

8 Because aluminium alloy, when hot, expands more than steel, the gudgeon pin may be a very tight fit in the piston when they are cold.

9 To ease assembly the piston can be heated by lowering into very hot water to the depth of the gudgeon pin bore. On removal the gudgeon pin can be slid into position and the connecting rod engaged as the pin passes through.

10 Prior to reassembly lay the respective piston and connecting rods opposite each other to avoid confusion when fitting. Used pistons must be refitted to the bore from which they were removed. If fitting new pistons this rule only applies to the connecting rods.

11 Remember that as each piston and connecting rod are assembled the FRONT marking on the piston crown (photo) must face towards the front of the engine and the gudgeon pin bolt hole in the connecting rod small-end faces towards the camshaft.

12 As each gudgeon pin is slid into its piston and connecting rod arrange the position of the cutaway on the gudgeon pin so that it will align with the retaining bolt hole.

13 When the gudgeon pin is centrally located within the piston and connecting rod bolt hole is aligned with the gudgeon pin cutaway, insert the retaining bolt with a new spring washer located under the bolt head. If the hole is not in exact alignment with the slot, the bolt will be difficult to locate in which case position a nut at each end of the gudgeon pin and clamp the pin in the jaws of a vice (see photo 18.3). The piston and connecting rod must be free to rotate. Align the hole and slot enabling the bolt to be inserted.

14 Tighten the bolt to the specified torque wrench setting. To avoid distorting the connection rod when tightening, the assembly should be located in a vice as described in paragraph 13. When the pistons and connecting rods are assembled, it's advisable to have their alignment checked if possible. A special jig is required to do this and it should therefore be entrusted to an automotive engineer who will be able to make any adjustments required. Considering the small amount of extra time and relative cost involved this is well worthwhile.

43 Pistons and connecting rods – refitting

1 With a wad of clean rag wipe the cylinder bores clean.

41.4 Locate the upper bearing shells and lubricate

41.6 Lower the crankshaft into position

41.7a Side thrust washers – note location tag of lower half

41.7b Locating the upper washer

41.8 Fit the main bearing shells to the caps

41.9a Locate the lower side thrust washers onto centre main bearings cap – note oil grooves face away from cap

41.9b Locating the centre main bearing cap

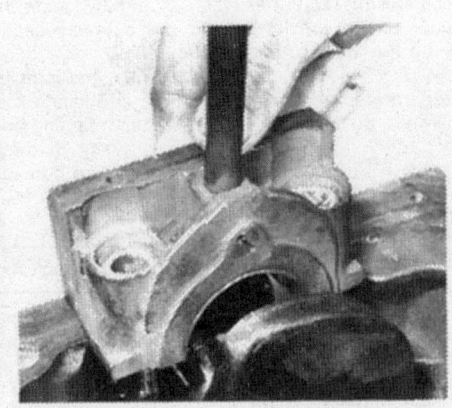

41.9c Locate the rear main bearing cap

41.9d Locate the front main bearing cap

41.10 Check the crankshaft endfloat using feeler gauges

41.11 Tighten the main bearing nuts to the specified torque

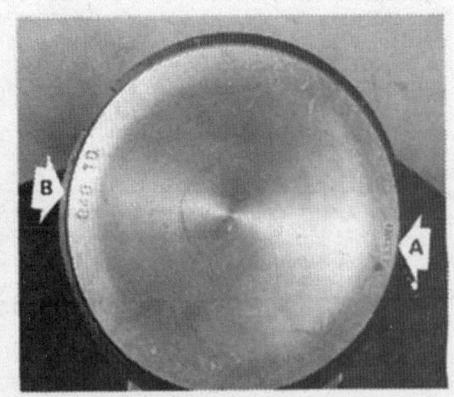

42.11 The piston front marking 'A' and oversize marking 'B'

2 Lubricate the cylinder bores and piston assemblies prior to fitting with clean engine oil.
3 The pistons, complete with connecting rods, are fitted to their bores from above.
4 As each piston is inserted into its bore ensure that it is the correct piston/connecting rod assembly for that particular bore and that the connecting rod is the right way round, the front of the piston towards the front of the bore ie towards the front of the engine.
5 The piston will only slide into the bore as far as the oil control ring. It is then necessary to compress the piston rings into a clamp and to gently tap the piston into the cylinder bore with a wooden or plastic hammer. If a proper piston ring clamp is not available then a suitable worm drive clip will suffice.
6 As the pistons are pushed down into their respective bores, guide each connecting rod into position onto the crankshaft journals and between the webs.

44 Connecting rods to crankshaft – refitting

1 Wipe clean the connecting rod big-end and also the big-end bearing cap. Wipe any protective coatings from the shell bearings before fitting.
2 Locate the shell bearings into position in the connecting rods and caps with the location torque of each bearing half shell engaged in the groove of its rod/cap.
3 All rods are fitted in the same manner, being offset to the distributor side with the caps fitted from the camshaft side.
4 If the old bearings are in good condition and are being refitted make sure that they are relocated in their correct rod and cap positions.
5 Generously lubricate the crankpin journals with engine oil, and turn the crankshaft so that the crankpin is in the most advantageous position for the connecting rod to be drawn onto it.
6 Generously lubricate the shell bearing and offer up the connecting rod bearing cap the the connecting rod.
7 Fit the connecting rod bolts with the one-piece locking tab under them and tighten the bolts with a torque spanner to the specified torque. With a cold chisel or pair of pliers knock up the locking tabs against the bolt head.
8 When all the connecting rods have been fitted, rotate the crankshaft to check that everything is free, and that there are no high spots causing binding.

45 Camshaft and engine front plate – refitting

1 Smear the front face of the crankcase with sealant and locate the gasket and front plate (photo). Insert the retaining bolts and tighten progressively.
2 Stand the engine in the upright position and locate a suitable block under the crankcase. Camshaft installation and the subsequent engine reassembly procedures will be easier with the engine in this position.
3 Wipe the camshaft bearing journals clean and lubricate them generously with engine oil.
4 Insert the camshaft into the crankcase gently, taking care not to damage the camshaft bearings with the cams (photo).
5 With the camshaft inserted into the block as far as it will go, rotate it slightly to ensure the skew gear has mated with the tachometer drivegear.
6 Refit the camshaft locating plate and tighten down the three retaining bolts and washers (photo).
7 Check that the camshaft rotates freely.

46 Oil pump – reassembly and refitting

1 Fit the outer rotor in the body of the pump so the chamfered end is at the driving end of the rotor pocket in the body of the pump.
2 Refit the inner rotor together with the oil pump shaft and fill the pump with oil to thoroughly lubricate it.
3 Fit the cover in position over the dowels on the joint face and use a new gasket. Refit and tighten the securing bolts. Check that the pump turns freely.
4 Fit the pump and shaft to the crankcase using a new gasket (photo) and insert and tighten up the three nuts which hold the pump in place.

47 Gauze strainer/oil pump unit and rear end plate – refitting

1 The gauze strainer and suction pipe should be thoroughly cleaned in petrol, and then blown dry with a compressed air line.
2 Reassembly consists of refitting the centre nut and bolt and the two delivery pipe flange bolts and then inserting and doing up the two bolts which hold it to the pump (photo).
3 Do not forget to refit the distance tube and ensure the locating tongue on the side of the cover is correctly positioned.
4 Relocate the engine plate at the rear together with a new gasket. Insert the respective bolts and tighten them fully.

48 Flywheel – refitting

1 When refitting the flywheel it is important to ensure that it is placed in the correct relative position with the crankshaft.
2 To do this, turn the crankshaft until piston Nos. 1 and 4 are at the top of their bores and lock the crankshaft in this position with a wedge of wood between the crankshaft and the crankcase.
3 Wipe the mating surfaces of the crankshaft flange and flywheel clean, and then fit the flywheel so the marks '1/4' on the flywheel periphery are at the top. (See photograph 20.5).
4 Screw in the six bolts and locking plates and tighten the bolts to the specified torque. Bend up the locking tabs on the locking plates (photo) and refit the clutch as described in Chapter 5.

49 Sump – refitting

1 Ensure that the sump is perfectly clean with all traces of the old gasket removed from the mating flanges.
2 Carefully locate the main bearing cap cork seal strips into position in the cutaway sections of the front and rear main bearing caps (photo).
3 Smear the joint faces of the sump and crankcase with grease or sealant and locate the gasket. Refit the sump, aligning the holes and insert the retaining bolts with washers (photo). Note that the four bolts having a slot in their head are fitted to the rear face (enabling a screwdriver to be used for their initial installation). Tighten the sump bolts.

50 Timing sprockets, chain, tensioner and cover – refitting

1 Before reassembly begins check that the packing washers are in place on the crankshaft nose. If new gearwheels are being fitted it may be necessary to fit alternative washers. These washers ensure that the crankshaft gearwheel lines up correctly with the camshaft gearwheel.
2 This can be checked by locating the two sprockets onto their respective shafts and laying a straight edge rule across their front faces (photo). Add or reduce the crankshaft washer thicknesses accordingly to align the sprockets. Remove the sprockets.
3 Refit the Woodruff keys in their respective slots in the crankshaft and camshaft and ensure that they are fully seated. If their edges are burred they must be cleaned with a fine file.
4 Lay the gearwheels on a clean surface so that the two timing dots are adjacent to each other. Slip the timing chain over them and pull the gearwheels back into mesh with the chain so that the timing dots, although further apart, are still adjacent to each other (photo).
5 Rotate the crankshaft so that the Woodruff key is at top dead centre. (The engine should be standing upright on its sump).
6 Rotate the camshaft so that when viewed from the front the Woodruff key is at the two o'clock position.
7 Fit the timing chain and gearwheel assembly onto the camshaft and crankshaft, keeping the timing marks adjacent. If the camshaft and crankshaft have been positioned accurately it will be found that the keyways on the gearwheels will match the position of the keys, although it may be necessary to rotate the camshaft a fraction to ensure accurate lining-up of the camshaft gearwheel (photo).
8 Press the gearwheels into position on the crankshaft and camshaft as far as they will go. Refit the camshaft sprocket retaining nut with

43.5 Inserting pistons and rods using a ring clamp to compress the piston rings

44.7 Tighten the connecting rod/cap bolts to the specified torque

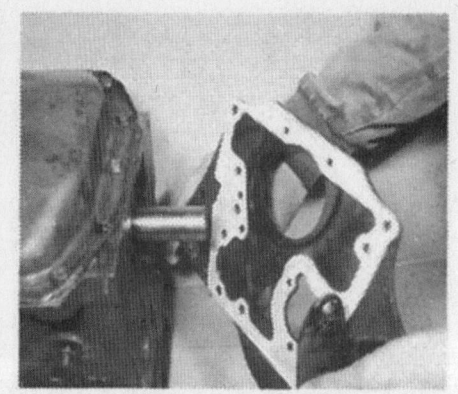

45.1 Relocate the front plate and gasket

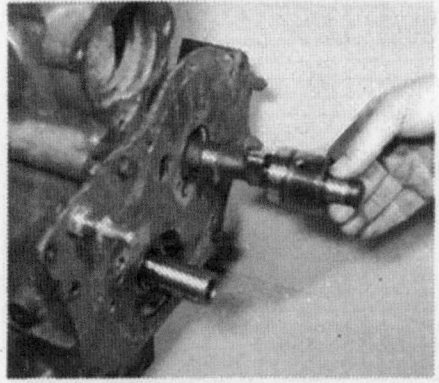

45.2 Insert the camshaft

45.6 Refit the location plate

46.4 Locate a new pump to crankcase gasket

47.2 Refit gauze strainer to pump pick-up

48.4 Flywheel retaining nuts and locktab washers

49.2 Locate the cork seal strips

49.3 Refit the sump using a new gasket

50.2 Check sprockets for alignment

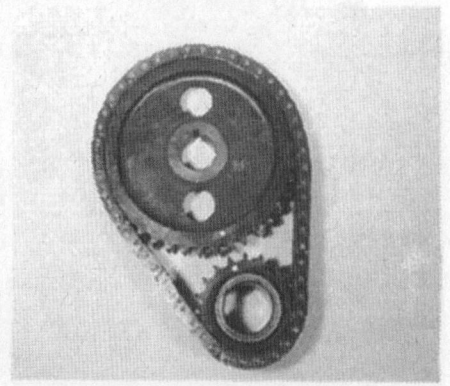

50.4 Locate the chain onto the sprockets and align timing dots

50.7 Refit the sprockets and chain – note keyway positions for timing

50.8 Bend over the lockwasher to secure the nut

50.11 Refit the chain tensioner unit and bend over locktabs to secure bolts

50.15 Install a new timing cover oilseal using a socket to drive squarely into position

50.16 Refit timing cover with new gasket

50.18 Locate crankshaft pulley and starter dog bolt with tab washer to secure

51.2 Insert valve

51.4 Locate valve spring cap and shroud over stem

51.5a Compress the valve springs to locate the collets

51.5b Retain collets with spring clips

52.2 The split pin and washer retaining the rocker assembly

53.1 Insert the tappets

lock washer (photo).

9   Next assemble the chain tensioner by inserting one end of the spring into the plunger and fit the other end of the spring into the cylinder.

10 Compress the spring until the cylinder enters the plunger bore and ensure the peg in the plunger engages the helical slot. Insert and turn the Allen key clockwise until the end of the cylinder is below the peg and the spring is held compressed.

11 Fit the unit into position with its plate and locate the two retaining bolts with a common lock washer. Tighten the bolts and turn over the lockwasher tabs to secure (photo).

12 With the timing chain in position, the tensioner can now be relaxed. Insert the Allen key and turn it clockwise so the slipper head moves forward under spring pressure against the chain. Do not under any circumstances turn the key anti-clockwise or force the slipper head into the chain. Check that the slipper head is free to move and doesn't rub against the back plate.

13 Locate the oil thrower washer onto the front of the crankshaft with its concave side to the front.

14 Generally lubricate the timing chain and sprockets with engine oil.

15 Check that the timing cover and the mating flanges are clean. If a new oilseal is to be fitted into the timing cover, support it on its underside and using a tube drift of suitable diameter drive the new seal into its aperture (photo). On early engines, renew the felt washer and smear it with engine oil.

16 Lubricate the seal and smear the mating flange of the cover with sealant or grease. Locate the new gasket and refit the cover onto the front of the engine (photo).

17 Insert the respective retaining bolts and washers but don't fully tighten them until the crankshaft pulley is fitted as the pulley shoulder centralises the seal.

18 Refit the crankshaft pulley onto the crankshaft front end engaging the pulley with the Woodruff key in the shaft. Fit the pulley retaining bolt and lockwasher and tighten to the specified torque. Bend over the lockwasher tab to secure (photo).

19 Tighten the timing case retaining bolts.

51 Valves and springs – reassembly to cylinder head

1   Rest the cylinder head on its side, or if the manifold studs are still fitted, with the gasket surface downwards.

2   Fit each valve and valve springs in turn wiping down and lubricating each valve stem as it is inserted into the same valve guide from which it was removed (photo).

3   Move the cylinder head towards the edge of the work bench if it is facing downwards and slide it partially over the edge of the bench so as to fit the bottom half of the valve spring compressor to the valve head.

4   Slip the valve springs, shroud and cap over the valve stem (photo).

5   With the base of the valve compressor on the valve head, compress the valve springs until the oil sealing ring can be located in the bottom of the cotter groove, and the cotters above. Gently release the compressor and fit the circlip in position in the grooves in the cotters (photos).

6   Repeat this procedure until all eight valves and valve springs are fitted.

52 Rocker shaft – reassembly

1   To reassemble the rocker shaft fit the split pin, flat washer, and spring washer at the rear end of the shaft and then slide on the rocker arms, rocker shaft pedestals, and spacing springs in the same order in which they were removed.

2   With the front pedestal in position, screw in the rocker shaft locating screw and slip the locating plate into place. Finally, fit to the front of the shaft the spring washer, plain washer, and split pin, in that order (photo).

53 Tappets and tappet covers – refitting

1   Generously lubricate the tappets internally and externally and insert them in the bores from which they were removed through the tappet chest (photo).

2   Before refitting the covers the cylinder head and pushrods should be refitted. When the covers are fitted check that the mating surfaces of the covers and crankcase are clean and free of old gasket.

3   Smear the flanges of the covers with sealant or grease and locate the gaskets. Fit the covers and retain with bolts and washers but do not overtighten.

54 Cylinder head – refitting

1   After checking that both the cylinder block and cylinder head mating faces are perfectly clean, generously lubricate each cylinder with engine oil.

2   Always use a new cylinder head gasket as the old gasket will be compressed and not capable of giving a good seal.

3   The cylinder head gasket is marked 'FRONT' and 'TOP' and should be fitted in position according to the markings (photo).

4   With the gasket in position carefully lower the cylinder head onto the cylinder block (photo).

5   With the head in position fit the cylinder head nuts and washers finger tight to the cylinder head holding down studs, which remain outside the rocker cover. It is not possible to fit the remaining nuts to the studs inside the rocker cover until the rocker assembly is in position.

6   Refit the respective pushrods into their original locations in the engine.

7   The rocker shaft assembly can now be lowered over its locating studs. Take care that the rocker arms are the right way round. Lubricate the balljoints, and insert the rocker arm balljoints in the pushrod cups (photo).

Note: *Failure to place the balljoints in the cups can result in the balljoints seating on the edge of a pushrod or outside it when the head and rocker assembly is tightened down.*

8   Fit the rocker pedestal nuts and washers, and then the cylinder head stud nuts and washers which also serve to hold down the rocker pedestals. Tighten the nuts down evenly, but without tightening them.

9   When all is in position, the cylinder head nuts and the rocker pedestal nuts can be tightened down in the order shown in Fig. 1.1. Turn the nuts a quarter of a turn at a time to the specified torque. Tighten the remaining rocker assembly nuts to the specified torque.

10 Now refit the tappet covers and gaskets.

55 Valve clearances – adjustment

1   The importance of correct valve clearances cannot be overstressed as they vitally affect the performance of the engine.

2   If the clearances are set too open, the efficiency of the engine is reduced as the valves open late and close earlier than was intended. If, on the other hand the clearances are set too close there is a danger that the stems will expand upon heating and not allow the valves to close properly which will cause burning of the valve head and seat and possible warping.

3   If the engine is in the car to get at the rockers it is merely necessary to remove the holding down nuts from the rocker cover, and then to lift the rocker cover and gasket away.

4   It is important that the clearance is set when the tappet of the valve being adjusted is on the heel of the cam, (ie opposite the peak). This can be done by carrying out the adjustments in the following order, which also avoids turning the crankshaft more than necessary.

Valve fully open	Check and adjust
Valve No. 8	*Valve No. 1*
Valve No. 6	*Valve No. 3*
Valve No. 4	*Valve No. 5*
Valve No. 7	*Valve No. 2*
Valve No. 1	*Valve No. 8*
Valve No. 3	*Valve No. 6*
Valve No. 5	*Valve No. 4*
Valve No. 2	*Valve No. 7*

5   The correct valve clearance is given in the Specifications and obtained by slackening the hexagon locknut with a spanner while holding the ball pin against rotation with the screwdriver. Then, still pressing down with the screwdriver, insert a feeler gauge in the gap between the valve stem head and the rocker arm and adjust the ball pin until the feeler gauge will just move in and out without nipping.

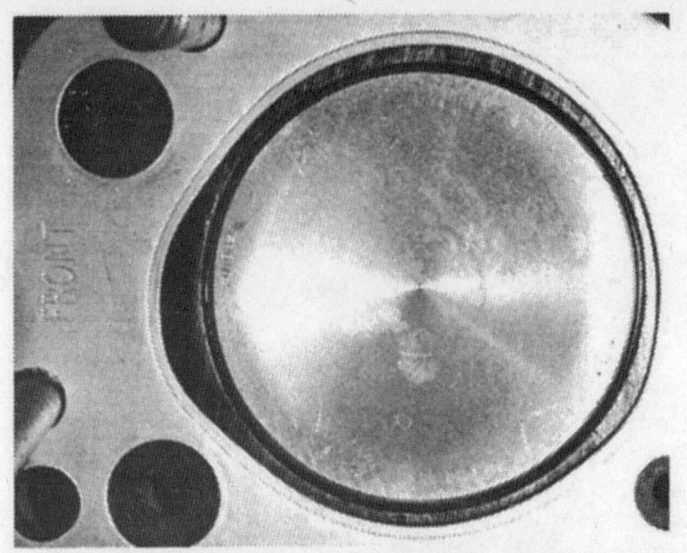

54.3 The cylinder head gasket FRONT marking

54.4 Lower the cylinder head into position

54.7 Locate the rocker assembly and pushrods

55.5 Adjust the valve clearances

56.8 Locate the housing and retaining screw

57.1a Refit the oil pressure pipe and filter feed pipe unions

57.1b Refit the tachometer drive unit

58.5 Relocating the engine and gearbox with the units removed from the car

Then, still holding the ball pin in the correct position, tighten the locknut (photo).
6 An alternative method is to set the gaps with the engine running, and although this may be faster it is no more reliable. The main advantage of this method is that an excessively noisy tappet 'knock' can be located and eliminated. However care must be taken not to overtighten the adjusters and this method is not generally recommended to the inexperienced.

56 Distributor drive gear and distributor – refitting

1 It is important to set the distributor drive correctly as otherwise the ignition timing will be totally incorrect. It is easy to set the distributor drive gear in apparently the right position, but, exactly 190° out by omitting to select the correct cylinder which must not only be at TDC but must also be on its firing stroke with both valves closed. The distributor drive gear should therefore not be fitted until the cylinder head is in position and the valves can be observed. Alternatively, if the timing cover has not been refitted, the distributor drive can be refitted when the dots on the timing wheels are adjacent to each other.
2 Rotate the crankshaft so that No. 1 piston is at TDC and on its firing stroke (the dots in the timing gears will be adjacent to each other). When No. 1 piston is at TDC the inlet valve on No. 4 cylinder is just opening and the exhaust valve closing.
3 When the marks '1/4' on the flywheel are at TDC, or when the dimple on the crankshaft pulley wheel is in line with the pointer on the timing gear cover, then Nos. 1 and 4 pistons are at TDC.
4 Screw a ⅜ in UNF bolt into the head of the distributor drive gear.
5 Referring to Section 15, set the engine timing as described in paragraphs 2 and 3.
6 Insert the distributor drive gear into the housing with the slotted section in the top face on the horizontal, the larger segment being at the top.
7 As the drive gear engages with the gear on the camshaft the drive gear will rotate anti-clockwise and when fully located the slot will be in the one o'clock position.
8 Unscrew and remove the bolt from the drive gear and then fit the distributor housing, securing it with the special countersunk setscrew (photo).
9 The distributor can now be refitted and the two securing bolts and spring washers which hold the distributor clamping plate to the distributor housing, tightened. If the clamp bolt on the clamping plate was not previously loosened and the distributor body was not turned in the clamping plate, then the ignition timing will be as previously set. If the clamping bolt has been loosened, then it will be necessary to retime the ignition as described in Chapter 4.

57 Engine final assembly prior to refitting

1 Where possible the engine must be reassembled as much as possible before refitting into the car. In general the items to be refitted are a reversal of those removed in Section 8 (photos).
2 Certain items must not be assembled before refitting the engine as they will impair the refitting procedures. The inlet/exhaust manifolds and carburettors for example must be refitted once the engine is in position in the car.
3 The dynamo is best left until the engine is refitted since it will impede and prevent fitting and location of the right-hand engine mounting if fitted before installation.
4 The oil filter assembly is best fitted before installation as is the starter motor where the engine and gearbox are being fitted together.
5 Refit the water pump and thermostat unit referring to Chapter 2 for detailed information.

58 Engine – installation

1 Although the engine can be refitted with one man and a suitable winch, it is easier if two are present. One to lower the engine into the engine compartment and the other to guide the engine into position and to ensure that it does not foul anything.
2 Generally speaking, engine replacement is a reversal of the procedures used when removing the engine, (see Sections 5 and 6).
3 Ensure all the loose leads, cables etc., are tucked out of the way. If not it is easy to trap one and so cause much additional work after the engine is refitted.
4 It will be assumed that the clutch bellhousing will have been wiped clean and any defective clutch and/or clutch release components renewed. If oil was apparent in the clutch housing when dismantled it may have been caused by oil leaking through the front seal in the gearbox (input shaft seal) and this must obviously be removed before refitting the engine.
5 When aligning the engine and gearbox (photo), engage the input shaft in the clutch disc hub splines taking care not to allow the weight of the engine to rest on the shaft until the engine and gearbox are fully assembled.
6 If trouble is experienced in engaging the input shaft into the clutch the clutch disc may need centralising in which case refer to Chapter 5. Try turning the engine over (spark plugs removed and turning the flywheel) to align the splines whilst applying a moderate pressure on the front of the engine.
7 Once in position, relocate all mounting bolts and fittings before tightening them to the specified torque wrench settings.

8 Check that all wiring is in good condition and securely located when reconnected.
9 Refit and connect the inlet/exhaust manifolds, carburettors and fuel and exhaust pipes (Chapter 3).
10 Refit the radiator and connect the respective hoses. Renew any hoses showing signs of defectiveness.
11 Check that all drain taps are closed and then refill the cooling system and engine/gearbox oils.

59 Initial start-up after major overhaul

1 Make sure that the battery is fully charged and that all lubricants, coolant and fuel are replenished.
2 As soon as the engine fires and runs, keep it going at a fast tickover only (no faster), and bring it up to the normal working temperature.
3 As the engine warms up there will be odd smells and some smoke from parts getting hot and burning off oil deposits. The signs to look for are leaks of water or oil which will be obvious if serious. Check also the exhaust pipe and manifold connections, as these do not always 'find' their exact gas tight position until the warmth and vibration have acted on them, and it is almost certain that they will need tightening further. This should be done of course, with the engine stopped.
4 When normal running temperature has been reached adjust the engine idling speed, as described in Chapter 3.
5 Stop the engine and wait a few minutes to see if any lubricant or coolant is dripping out when the engine is stationary.
6 Road test the car to check that the timing is correct and that the engine is giving the necessary smoothness and power. Do not race the engine — if new bearings and/or pistons have been fitted it should be treated as a new engine and run in at a reduced speed for the first 500 miles (800 km). The maximum speed should not exceed 45 mph (72 km/h) in top gear whilst the speeds in the lower gears should also be restricted. On the other hand do not let the engine labour (ie in a high gear when going up a steep hill for example).
7 After an initial mileage has been covered further minor adjustments may be necessary to the carburettor and possibly distributor timing. A new fan belt (if fitted) will stretch initially and its tension should also be checked and adjusted if necessary.
8 After 500 miles have been completed remove the rocker cover and check the cylinder head nuts for tightness at the specified torque. If further tightening was necessary check the valve clearances and adjust as required. Change the engine oil and filter if new bearings and/or pistons were fitted.

60 Fault diagnosis — overhead valve engines

Symptom	Reason/s
Engine fails to turn over when starter control operated	
No current at starter motor	Flat or defective battery
	Loose battery leads
	Defective starter solenoid or switch or broken wiring
	Engine earth strap disconnected
Current at starter motor	Jammed starter motor drive pinion
	Defective starter motor
Engine turns over but will not start	
No spark at spark plug	Ignition damp or wet
	Ignition leads to spark plugs loose
	Shorted or disconnected low tension leads
	Dirty, incorrectly set, or pitted contact breaker points
	Faulty condenser
	Defective ignition switch
	Ignition leads connected wrong way round
	Faulty coil
	Contact breaker point spring earthed or broken
No fuel at carburettor float chamber or at jets	No petrol in petrol tank
	Vapour lock in fuel line (in hot conditions or at high altitude)
	Blocked float chamber needle valve
	Fuel pump filter blocked
	Faulty fuel pump
Engine stalls and will not start	
Excess of petrol in cylinder or carburettor	Too much choke allowing too rich a mixture to wet plugs
	Float damaged or leaking or needle not seating
	Float lever incorrectly adjusted
No spark at spark plug	Ignition failure — sudden
	Ignition failure — misfiring precludes total stoppage
	Ignition failure — in severe rain or after traversing water splash
Engine misfires or idles unevenly	
Intermittent spark at spark plug	Ignition leads loose
	Battery leads loose on terminals
	Battery earth strap loose on body attachment point
Intermittent sparking at spark plug	Engine earth lead loose
	Low tension leads to SW and CB terminals on coil loose
	Low tension lead from CB terminal side to distributor loose
	Dirty, or incorrectly gapped plugs

Chapter 1 Engine

Symptom	Reason/s
Intermittent sparking at spark plug (continued)	Dirty, or incorrectly set, or pitted contact breaker points Tracking across inside of distributor cover Ignition too retarded Faulty coil
Fuel shortage at engine	Mixture too weak Air leaks in carburettor Air leak at inlet manifold to cylinder head, or inlet manifold to carburettor
Lack of power and poor compression Mechanical wear	Incorrect valve clearances Burnt out exhaust valves Sticking or leaking valves Weak or broken valve springs Worn valve guides or stems Worn pistons and piston rings
Fuel/air mixture leaking from cylinder	Burnt out exhaust valves Sticking or leaking valves Worn valve guides and stems Wear or broken valve spring Blown cylinder head gasket (accompanied by increase in noise) Worn pistons and piston rings Worn or scored cylinder bores
Incorrect adjustments	Ignition timing wrongly set. Too advanced or retarded Contact breaker points incorrectly gapped Incorrect valve clearances Incorrectly set spark plugs Carburation too rich or too weak
Carburation and ignition faults	Dirty contact breaker points Fuel filters blocked causing poor top end performance through fuel starvation Distributor automatic balance weights or vacuum advance and retard mechanisms not functioning correctly Faulty fuel pump giving top end fuel starvation
Excessive oil consumption	Excessively worn valve stems and valve guides Worn piston rings Worn pistons and cylinder bores Excessive piston ring gap allowing blow-by Piston oil return holes choked
Oil being lost due to leaks	Leaking oil filter gasket Leaking rocker cover gasket Leaking timing gear cover gasket Leaking sump gasket Loose sump plug
Unusual noises from engine Excessive clearances due to mechanical wear	Worn valve gear (noisy tapping from rocker box) Worn big-end bearing (regular heavy knocking) Worn timing chain and gears (rattling from front of engine) Worn main bearings (rumbling and vibration) Worn crankshaft (knocking, rumbling and vibration)

Chapter 1 Engine

Part B TWIN CAM ENGINE

61 General description

The engine is a four cylinder, in line, water cooled, double overhead camshaft type of 1588 cc (96.9 cu in) capacity. The cylinder head, which is manufactured in aluminium alloy, is of a crossflow design with two valves per cylinder.

Bucket type tappets are fitted and these locate over the respective valve stems and provide the contact face for the cams to actuate on. The valve clearances are adjustable by means of shims which can be added or subtracted from their location between the valve stem end face and the tappet under face. Various shim thicknesses are available as required, the shims being numerically numbered to denote thickness.

The camshafts run in shell type bearings, three to each shaft and are chain driven. The chain is driven by a half speed shaft sprocket which has a reduction gear mounted on its front end. This reduction gear is driven by the crankshaft gear.

The half speed shaft also drives the oil pump, distributor and tachometer. From the half speed sprocket the chain runs round a fixed guide sprocket and up to the inlet and exhaust camshaft sprockets and thence back to the half speed sprocket via a chain tensioner sprocket. The chain tensioner is adjusted manually through the oil filler hole at the front end of the cam cover on the left-hand side.

The aluminium alloy pistons each have three compression and one oil control ring. The standard pistons give an 8.3 : 1 compression ratio and unless the vehicle is being used purely for competition events, these are generally recommended, their BMC part number being AEH690.

High compression competition type pistons are available which give a compression ratio of 9.9 : 1, their part number being AEH681. However with these pistons fitted, 100 octane fuel must be used and the static ignition setting is TDC instead of the normal 8° BTDC for the normal compression ratio.

The pistons are located with their connecting rods by means of fully floating gudgeon pins. The gudgeon pins are located by circlips and the small-end bush in the connecting rod is renewable.

The connecting rod big-end bearings are shell type as also are the crankshaft main bearings, of which there are three. The counter balanced crankshaft is manufactured in forged steel and its end thrust is adjustable by means of thrust washers fitted each side of the centre main bearing.

A forced feed lubrication system is employed, the oil pump being located within the crankcase. The pump is of the eccentric rotor type and oil drawn into it from the sump is filtered through a gauze strainer. The main relief valve for engine oil pressure is fitted in the rear of the crankcase and consists of a plunger and spring. The externally mounted oil filter unit also has two relief valves which are only actuated should the filter become blocked. They enable the oil flow to by-pass the filter and continue through the main oil galleries. A renewable filter is fitted within the canister.

The sump is finned to aid engine oil cooling and the capacity of oil in the sump should never exceed the recommended amount (see Specifications), or be allowed to drop below the minimum level marking on the dipstick.

Modifications to the engine
Engine mountings

From chassis number MGA528 a packing plate with longer setscrews were fitted under the left-hand engine mounting to allow an increase in the clearance between the crankshaft starter dog and the steering rack housing. This packing plate (Part number AHH5896) can be fitted together with longer setscrews to models previous to the chassis number mentioned if required.

Half speed shaft and oil pump drive spindle

From engine number 315, and also on engine number 313, the half speed shaft and pump drive spindle were modified. The pump drive spindle teeth are increased to 11 (instead of 10) and the half speed shaft gear teeth increased to 10 (instead of 9). Where badly worn, the later type shaft and spindle units can be fitted to earlier models, but only as a pair.

Crankcase breather pipe

At engine number 657 a new crankcase breather pipe was fitted to prevent oil leakage from the engine breather onto the exhaust system. When fitting this breather to engines previous to this number, you will need to fit a longer clip and bellhousing bolt to secure the pipe to the crankcase. The pipe is retained to the vent pipe on the engine side cover at the rear and at the gearbox mounting plate.

Tappets

Larger tappets were used on cars from engine number 1087 and this was necessary to prevent tappet failure. Only assemble complete sets of one type or the other when assembling the engine – do not intermix them. At engine number 1587 tappet bushes were introduced to lessen tappet wear, each bush being located in the cylinder head by a screwed plug.

Timing cover gasket

A four section timing cover gasket was fitted to later models to eliminate the necessity to completely dismantle the timing gear when fitting a new cover gasket. This gasket has the advantage of being able to have the offending section renewed as necessary.

62 Major operations possible with the engine fitted

The following operations may be undertaken with the engine fitted in the car:

(a) *Cylinder head and associate components – removal and refitting*
(b) *Sump – removal and refitting (but only if engine mountings disconnected and engine raised sufficiently enough to allow sump removal)*
(c) *Big-end bearings – removal and refitting*
(d) *Pistons and connecting rods – removal and refitting*
(e) *Timing case, chain and sprockets – removal and refitting (steering box must be moved forward – see Chapter 11)*
(f) *Camshafts – removal and refitting*
(g) *Oil pump – removal and refitting*
(h) *Half speed shaft – removal and refitting*

63 Major operations only possible with the engine removed

The following operations can only be undertaken with the engine removed from the car:

(a) *Crankshaft and main bearings – removal and refitting*
(b) *Flywheel and clutch unit – removal and refitting*

64 Engine without gearbox – removal

1 Removal of the Twin Cam engine is not the easiest of jobs due to its somewhat confined location. The main problem is in disengaging the engine from the input shaft of the gearbox. It is not possible to move the engine forward sufficiently to achieve this as the steering box is in the way. The gearbox must also therefore be disengaged from its location sufficiently enough to be moved rearwards by about 3 inches in order to disengage the input shaft from the flywheel and clutch. If this is done the engine can be lifted straight up and out of the engine compartment.
2 The alternative to this method is to remove the engine and gearbox together as a unit. This method was recommended by MG and is described in Section 65.
3 To disconnect the engine refer to Section 65 and follow the instructions given in paragraphs 1 to 13 inclusive.
4 Disconnect the gearbox referring to Section 65, paragraphs 15 to 28 inclusive. When the gearbox is being disconnected from its mounting location support it with a jack (trolley type if available) so that it can be lowered as required to pull it rearwards to disengage from the engine when ready.
5 Unscrew the gearbox to engine clutch housing bolts and pull the gearbox rearwards to disengage it from the engine. Ensure that the gearbox is well supported.
6 Disconnect the engine mountings and lift the engine directly upwards through the bonnet aperture. Arrange the lifting sling so that

Chapter 1 Engine

when lifted the engine is kept horizontal and get an assistant to help guide the engine out of its compartment to avoid damaging any of the adjacent fittings.
7   Ensure during removal that the gearbox is well supported underneath.
8   Once lifted from the car, remove the engine to a suitable work area where it can be cleaned off and dismantled as necessary.
9   Remove the clutch (Chapter 5).

65 Engine and gearbox – removal

1   Disconnect the battery positive lead.
2   Mark the bonnet to hinge relative positions with a pencil and get an assistant to support the bonnet whilst it is detached from the hinges. Lift it clear and store in a safe place where it will not get in the way.
3   Refer to Chapter 2 and drain the radiator and cylinder block.
4   Position a suitable container under the sump drain plug, remove the plug and drain the oil. Remove the oil filter.
5   With the radiator drained, detach the hoses to the radiator, unbolt the radiator (three bolts each side) and carefully lift the radiator clear. As with the bonnet, place it safely out of the way.
6   Refer to Chapter 3 and remove the air cleaners and carburettors.
7   Disconnect and remove the heater air inlet pipe.
8   Loosen off the thermostat housing to header tank hose clips, and then remove the header tank retaining screws at the bracket. Detach the overflow pipe at the filler neck connection and remove the header tank.
9   Remove the thermostat housing (see Chapter 2).
10 Disconnect the exhaust pipes from the manifold connections and also from the steady bracket on the engine mounting plate at the rear. Loosen the exhaust downpipe to rear pipe clamp bolt and disconnect the downpipe.
11 Unscrew and disconnect the tachometer (rev counter) drive cable from the connection point on the cylinder block rear face (photo).
12 Unscrew the oil pressure gauge pipe union at its connection on the cylinder block rear face (right-hand side).
13 Disconnect the following wires from their respective connecting points and take a note of their relative locations to ensure correct reassembly:

   (a) The dynamo wires (then remove the dynamo – see Chapter 10)
   (b) Detach the distributor cap and remove it complete with HT leads, disconnecting the leads from the spark plugs and coil
   (c) Detach the low tension lead from the coil at the distributor
   (d) The starter motor wires

14 Unscrew and remove the gearbox drain plug and drain the gearbox oil into a suitable container. Once drained refit the drain plug to prevent oil emerging when lifting clear.
15 Disconnect and lift out both front seats and their frames. Unclip the carpets and remove them from the floor panels and gearbox housing cover.
16 Disconnect and lift out the floor panels and also the propeller shaft cover.
17 Release the handbrake and loosen off its cable adjuster nut (see Chapter 9). Detach the handbrake cable from the relay lever.
18 The propeller shaft to gearbox output shaft flange must now be disconnected, but make an alignment mark across the flange outer faces to show their relative locations to each other on reassembly.
19 Unscrew the gear lever knob and then withdraw the rubber draught excluder.
20 Refer to Chapter 6 and disconnect the gear lever remote control cover.
21 Unscrew and remove the gearbox cover to frame screws, and the four nuts, bolts and spring washers retaining the cross-brace plates on the left side to the gearbox cover. 'Spring' out the rear end of the gearbox cover and pull the crossbrace plates clear past the propeller shaft.
22 Unscrew the speedometer drive cable from the gearbox connections.
23 Detach the clutch slave cylinder from the gearbox. It is secured by two setscrews. When the cylinder has been unscrewed pull it free from the pushrod. The pushrod can be left attached to the clutch operating lever and the slave cylinder to the hydraulic hose.
24 Refer to Chapter 6 and remove the gearbox remote control unit from the gearbox.
25 Refer to Chapter 11 and remove the steering column.
26 Disconnect and remove the dip switch mounting bracket.
27 Detach the petrol pipe clip from the steering column dust seal retaining plate and then extract the throttle cable.
28 Remove the toe board support plate which is secured by nine setscrews with washers.
29 Unscrew and remove the four engine mounting bolts each side.
30 Locate the lifting sling into position around the engine and arrange it so that it will tilt the engine upwards at the front. With the sling in position connect to the hoist and raise it just sufficiently to take the weight of the engine without actually lifting it.
31 Unscrew and remove the nut, bolt and spring washer retaining the gearbox to the mounting bracket on the frame crossmember.
32 Before lifting the engine and gearbox clear, make a final check to ensure that all fittings and connections to the engine and gearbox are detached.
33 The engine and gearbox can now be lifted carefully upwards through the bonnet aperture. Move the engine forward a little to start with, then raise it tilting it upwards at the front and manoeuvre it clear. An assistant will be useful to help guide the gearbox and prevent the unit from swaying against the body panels. Once clear of the engine compartment, wheel the car backwards or pull the power unit clear.
34 Remove the gearbox from the engine as follows.
35 Remove the starter motor (see Chapter 10).
36 Ensure that the engine and gearbox are well supported. Undo and remove the nuts and bolts securing the gearbox bellhousing to the engine. Do not allow the weight of the gearbox to rest on the input shaft.
37 Withdraw the gearbox from the engine keeping the gearbox flange parallel with the crankcase face until the input shaft is clear of the clutch.
38 Remove the clutch (Chapter 5).

66 Engine dismantling – general

Refer to Section 7 in Part A of this Chapter and note the general instructions regarding the engine dismantling procedures.

67 Engine ancillary components – removal

1   With the engine cleaned down and suitably supported, the various ancillary items can be removed, the extent of which depends on the items left attached during removal from the car and the tasks to be performed. Assuming the engine is to be completely stripped remove the following:

   (a) The distributor (see Chapter 4)
   (b) The inlet and exhaust manifolds
   (c) Unbolt and remove the oil filter and container allowing for a certain amount of oil spillage (if not already removed)
   (d) Water pump (see Chapter 2)

68 Cylinder head – removal

If the cylinder head is being removed with the engine removed, proceed from paragraph 9
1   Drain the cooling system as described in Chapter 2 and then disconnect the header tank and thermostat housing hoses.
2   Remove the header tank and thermostat housing (Chapter 2).
3   Disconnect the heater inlet pipe (where fitted).
4   Disconnect each exhaust downpipe from its respective manifold connection and detach the pipe steady bracket from the gearbox mounting plate.
5   Unscrew and remove the exhaust manifold retaining nuts and washers and carefully withdraw the exhaust manifold from the cylinder head.
6   Refer to Chapter 3 and remove the air cleaner units and carburettors.
7   Disconnect the oil feed pipe to the cylinder head on the right-hand side at the rear.
8   Disconnect the HT cables from the spark plugs. Unscrew and

Chapter 1 Engine 51

65.11 Detach the tachometer cable from the cylinder block

68.10 Remove the cam covers

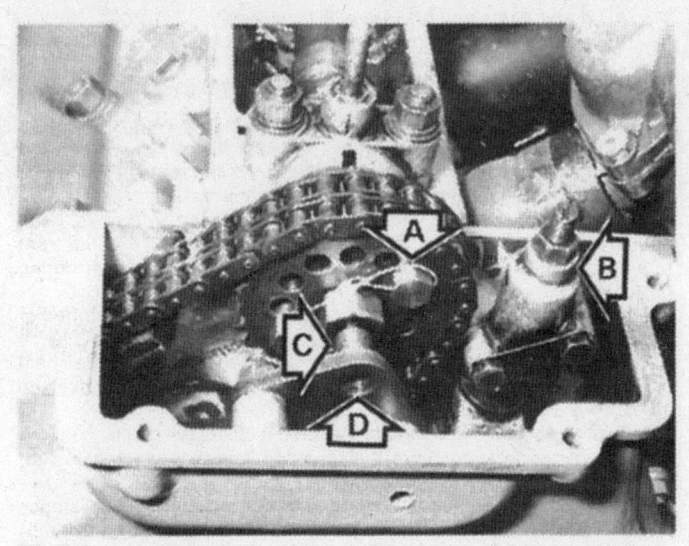

68.13 Remove the lockwire (A) from the set bolts of each camshaft sprocket. Note the chain tensioner (B). Spindle thread (C) locates in support plate (D) to disengage sprocket from camshaft

68.16 The cylinder head bolts loosening/tightening sequence (arrow indicates front of engine)

remove the respective spark plugs.
9   Disconnect the coolant intake pipe to the cylinder head at the rear which is retained by two bolts with spring and plain washers.
10 Unscrew and remove the three cam cover retaining set screws with spring and plain washers from the front end face of each camshaft cover. Remove the three domed nuts and copper washers from the top face of the covers and carefully lift the covers clear (photo).
11 Mark the relative positions of the camshaft sprockets and the drive flanges to ensure correct refitting on assembly.
12 Loosen off the timing chain tensioner adjustment screws.
13 Extract the locking wire from the setscrews retaining the camshaft drive sprockets to the flanges and loosen off the setscrews (photo).
14 Loosen the two nuts holding each of the camshaft sprocket support plates to the timing case.
15 Now pull sprockets and spindles from the flanges and locate each spindle thread within its support plate (as shown in photo 68.13), and remove the drive sprocket setscrews from each drive sprocket. **Note:** *The camshaft drive sprockets must always be disconnected from their drive flanges whenever the cylinder head or camshafts are to be removed.*
16 Loosen off the cylinder head retaining nuts in a progressive fashion and in the sequence shown (photo). When all the nuts are loosened off remove them.
17 Lift the cylinder head directly upwards to clear the studs. If it is

stuck in position, fully tap the head underside with a soft head mallet, but take care not to damage the castings. Do not try to lever the cylinder head off by inserting a tool in the gasket joint as this may damage the mating faces of the block and cylinder head.

69 Camshafts – removal

1   The camshaft can be removed with the engine in the car and if this is the case first refer to the previous section and remove the camshaft covers and detach the drive sprockets from the flanges.
2   Loosen off the camshaft bearing cap nuts in a progressive manner, one turn at a time. This procedure allows the camshaft to rise evenly on the studs and prevents the possibility of damage or distortion. **Note:** *Unscrew the rear bearing nuts first and work towards the front.*
3   As the bearing caps are removed note that they are marked for position so that they can be correctly relocated on reassembly.
4   Remove the camshaft and repeat the procedure for the remaining camshaft.

70 Valves – removal

1   Having removed the cylinder head and camshafts, as described in the previous two Sections, the valve tappets can now be removed.

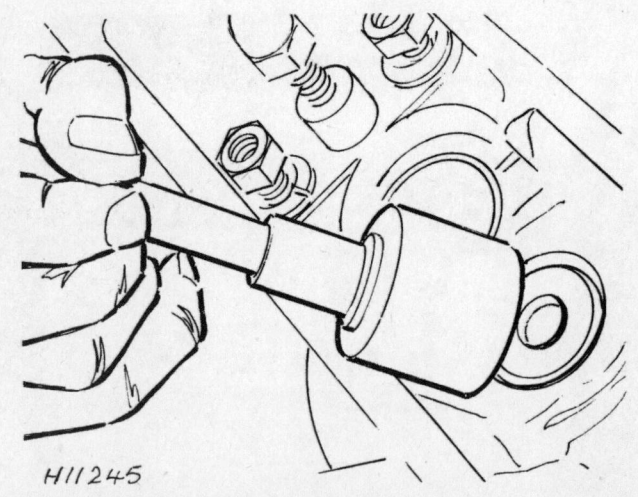

Fig. 1.7 Method of extracting a tappet using a valve grinder suction tool. Arrow indicates position of adjuster shim (Sec 70)

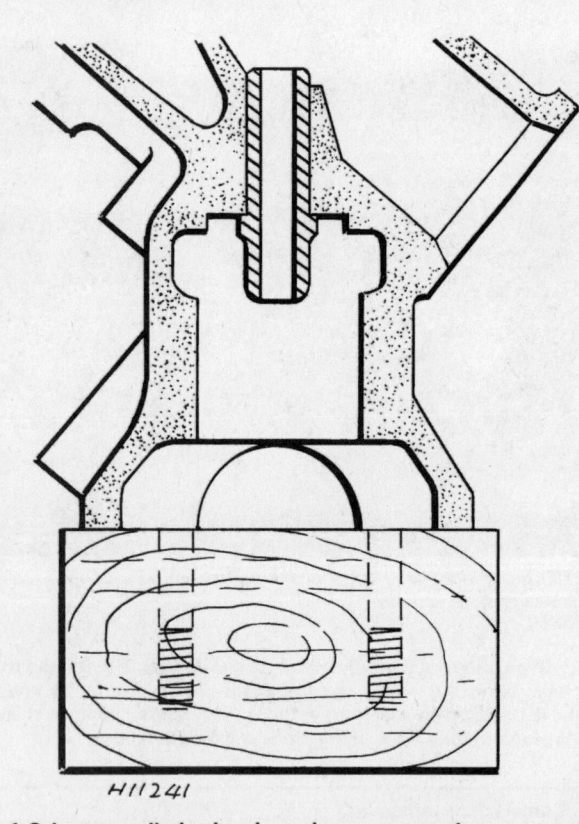

Fig. 1.8 Locate cylinder head as shown, supporting on wooden block when removing the valve guides. Note that pressure is taken on cam cover faces – not the studs (Sec 71)

Each valve assembly and tappet must be kept in order of appearance on removal so that they can be refitted to their original location.
2 The tappets are best removed using a valve grinder suction pad tool, (Fig. 1.7). As the tappets are removed keep the respective adjuster shims with them.
3 Removal of the valves necessitates the use of a suitable valve spring compressor. With the compressor in position tighten it sufficiently to allow the valve retainers to be extracted, then release the pressure on the compressor and remove it together with the valve spring cup, the inner and outer valve springs and the bottom thrust washer.
4 The valve can now be extracted from its guide and the procedure repeated with the other valves.

71 Valve guides – removal

1 With the valve assemblies removed the guides can be driven out using a shouldered drift of suitable diameter.
2 Support the head on a wooden block with the camshaft cover joint face down (Fig. 1.8). The camshaft bearing cap studs must be kept clear of the support area as it is important that they are not subjected to any pressure during removal of the guide.
3 Drive the guide out from the combustion chamber side so that it exits towards the camshaft chamber.
4 Where a guide proves particularly tight to remove it, it is advisable to have it extracted by a Leyland dealer or local automotive engineer.

72 Timing cover, sprockets and chain – removal

1 If the engine is removed from the car, proceed from paragraph 4.
2 Where the engine is in the car commence by draining the cooling system and removing the radiator (Chapter 2).
3 Loosen off the steering column upper universal joint clamp and then remove the four nuts and bolts retaining the steering rack to the frame. With all the bolts removed, pull the rack forwards so that it is clear of the crankshaft pulley.
4 Remove the following items:

(a) Water pump and by-pass pipe (Chapter 2)
(b) The distributor, distributor drive gear and housing (Chapter 4 and Section 110 of this Chapter)
(c) The camshaft covers (Section 68 in this Chapter)

5 The starting dog nut retaining the crankshaft pulley is locked in position by a tab washer. Bend back the ears of the tab washer and then using a suitable spanner (wrench) unscrew and remove the nut.
6 Withdraw the pulley from the front of the crankshaft.
7 Unscrew and remove the timing cover retaining setscrews, bolts and nuts with washers and carefully prise the cover free from the front mounting plate. Take care not to damage or distort the cover during removal.
8 If crankshaft oil seal in the cover needs renewal it can be drifted or prised out of its location.
9 To remove the timing chain, bend over the lock tabs of the chain adjuster retaining bolt washers. Unscrew the bolts and remove the adjuster.
10 Pivot the adjuster sprocket fork so that it clears the chain.
11 Extract the lockwire from the retaining screws of each camshaft sprocket and withdraw the sprockets.
12 Unscrew and remove the bolt and lockwasher with distance pieces from the half-speed shaft gear and distributor drive gear. Withdraw the respective gears and their Woodruff keys keeping them with each accordingly.
13 Remove the timing chain. Note: *Do not rotate the crankshaft if the timing chain is removed and the cylinder head is still in position.*

73 Engine front plate – removal

1 The engine must be removed from the car to detach the front plate. Refer to Section 64 to remove the engine.
2 Refer to the previous Section and remove the timing cover and chain assembly.
3 Remove the chain sprocket from the half speed shaft.
4 Unscrew and remove the three setscrews from the half speed shaft and then withdraw the shaft with locating washer and shims.
5 Unscrew and remove the oil feed pillar retaining bolt and oil pipe banjo bolt.
6 Detach the engine mounting brackets.
7 Unscrew and remove the setscrews with spring washers that retain the engine front plate in position and remove the plate.

74 Sump, oil pump and strainer – removal

1 If the engine is in the car, position a container under the sump drain plug and remove the plug to drain the engine oil.
2 Unscrew and remove the respective sump retaining bolts.
3 Lower the sump clear of the engine crankcase.
4 Remove the oil strainer unit from the oil pump cover by unscrew-

ing the three retaining bolts.
5   Unscrew and remove the three pump unit retaining nuts and withdraw the unit together with the drive shaft.

75 Pistons and connecting rods – removal

1   To remove the piston and connecting rod assemblies with the engine fitted in the car first remove the cylinder head, sump, and oil strainer as previously described in Sections 68 and 74.
2   The pistons and connecting rods can only be withdrawn upwards through the top of the cylinder block.
3   The removal procedure is identical to that given in Section 17 of Part A of this Chapter but note that the big-end caps face towards the half speed shaft.

76 Gudgeon pins and connecting rod small-end bushes – removal

1   The gudgeon pins are retained in position in the pistons by means of circlips and therefore suitable circlip pliers will be needed to contract the clips and extract them from the pistons.
2   Before removing the gudgeon pin note the piston position on the connecting rod and if not already numerically marked on the piston crown mark each piston accordingly on the same side of the crown as the connecting rod/cap numbers. This ensures correct reassembly.
3   Push the gudgeon out of the piston and connecting rod.
4   If the small-end bushes in the connecting rods are to be renewed they are best pressed out using a shouldered drift of suitable diameter whilst supporting the connecting rod at the piston end. This operation is really best left to an automotive machine shop as the new bushes will have to be reamed to size when fitted into the connecting rods. Oversize gudgeon pins are not available.

77 Half speed shaft – removal

1   This can be removed with the engine in the car. To do this remove the timing case and chain as given in Section 72. Remove the chain driving sprocket using a puller. Drain the oil and lower the sump. Remove the oil pump and pump drive shaft (see Section 74).
2   Remove the half speed shaft location plate which is retained by three setscrews and shakeproof washers.
3   Withdraw the half speed shaft and note any shims located at the rear of the location plate which allow the correct shaft endfloat.
4   Should the half speed shaft bearings be in need of replacement they can be renewed but the task is best left to an automotive machine shop who will be able to ream out the new bearings accordingly when fitted. It is essential that the new bearings are reamed accurately and also that the oil holes in the bearings are in alignment when fitted.

78 Flywheel/starter ring – removal

1   The engine must be removed before the flywheel is accessible, therefore refer to Section 65.
2   If not already removed, disconnect and withdraw the clutch unit, but mark the clutch to flywheel relative positions (if not already marked) before progressively unscrewing the six clutch retaining setscrews.
3   Mark the relative flywheel to crankshaft flange positions, unlock the tab washers under the retaining nuts and unscrew the nuts. The flywheel may have to be locked in position with a wedge of wood to stop it turning before the nuts can be undone.
4   Remove the flywheel from the flange.
5   To renew the starter ring refer to Section 39. Note that to remove the flywheel bolts, the sump and rear main bearing cap must also be removed.

79 Crankshaft and main bearings – removal

1   Remove the engine from the car as described in Section 64 and remove the following items:

   (a) Sump and oil strainer (Section 74)
   (b) Timing cover and timing chain assembly (Section 72)
   (c) Front engine plate (Section 73)
   (d) Clutch and flywheel (Section 78) and gearbox mounting plate
   (e) Big-end bearing caps (Section 76)

2   Unbolt and remove the main bearing caps. If not already marked, scribe or punch mark the number of each main bearing cap.
3   Carefully lift out the crankshaft and remove the upper main bearing shells. If the main bearing shells are to be reused (not recommended unless fairly new and in good condition) keep them with their respective caps or mark the back face of them with a felt tip pen to identify their location for reassembly. They must *not* be refitted to any other position other than that from which they were removed.
4   As the crankshaft is removed note the half thrust washers located each side of the centre main bearing. It will be seen that two of the half washers have a lug which locates into the slotted recess in the bearing cap whilst the other two halves are plain. Again, do not get these thrust washers mixed up if they are being refitted.

80 Engine lubrication system – description

1   A forced feed system of lubrication is fitted with oil circulated round the engine from the sump below the block. The level of engine oil in the sump is indicated on the dipstick which is fitted on the left-hand side of the engine. It is marked to indicate the optimum level which is the maximum mark. The oil level should always be kept up to and should never exceed this mark. The oil filler cap is at the front of the exhaust camshaft cover.
2   The eccentric type oil pump is located within the crankcase and is driven by the half speed shaft via a short vertical connecting shaft. The pump draws up the oil from the sump through a gauze strainer and then transmits it to the oil relief valve situated at the rear on the left side. The relief valve is the plunger type and is not adjustable.
3   The oil is directed from the relief valve through an integral oilway at the rear to an external pipe which delivers it to the oil filter located on the outside of the crankcase.
4   From the filter the oil passes on into the main oil gallery where it is dispersed to the crankshaft main and big-end bearings and also to the bearings of the half speed shaft. The main gallery also diverts oil via an external pipe to the bearings of the camshafts. An oil distributor pillar secured to the front engine plate sprays the timing sprockets with oil. The timing chain idler sprocket bearing and chain tension adjusting sprocket pivot bearing are also lubricated with oil delivered by pipes from the distributor pillar on the front plate.
5   At normal road speeds the oil pressure should never drop below 30 lbf/in^2 (2.1 kgf/cm^2) whilst 10 lbf/in^2 (0.7 kgf/cm^2) is the recommended idle speed pressure.

81 Oil filter – renewal

Refer to Section 23 in Part A of this Chapter.

82 Oil pressure relief valve – removal, inspection and refitting

1   The oil pressure relief valve is located at the rear of the crankcase on the left-hand side. It is retained in position by a domed head nut and sealing is by the use of two fibre washers.
2   The relief valve is non-adjustable and its object is to regulate the engine oil pressure under the various operating conditions and temperatures.
3   To remove the relief valve unscrew the domed nut and remove it complete with the two fibre washers. Extract the spring and valve cup.
4   Clean the respective components and also the machined face within the crankcase against which the valve cup contacts.
5   Check the contact surface areas of the valve cup for scratches or distortion. The spring tension is most important and this can be checked for effectiveness by measuring the spring length which should not be under 3 in (76 mm). The correct relief pressure is 50 lbf/in^2 (3.52 kgf/cm^2). If the cup or spring are found to be defective renew them.
6   Refitting is a reversal of the removal procedure. Use new fibre washers under the domed nut to ensure a good seal.

83 Engine components – examination and renovation

Refer to Section 25 in Part A of this Chapter.

84 Crankshaft and main bearings – examination and renovation

Refer to the procedures given in Section 26 of Part A of this Chapter for the method of inspection and the Specifications for Twin Cam engine for the dimensional checks.

85 Connecting rods and big-end bearings – examination and renovation

Refer to the procedure given in Section 27 Part A of this Chapter for the method of inspection but the Twin Cam specifications for dimensional checks. The connecting rods must weigh within 1 oz (28.35 gm) of the standard weight of 1 lb 15 oz 6 dr (889.47 gm).

86 Cylinder bores – examination and renovation

Refer to Section 28 Part A of this Chapter for the inspection procedures and to the Specifications for the Twin Cam for the dimensional checks.

87 Crankcase and engine mountings – examination and renovation

Refer to Section 28 in Part A of this Chapter.

88 Pistons and piston rings – examination and renovation

Refer to the procedure given in Section 29 Part A of this Chapter and to the specifications for the Twin Cam for the dimensional checks.

89 Camshafts and camshaft bearings – examination and renovation

Refer to the procedure given in Section 30 of Part A of this Chapter. Check the endfloat as given in the Specifications of the Twin Cam.

90 Timing chain, sprockets and tensioner – examination and renovation

1 Inspect the general condition of the chain and its tensioner assembly. If excessively worn or defective renew as applicable.
2 If the chain is generally worn then it's almost certain that the corresponding drive sprockets will also be the worse for wear.
3 Although the chain can be adjusted for tension to take up a certain amount of wear, this facility has its limits and therefore renew when necessary.

91 Timing gears and half speed shaft – examination and renovation

1 Check the timing gear teeth for signs of excessive wear on their contact faces. If the teeth are damaged or very worn then they must be renewed and if possible replace them as a pair.
2 Check the half speed shaft and its bearings for signs of excessive wear or damage. If renewing the bearings refer to Section 77.

92 Cylinder head, valves and valve seats – decarbonising and servicing

Refer to Sections 35 and 36 Part A of this Chapter and follow the procedure given for the overhead valve engine version, but take extra care when scraping the carbon from the cylinder head, which is manufactured in aluminium alloy and will be easily damaged.

93 Sump and oil pump assembly – examination and renovation

1 Thoroughly wash out the sump with petrol or suitable solvent and similarly clean the filter gauze and the oil pump components; the oil pump rotors are removed after unscrewing the two bolts.
2 Check that the sump is not damaged and particularly that the joints surface is cleaned of the old gasket and in good condition. Make sure that the external cooling fins are cleaned out thoroughly.
3 Inspect the oil pump components for damage or excessive wear. Check the inner rotor drive shaft for true. If badly worn, damaged or scored then the pump should be renewed.
4 Where the pump has been removed and is to be renewed with the engine in the car, it will also be necessary to remove the half speed shaft in order that the pump gear endfloat and 'free spin' can be checked. To do this mount the pump with its drive gear and thrust washer. Secure to the correct torque figure of 23 lbf ft (3.2 kgf m). Now ensure that the shaft is free to rotate without binding and that no excessive endfloat is apparent.
5 Although the oil pump is assembled 'dry', lubricate the pump drive spindle in the crankcase. Refit the half speed shaft if applicable and check its endfloat as in Section 103.
6 It should be noted that when the oil pump driving spindle is being renewed, that a modified shaft and spindle were employed from engine No 315 (also engine No 313). The modified shaft, part No. AEH619 and spindle, part No. AEH620 can be fitted to engines produced previous to the above mentioned but only as a pair.

94 Oil seals – renewal

1 At the time of a major overhaul the crankshaft rear main bearing oil seal and timing cover oil seal should always be renewed as a matter of course.
2 Prise the old seals out of position with a screwdriver, and thoroughly clean out the housings before fitting the new ones.

95 Flywheel and starter ring – examination and renovation

Refer to the procedure given in Part A Section 39 and inspect the flywheel and starter ring. Renew as applicable.

96 Engine reassembly – general

Refer to the procedure given in Part A Section 40 of this Chapter.

97 Crankshaft and main bearings – reassembly

1 Ensure that the crankcase is thoroughly clean and that all oilways are clear. A thin-twist drill is useful for cleaning them out. If possible, blow them out with compressed air.
2 Repeat the above procedure with the crankshaft oilways and then inject the oilways with clean engine oil.
3 If the old main bearing shells are to be replaced, (a false economy unless they are virtually as new), fit the three upper halves of the main bearing shells to their location in the crankcase, after wiping the locations clean.
4 Note that at the back of each bearing is a tab which engages in locating grooves in either the crankcase or the main bearing cap housings.
5 If new bearings are being fitted, carefully clean away all traces of the protective grease with which they are coated.
6 With the three upper bearing shells securely in place, wipe the lower bearing cap housings and fit the three lower shell bearings to their caps ensuring that the right shell goes into the right cap if the old bearings are being refitted.
7 Wipe the recesses either side of the centre main bearing which locate the upper halves of the thrust washers.
8 Generously lubricate the crankshaft journals and the upper and

lower main bearing shells and carefully place the crankshaft in position.

9   Introduce the upper halves of the thrust washers (the halves without tabs) into their grooves either side of the centre main bearing, rotating the crankshaft in the direction towards the main bearing tabs (so that the main bearing shells do not slide out). At the same time feed the thrust washers into their locations with their oil grooves outwards away from the bearing.

10   Fit the main bearing caps in position ensuring they locate properly. The mating surfaces must be spotlessly clean or the caps will not seat correctly. Make sure that the flywheel bolts are located on the crankshaft flange.

11   When fitting the centre main bearing cap ensure the thrust washers, generously lubricated, are fitted with their oil grooves facing outwards, and the locating tab of each washer is in the slot in the bearing cap as shown.

12   Locate the locking strip or plates over the cap and insert the bearing cap bolts. Tighten them to the specified torque settings and then bend up the tabs of the lockplates/strips to secure.

13   Test the crankshaft for freedom of rotation. Should it be very stiff to turn or possess high spots a most careful inspection must be made, preferably by a qualified mechanic with a micrometer to get to the root of the trouble. It is very seldom that any trouble of this nature will be experienced when fitting the crankshaft.

98 Pistons and connecting rods – reassembly

1   If the same pistons are being used, then they must be mated to the same connecting rod with the same gudgeon pin. If new pistons are being fitted it does not matter which connecting rod they are used with, but, the gudgeon pins should be fitted on the basis of selective assembly where supplied separate to the pistons.

2   This involves trying each of the pins in each of the pistons in turn and fitting them to the ones they fit best. Gudgeon pins should be a hand push fit at an air temperature of about 68° F (20° C).

3   If new small-end bushes have been fitted, ensure that the oil hole in the bush corresponds with the oil hole in the rod. New bushes must also be reamed to suit the gudgeon pin and as mentioned in Section 29 this is best left to an automotive machinist.

4   Lay the correct piston adjacent to each connecting rod and remember that the same rod and piston must go back into the same bore. If new pistons are being used it is only necessary to ensure that the right connecting rod is placed in each bore.

5   To assemble the pistons to the connecting rods, first locate the small-end of the connecting rod in the piston. The FRONT mark on the piston crown must face towards the front of the engine and the connecting rod situated so that the big-end cap is offset towards the half speed shaft side of the engine.

6   With the gudgeon pin bores of the pistons and small-end in alignment, press the gudgeon pin into position so that it is located within the grooves for the circlips each side. Insert the circlips to retain the pin in position and ensure that both clips are securely positioned in their grooves.

7   Check that the piston is free to pivot on the pin whilst holding the rod. Repeat the procedure for the remaining pistons and rods. **Note**: *Where a connecting rod is being fitted ensure that it weighs within 3 dr (5.32 gm) of the other rods in the set. Where possible have the rods checked for alignment before fitting into the crankcase.*

99 Piston rings – refitting

Refer to Section 42 in Part A this Chapter and follow the procedure described in the relevant paragraph.

100 Pistons and connecting rods – refitting

Refer to the procedures given in Section 42 Part A of this Chapter. The connecting rods are reassembled to the crankshaft in the same manner as that described in Section 44 Part A of this Chapter.

101 Oil pump and gauze strainer – refitting

1   Before reassembling the oil pump and gauze strainer ensure that they are perfectly clean.

2   Where a new oil pump is being fitted it will be assumed that the half speed shaft has been removed for reasons outlined in Section 93 (paragraph 4).

3   The oil pump is assembled 'dry' but lubricate the drive gear spindle where it locates in the crankcase. Always use a new pump joint washer when refitting the pump.

4   Reassembly is a reversal of the removal procedure but torque tighten the pump fixings to 23 lbf ft (3.2 kgf m). When fitted, check that the drive shaft is free to rotate without binding and that the endfloat is not excessive.

5   When refitting the half speed shaft check and adjust its endfloat as necessary by means of the shims behind the locating plate.

6   Relocate the oil strainer and bolt it into position to secure.

7   Check that the crankcase and sump flange faces are clean. Use a new gasket between them.

8   Make a final check in the crankcase to ensure that all fastenings are secure and that no tools have been left in position. Locate the cork seals on the front and rear main bearing caps.

9   Smear the mating flanges with grease or a suitable sealant and locate the gasket and sump. Refit and progressively tighten the retaining bolts.

102 Flywheel – refitting

1   Before refitting the flywheel onto the crankshaft rear flange ensure that both mating surfaces are perfectly clean.

2   Locate the flywheel onto the crankshaft flange and align the marks made when dismantled.

3   Fit the retaining plates over the studs and refit the nuts. Tighten the nuts progressively and bend over the locktabs to secure. The flywheel may have to be locked with a wooden wedge to stop it rotating before the nuts can be tightened.

4   Refer to Chapter 5 concerning the refitting of the clutch unit.

103 Engine front plate and half speed shaft – refitting and adjustment

1   Clean the mating faces of the front engine plate and crankcase.

2   Locate the plate against the crankcase with a new gasket and insert the setscrews with spring washers, tighten them securely.

3   Relocate the engine mounting brackets.

4   Refit the oil feed pillar with retaining bolt and the oil pipe banjo bolt.

5   Refit the half speed shaft with its endfloat adjustment shims and insert the three retaining setscrews with new shakeproof washers. Check the endfloat of the half speed shaft, and if it does not comply with the recommended settings given in the Specifications, readjust it accordingly by adding or subtracting shims as required.

104 Cylinder head – refitting

1   First ensure that the mating surfaces of the cylinder head and crankcase are perfectly clean.

2   A new cylinder head gasket should always be used wherever possible. The front camshaft bearing seals should also be renewed, unless the old ones are relatively new and in good condition.

3   If the camshafts are already fitted to the cylinder head, rotate the crankshaft to position all pistons about half way down their bores to avoid any possibility of enforced contact between an open valve and piston crown.

4   Smear the gasket face on each side with clean grease and locate it over the headstuds. Take care not to distort or damage it on the stud threads as it is lowered into position.

5   Now locate the cylinder head into position over the studs. Refit the retaining nuts and tighten them evenly and progressively in the sequence shown in photo 68.16 to the specified torque figure.

105.3 Align the cap timing slot and camshaft flange slot

106.4 Checking the tappet clearances using a feeler gauge

105 Camshafts – refitting

1   Position the crankshaft so that it is approximately 90° before top dead center (TDC) on number 1 cylinder (to ensure that an open valve doesn't make contact with the piston crown).
2   Check that the camshaft bearings and journals are perfectly clean before fitting. Also ensure that each tappet and its respective adjustment shims are located over the respective valves.
3   Lubricate each camshaft with clean engine oil before fitting. Once in position refit each bearing cap to its numbered position and align the cap timing slots with the camshaft flange slots (photo).
4   Refit the cap retaining nuts and tighten them progressively and evenly one turn at a time starting at the front bearing. Tighten the nuts to the specified torque setting and check that the thrust flanges do not foul the thrust slots.
5   Align the relative marks of the camshaft flanges and sprockets and refit the retaining setscrews.
6   Do not lockwire the setscrews or refit the cam covers until after the timing chain, tappets, and valve timing adjustments have been made.

106 Tappet clearances – checking and adjustment

1   The accuracy of the tappet clearance settings is of utmost importance for both engine efficiency and also to prevent tappet 'chatter'. The clearances are checked in the normal way by inserting a feeler gauge between the tappet and camshaft lobe being checked. The valve being checked must of course be in the fully closed position.
2   Adjustments are made by changing the thickness of shims located between the valve stem and the tappet underside. The shims available range in thickness graduations of 0.002 in (0.05 mm) from a minimum of 0.086 in (2.182 mm) up to 0.116 in (2.948 mm). The shims are numbered from 1 to 16 for thickness identification, ie No. 1 = 0.086 in (2.182 mm), No. 2 = 0.088 (2.232 mm) etc.
3   Remove the cam covers (Section 68).
4   To check the tappet clearances turn the engine over and set at the position where the valve to be measured is fully closed, and the cam lobe peak concerned is 180° from the valve stem head. Calculate the clearance with feeler gauges and make a note of the valve number and its clearance (photo).
5   Now repeat this procedure with the other valves in the bank concerned, and if any are in need of adjustment first make sure that you have the necessary spare shim requirements to correct the clearances.
6   Mark the camshaft flange to sprocket relative positions and remove the camshaft concerned as described in Section 69.
7   Any tappets requiring adjustment can now be removed and alternative shims fitted to correct the clearances. A valve grinding suction plunger is ideally suited for removing the tappets.

8   When the respective tappets have been adjusted the camshaft can be relocated (see previous Section) and the clearances rechecked.
9   The procedure is then repeated on the opposing camshaft bank and the cam covers refitted on completion.
10 If the substantial tappet adjustments have been made it is advisable to check and if necessary adjust the valve timing as given in Section 109.

107 Timing sprocket and chain – refitting

1   Refit the half speed shaft chain sprocket onto its shaft and locate then locate the chain onto the sprocket, passing it up through each side of the vertical chain guide.
2   Refit the timing gears to the half speed shaft and crankshaft, engaging each gear onto it's Woodruff key. Align the respective gear T-marking on the front faces which gives the correct timing (number 1 piston at TDC).
3   Refit the distributor drive gear and Woodruff key onto the front end of the half speed shaft, locate the distance washer, lock washer and bolt. Tighten the bolt and bend over the lockwasher tab to secure.
4   If the chain guide sprocket has been removed, relocate it onto its shaft, refit the washer and castle nut. Insert a new split pin to secure. Check that the sprocket rotates freely.
5   Insert the camshaft sprockets into the timing chain and position so that when fitted to the camshafts the timing setting marks will be aligned. The camshaft sprockets are secured via two retaining bolts which are then lockwired. Do not lockwire them at this stage but first refit and adjust the chain tensioner and check the valve timing as given in Sections 108 and 109 respectively.
6   Refit the tensioner unit and relocate the oil feed pipe from the oil distributor pillar. The chain tensioner adjustment screw must be loosened right off. Bend over the lock washer tabs of the adjuster unit retaining bolts once they are tightened.

108 Timing chain – adjustment

1   The tension of the timing chain is adjustable if necessary via an adjuster screw and locknut accessible through the oil filler aperture (photo).
2   The chain tension is most important since excessive play will have adverse effects on the timing of the engine.
3   Over a period of time the timing chain will stretch and need periodic adjustment for tension. When a new timing chain has been fitted it must be adjusted initially and then checked and readjusted as necessary after the engine has been run for a short period to take up any stretch.
4   To adjust the chain remove the oil filler cap on the exhaust cam cover. Using a suitable box spanner loosen off the adjuster screw locknut and then slowly tighten the adjuster screw until a resistance is

Chapter 1 Engine

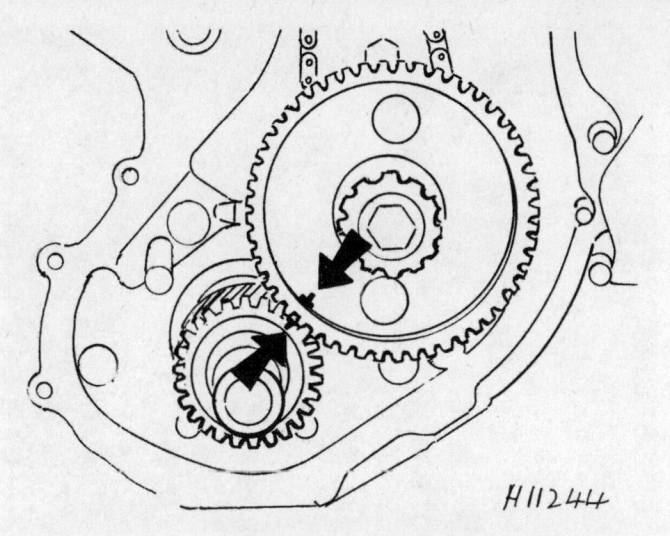

Fig. 1.9 Align the T marks of the timing gears (Sec 107)

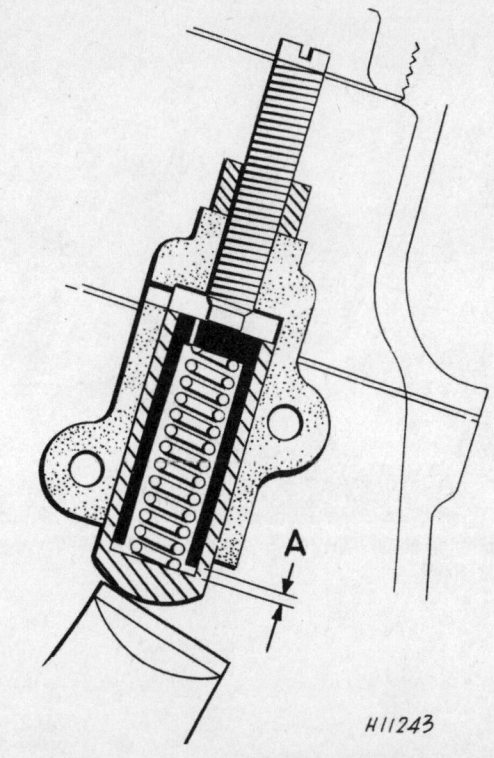

Fig. 1.10 Timing chain adjuster to allow a clearance of 0.031 in (0.80 mm) between the inner sleeve and plunger base (A) (Sec 108)

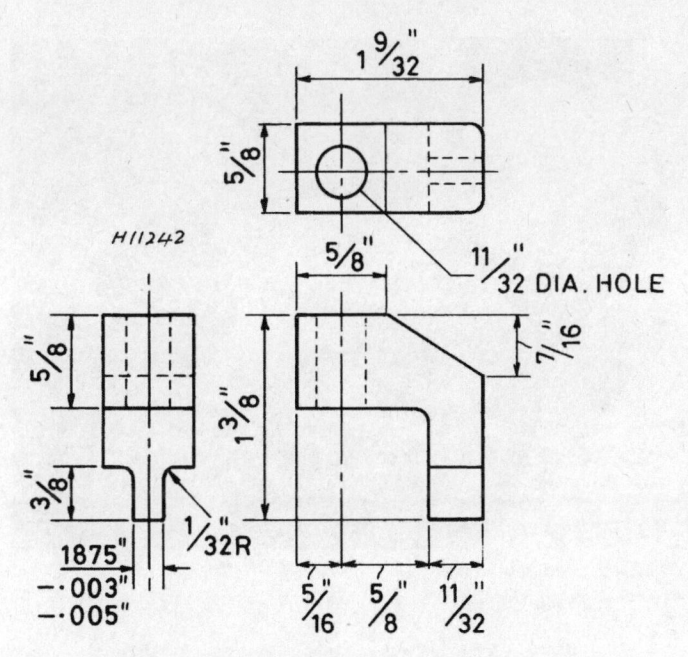

Fig. 1.11 The camshaft lock tool dimensions. This tool will be required when adjusting the timing (Sec 109)

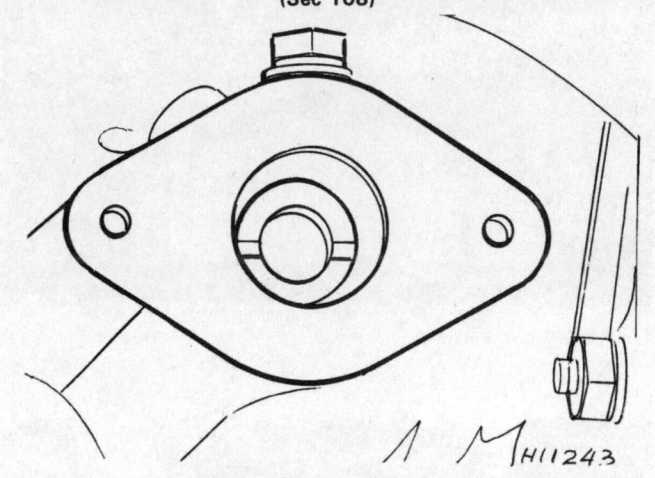

Fig. 1.12 Correct position of distributor drive slot – horizontal with large section at top (Sec 110)

felt. At this point the adjuster screw is then unscrewed ¾ of a turn and held in this position whilst the locknut is tightened to set the screw in a position where it allows a clearance of 0.031 in (0.80 mm) between the adjuster inner sleeve and plunger base inside (Fig. 1.10).
5 Where no more adjustment is possible the chain must be renewed and if the adjuster housing threads are worn or defective then this must be renewed.
6 Where the chain adjustment necessary was considerable, it is advisable to recheck the valve timing as given below (Section 109).

109 Valve timing – checking and adjustment

1 This can be undertaken with the engine in or out of the car, the most important requirements being that of a dial indicator gauge and a special MG tool, number 18G551, if available, with which to lock the camshafts in position. If this tool is not available a similar tool can be made and the dimensions of which are given in Fig. 1.11.

2 Before checking the valve timing, the tappets and timing chain tension adjustments must be known to be correct, (see previous Sections).
3 If in position, remove the camshaft covers.
4 Position the dial indicator on a suitable point on the cylinder head and arrange the indicator probe so that it is just in contact with the number 1 cylinder inlet valve tappet. The cam must not be in contact with the tappet. When in this position, zero the indicator reading and then rotate the crankshaft to locate the 4 piston at top dead centre (TDC) on its compression stroke. In this position the valves of number 1 cylinder will just be rocking. Align the notch in the crankshaft pulley with the timing mark indicator on the timing cover.
5 Now check the dial indicator reading. The number 1 inlet valve tappet should have moved between 0.072 and 0.083 in (1.831 and 2.108 mm).
6 Leave the crankshaft set at the TDC position and move the dial indicator to bear against the number 1 exhaust tappet. When the indicator is in position set the probe onto the tappet and zero the dial reading.

Chapter 1 Engine

108.1 The timing chain adjuster viewed through the oil filler aperture with cap removed

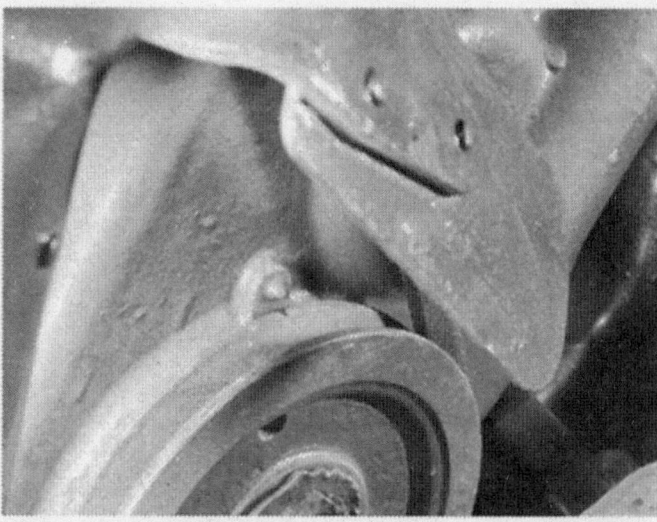

109.4 Align groove in pulley with mark on timing case to set at TDC

112.4a Refit dynamo and ...

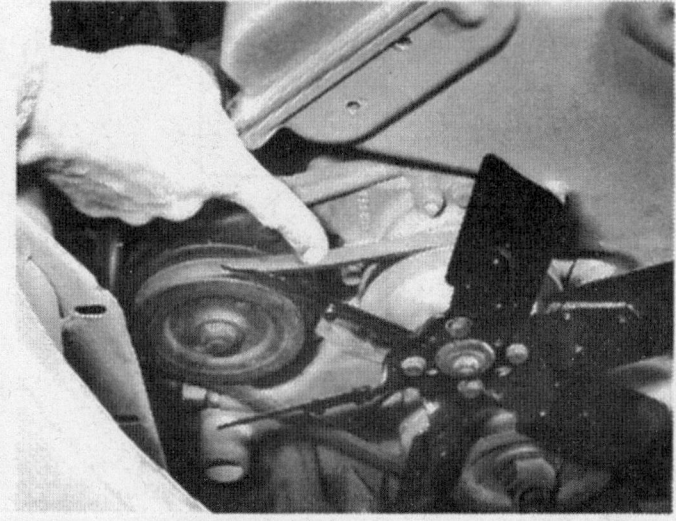

112.4b ... adjust fan belt ...

112.4c ... before refitting the radiator

7   Now rotate the crankshaft to fully close the exhaust valve at which point the cam will clear the tappet. The dial gauge indication should be within the same tolerance margin allowed for the inlet valve (see paragraph 5).
8   If the timing readings are found to be incorrect adjustment can be made in the following manner.
9   Refer to Section 72 and remove the timing chain cover.
10 Bend back the lockwasher tabs of the bolts retaining the chain adjuster, unscrew the bolts and remove the adjuster unit.
11 Pivot the adjuster sprocket unit away from the chain.
12 Rotate each camshaft in turn so that the inner flange slots align with slots in the bearing housing slots (camshaft front end). If for any reason the timing chain has been removed rotate the crankshaft so that the pistons are located about half way in the bores. This prevents the possibility of an open valve fouling the crown of a piston when the camshafts are rotated.
13 With the slots of the camshaft and bearing housings in alignment the camshaft's must be locked in position. Special MG service tool, number 18G551 is ideal for this purpose if still available, if not, a similar tool can be fabricated the dimensions of which are shown in Fig. 1.13.
14 When the camshafts are locked in position, check that the T-marks on the half speed and crankshaft drive gears are in alignment (Fig. 1.9)

when the number 1 piston is at TDC.
15 Unscrew and remove the camshaft sprocket retaining screws from both camshafts and loosen the sprocket support spindles.
16 Now rotate the inlet camshaft sprocket clockwise to take up the chain tension between the half speed sprocket and itself. In this position the two opposing holes in the camshaft sprocket should be in alignment with the corresponding tapped holes in the mating flange of the inlet camshaft.
17 Where the holes don't line up it will be necessary to lift the chain from the sprocket and rotate the sprocket so that a pair of the sprocket holes do align with the tapped holes in the flange whilst correspondingly taking up any slack in the chain between the two sprockets (half speed and inlet camshaft).
18 Having aligned a suitable pair of holes, refit the sprocket setscrews and retighten the sprocket spindle.
19 The exhaust camshaft timing is now checked and if necessary adjusted in a similar manner, but the chain must be kept tight between the exhaust, inlet and half speed sprockets.
20 When the exhaust camshaft has been readjusted and relocated, pivot the chain tensioner sprocket back into position and refit the tensioner. Adjust the tension as given in Section 108 after removing the special tool.
21 Now recheck the valve timing as described previously using the dial gauge and if necessary make further slight adjustments by advancing or retarding by one hole.
22 Use new lockwire and wire the sprocket setscrews.
23 Refit the timing case and cam covers ensuring that the gaskets and their mating faces are clean.

110 Distributor drive gear – refitting

1 Rotate the crankshaft to locate the number 4 pistons at TDC on its firing (compression) stroke at which point the number 1 cylinder valves are rocking – exhaust closing and inlet opening. At this point the crankshaft pulley timing notch should be in line with the timing indicator on the timing cover.
2 Rotate the distributor drive gear so that the large segment is uppermost as shown in Fig. 1.12 and the engagement slot is horizontal.
3 When the driven gear contacts the half speed shaft the slot will rotate anti-clockwise to the two o'clock position. Relocate the housing nuts, with flat and spring washers.
4 Refit the distributor and its clamp plate. If for any reason the clamp plate was disturbed, refer to Chapter 4, concerning timing the distributor (static ignition timing).

111 Engine – final assembly

1 The camshaft covers can now be refitted and secured, if not already in place. Use new copper washers under the domed head nuts.
2 Refer to Chapter 5 and refit the clutch unit.
3 Refer to Chapter 2 and refit the water pump unit.

4 If fitting the engine and gearbox as a unit, locate the starter motor before fitting the engine and gearbox.
5 Refer to Section 23 and refit the oil filter unit.
6 Refit the inlet and exhaust manifolds. Ensure that both manifold and cylinder head mating faces are perfectly clean and free from all traces of the old gaskets. Use new gaskets.
7 Refit the carburettors, ensuring that the joint faces are perfectly clean and use new gaskets.
8 Do not refit the dynamo until after the engine has been installed and the engine mounting tightened on the right-hand side otherwise it is inaccessible.
9 Refer to Chapter 4 and relocate the distributor.
10 Refit the external oil feed pipes using new joint washers.
11 Refit the oil relief valve spring and plunger and secure with the domed nut and two fibre washers.

112 Engine – refitting

Although the engine can be replaced with one man and a suitable winch, it is easier if two are present. One to lower the engine into the engine compartment and the other to guide the engine into position and to ensure that it does not foul anything. Generally speaking, engine or engine/gearbox replacement is a reversal of the procedures used when removing the engine, (see Sections 64 and 65 as applicable), but one or two added tips may come in useful.

1 Ensure all the loose leads, cables, etc., are tucked out of the way. It is easy to trap one and so cause much additional work after the engine is replaced, if this is not attended to beforehand.
2 Once the unit is in position loosely locate the respective fastenings until they are all engaged, and then tighten them.
3 Don't forget to relign the mating marks of the gearbox output and propeller shaft front flanges before bolting them together (when applicable).
4 When the engine mountings are tightened, refit the dynamo and adjust the fan belt before refitting the radiator (photos).

113 Initial start-up after major overhaul

Refer to Section 59 in Part A of this Chapter and observe the suggested procedures.

114 Fault diagnosis – Twin Cam engines

In general the faults diagnosis chart given in Part A (Section 60) of this Chapter applies to both the overhead valve and Twin Cam engines. However as the Twin Cam engine is more highly developed it is apt to be more temperamental if not tuned regularly, particular attention being paid to the ignition timing and carburettor timing. Both of these items must be set up correctly for the engine to perform as it was designed and therefore should problems occur, particular attention should be paid to checking both of these items carefully.

Chapter 2 Cooling system

Contents

Antifreeze mixture	11
Cooling system – draining	2
Cooling system – filling	4
Cooling system – flushing	3
Fan belt – adjustment	12
Fan belt – removal and refitting	13
Fault diagnosis – cooling system	15
General description	1
Header tank (Twin Cam engine) – dismantling and reassembly	7
Radiator – removal and refitting	5
Temperature gauge – general	14
Thermostat – removal, testing and refitting	6
Water pump (overhead valve engines) – dismantling and reassembly	9
Water pump – removal and refitting	8
Water pump (Twin Cam engine) – dismantling and reassembly	10

Specifications

System type
Pressurised, pump impeller and fan assisted

Thermostat setting
15GB and 15GD engines	70 to 75°C (158 to 167°F)
16GA engine:	
Opens at	68°C (154°F)
Fully open at	83°C (181°F)
16GC engine	66°C (150°F)
BC16GB Twin Cam engine	50 to 55°C (122 to 131°F)

Water pump
Water pump type	Centrifugal
Water pump drive	Belt from crankshaft pulley

Drive belt tension adjustment
1 in (2·5 cm) measured side to side at centre of longest run

Torque wrench setting
	lbf ft	kgf m
Water pump bolts	25	3·45

1 General description

Overhead valve engines

The engine cooling water is circulated by a thermo-siphon, water pump assisted system, and the coolant is pressurised. This is to both prevent the loss of water down the overflow pipe with the radiator cap in position and to prevent premature boiling in adverse conditions.

The radiator cap is pressurised to 7 lbf/in² (0·5 kgf/cm²) and increases the boiling point to 107°C (225°F). If the water temperature exceeds this figure and the water boils, the pressure in the system forces the internal part of the cap off its seat, thus exposing the overflow pipe down which the steam from the boiling water escapes thus relieving the pressure.

It is, therefore, important to check that the radiator cap is in good condition and that the spring behind the sealing washer has not weakened. Most garages have a special machine in which radiator caps can be tested.

The cooling system comprises the radiator, top and bottom water hoses, heater hoses (if heater/demister fitted), the impeller water pump, (mounted on the front of the engine it carries the fan blades and is driven by the fan belt), the thermostat and the two drain taps.

The system functions in the following fashion. Cold water in the bottom of the radiator circulates up the lower radiator hose to the water pump where it is pushed round the water passages in the cylinder block, helping to keep the cylinder bores and pistons cool.

The water then travels up into the cylinder head and circulates round the combustion spaces and valve seats absorbing more heat, and then, when the engine is at its proper operating temperature, travels out of the cylinder head, past the open thermostat into the upper radiator hose and so into the radiator header tank.

The water travels down the radiator where it is rapidly cooled by the in-rush of cold air through the radiator core, which is created by both the fan and the motion of the car. The water, now cold, reaches the bottom of the radiator, when the cycle is repeated.

When the engine is cold the thermostat (a valve which opens and closes according to the temperature of the water) maintains the circulation of the same water in the engine.

Only when the correct minimum operating temperature has been reached, as shown in the specification, does the thermostat begin to open, allowing water to return to the radiator.

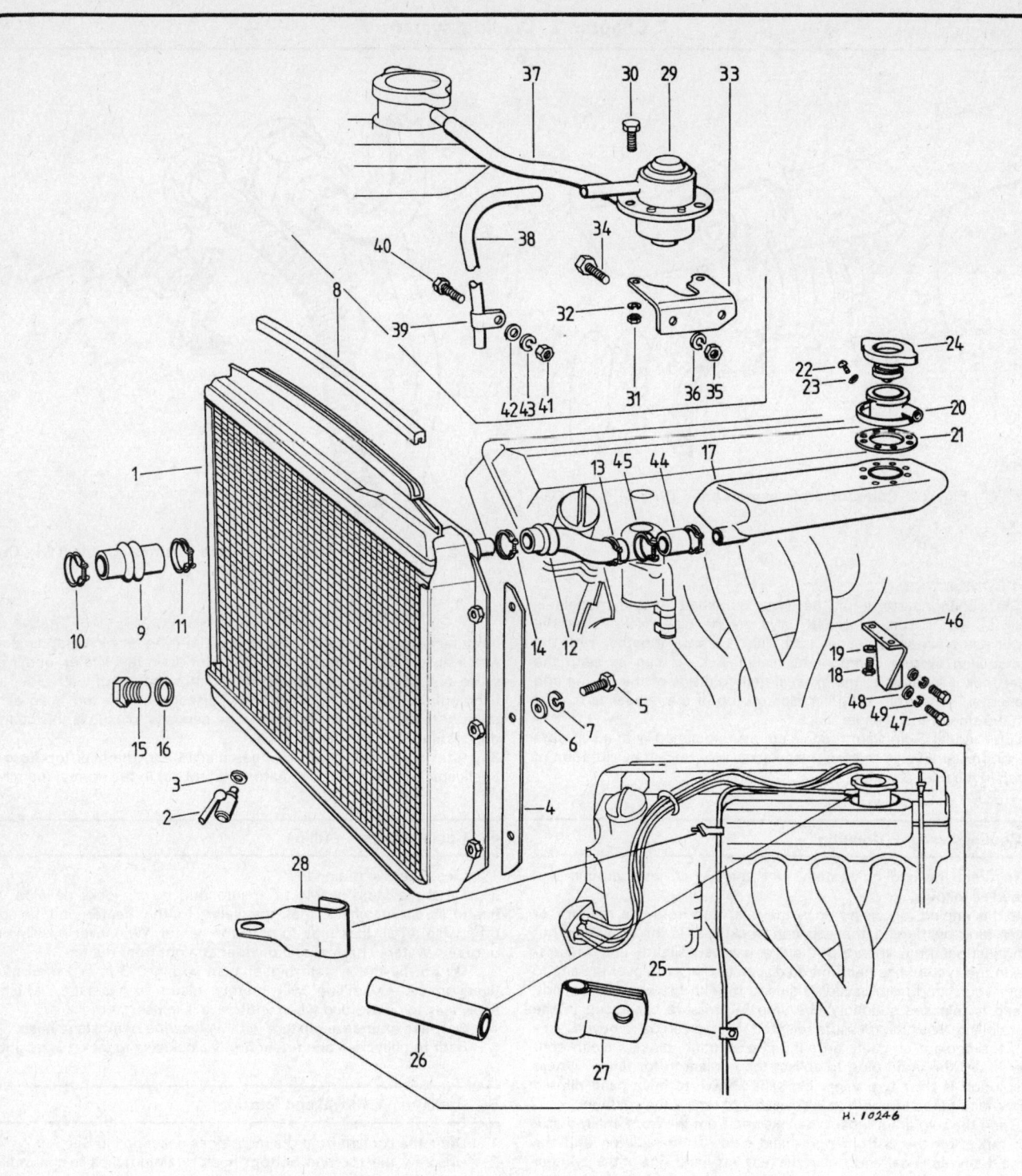

Fig. 2.1 The cooling system components of the Twin Cam engine (Sec 1)

1 Radiator	14 Small clip	26 Overflow pipe connection	38 Overflow tube
2 Drain tap	15 Plug	27 Clip	39 Bracket
3 Washer	16 Washer	28 Clip	40 Screw
4 Packing piece	17 Header tank	29 Relief valve and cage	41 Nut
5 Screw	18 Screw	30 Screw	42 Washer
6 Washer (plain)	19 Washer	31 Nut	43 Washer
7 Washer (spring)	20 Filler neck	32 Washer	44 Hose
8 Radiator air seal rubber	21 Filler neck gasket	33 Valve bracket	45 Clip
9 Bottom hose	22 Screw	34 Screw	46 Bracket
10 Large clip	23 Washer	35 Nut	47 Screw
11 Small clip	24 Header tank cap	36 Washer	48 Washer
12 Top hose	25 Overflow pipe	37 Hose	49 Washer
13 Large clip			

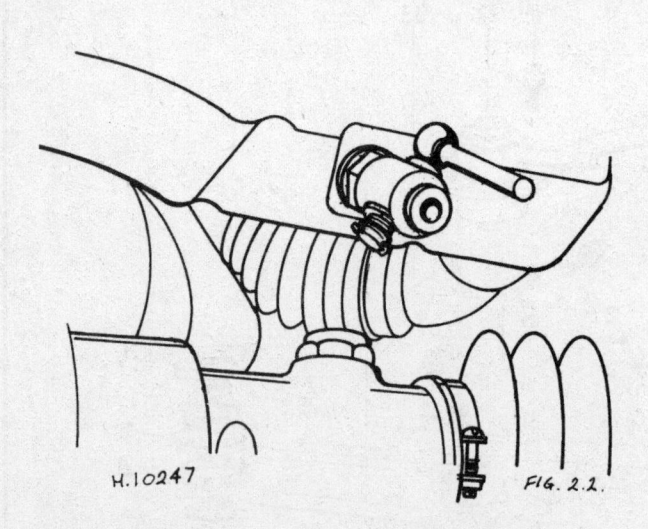

Fig. 2.2 Radiator drain cap location (Sec 2)

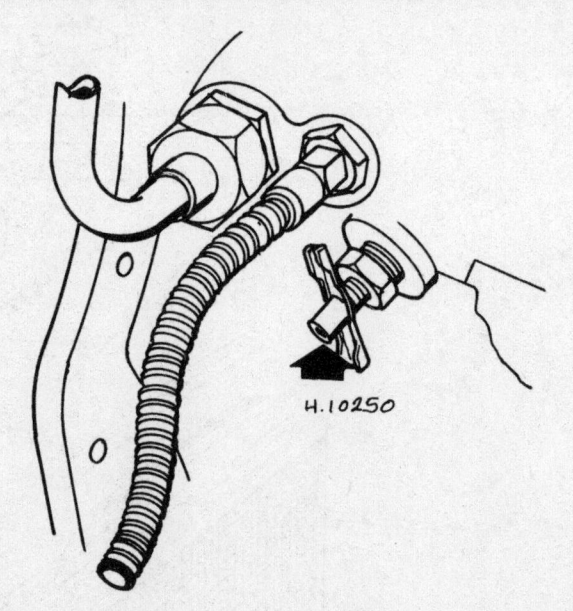

Fig. 2.3 The cylinder block drain tap position on the Twin Cam engine (Sec 2)

Twin Cam engine

The cooling system for the Twin Camshaft engine models is similar to that of the overhead valve engine type except that the radiator has a separate header tank. This is shown together with the other cooling system components in Fig. 2.1. As can be seen the header tank is located on the exhaust manifold side of the engine and the overflow pipe from the filler pipe on top of the header tank runs down the side of the cylinder block.

Later model Twin Cam models are also equipped with a separate radiator pressure valve to stop the coolant boss caused by vibration of the cap in the filler cap.

2 Cooling system – draining

1 To drain the cooling system, park the car on level ground and proceed as follows.
2 If the engine is cold remove the filler cap from the radiator or header tank by turning the cap anti-clockwise. If the engine is hot having just been run, then turn the filler cap very slightly until the pressure in the system has had time to disperse. Use a rag over the cap to protect your hand from escaping steam. If, with the engine very hot, the cap is released suddenly, the drop in pressure can result in the water boiling. With the pressure released the cap can be removed.
3 If the coolant contains an antifreeze solution, place a clean container under the drain plug to collect the coolant for reuse. Where the solution is over two years old or is known to have been diluted below the required strength, it is advisable to renew the solution.
4 Open the two drain taps. When viewed from the front, the radiator drain tap is on the bottom right-hand side of the radiator, and the engine drain tap is halfway down the rear left-hand side of the cylinder block (on Twin Cam engines the radiator drain tap is on the bottom left-hand side when viewed from the front).
5 A short length of rubber tubing over the radiator drain tap nozzle will assist draining the coolant into a container without splashing.
6 When the water has finished running, probe the drain tap orifices with a short piece of wire to dislodge any particles of rust or sediment which may be blocking the taps and preventing all the water draining out.

3 Cooling system – flushing

1 With time the cooling system will gradually lose its efficiency as the radiator becomes choked with rust scales, deposits from the water and other sediment. To clean the system out, remove the radiator/header tank cap and the drain tap and leave a hose running in the radiator cap orifice for ten to fifteen minutes.
2 In very bad cases the radiator should be reverse flushed. This can be done with the radiator in position. The cylinder block tap is closed and a hose placed over the open radiator drain tap. Water, under pressure, is then forced up through the radiator and out of the header tank filler orifice. On Twin Cam models, disconnect the top hose at the radiator to allow the water and sludge deposits to exit via this connection instead of at the header tank.
3 After reverse flushing the hose placed into the filler/top hose (as applicable) orifice and the radiator washed out in the normal manner.

4 Cooling system – filling

1 Close the two drain taps.
2 Fill the system slowly to ensure that no air locks develop. If a heater is fitted, check that the valve to the heater unit is open, otherwise an air lock may form in the heater. Whenever possible use pure rain water in preference to water straight from the tap.
3 Do not fill the system higher than within 0·5 in (13 mm) of the filler orifice. Overfilling will merely result in wastage, which is especially to be avoided when antifreeze is in use.
4 Only use antifreeze mixture with a glycerine or ethylene base.
5 Refit the filler cap and turn it firmly clockwise to lock it in position.

5 Radiator – removal and refitting

1 Drain the coolant from the radiator as described in Section 2.
2 Unscrew the top and bottom hose retaining clips to the radiator and disconnect the hoses. If when the hoses are disconnected they crack or are obviously defective remove and renew them on reassembly.
3 The radiator is secured in position by means of three bolts on each side. Unscrew and remove these bolts and then carefully lift the radiator from the car (photo).
4 Once out of the car the radiator can be cleaned and inspected. Blow through from the rear with an air line and hose through to remove the usual insects and dust in the core. Flush the radiator out as previously described.
5 If the radiator suffers from a serious leak due to damage to the core or decay then its repair is best entrusted to a specialist or where possible renewed.
6 There are also a number of 'anti leak' products on the market which are designed to be diluted with the coolant and if the manufacturers instructions are followed closely, will often stop quite sizeable leaks.
7 Check that the drain tap is securely located and in good condition.

Chapter 2 Cooling system

5.3 Lift the radiator clear (1500 engine)

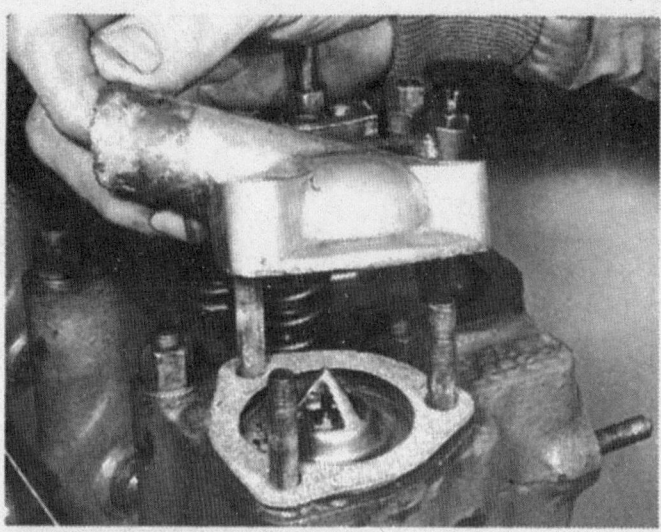

6.2a Remove the housing and cork gasket

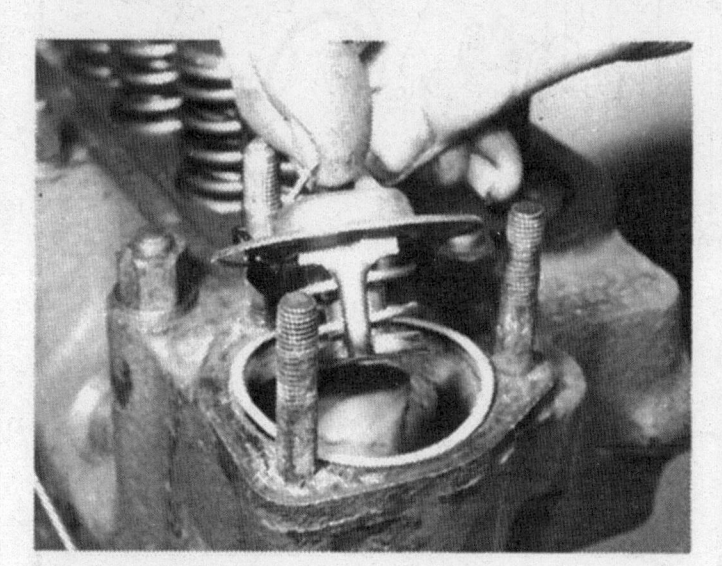

6.2b Remove the thermostat and paper gasket

6.9 The Twin Cam thermostat housing

Renew it if necessary and fit a new sealer washer.

8 The radiator cap is designed to work at a given pressure and if suspect, can be tested at most garages. Check that the cap is of the correct pressure rating of 7 lbf/in^2 (3·175 kgf/cm^2). The pressure rating is marked on the top of the cap.

9 Refitting the radiator is a reversal of the removal procedure, special care being taken to lift it into position without damaging it. Locate all of the retaining bolts and packing strips each side before finally tightening them.

10 Once the hoses have been reconnected and the coolant level topped-up, run the engine up to its normal operating temperature and check for any signs of leaks, particularly from the hose connections.

6 Thermostat – removal, testing and refitting

Overhead valve engines

1 To remove the thermostat partially drain the cooling system (4 pints is enough), loosen the upper radiator hose at the thermostat elbow end and pull it off the elbow.

2 Unscrew the three set bolts and spring washers from the thermostat housing and lift the housing and cork gasket away. Take out the thermostat, and paper gasket (photos).

3 Test the thermostat for correct functioning by immersing it in a saucepan of cold water together with a thermometer.

4 Heat the water and note when the thermostat begins to open. The opening temperature for your particular model is given in the Specifications.

5 Discard the thermostat if it opens too early. Continue heating the water until the thermostat is fully open. Then let it cool down naturally. If the thermostat will not open fully in boiling water, or does not close down as the water cools, then it must be exchanged for a new one.

6 If the thermostat is stuck open when cold this will be apparent when removing it from the housing.

7 Refitting the thermostat is a reversal of the removal procedure. Remember to use a new gasket between the thermostat housing elbow and the thermostat. Renew the thermostat elbow if it is badly corroded.

Twin Cam engine

8 The thermostat removal and testing procedures for this engine are similar to that for the overhead valve engine.

9 The thermostat and its housing assembly are shown in Fig. 2.4. Where the housing is to be removed, disconnect the heater inlet pipe (where fitted) and remove the retaining nuts and bolts (photo).

10 Refitting is a reversal of the removal procedure. Check for signs of leaks on completion when the system has been topped-up.

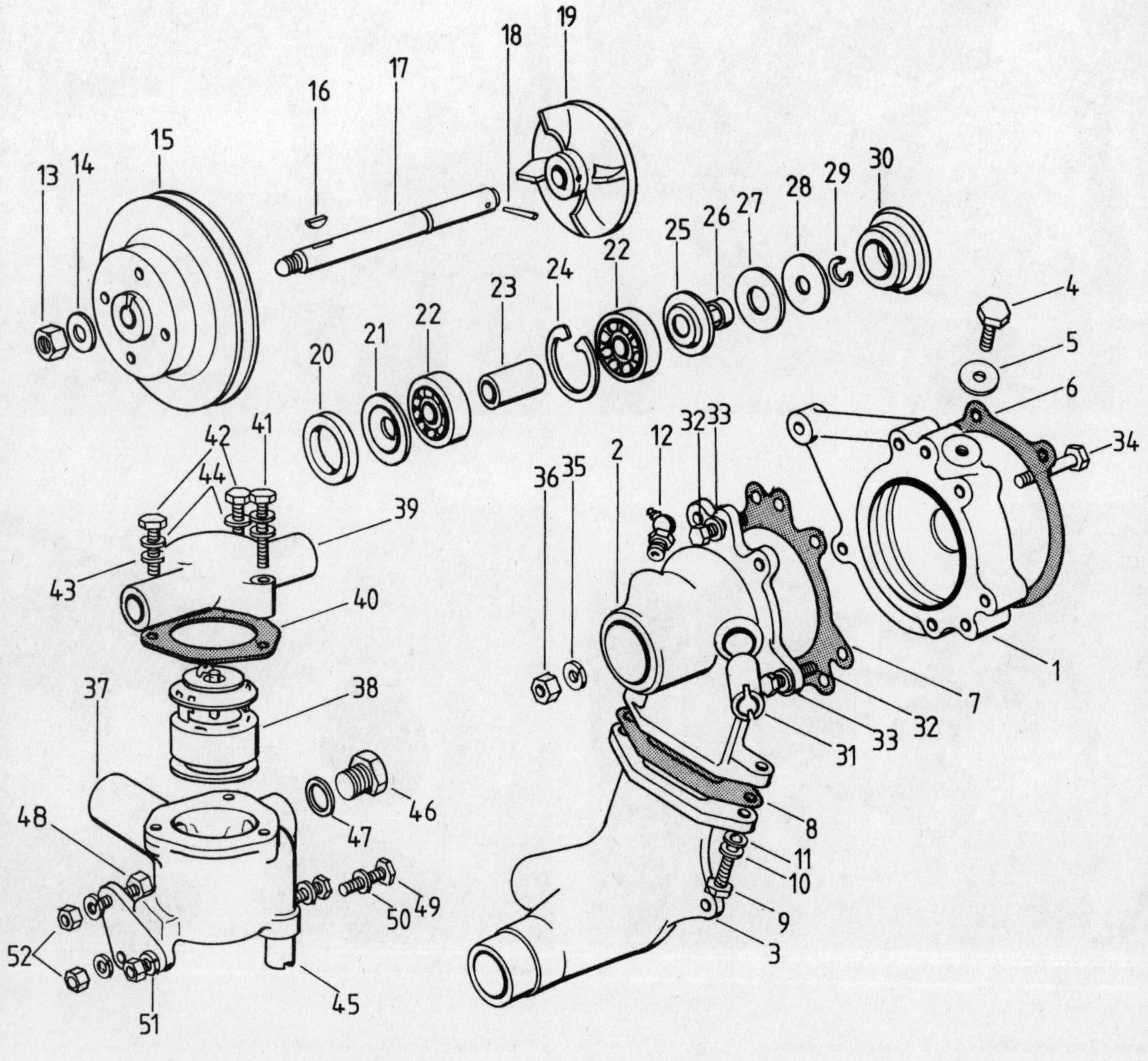

Fig. 2.4 The components of the water pump and thermostat fitted to Twin Cam engines (Sec 6)

1 Scroll	14 Lockwasher	27 Felt washer	40 Joint for cover
2 Body	15 Fan pulley	28 Dust cover	41 Bolt
3 Inlet pipe	16 Spindle key	29 Circlip	42 Set screw
4 Vent plug	17 Spindle	30 Seal	43 Plain washer
5 Washer	18 Vane taper pin	31 Hose connection	44 Spring washer
6 Gasket	19 Vane	32 Setscrew	45 Thermostat by-pass pipe
7 Gasket	20 Felt washer	33 Spring washer	46 Plug (heater take-off)
8 Gasket	21 Dust cover	34 Bolt	47 Washer for plug
9 Set screw	22 Bearing	35 Spring washer	48 Bolt
10 Spring washer	23 Bearing distance tube	36 Nut	49 Setscrew
11 Plain washer	24 Circlip	37 Thermostat housing	50 Plain washer
12 Bearing grease nipple	25 Dust cover	38 Thermostat	51 Spring washer
13 Nut	26 Collar	39 Housing cover	52 Nut

Chapter 2 Cooling system 65

8.5 The water pump location on the Twin Cam engine (arrowed)

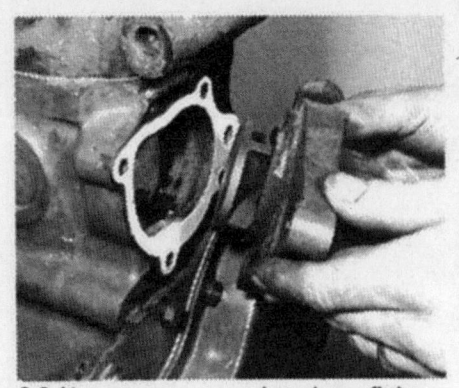

8.6 Always use a new gasket when refitting the water pump

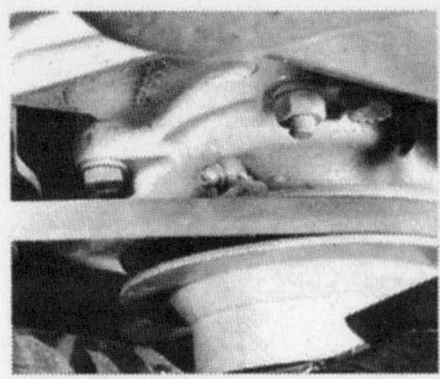

10.8 The Twin Cam water pump lubrication nipple

7 Heater tank (Twin Cam engine) – removal and refitting

1 Partially drain the cooling system to lower the level sufficiently to disconnect the feed pipe to the thermostat housing cover.
2 Disconnect the hose at the header tank.
3 Detach the heater air inlet pipe.
4 Detach the overflow pipe at the filler neck.
5 Unscrew and remove the two header tank retaining set screws with spring and flat washers and lift the tank clear.
6 Refitting is a reversal of the removal procedure. Check for leaks on completion of assembly and topping-up.

8 Water pump – removal and refitting

1 Refer to Section 2 and drain the cooling system.
2 Refer to Section 5 and remove the radiator.
3 Loosen the dynamo attachment bolts and pivot it inwards towards the engine. Disconnect the drive belt from the pulleys. Remove the dynamo mounting bolts and adjuster strap bolts and place the dynamo to one side.
4 Unscrew the four bolts retaining the cooling fan and pulley to the water pump spindle flange and detach the fan and pulley.
5 Unscrew and remove the water pump retaining bolts (and nuts if fitted) and withdraw the pump from the front face of the cylinder block (photo).
6 Refitting is a reversal of the removal procedure. Always use new gaskets (photo) and ensure that the mating surfaces are perfectly clean on both the pump and cylinder block.
7 Retension the drive belt as described in Section 12.

9 Water pump (overhead valve engines) – dismantling and reassembly

Early type

1 To dismantle the pump unit, unscrew the central nut, then tap or pull off the hub from the spindle but take care not to damage it. Remove the Woodruff key and deburr it with a file.
2 Extract the dished oil seal washer and retaining circlip.
3 Use a soft head hammer and carefully tap the pump spindle out of the body (rearwards) and remove the seal gland.
4 The ball bearings can be removed using suitable pullers. Remove the front bearing first followed by the distance piece and then the rear bearing.
5 Remove the rear bearing felt washer and its retainers. Although not normally necessary, the rear distance piece can be removed to complete the dismantling.
6 Reassembly is a direct reversal of the removal procedure but note the following:

  (a) Ensure that all items are perfectly clean before assembly
  (b) Repack the bearings with grease or equivalent
  (c) Always renew the oilseal and felt oilseal washer

Later type pump dismantling

7 On later models from engine number 15GB/U/H39526 on (and some earlier models) the water pump was modified to incorporate a one piece bearing. The later type of pumps can be refitted in place of the early type on models previous to the given engine number but only as a complete unit. Dismantle the later type as follows.
8 With the fan blades and fan pulley removed, pull or tap off the hub from the end of the spindle, taking great care not to damage it.
9 Then pull out the bearing retaining wire.
10 The spindle and bearing assembly are combined (and are only supplied on exchange as a complete unit), and should now be gently tapped out of the rear of the water pump.
11 The oil seal assembly and the impeller will also come out with the spindle and bearing assembly.
12 The impeller vane is removed from the spindle by judicious tapping and levering, or preferably, to ensure no damage and for ease of operation, with an extractor. The oil seal assembly can then be slipped off.
13 Reassembly of the water pump is a reversal of the above sequence. Three points should be noted which have not already been covered:-

  (a) If the oil seal assembly shows any sign of damage or wear it should be renewed, and the block should be renewed every time the pump is removed
  (b) There is a small hole in the bearing body cover. When assembled it is vital that this hole lines up with the lubrication hole in the pump body. To check that this is so, prior to reassembly remove the greasing screw and check visually that the hole is in the correct position directly below the greasing aperture (Fig. 2.6).
  (c) Regrease the bearing by pushing a small amount of grease into the greaser and then screwing in the greasing screw. Under no circumstances should grease be applied under pressure as it could ruin the efficiency of the oil seal

10 Water pump (Twin Cam engine) – dismantling and reassembly

1 Unscrew and remove the hub nut with its spring washer from the spindle. Carefully withdraw the hub using a suitable extractor.
2 Unscrew and remove the two bolts retaining the inlet pipe and detach the pipe.
3 Prise the felt seal and Woodruff key from the spindle. Any burrs on the key must be removed with a fine file.
4 Extract the dished oil seal washer.
5 Unscrew the four bolts that hold the pump body to the scroll casing. Separate the pump body from the scroll casing and then tap the spindle out rearwards. Remove the seal washer, felt seal and dished seal washer followed by the rubber gland seal with circlip.
6 To remove the bearings employ a suitable puller/extractor. The rear bearing can only be extracted after removing the central spacer and circlip.
7 Assembly is a reversal of the removal procedure but prior to fitting the pump body to the scroll case check the body to pump valve clearance which should be as shown in Fig. 2.7. No adjustment is possible and a new pump is the alternative.
8 Always repack the bearings with grease and use new seals, gaskets and washers (photo).

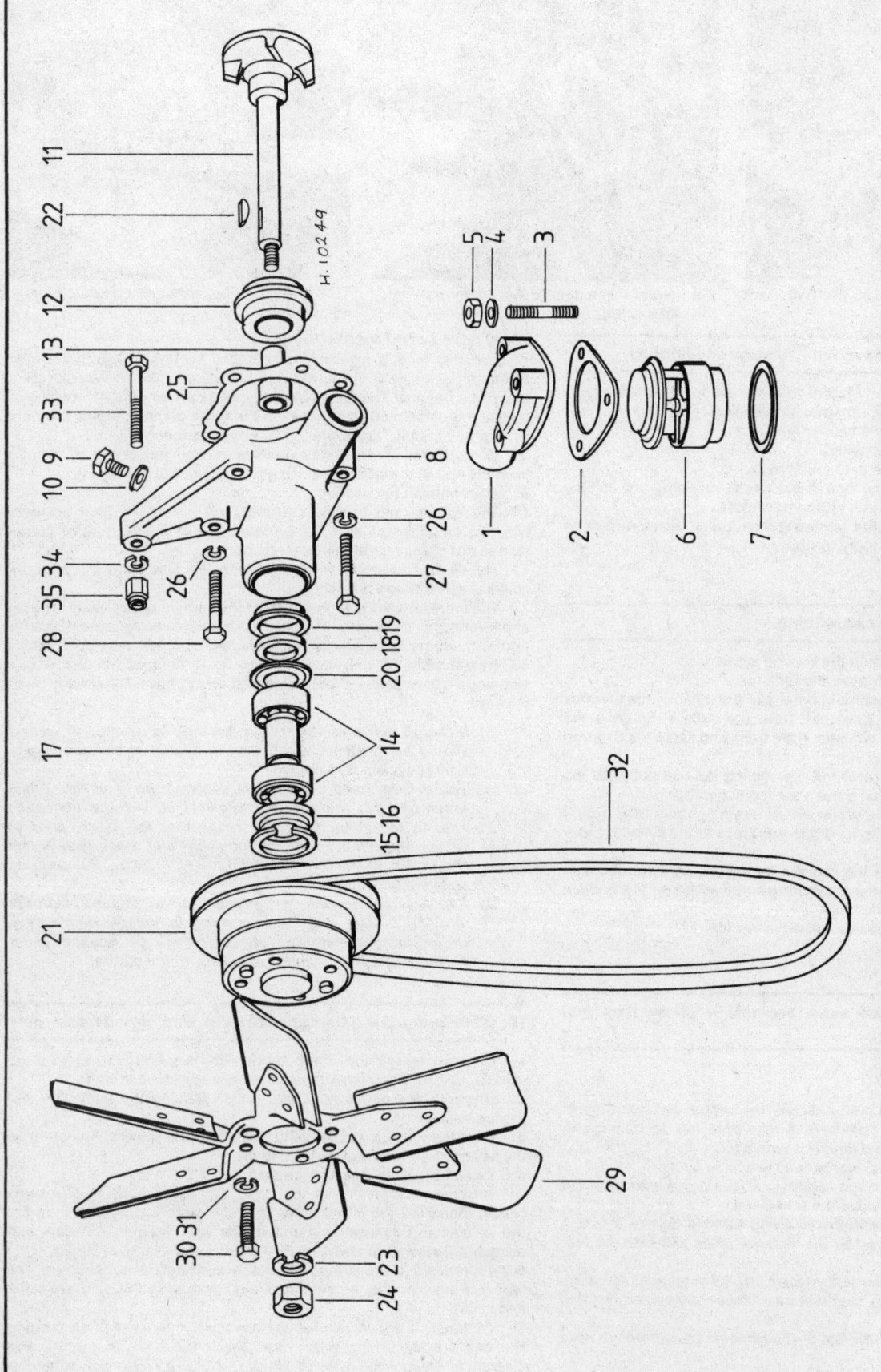

Fig. 2.5 The components of the water pump and thermostat units fitted on overhead valve engines (Sec 8)

1 Water outlet elbow
2 Gasket
3 Stud
4 Washer
5 Nut
6 Thermostat
7 Gasket
8 Body
9 Plug
10 Washer
11 Spindle and vane
12 Seal
13 Distance piece
14 Bearing
15 Spring ring
16 Grease retainer
17 Distance piece
18 Felt washer
19 Retainer (felt washer inner)
20 Retainer (felt washer outer)
21 Pulley and fan
22 Key
23 Spring washer
24 Nut
25 Pump to block gasket
26 Spring washer
27 Setscrew (long)
28 Setscrew (short)
29 Fan complete
30 Setscrew
31 Spring washer
32 Belt
33 Bolt
34 Spring washer
35 Nut

Chapter 2 Cooling system

9 Check that the mating faces are perfectly clean before assembly.

11 Antifreeze mixture

1 In circumstances where it is likely that the temperature will drop to below freezing it is essential that some of the water is drained and an adequate amount of ethylene glycol antifreeze is added to the cooling system.
2 Always use a universal antifreeze and in the case of the Twin Cam engine one which is suitable of aluminium alloy cylinder heads. Never use an antifreeze with an alcohol base as evaporation is too high.
3 Antifreeze with an anti-corrosion additive can be left in the cooling system for up to two years, but after six months it is advisable to have the specific gravity of the coolant checked at your local garage, and thereafter once every three months.
4 Listed are the amounts of antifreeze which should be added to ensure adequate protection down to the temperature given.

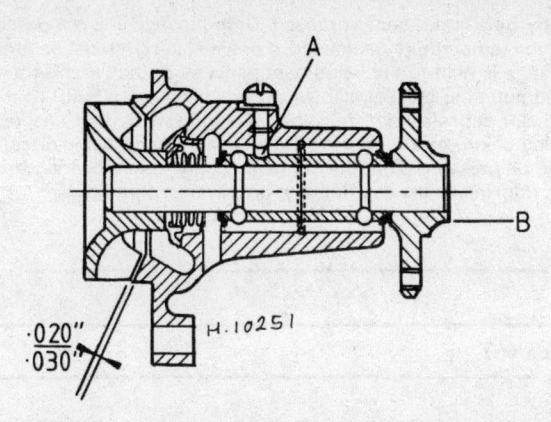

Fig. 2.6 Ensure the hole in the bearing 'A' aligns with the lubricating hole in the pump body. The end of the spindle should be flush with the face of the hub 'B' (Sec 9)

Protection level	Antifreeze requirement	
	Overhead valve engines	Twin Cam engine
15° frost	1 Imp pint (0·57 litre)	1·5 Imp pints (0·85 litre)
25° frost	1·5 Imp pints (0·85 litre)	2·0 Imp pints (1·14 litre)
35° frost	2·0 Imp pints (1·14 litre)	3·5 Imp pints (2·0 litre)

12 Fan belt – adjustment

1 The fan belt tension must be kept to the specified amount at all times. When the belt is loose it will slip, wear rapidly and cause the dynamo and water pump to malfunction. If the belt is too tight the dynamo and water pump bearings will wear rapidly causing premature failure of these components.
2 The fan belt tension is correct when there is 1·0 inch (25 mm) of play measured side to side at the midpoint position of the belt at its longest run. This measurement applies to both overhead valve and Twin Cam engine versions.
3 On early models the radiator is best removed for accessibility.
4 To adjust the fan belt, slacken the dynamo securing bolts and move the dynamo either in or out until the correct tension is obtained (Fig. 2.8). It is easier if the dynamo bolts are only slackened a little so it requires some force to move the dynamo. In this way the tension of the belt can be arrived at more quickly than by making frequent adjustments.
5 If difficulty is experienced in moving the dynamo away from the engine a long spanner placed behind the dynamo and resting against the block serves as a very good lever and can be held in this position while the dynamo bolts are tightened.

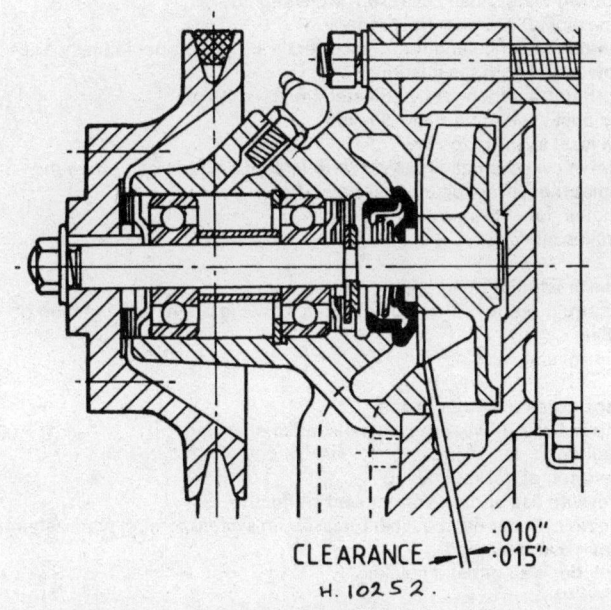

Fig. 2.7 Clearance between body and pump vane on Twin Cam models to be as shown, 0.010 to 0.015 in (0.254 to 0.381 mm) (Sec 10)

13 Fan belt – removal and refitting

1 The most common reason for renewing the fan belt is when it breaks in service and for this reason it is strongly recommended that a spare belt be carried in the car at all times. Other reasons for renewing the belt are if it is generally worn, cracked and is stretched unduly.
2 To remove the old belt, loosen the dynamo mounting/pivot bolts and loosen off the adjustment by pushing the dynamo inwards towards the engine. Disengage the belt from the pulleys.
3 Where a new belt is replacing a broken one, the dynamo mounting bolts must be loosened and pivoted inwards to enable the new belt to be fitted.
4 Fit the belt over the respective pulleys and then pivot the dynamo away from the engine and adjust the belt tension before tightening the bolts (see previous Section). **Note:** *A new fan belt will stretch initially when it is first used and therefore a recheck should be made on its tension adjustment after approximately 250 miles (400 km).*

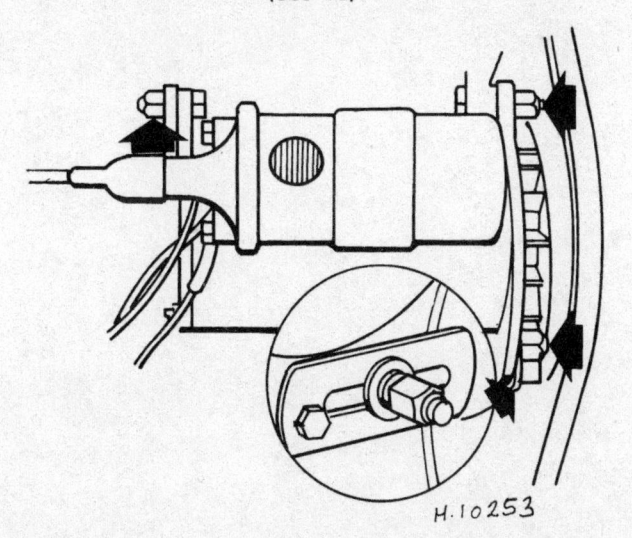

Fig. 2.8 The dynamo mounting/adjustment bolts (Sec 12)

14 Temperature gauge – general

1   The temperature gauge is located on the instrument panel and the oil pressure gauge is also fitted in the same unit. The temperature gauge is connected by a capillary tube to a sensor capsule located in the cylinder head.

2   If the temperature gauge develops a fault, first check that the capillary tube is not bent or broken. Unfortunately it is not possible to repair the temperature gauge and, if proved faulty, it must be renewed. The gauge is held to the instrument panel by a small bracket and two knurled nuts; the bracket also supports a panel lamp bulb. To remove the sensor capsule first drain the cooling system then unscrew the retaining union. After removing the two capillary clips and disconnecting the oil pressure pipe, the complete gauge assembly can be withdrawn from inside the car. Refitting is a reversal of removal.

15 Fault diagnosis – cooling system

Symptom	Reason/s
Engine runs too hot	Insufficient water in cooling system
	Fan belt slipping (accompanied by a shrieking noise on rapid engine acceleration)
	Radiator core blocked or radiator grille restricted
	Bottom water hose collapsed, impeding flow
	Thermostat not opening properly
	Ignition advance and retard incorrectly set (accompanied by loss of power and perhaps misfiring)
	Carburettors incorrectly adjusted (mixture too lean)
	Exhaust system partially blocked
	Oil level in sump too low
	Blown cylinder head gasket (water/steam being forced down the radiator overflow pipe under pressure)
	Engine not yet run-in
	Brakes binding
Engine runs too cool	Thermostat jammed open
	Incorrect grade of thermostat fitted allowing premature opening of valve
	Thermostat missing
Coolant level consistently drops	Loose clips on water hoses
	Top or bottom water hoses perished and leaking
	Radiator core leaking
	Thermostat gasket leaking
	Pressure cap spring worn or seal ineffective
	Blown cylinder head gasket (pressure in system forcing water/steam down overflow pipe)
	Cylinder wall or head cracked

Chapter 3 Fuel and exhaust systems

Contents

Air cleaners – removal, maintenance and refitting	2
Carburettor jet – adjusting and timing	10
Carburettor jet – centralizing	9
Carburettors – dismantling	7
Carburettors – inspection and renovation	8
Carburettors – removal and refitting	6
Carburettors – synchronisation	11
Exhaust system and manifolds	18
Fault diagnosis – fuel system	19
Float chamber unit – removal, overhaul, fuel level adjustment	
and refitting	5
Fuel gauge sender unit – removal and refitting	16
Fuel pump – maintenance and fault checks	14
Fuel pump – removal and refitting	13
Fuel tank – cleaning	17
Fuel tank – removal and refitting	15
General description	1
SU carburettor – general description	3
SU carburettor – main faults and remedies	4
SU electric fuel pump – description	12

Specifications

Carburettors (overhead valve engine)
Make and model	Twin SU H4 semi-downdraught
Choke diameter	1·5 in (38·1 mm)
Needle type:	
1500 engine	GS
1600 engine	No. 6
Jet size	0·090 in (2·29 mm)
Piston spring	Red

Carburettors (Twin Cam engines)
Make and model	Twin SU H6 semi-downdraught
Choke diameter	1·750 in (44·45 mm)
Needle types available:	
Standard	OA6
Rich	RH
Weak	OA7
Jet size	0·10 in (2·54 mm)
Piston spring	Red 4·5 oz (128 gm)

Carburettor air cleaners
Vokes – oil soaked type

Fuel pump
SU electric

Delivery rate:
Overhead valve engines	10·0 gals/hr (45·4 litres/hr)
Twin Cam engine	12·5 gals/hr (54·28 litres/hr)
Suction lift	33 in (83·8 cm)
Output lift	48 in (121·9 cm)

1 General description

The main components of the fuel system are the fuel tank at the rear of the car, the electrical fuel pump and the twin SU semi-downdraught type carburettors.

The system is basically the same on all models, the only differences being the higher rating fuel pump and larger SU carburettors used on the twin cam model.

The fuel tank is located under the boot floor at the rear and fuel from it is sucked along the connecting pipe to the electrical fuel pump. The pump unit is housed at the rear by the right-hand side battery. As the fuel passes through the pump it is filtered through a gauze element to help prevent any fuel tank sediment being passed on to the carburettors.

The fuel supply pipe junction at each carburettor also incorporates a gauze type fuel strainer. The filters of the carburettors and fuel pump must be cleaned out occasionally or eventually the fuel supply will be restricted.

The twin SU type carburettors are of the semi-downdraught vari-

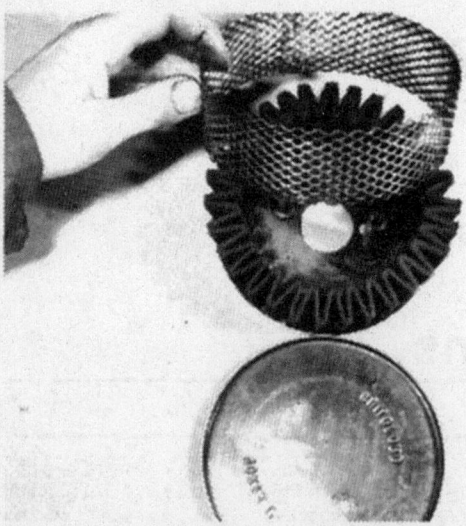

Chapter 3 Fuel and exhaust systems

2.2 The air cleaner element components

2.6 Refitting the rear filter

able choke type, each having its own separate air filter.

2 Air filters – removal, maintenance and refitting

1 At the specified mileage intervals of 3000 miles (4800 km), each air cleaner unit must be dismantled and the filter cleaned.
2 The relative parts of each filter are shown in the accompanying photo.
3 Remove the two outer cover retaining bolts and tap the cover free together with its seal ring. Extract the element from the filter body.
4 Wash each element in petrol and then carefully tap the filter by hand to eject most of the petrol and finally dry it by blowing through using an air line or allow to drain and dry.
5 Immerse the cleaned element/s in some SAE 20 engine oil and allow them to drain off.
6 Before refitting each filter element, clean out the housings. Note that the front filter element is fitted with its corrugations clear of the breather spigot in the filter body. Refit the cover with its seal and secure with the retaining nuts and spring washers.
7 Check that the gasket seal is in good condition and renew if necessary (photo).

3 SU carburettors – general description

The variable choke SU carburettor is a relatively simple instrument and is basically the same irrespective of its size and type. If differs from most other carburettors in that instead of having a number of various sized fixed jets for different conditions, only one variable jet is fitted to deal with all possible conditions.

Air passing rapidly through the carburettor choke draws petrol from the jet so forming the petrol/air mixture. The amount of petrol drawn from the jet depends on the position of the tapered carburettor needle, which moves up and down the jet orifice according to engine load and throttle opening, thus effectively altering the size of the jet so that exactly the right amount of fuel is metered for the prevailing road conditions.

The position of the tapered needle in the jet is determined by engine vapours. The shank of the needle is held at its top end in a piston which slides up and down the dashpot in response to the degree of manifold vacuum. This is directly controlled by the position of the throttle.

With the throttle fully open, the full effect of inlet manifold vacuum is felt by the piston which has an air bleed into the choke tube on the outside of the throttle. This causes the piston to rise fully, bringing the needle with it. With the accelerator partially closed only slight inlet manifold vacuum is felt by the piston (although, of course, on the engine side of the throttle the vacuum is now greater), and the piston only rises a little, blocking most of the jet orifice with the metering needle.

To prevent the piston fluttering, and to give a richer mixture when the accelerator is suddenly depressed, an oil damper and light spring are fitted inside the dashpot.

The only portion of the piston assembly to come into contact with the piston chamber or dashpot is the actual central piston rod. All the other parts of the piston assembly, including the lower choke portion, have sufficient clearances to prevent any direct metal to metal contact which is essential if the carburettor is to work properly.

The correct level of the petrol in the carburettor is determined by the level of the float in the float chamber. When the level is correct the float rises and by means of a lever resting on top of it closes the needle valve in the cover of the float chamber. This closes off the supply of fuel from the pump. When the level in the float chamber drops as fuel is used in the carburettor the float sinks. As it does, the float needle comes away from its seat so allowing more fuel to enter the float chamber and restore the correct level.

4 SU carburettors – main faults and remedies

1 The SU carburettor generally speaking is most reliable, but even so it may develop one of several faults which may not be readily apparent unless a careful inspection is carried out. The common faults the carburettor is prone to are:

   (a) Piston sticking
   (b) Float needle sticking
   (c) Float chamber flooding
   (d) Water and dirt in the carburettor

Any of these malfunctions can be checked without removing the carburettor from the car.

Piston sticking

2 The hardened piston rod which slides in the centre guide tube in the middle of the dashpot is the only part of the piston assembly (which comprises the jet needle, suction disc, and piston choke) that should make contact with the dashpot.
3 The piston rim and the choke periphery are machined to very fine tolerances so that they will not touch the dashpot or the choke tube walls.
4 After high mileages, wear in the centre guide tube may allow the piston to touch the dashpot wall. This condition is known as sticking.
5 If the piston sticking is suspected or it is wished to test for this condition, rotate the piston about the centre guide tube at the same time sliding it up and down inside the dashpot.
6 If any portion of the piston makes contact with the dashpot wall then that portion of the wall must be polished with metal polish until clearance exists. In extreme cases, fine emery cloth can be used.
7 The greatest care should be taken to remove only the minimum

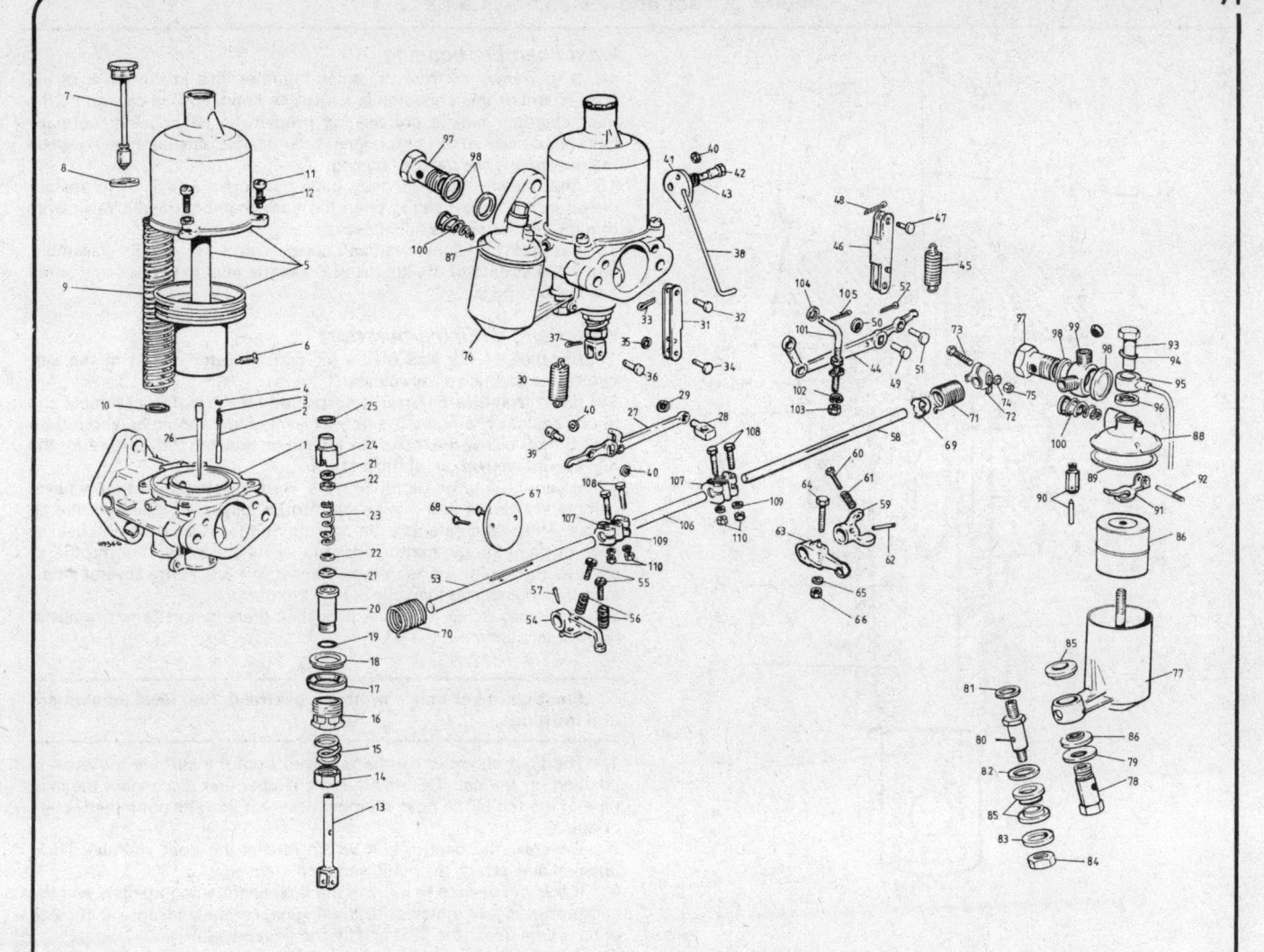

Fig. 3.1 The twin SU carburettors and linkage components (Sec 3)

1 Rear carburettor body	29 Washer (starlock)	57 Pin	84 Nut
2 Piston lifting pin	30 Jet lever return spring	58 Throttle spindle	85 Grommet (rubber)
3 Spring	31 Jet lever linkage	59 Lever	86 Float
4 Circlip	32 Pin	60 Stop adjusting screw	87 Lid (float-chamber)
5 Chamber and piston	33 Split pin	61 Spring	88 Lid (float chamber)
6 Screw	34 Pin (link to lever)	62 Pin	89 Lid washer
7 Cap and damper	35 Washer (starlock)	63 Throttle lever	90 Needle and seat assembly
8 Washer (fibre)	36 Pin (lever to jet)	64 Bolt	91 Lever
9 Spring (red)	37 Split pin	65 Washer (spring)	92 Pin
10 Washer	38 Link tension	66 Nut	93 Cap nut
11 Screw	39 Swivel pin	67 Throttle disc	94 Washer (aluminium)
12 Washer	40 Washer (starlock)	68 Screw	95 Banjo vent and drain pipe
13 Jet assembly	41 Cam plate	69 Plate	96 Washer (fibre)
14 Adjusting nut	42 Bolt	70 Spring	97 Bolt
15 Spring	43 Washer (spring)	71 Spring	98 Washer (fibre)
16 Gland seal nut	44 Jet lever	72 Clip	99 Union (double banjo)
17 Aluminium seal ring	45 Spring	73 Bolt	100 Filter
18 Cork seal ring	46 Jet lever linkage	74 Washer (plain)	101 Link rod
19 Copper washer	47 Pin	75 Nut	102 Washer (spring)
20 Bearing (bottom)	48 Split pin	76 Float chamber	103 Nut
21 Cork gland washer	49 Pin	77 Float chamber	104 Brass washer
22 Brass washer	50 Washer (starlock)	78 Bolt	105 Split pin
23 Spring (gland)	51 Pin	79 Washer (fibre)	106 Throttle connecting rod
24 Top bearing	52 Split pin	80 Pillar	107 Rod coupling
25 Copper top bearing washer	53 Throttle spindle	81 Washer	108 Coupling bolt
26 Needle (M6) standard jet	54 Throttle stop lever	82 Washer (inner)	109 Washer
27 Jet lever	55 Stop adjusting screw	83 Washer (outer)	110 Nut
28 Trunnion for lever	56 Spring		

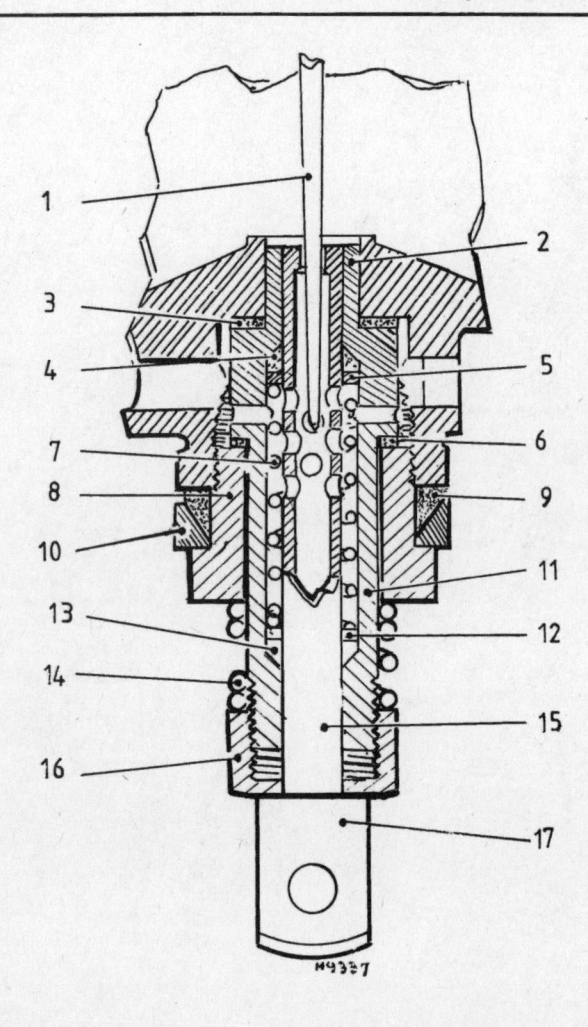

Fig. 3.2 Sectional view of the SU jet assembly (Sec 3)

1. Needle
2. Tap bearing
3. Copper washer
4. Gland washer
5. Gland washer
6. Copper washer
7. Spring
8. Jet nut
9. Washer
10. Bevelled washer
11. Bottom washer
12. Washer
13. Washer
14. Spring
15. Jet
16. Adjusting nut
17. Jet head

amount of metal to provide the clearance, as too large a gap will cause air leakage and will upset the functioning of the carburettor.
8 Clean down the walls of the dashpot and the piston rim and ensure that there is no oil on them. A trace of oil may be judiciously applied to the piston rod.
9 If the piston is sticking under no circumstances try to clear it by trying to alter the tension of the light return spring.

Float needle sticking

10 If the float needle sticks the carburettor will soon run dry and the engine will stop despite there being fuel in the tank.
11 The easiest way to check a suspected sticking float needle is to remove the inlet pipe at the carburettor, and turn on the ignition.
12 If fuel spurts from the end of the pipe (direct it towards the ground or into a wad or cloth or jar), then the fault is almost certain to be a sticking float needle.
13 Remove the float chamber cover, flood the chamber with petrol to raise the float and extract it from the chamber. Empty the fuel and clean the chamber out thoroughly. Remove the needle from the cover and wash it and its housing in petrol.

Float chamber flooding

14 If fuel emerges from the small breather hole in the cover of the float chamber this condition is known as flooding. It is caused by the float chamber needle not seating properly in its housing; normally because a piece of dirt or foreign matter has become jammed between the needle and the needle housing.
15 Alternatively the float may have developed a leak or be maladjusted so that it is holding open the float chamber needle valve even though the chamber is full of petrol.
16 Remove the float chamber cover, clean the needle assembly, check the setting of the float, and shake the float to verify if any petrol has leaked into it.

Water and dirt in carburettor

17 Because of the size of the jet orifice, water or dirt in the carburettor is normally easily cleared.
18 If dirt in the carburettor is suspected lift the piston assembly and flood the float chamber. The normal level of fuel should be about 0.06 in (1.6 mm) below the top of the jet and on flooding the carburettor the fuel should well up out of the jet hole.
19 If very little or no petrol appears, start the engine (the jet is never completely blocked) and with the throttle fully open, blank off the air intake. This will create a partial vacuum in the choke tube and help to suck out any foreign matter from the jet tube. Release the throttle as soon as the engine starts to race. Repeat this procedure several times, stop the engine, and then check the carburettor.
20 If this has failed to do the trick then there is no alternative but to remove and blow out the jet.

5 Float chamber unit – removal, overhaul, fuel level adjustment and refitting

1 The float chamber can be removed from the carburettor when in position on the car. To remove the chamber first disconnect the inlet pipe at the top of the float chamber cover, (if this has not already been done).
2 Unscrew the central bolt which retains the float chamber lid in position and detach the banjo vent and drain pipe.
3 If it is not wished to remove the float chamber completely and the carburettor is still attached to the engine, carefully insert a thin piece of bent wire under the float and lift the float out.
4 To remove the float chamber unscrew and remove the chamber to carburettor body retaining bolt.
5 Make a careful note of the rubber grommets and washer and on reassembly ensure they are refitted in the correct order. If the float chamber is removed completely it is a simple matter to turn it upside down to drop the float out. Check that the float is not cracked or leaking. If it is, it must be repaired or renewed.
6 The float chamber cover contains the needle valve assembly which regulates the amount of fuel which is fed into the float chamber (photo).
7 One end of the float lever rests on top of the float, rising and falling with it, while the other end pivots on a hinge pin which is held by two lugs. On the float cover side of the float lever is a needle which rises and falls in its brass seating according to the movement of the lever.
8 With the cover in place the hinge pin is held in position by the walls of the float chamber. With the cover removed the pin is easily pushed out so freeing the float lever and the needle.
9 Examine the tip of the needle and the needle seating for wear. Wear is present when there is a discernible ridge in the chamfer of the needle. If this is evident then the needle and seating must be renewed. This is a simple operation and the hexagon head of the needle housing is easily screwed out.
10 Never renew either the needle or the seating without the other parts as otherwise it will not be possible to get a fuel tight joint.
11 Clean the fuel chamber out thoroughly. Reassembly is a reversal of the dismantling procedure. Before refitting the float chamber cover, check that the fuel level setting is correct otherwise excessive fuel consumption may occur (photo).

Float level check

12 To check the float level invert the float chamber lid so that the needle valve is closed. It should now be just possible to place a 0.44 in (11.1 mm) diameter bar across the middle diameter of the machined float chamber lip parallel to the float lever hinge, so the face of the

Chapter 3 Fuel and exhaust systems

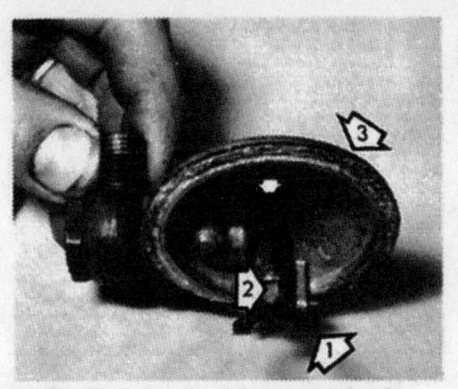

5.6 The float chamber lid removed showing
1 Float level lever
2 Needle and seat assembly
3 Gasket

5.11 Extract the float to clean out the float chamber and check float for leaks

6.8 Removing the carburettors from the manifold studs – note the heat shield which can stay in position

float lever just rests on the bar, when the float needle is held fully on its seating.
13 If the bar lifts the lever or if the lever stands proud of the bar then it is necessary to bend the lever at the bifurcation point between the shank and the curved portion until the clearance is correct. Never bend the flat portion of the lever.
14 When refitting the chamber lid, make sure that the mating surfaces of the chamber and lid are perfectly clean and where possible use a new seal gasket.
15 When fastening the retaining bolt the aluminium washer fits directly under the bolt head whilst the fibre washer locates between the banjo and the chamber lid.
16 Clean out the filter before reconnecting the fuel supply pipe.

6 Carburettors – removal and refitting

Overhead valve engines

1 Release the clip securing the breather hose to the rocker cover and detach the hose from the pipe protruding from the cover.
2 Refer to Section 2 and remove the air cleaner units.
3 Disconnect the main fuel line connection to the carburettors in front of the bulkhead.
4 Unscrew the vacuum pipe union nut at its connection to the rear carburettor body and carefully bend it out of the way.
5 Extract the split pin from the clevis pin retaining the mixture control cable to its linkage. Withdraw the pin and retain the small flat washer refitting it onto the pin with split pin. The mixture control outer cable can now be detached from the location bracket.
6 Disconnect the throttle return spring and detach the cable.
7 Unscrew the nut retaining the vent pipe to the top of each carburettor float chamber. Remove the nuts and washers and detach the vent pipes.
8 Unscrew and remove the carburettor to manifold flange nuts. Carefully remove the carburettors from the manifold (photo).
9 Refitting the carburettors is a direct reversal of the removal procedure. Always use new flange gaskets where possible. Check and adjust as necessary the choke and throttle connections as given in Section 10. Check and seal any fuel leaks.

Twin Cam engine

10 The removal and refitting procedure for the Twin Cam models is the same as for the overhead valve models previously described except for the following points.
   (a) Disconnect the jet lever interconnecting link
   (b) The vacuum control pipe to the ignition is attached to the front carburettor
   (c) The carburettors cannot be removed with the inlet manifold, since the manifold is retained in position via two nuts on studs in line with the respective carburettor flange housings within the manifold

7 Carburettors – dismantling

1 The SU carburettor with only two normally moving parts – the throttle valve and the piston assembly – makes it a straightforward instrument to service, but at the same time it is a delicate unit and clumsy handling can cause much damage. In particular it is easy to knock the finely tapered needle out of true, and the greatest care should be taken to keep all the parts associated with the dashpot scrupulously clean. Keep the respective ports of each carburettor separate when dismantling the two.
2 Remove the oil dashpot plunger nut from the top of the dashpot.
3 Before removing the dashpot from each carburettor scribe a relative alignment mark between the dashpot and flange face of the carburettor body to ensure correct reassembly.
4 Unscrew the set screws holding the dashpot to the carburettor body, and lift away the dashpot, light spring, and piston and needle assembly (photo).
5 To remove the metering needle from the choke portion of the piston unscrew the sunken retaining screw from the side of the piston choke and pull out the needle. When refitting the needle ensure that the shoulder is flush with the underside of the piston.
6 Release the float chamber from the carburettor by releasing the clamping bolt and sealing washers from the side of the carburettor base.
7 Normally, it is not necessary to dismantle the carburettor further, but if because of wear or for some other reason it is wished to remove the jet, this is easily accomplished by removing the clevis pin holding the jet operating lever to the jet head, and then just removing the jet by extracting it from the base of the carburettor. The jet adjusting nut can then be unscrewed together with the jet adjusting nut locking spring.
8 If the larger locking nut above the jet adjusting nut is removed, then the jet will have to be recentred when the carburettor is reassembled. With the jet nuts removed it is a simple matter to release the jet bearing together with the gland packing washers and seals.
9 To remove the throttle and actuating spindle release the two screws holding the throttle in position in the slot in the spindle, slide the throttle out of the spindle and then remove the spindle.
10 The respective carburettor parts can now be cleaned and laid out in order of appearance for inspection.

8 Carburettors – inspection and renovation

1 Examine the component parts of each carburettor in turn and keep them separate – they must not be interchanged.
2 Carefully inspect the internal and external carburettor body for cracks, particularly around the bolt holes of the mounting flanges. If any cracks are found the complete carburettor should be renewed.
3 Check the respective mating flanges for flatness using a straight edge. Minor distortions may possibly be removed using a sheet of fine emery cloth on a perfectly flat surface and lightly rubbing the face concerned on it until smooth.
4 Check that the throttle spindle rotates freely but with no radial play. Where radial play is found, either the throttle spindle or its aperture in the carburettor body is worn, possibly both, in which case the body should be renewed. Any air leaks through the spindle area will upset the operation of the carburettor making it difficult to tune.
5 Inspect the needle and check it for alignment by rolling the shank (top section) on a flat surface and watch the needle end for signs of distortion. If bent the needle must be renewed (photo). The needle

Chapter 3 Fuel and exhaust systems

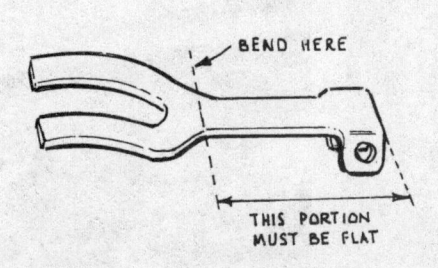

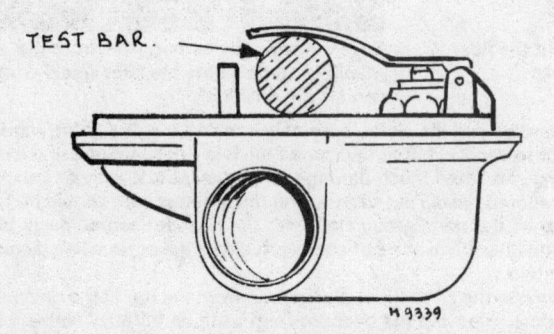

Fig. 3.3 Bend lever as shown to adjust for correct float level (Sec 5)

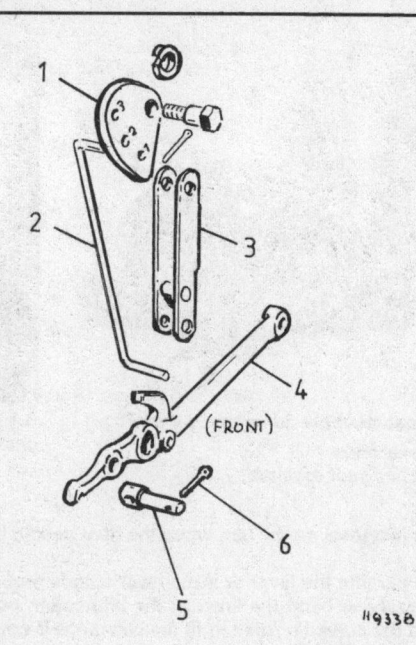

Fig. 3.4 The carburettor fast idle control linkage (Sec 10)

1 Cam
2 Link rod
3 Link
4 Jet lever
5 Pivot pin
6 Split pin

type identification code letter is stamped on the shank and this should be one of the types recommended, (see the Specifications). If renewing the needle the jet should also be renewed.
6 Check that the jet is a good sliding fit in its holder, (with glands removed).
7 Return the piston and suction chamber unit. The piston must be a good sliding fit in the chamber and they must both be perfectly clean and free from cracks or burrs. If the piston spring is distorted it must be renewed.
8 Inspect the float chamber and its components for defects. To check the float for leakage immerse it in boiling water and any signs of small bubbles emerging from it means that it leaks and must be repaired or renewed.
9 Check the float needle and hinged lever for freedom of operation. Take care not to bend the lever as this will effect the float level setting.
10 Renew any suspect or defective parts. Depending on the extent of dismantling you will need to get a gasket pack and possibly an overhaul pack if the gland seals have been removed from the jet housing assembly.
11 Before reassembling the carburettor ensure that all parts are perfectly clean.
12 The jet will have to be centred on reassembly and the details on this are discussed in the following Section.

9 Carburettor jet – centralizing

1 The carburettor metering needle is used as a pilot for centring the jet. The piston must therefore be in position with the dashpot in place before the jet is centred.
2 Extract the operating lever to jet head location clevis pin and withdraw the jet.
3 Unscrew the adjuster nut and remove it with the spring. Remove the spring and refit the nut, tightening to its highest position and then relocate the jet so that its head is flush against the adjuster nut.
4 Now raise and lower the piston to check it for freedom of operation. If it binds at any point within its range, loosen the large hexagon jet nut (above the adjuster nut) and gripping the two manipulate them to centralise the jet around the needle as required.
5 Move the jet until the carburettor needle will enter into it fully, and can also be raised and lowered and will fall under its own weight with a soft click. When fully lowered the needle must not foul the jet at any point. When this is achieved the jet is centralised.
6 Retighten the large hexagon nut retaining the jet, remove the

adjuster nut and refit the spring. When reassembled recheck that the piston drops fully without binding.
7 Adjust the carburettor mixture strength.

10 Carburettor – adjustments and tuning

1 To adjust and tune the SU carburettor proceed in the following manner:- Check the colour of the exhaust at idling speed with the choke fully in.
2 If the exhaust tends to be black, and the tailpipe interior is also black it is a fair indication that the mixture is too rich.
3 If the exhaust is colourless and the deposit in the exhaust pipe is a very light grey it is likely that the mixture is too weak.
4 This condition may also be accompanied by intermittent misfiring, while too rich a mixture will be associated with 'hunting'. Ideally the exhaust should be colourless with a medium grey pipe deposit.
5 Once the engine has reached its normal operating temperature, disconnect the carburettors so each can be worked on independently by slackening the nut on the folded metal clamp on the interconnecting shaft.
6 Only two adjustments are provided on the SU carburettor. Idling speed is governed by the throttle adjusting screw, and the mixture strength by the jet adjusting screw. The SU carburettor is correctly adjusted for the whole of its engine revolution range when the idling mixture strength is correct.
7 Idling speed adjustment is effected by the idling adjusting screw. To adjust the mixture set the engine to run at about 1000 rpm by screwing in the idling screw. Repeat this procedure for each instrument in turn.
8 Check the mixture strength by lifting the piston of the carburettor approximately 0.03 in (0.79 mm) with the piston lifting pin, when if:

(a) the speed of the engine increases appreciably the mixture is too rich
(b) the engine speed immediately decreases the mixture is too weak
(c) the engine speed increases very slightly the mixture is correct

9 To enrich the mixture rotate the adjusting screw, which is the screw at the bottom of the carburettor, in an anti-clockwise direction, ie downwards. To weaken the mixture rotate the jet adjusting screw in a clockwise direction, ie upwards. Only turn the adjusting screw a flat at a time and check the mixture strength between each turn. It is likely that there will be a slight increase or decrease in rpm after the mixture

Chapter 3 Fuel and exhaust systems

7.4a Remove the dashpot with care ...

7.4b ... followed by the piston unit and needle

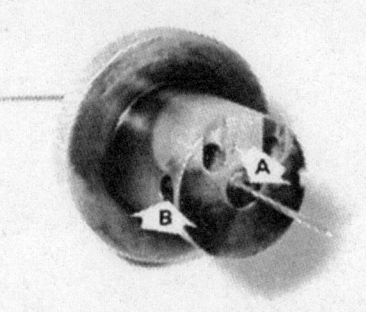

8.5 Check needle fitting in piston – needle shank shoulder to be flush with base of piston at A. Note needle retaining screw position B

adjustment has been made so the throttle idling adjusting screw should now be turned so that the engine idles at between 600 and 700 rpm.

11 Carburettors – synchronisation

1   First ensure that the mixture is correct in each carburettor. With twin SU carburettors, in addition to the mixture strength being correct for each carburettor, the idling suction must be equal on both . It is best to use a vacuum synchronising device. If this is not available, it is possible to obtain fairly accurate synchronisation by listening to the hiss made by the air flow into the intake throats of each carburettor using a length of plastic or rubber tube.
2   The aim is to adjust the throttle butterfly disc so that an equal amount of air enters each carburettor. Loosen the screw on the folded clamp which connects the two throttle disc spindles. Listen to the hiss from each carburettor and if a difference in intensity is noticed between them, then unscrew the throttle adjusting screw on the other carburettor until the hiss from both the carburettors is the same.
3   With a vacuum synchronisation device all that it is necessary to do is to place the instrument over the mouth of each carburettor in turn and adjust the adjusting screws until the reading on the gauge is identical for both carburettors.
4   Tighten the screw on the folded clamp to connect the throttle disc of the two carburettors together, at the same time holding down the throttle adjusting screws against their idling stops. Synchronisation of the two carburettors is now complete.
5   After adjusting the carburettors check that the accelerator and choke control cables are correctly adjusted. The choke linkage below each carburettor must be fully applied when the choke knob is fully pulled out, and must be fully released when the knob is pushed in. Similarly the throttle valve on each carburettor must be fully open with the accelerator pedal fully depressed, and fully closed with the pedal released. Adjustment of either cable is made by loosening the clamp nut at the carburettor end, and repositioning the inner cable as necessary.

12 SU Electric fuel pump – description

1   Two types of SU electric fuel pump have been fitted, the HP type which is fitted to all overhead valve models and the LCS type which is fitted to the Twin Cam models.
2   Although both types of pump operate on the same principal the main difference between the two is the design layout of the pump body each being shown in Figs. 3.5 and 3.6.
3   The HP type and LCS type pumps both consist of a long outer body casing housing and diaphragm, armature and solenoid assembly, with at one end the contact breaker assembly protected by a bakelite cover, and at the other end a short casting containing the inlet and outlet ports, filter, valves, and pumping chamber. The joint between the bakelite cover and the body casing is protected with a rubber sheath.
4   The pump operates in the following manner. When the ignition is switched on current travels from the terminal on the outside of the bakelite cover through the coil located round the solenoid core which becomes energised and acting like a magnet draws the armature towards it. The current then passes through the points to earth.
5   When the armature is drawn forward it brings the diaphragm with it against the pressure of the diaphragm spring. This creates sufficient vacuum in the pump chamber to draw in fuel from the tank through the fuel filter and non-return inlet valve.
6   As the armature nears the end of its travel a 'throw-over' mechanism operates which separates the points so breaking the circuit.
7   The diaphragm return spring then pushes the diaphragm and armature forwards into the pumping chamber so forcing the fuel in the chamber out to the carburettor through the non-return outlet valve. When the armature is nearly fully forward the throw over mechanism again functions, this time closing the points and re-energising the solenoid, so repeating the cycle.

13 Fuel pump – removal and refitting

1   Raise the car soft-top and tilt the seats forward.
2   Withdraw the spare wheel from its location in the boot.
3   Disconnect the quick release soft-top stowage compartment floor retaining screws, turning them each a quarter of a turn. Remove the floor panel for access to the pump (photo).
4   Detach the earth lead and supply lead to the pump.
5   Unscrew and disconnect the inlet and outlet pipe connections and plug each to prevent leakage and the ingress of dirt.
6   Remove the bolts retaining the pump unit to the bracket on the frame crossmember and withdraw the pump.
7   Refit in the reverse order and check for signs of leakage around the pipe union connections on completion.

14 Fuel pump – maintenance and faults check

1   Being an extremely reliable unit, the pump often gets neglected where maintenance is concerned. The only things to be checked are the contact points which must be clean and correctly gapped, and the fuel filter which should be periodically cleaned together with the points at about 12 000 mile (19 000 km) intervals.
2   Should the fuel pump fail to operate the following points can be checked easily and without fully dismantling the complete unit. Complete dismantling of the pump is not generally recommended anyway since the relatively low cost of a new unit makes it impractical and new parts will possibly be difficult to get anyway.
3   The most common fault with this type of pump is dirty points, access to which is gained after removing the front cover.
4   The contact faces of the points can be cleaned using a very fine emery paper but care must be taken not to distort the spring blade. A points gap of 0.030 in (0.76 mm) must exist and this can be checked with a feeler gauge.
5   A separate fuel filter is fitted within the underside of the pump body and on the HP model pump this is retained in position by a hexagon head plug. Unscrew the plug and extract the filter. Clean the gauze using petrol and blow it dry. Refit it and locate with its fibre seal

Fig. 3.5 The SU fuel pump HP type (Sec 12)

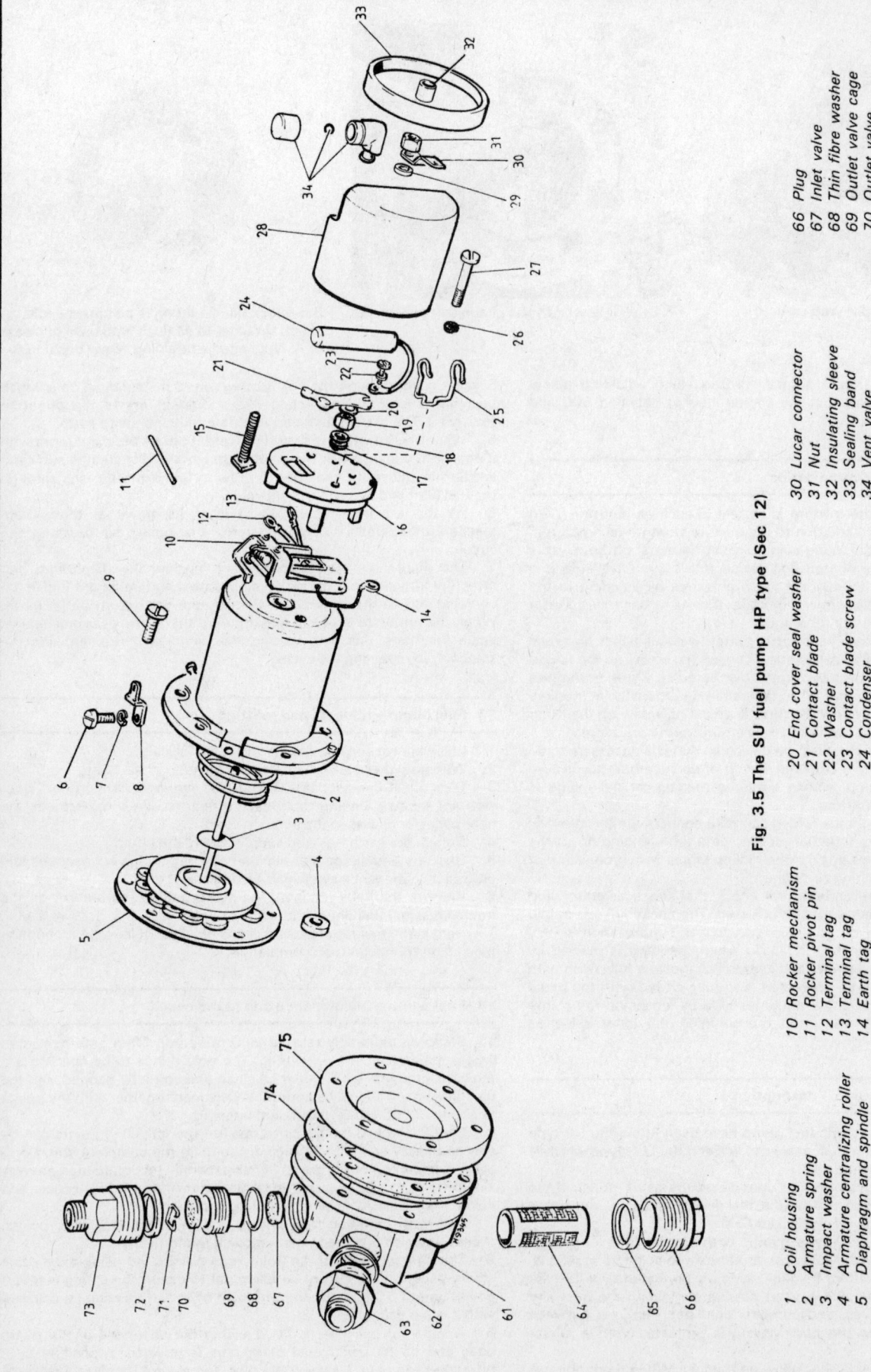

1. Coil housing
2. Armature spring
3. Impact washer
4. Armature centralizing roller
5. Diaphragm and spindle assembly
6. Set screw
7. Spring washer
8. Earth connector
9. Set screw
10. Rocker mechanism
11. Rocker pivot pin
12. Terminal tag
13. Terminal tag
14. Earth tag
15. Terminal stud
16. Pedestal
17. Spring washer
18. Lead washer
19. Terminal nut
20. End cover seal washer
21. Contact blade
22. Washer
23. Contact blade screw
24. Condenser
25. Condenser clip
26. Spring washer
27. Pedestal screw
28. End cover
29. Shakeproof washer
30. Lucar connector
31. Nut
32. Insulating sleeve
33. Sealing band
34. Vent valve
61. Pump body
62. Fibre washer
63. Outlet connection
64. Filter
65. Washer
66. Plug
67. Inlet valve
68. Thin fibre washer
69. Outlet valve cage
70. Outlet valve
71. Spring clip
72. Medium fibre washer
73. Outlet connection
74. Gasket
75. Sandwich plate

Fig. 3.6 The SU fuel pump, LCS type (Sec 12)

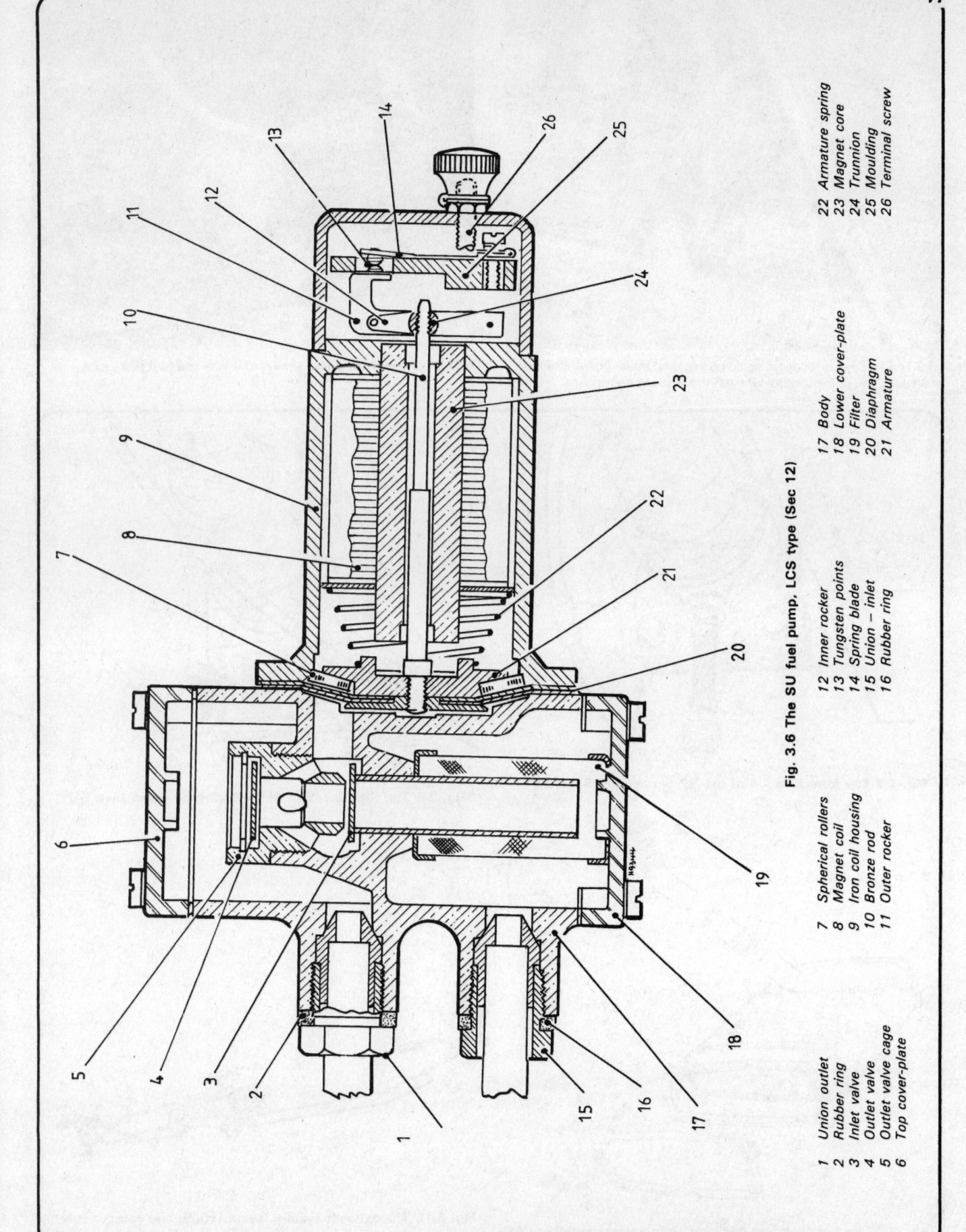

1 Union outlet	7 Spherical rollers	12 Inner rocker	22 Armature spring
2 Rubber ring	8 Magnet coil	13 Tungsten points	23 Magnet core
3 Inlet valve	9 Iron coil housing	14 Spring blade	24 Trunnion
4 Outlet valve	10 Bronze rod	15 Union – inlet	25 Moulding
5 Outlet valve cage	11 Outer rocker	16 Rubber ring	26 Terminal screw
6 Top cover-plate		17 Body	
		18 Lower cover-plate	
		19 Filter	
		20 Diaphragm	
		21 Armature	

13.3 The fuel pump location, showing inlet and outlet pipes, and the earth wire, the connection of which must be clean and secure

15.5 Disconnect the gauge sender unit wire and fuel pipe

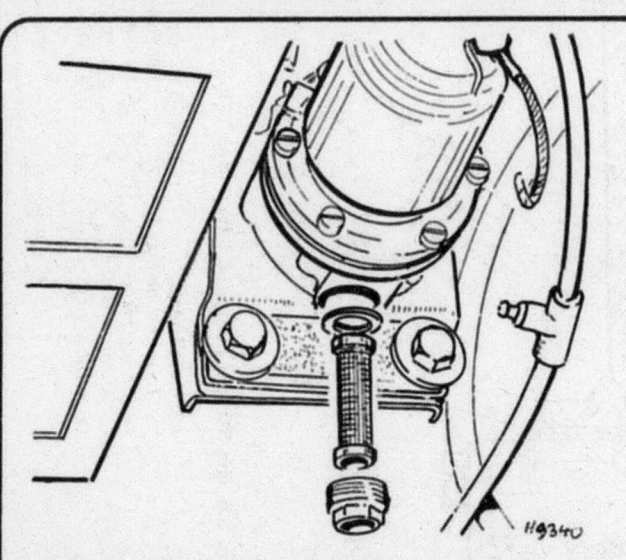

Fig. 3.7 The filter location of the HP type pump (Sec 14)

Fig. 3.8 The filter location of the LCS type pump (Sec 14)

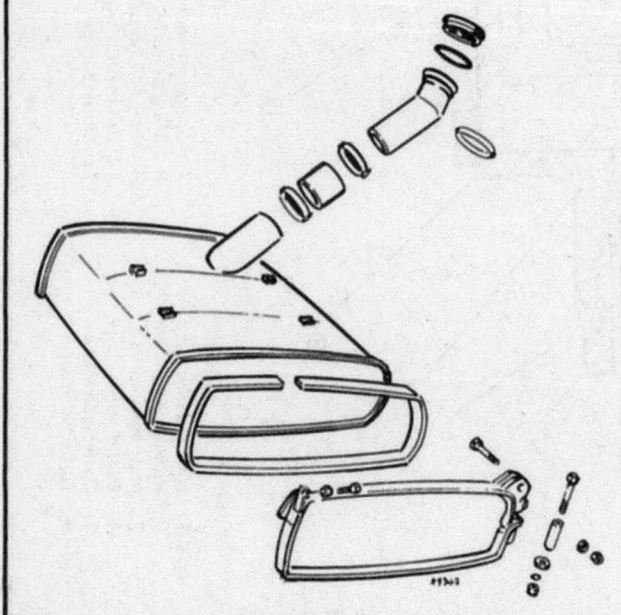

Fig. 3.9 The fuel tank and retaining strap components (Sec 15)

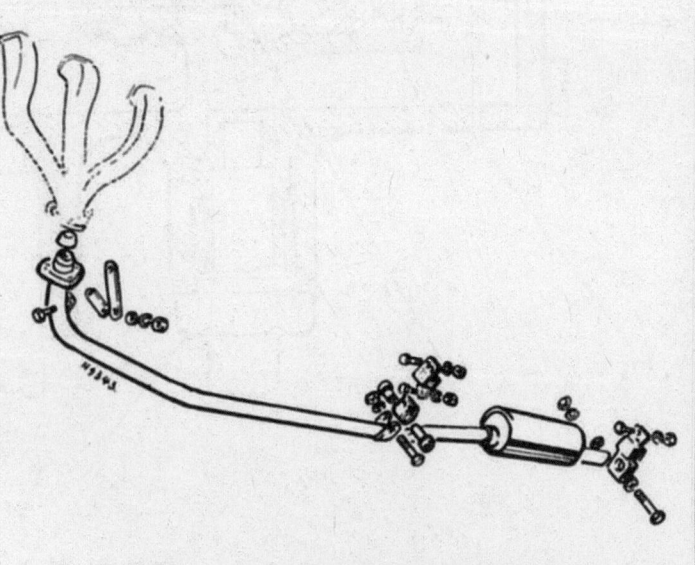

Fig. 3.10 The exhaust system layout (1500) and components (Sec 18)

Chapter 3 Fuel and exhaust systems

18.5 Locate the exhaust support hangers loosely at first – tighten when system is fully located

18.7 Inlet and exhaust manifold refitting with new gasket

washer. On the LCS pump the filter is retained in the pump body by means of the lower cover. Remove the cover plate screws and prise the cover free to extract the filter for cleaning. When refitting the filter and cover the cover gasket must be renewed if it was broken or faulty on removal.

6   Check that the pump electrical connections are in order. Use a test bulb to ensure that current is reaching the pump connecting terminal on the front cover when the ignition is switched on. Check that the pump is earthed cleanly.

7   Loosen the pump outlet feed pipe union connection and then turn on the ignition. Fuel should be pumped in regular spurts from the outlet; if not it can be assumed that the pump is faulty. If the pump operates but fuel is not being delivered to the carburettors it can be assumed that there is a blockage in the main fuel supply line between the pump and the carburettors. The blockage must be cleared or the pipe be renewed.

8   If after the above checks the pump still fails to operate then it should be removed and a new unit fitted.

15 Fuel tank – removal and refitting

1   The fuel tank is located under the boot floor and attached to the chassis by straps (see Fig. 3.9).
2   To remove the tank, place a suitable size container under the drain plug and remove the plug to empty the tank.
3   Loosen off the filler neck hose retaining clips and extract the filler extension piece.
4   Withdraw the tank hose and take out the three filler neck retaining screws. Remove the neck seal and its clamping plate.
5   Disconnect the fuel gauge wire connections on the right-hand side (photo).
6   Detach the fuel supply pipe on the right-hand side.
7   Loosen the tank retaining bolts, two to the frame anchorage brackets at the rear and two to the frame at the front of the tank.
8   Support the tank and remove the bolts and distance tubes and then carefully remove the tank.
9   Refitting is a reversal of the removal procedure. Check that all connections are secure on completion and when refilled with fuel check for leaks.

16 Fuel gauge sender unit – removal and refitting

1   Disconnect the earth lead from the battery (positive terminal).
2   The sender unit is located on the right-hand side of the petrol tank.
3   Disconnect the gauge wire and undo the screws which hold the sender unit to the tank.
4   Carefully lift the complete unit away making sure that the float lever is not bent or damaged in the process.

5   Refitting the unit is a reversal of the removal procedure. To ensure a fuel tight joint, scrape both the tank and sender gauge mating flanges clean, and always use a new joint gasket.

17 Fuel tank – cleaning

1   With time it is likely that sediment will collect in the bottom of the fuel tank. Condensation, resulting in rust and other impurities, will usually be found in the fuel tank of any car more than three of four years old.
2   When the tank is removed it should be vigorously flushed out and turned upside down, and if facilities are available, steam cleaned.

18 Exhaust system and manifolds

1   As with most sports cars, the exhaust system takes more than its fair share of punishment due to its close proximity to the ground. A regular check should therefore be made to ensure that the system is in good condition, leak free around the joints and securely located.
2   To remove the system the car is best run up onto ramps or over a work pit for accessibility. If jacking it up, supplement with axle-stands and or blocks.
3   Disconnect the downpipe(s) from the manifold(s) and the pipe sections from their respective hangers. As the fastenings will probably be rusted in position try cleaning and applying some penetrating fluid to shift them. If this fails cut them through with a hacksaw as they will need renewing anyway.
4   With the system removed, the offending section can be separated and renewed. Apply some exhaust sealant around the joints to help give it a perfect seal.
5   When refitting the exhaust system locate the fastenings loosely and when in position fully tighten them (photo). Check that the system is not rubbing or chafing against any adjacent chassis components or wiring and run the engine to check for leaks.

Manifolds

6   Normally the only time that the manifolds have to be removed is when a gasket blows or during a cylinder head/engine overhaul. To remove the manifolds, (the inlet and exhaust being separate but located on the same joint face on overhead valve engines and on separate sides of the cylinder head on Twin Cam engines) first remove the carburettors. The manifolds can then be disconnected from the cylinder head and the exhaust down pipe.
7   When refitting the manifolds be sure to clean off the mating surfaces of both the cylinder head and manifolds removing any portions of the old gasket which may have stuck in position. Use a new gasket and tighten the securing nuts evenly and progressively (photo). Note that the four central studs are fitted with the large washers on overhead valve engines.

17 Fault diagnosis – fuel system

Symptom	Reason/s
Smell of petrol when engine is stopped	Leaking fuel lines or unions Leaking fuel tank
Smell of petrol when engine is idling	Leaking fuel line unions between pump and carburettor Overflow of fuel from float chamber due to wrong level setting, ineffective needle valve or punctured float
Excessive fuel consumption for reasons not covered by leaks or float chamber faults	Worn jet
Difficult starting, uneven running, lack of power, cutting out	Excessive sediment in float chamber Float chamber fuel level too low or needle valve sticking Fuel pump not delivering sufficient fuel Worn/damaged carburettor

Unsatisfactory engine performance and excessive fuel consumption are not necessarily the fault of the fuel system or carburettors. In fact they more commonly occur as a result of ignition and timing faults. Before acting on the following it is necessary to check the ignition system first. Even though a fault may lie in the fuel system it will be difficult to trace unless the ignition is correct. The faults below, therefore, assume that this has been attended to first (where appropriate)

Chapter 4 Ignition system

Contents

Condenser – removal, testing and refitting	4
Contact breaker points – removal and refitting	3
Distributor contact breaker points – adjustment	2
Distributor – dismantling	7
Distributor – inspection and repair	8
Distributor – lubrication	5
Distributor – reassembly	9
Distributor – removal and refitting	6
General description	1
Ignition system – fault diagnosis	12
Sparking plugs and leads	11
Static ignition timing	10

Specifications

Spark plugs
Overhead valve engines	Champion N5
Twin Cam engine	Champion N3 or Champion N58R (competition plug)
Plug size	14 mm
Plug electrode gap	0·024 to 0·026 in (0·625 to 0·660 mm)

Firing order
1 – 3 – 4 – 2

Coil type
Lucas HA12

Distributor
Type	Lucas DM2 or Lucas DM2 P4 (late models)
Rotational direction	Anticlockwise
Contact points gap setting	0·014 to 0·016 in (0·35 to 0·40 mm)

Static timing
1500 and 1600 Mk I	7° BTDC
1600 Mk II:	
High compression	10° BTDC (up to engine number 4003)
	5° BTDC (from engine number 4004)
Low compression	10° BTDC
Twin Cam engine:	
9·1 : 1 compression ratio	TDC
8·3 : 1 compression ratio	8° BTDC

Torque wrench setting
	lbf ft	kgf m
Spark plug	30	4·15

1 General description

In order that the engine can run correctly it is necessary for an electrical spark to ignite the fuel/air mixture in the combustion chamber at exactly the right moment in relation to engine speed and load. The ignition system is based on feeding low tension voltage from the batteries to the coil where it is converted to high tension voltage. The high tension voltage is powerful enough to jump the sparking plug gap in the cylinders many times a second under high compression pressures, providing that the system is in good condition and that all adjustments are correct.

The ignition system is divided into two circuits. The low tension circuit and the high tension circuit.

The low tension (sometimes known as the primary) circuit consists of the batteries, lead to the starter switch and control box, lead to the ignition switch, lead from the ignition switch to the low tension or primary coil windings (terminal SW), and the lead from the low tension coil windings (coil terminal CB) to the contact breaker points and condenser in the distributor.

The high tension circuit consists of the high tension or secondary windings, the heavy ignition lead from the centre of the coil to the centre of the distributor cap, the rotor arm, and the sparking plug leads and sparking plugs.

The system functions in the following manner. Low tension voltage is changed in the coil into high tension voltage by the opening and closing of the contact breaker points in the low tension circuit. High tension voltage is then fed via the carbon brush in the centre of the distributor cap to the rotor arm of the distributor. The rotor arm revolves inside the distributor cap, and each time it comes in line with one of the four metal segments in the cap, which are connected to the sparking plug leads, the opening and closing of the contact breaker points causes the high tension voltage to build up, jump the gap from the rotor arm to the appropriate metal segment and so via the sparking

2.4 Contact breaker arm on tip of cam lobe

2.6 Loosen contact plate screw

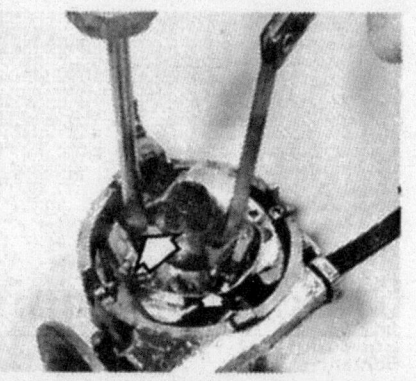

2.7 Adjusting the contact gap with screwdriver and feeler gauge

plug lead to the sparking plug, where it finally jumps the spark plug gap before going to earth.

The ignition is advanced and retarded automatically, to ensure the spark occurs at just the right instant for the particular load at the prevailing engine speed. On all early overhead valve models ignition advance is controlled both mechanically and by a vacuum system. Later twin cam models were fitted with a non vacuum advance distributor. The mechanical governor mechanism comprises two lead weights, which move out from the distributor shaft as the engine speed rises due to centrifugal force. As they move outwards they rotate the cam relative to the distributor shaft, and so advance the spark. The weights are held in position by two light springs and it is the tension of the springs which is largely responsible for correct spark advancement.

The vacuum control consists of a diaphragm, one side of which is connected via a small bore tube to the carburettor, and the other side to the contact breaker plate. Depression in the inlet manifold and carburettor, which varies with engine speed and throttle opening, causes the diaphragm to move, so moving the contact breaker plate, and advancing or retarding the spark. A fine degree of control is achieved by a spring in the vacuum assembly.

2 Distributor contact breaker points – adjustment

1   To adjust the contact breaker points to the correct gap, first pull off the two clips securing the distributor cam to the distributor body, and lift away the cap. Clean the cap inside and out with a dry cloth. It is unlikely that the four segments will be badly burned or scored, but if they are the cap will have to be renewed.
2   Push in the carbon brush located in the top of the cap once or twice to make sure that it moves freely.
3   Gently prise the contact breaker points open to examine the condition of their faces. If they are rough, pitted, or dirty, it will be necessary to remove them for resurfacing, or for new points to be fitted.
4   Presuming the points are satisfactory, or that they have been cleaned and refitted (or renewed), measure the gap between the points by turning the engine over until the contact breaker arm is on the peak of one of the four cam lobes (arrowed in photo).
5   A feeler gauge of the specified size should now just fit between the points.
6   If the gap varies from this amount, slacken the contact plate securing screw (arrowed in photo).
7   Adjust the contact gap by inserting a screwdriver in the notched hole (arrowed in photo) at the end of the plate. Turning clockwise to decrease and anti-clockwise to increase the gap. Tighten the securing screw and check the gap again (small arrow).
8   Refit the rotor arm and distributor cap and clip the spring blade retainers into position.

3 Contact breaker points – removal and refitting

1   If the contact breaker points are burned, pitted or badly worn, they must be removed and either renewed, or their faces must be filed smooth.
2   To remove the points unscrew the terminal nut and remove it together with the steel washer under its head. Remove the flanged nylon bush and then the condenser lead and the low tension lead from the terminal pin. Lift off the contact breaker arm and then remove the large fibre washer from the pivot pin and the small fibre washer from the terminal pin.
3   The adjustable contact breaker plate is removed by unscrewing the single retaining screw and removing it, complete with spring and flat washer. Some early models may have two screws.
4   To reface the points, rub their faces on a fine carborundum stone, or on fine emery paper. It is important that the faces are rubbed flat and parallel to each other so that there will be complete face to face contact when the points are closed. One of the points will be pitted and the other will have deposits on it.
5   It is necessary to completely remove the built-up deposits, but not necessary to rub the pitted point right down to the stage where all the pitting has disappeared, though obviously if this is done it will prolong the time before the operation of refacing the points has to be repeated.
6   To fit the points first position the adjustable contact breaker plate over the pivot pin (arrowed, see photo).
7   Secure the contact plate by screwing down the retaining screw together with its spring and flat washer (photo).
8   Locate the fibre washer over the pivot pin (photo).
9   Engage the contact breaker arm and spring over the pivot pin (photo).
10 Slide the fibre washer down the terminal pin and then bend the spring of the contact breaker arm round and engage it over the pin (photos).
11 Place the low tension lead and condenser lead over the pin and rest on top of the spring. The flanged nylon bush is now fitted onto the pin and is engaged in the two lead terminals and spring to centralise them (photo).
12 Locate the flat washer, lock washer and nut onto the pin and tighten to secure (photo).
13 With the points reassembled the points can be adjusted as described in the previous Section. Lightly smear the cams with a small portion of grease.
14 Before refitting the rotor arm and distributor cap check that the inside of the cap is clean and dry, that the central bush is free to slide within its housing and that the rotor arm contact and cap segments are clean.

4 Condenser – removal, testing and refitting

1   The purpose of the condenser, (sometimes known as a capacitor) is to ensure that when the contact breaker points open there is no sparking across them which would waste voltage and cause wear.
2   The condenser is fitted in parallel with the contact breaker points. If it develops a short circuit, it will cause ignition failure as the points will be prevented from interrupting the low tension circuit.
3   If the engine becomes very difficult to start or begins to miss after several miles running and the breaker points show signs of excessive burning, then the condition of the condenser must be suspect. A further test can be made by separating the points by hand with the ignition switched on. If this is accompanied by a flash it is indicative that the condenser has failed.
4   Without special test equipment the only sure way to diagnose condenser trouble is to renew a suspected unit with a new one and

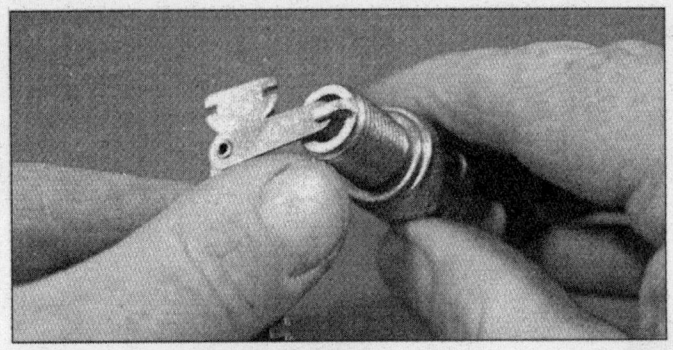

Measuring plug gap. A feeler gauge of the correct size (see ignition system specifications) should have a slight "drag" when slid between the electrodes. Adjust gap if necessary

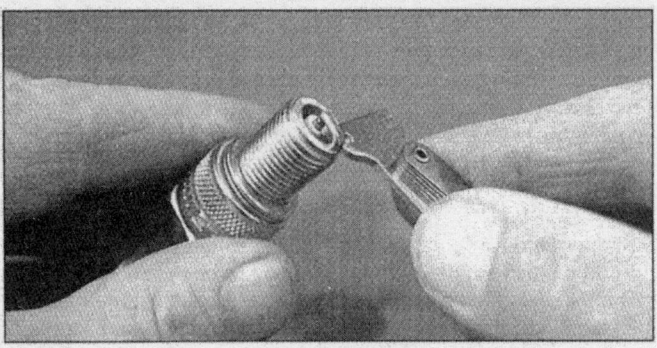

Adjusting plug gap. The plug gap is adjusted by bending the earth electrode inwards, or outwards, as necessary until the correct clearance is obtained. Note the use of the correct tool

Normal. Grey-brown deposits, lightly coated core nose. Gap increasing by around 0.001 in (0.025 mm) per 1000 miles (1600 km). Plugs ideally suited to engine, and engine in good condition

Carbon fouling. Dry, black, sooty deposits. Will cause weak spark and eventually misfire. Fault: over-rich fuel mixture. Check: carburettor mixture settings, float level and jet sizes; choke operation and cleanliness of air filter. Plugs can be re-used after cleaning

Oil fouling. Wet, oily deposits. Will cause weak spark and eventually misfire. Fault: worn bores/piston rings or valve guides; sometimes occurs (temporarily) during running-in period. Plugs can be re-used after thorough cleaning

Overheating. Electrodes have glazed appearance, core nose very white - few deposits. Fault: plug overheating. Check: plug value, ignition timing, fuel octane rating (too low) and fuel mixture (too weak). Discard plugs and cure fault immediately

Electrode damage. Electrodes burned away; core nose has burned, glazed appearance. Fault: pre-ignition. Check: as for "Overheating" but may be more severe. Discard plugs and remedy fault before piston or valve damage occurs

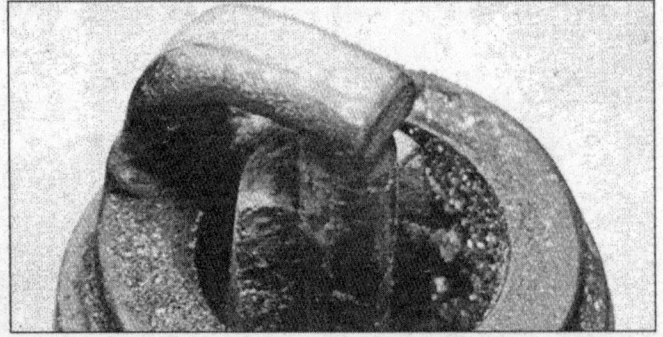

Split core nose (may appear initially as a crack). Damage is self-evident, but cracks will only show after cleaning. Fault: pre-ignition or wrong gap-setting technique. Check: ignition timing, cooling system, fuel octane rating (too low) and fuel mixture (too weak). Discard plugs, rectify fault immediately

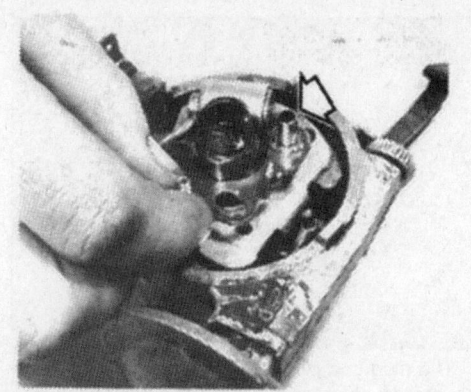

3.6 Fit contact plate over terminal pin

3.7 Tighten retaining screw

3.8 Locate fibre washer

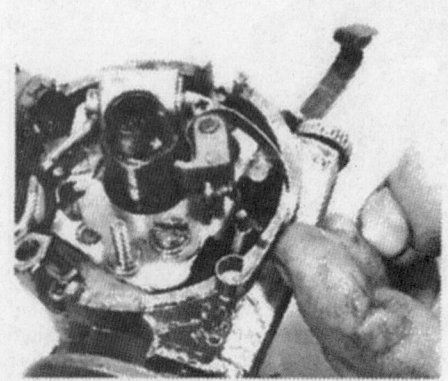

3.9 Fit contact breaker arm and spring unit

3.10a Locate fibre washer

3.10b Locate spring eye onto terminal pin

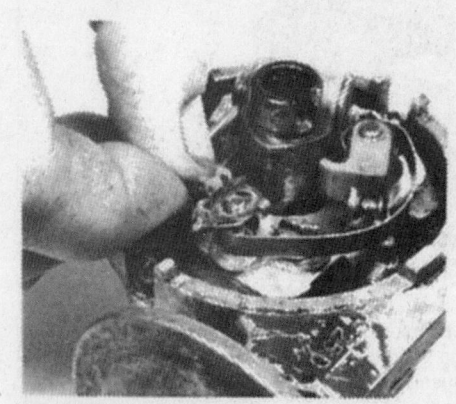

3.11a Refit terminals of low tension lead and condenser

3.11b Locate nylon bush

3.12a Fit the flat and star washers

3.12b Fit and tighten nut to secure

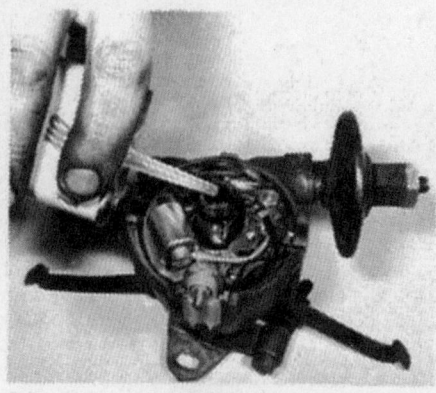

5.3 Lubricate the spindle

7.8 The spindle screw (arrowed) and centrifugal weights and springs

note if there is any improvement.
5   To remove the condenser from the distributor, remove the distributor cap and the rotor arm. Unscrew the contact breaker arm terminal nut, and remove the nut, washer, and flanged nylon bush and release the condenser lead from the bush. Unscrew the condenser retaining screw from the breaker plate and remove the condenser. Replacement of the condenser is simply a reversal of the removal procedure. Take particular care that the condenser lead does not short circuit against any portion of the breaker plate.

5 Distributor – lubrication

1   It is important that the distributor cam is lubricated with petroleum jelly at the specified mileages, and that the breaker arm, governor weights, and cam spindle, are lubricated with engine oil once every 1000 miles (1600 km). In practice it will be found that lubrication every 2000 miles (3200 km) is adequate, though once every 1000 miles (1600 km) is best.
2   Great care should be taken not to use too much lubricant, as any excess that finds its way onto the contact breaker points could cause burning and misfiring.
3   To gain access to the cam spindle, lift away the rotor arm. Drop no more than two drops of engine oil onto the screw head (photo). This will run down the spindle when the engine is hot and lubricate the bearings.
4   To lubricate the automatic timing control allow a few drops of oil to pass through the hole in the contact breaker base plate through which the four sided cam emerges. Apply not more than one drop of oil to the pivot post and remove any excess.

6 Distributor – removal and refitting

1   Unclip and detach the distributor cap, disconnect the four spark plug leads at the plugs and position the cap and leads out of the way. If the cap and leads are to be removed as well, disconnect the HT lead from the coil.
2   To prevent disturbing the distributor timing, use the starting handle and turn the engine over so that the rotor arm is pointing to the segment position for the spark plug lead of number 1 cylinder, (number 4 cylinder on Twin Cam models). The clamp plate pinch bolt must not be loosened during removal or refitting of the distributor as this will also upset the timing setting.
3   Disconnect the low tension lead from its location on the distributor body.
4   Carefully unscrew and detach the distributor vacuum advance pipe union (where fitted). Bend the pipe back a little so that it is clear of the distributor.
5   Unscrew the two clamp plate to crankcase retaining bolts and withdraw the distributor.
6   Refitting the distributor is a reversal of the removal procedure assuming that the engine has not been turned in the meantime. If for any reason the engine or timing has been disturbed the ignition will have to be retimed.

7 Distributor – dismantling

1   Remove the distributor from the car. Remove the distributor cap and rotor arm (if not already removed).
2   Remove the points from the distributor as described in Section 3.
3   Remove the condenser from the contact breaker plate by releasing its securing screw.
4   Unhook the vacuum unit spring from its mounting pin on the moving contact breaker plate. Some early models have a split pin.
5   Unscrew the two screws and lockwashers which hold the contact breaker base plate in position and remove the earth lead from the relevant screw. Remember to refit this lead on reassembly.
6   Lift out the contact breaker base plate.
7   Note the position of the slot in the rotor arm drive in relation to the offset drive dog at the opposite end of the distributor. It is essential that this is reassembled correctly as otherwise the timing may be 180° out.
8   Unscrew the cam spindle retaining screw, which is located in the centre of the rotor arm drive, and remove the cam spindle (photo).

9   Lift out the centrifugal weights together with their springs.
10   To remove the vacuum unit, spring off the small circlip which secures the advance adjustment nut which should then be unscrewed. With the micrometer adjusting nut removed, release the spring and the micrometer adjusting nut lock spring clip. This is the clip that is responsible for the 'clicks' when the micrometer adjuster is turned, and it is small and easily lost as is the circlip, so put them in a safe place. Do not forget to refit the lock spring clip on reassembly.
11   It is only necessary to remove the distributor drive shaft or spindle if it is thought to be excessively worn. With a thin punch drive out the retaining pin from the driving tongue collar on the bottom end of the distributor drive shaft. The shaft can then be removed. The distributor is now completely dismantled.

8 Distributor – inspection and repair

1   Check the points as described in Section 3. Check the distributor cap for signs of tracking, indicated by a thin black line between the segments. Renew the cap if any signs of tracking are found.
2   If the metal portion of the rotor arm is badly burned or loose, renew the arm. If slightly burnt clean the arm with a fine file.
3   Check that the carbon brush moves freely in the centre of the distributor cover.
4   Examine the fit of the breaker plate on the bearing plate and also check the breaker arm pivot for looseness or wear and renew as necessary.
5   Examine the balance weights and pivot pins for wear, and renew the weights or cam assembly if a degree of wear is found.
6   Examine the shaft and the fit of the cam assembly on the shaft. If the clearance is excessive compare the items with new units, and renew either, or both, if they show excessive wear.
7   If the shaft is a loose fit in the distributor bush and can be seen to be worn, it will be necessary to fit a new shaft and bush. The single bush is simply pressed out. Note that before inserting a new bush, it should be immersed in engine oil for at least 24 hours.
8   Examine the length of the balance weight springs and compare them with new springs. If they have stretched they must be renewed.

9 Distributor – reassembly

1   Reassembly is a straight reversal of the dismantling process, but there are several points which should be noted in addition to those already given in the section on dismantling.
2   Lubricate with S.A.E.20 engine oil the balance weights and other parts of the mechanical advance mechanism, the distributor shaft and the portion of the shaft on which the cam bears, during assembly. Do not oil excessively but ensure these parts are adequately lubricated.
3   On reassembling the cam driving pins with the centrifugal weights, check that they are in the correct position so that when viewed from above, the rotor arm slot should be at six o'clock position, and the small offset on the driving dog must be on the right.
4   Check the action of the weights in the fully advanced and fully retarded positions and ensure they are not binding.
5   Tighten the micrometer adjusting nut to the middle position on the timing scale (Fig. 4.2).
6   Finally, set the contact breaker gap to the correct clearance given in the Specifications.

10 Static ignition timing

1   If the clamp pinch bolt has been loosened on the distributor and the static timing lost, or if for any other reason it is wished to set the ignition timing, proceed as follows:-
2   The static advance is checked at the exact moment of opening of the points with regards to the position of the dimple in the crankshaft pulley in relation to the pointer/s on the bottom of the timing gear cover case.
3   On the overhead valve engine the longest pointer indicates TDC whilst the two shorter pointers indicate 5° and 10° BTDC respectively (Fig. 4.3). On the Twin Cam engine the dimple in the crankshaft pulley must align with the single projection mark in the timing case as shown in Fig. 4.4.
4   Check the 'Ignition specification' for the correct position of the

Chapter 4 Ignition system

crankshaft pulley wheel when the points should be just beginning to open. This is shown as 'static timing'.

5 Having determined whether your engine possesses a high or low compression ratio (by checking the engine number), turn the engine over so that No. 1 piston (overhead valve engines) or No. 4 piston (Twin Cam engines) is coming up to TDC on the compression stroke. (This can be checked by removing No. 1 (overhead valve) or No. 4 (Twin Cam) sparking plug and feeling the pressure being developed in the cylinder, or by removing the rocker cover and noting when the valves in No. 4 cylinder (No. 1 cylinder for Twin Cam engine) are rocking ie the inlet valve just opening and exhaust valve just closing. If this check is not made it is all too easy to set the timing 180° out, as both No. 1 and 4 cylinders come up to TDC at the same time, but only one is on the firing stroke.

6 Continue turning the engine until the dimple on the crankshaft

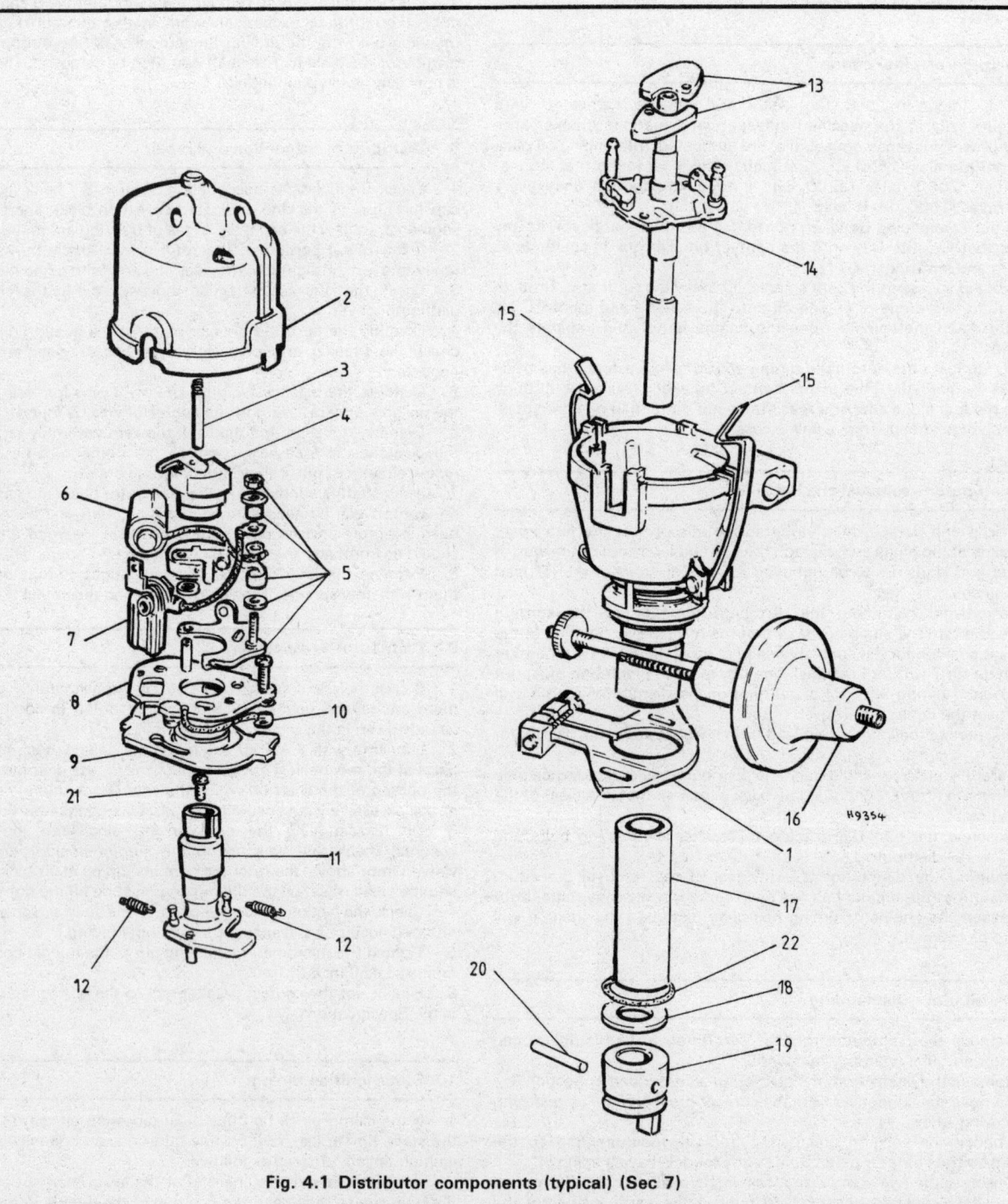

Fig. 4.1 Distributor components (typical) (Sec 7)

1	Clamping plate	7	Low tension terminal	13	Weight assembly	18	Thrust washer
2	Moulded cap	8	Moving contact breaker plate	14	Shaft and action plate	19	Driving dog
3	Brush and spring	9	Contact breaker base plate	15	Cap retaining clips	20	Parallel pin
4	Rotor arm	10	Earth lead	16	Vacuum unit	21	Cam screw
5	Contacts	11	Cam	17	Bush	22	O-ring oil seal
6	Condenser	12	Automatic advance spring				

Chapter 4 Ignition system

pulley is in line with the correct timing mark on the timing cover, or is on the correct position with regards to the pointers.

7 Remove the distributor cover, slacken off the distributor body clamp bolt, and with the rotor arm pointing towards the No. 1 terminal on overhead valve engines (or No. 4 terminal for the Twin Cam engine), insert the distributor into its housing. The drive shaft dog must line up with the slot in the distributor drive spindle.

8 Insert the two bolts holding the distributor in position.

9 With the engine set in the correct position and the rotor arm opposite the correct segment, (No. 1 or 4 as applicable), turn the advance/retard adjuster knob on the distributor until the contact breaker points are just beginning to open. Eleven clicks of the knurled micrometer adjuster nut represents 1° of timing movement.

10 If the range of adjustment provided by this adjuster is not sufficient it will be necessary to loosen the distributor retaining plate clamp adjuster bolt and rotate the distributor body. Sufficient adjustment will normally be found available using the distributor micrometer adjuster. When this has been achieved, the engine is statically timed.

11 Difficulty is sometimes experienced in determining exactly when the contact breaker points open. This can be ascertained most accurately by connecting a 12-volt bulb in parallel with the contact breaker points (one lead to earth and the other from the distributor low tension terminal). Switch on the ignition, and turn the advance and retard adjuster until the bulb lights up indicating that the points have just opened.

12 If a stroboscopic timing light is being used, attach one lead to No. 1 sparking plug or No 4 as applicable and attach the other lead into the free end of No. 1 or No. 4 plug ignition cable leading from the distributor. Start the engine and shine the light on the crankshaft pulley and timing indicators. If the engine idles at more than 600 rpm then the correct static timing will not be obtained as the centrifugal weights will have started to advance.

13 If the light shows the dimple in the pulley wheel to be to the right of the timing marks, when viewed from the front on OHV engines, then the ignition is too far advanced. If the dimple appears to the left of the timing marks, then the ignition is too far retarded. Turn the distributor body or micrometer adjuster until the timing dimple appears in just the right position in relation to the timing marks.

14 Tighten the clamp bolt and recheck that the timing is still correct, making any small correction necessary with the micrometer adjuster. A better result can sometimes be obtained by making slight readjustments with the engine running.

15 First start the engine and allow to warm up to normal temperature, and then accelerate in top gear from 30 to 50 mph, (48 to 80 km/h), listening for heavy pinking of the engine. If this occurs, the ignition needs to be retarded slightly until just the faintest trace of pinking can be heard under these operating conditions.

16 Since the ignition advance enables the firing point to be related correctly in relation to the grade of fuel used, the fullest advantage of any change of fuel will ony be attained by re-adjustment of the ignition settings.

17 This is done by varying the setting of the index scale on the vacuum advance mechanism one or two divisions, checking to make sure that the best all-round result is attained.

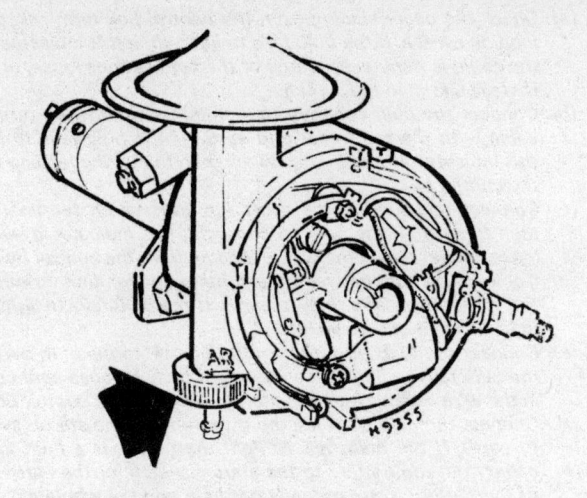

Fig. 4.2 The timing adjustment vernier (Sec 9)

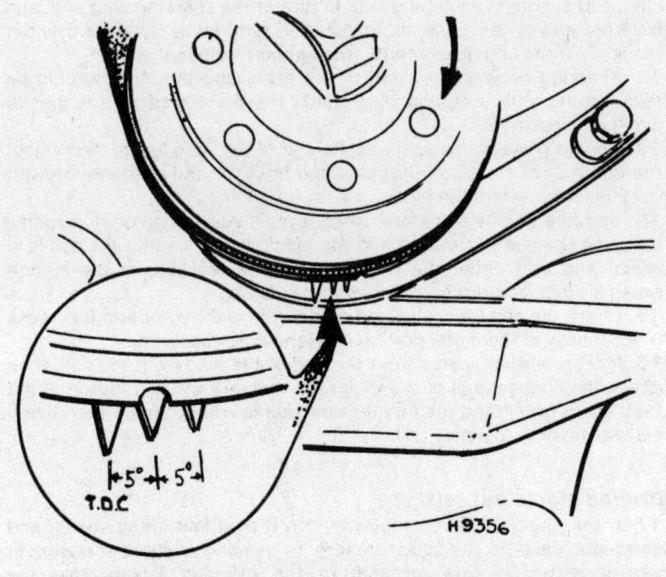

Fig. 4.3 The timing pointers and (inset) the crankshaft pulley notch – overhead valve engines (Sec 10)

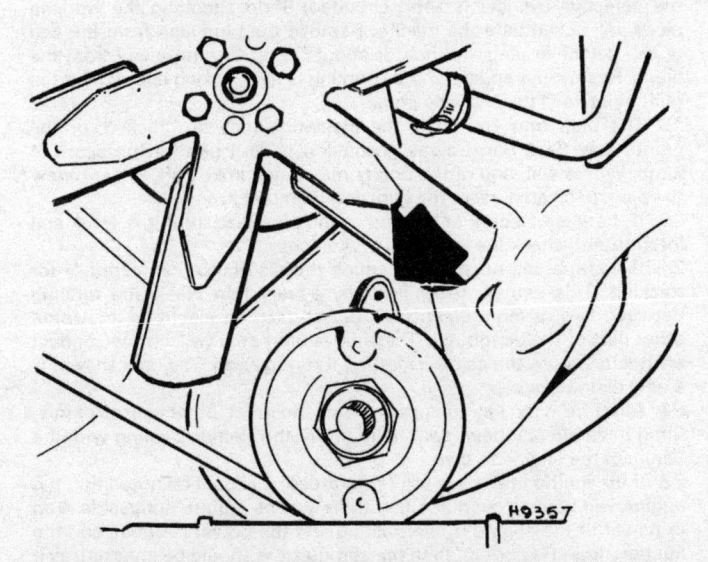

Fig. 4.4 The timing marks on crankshaft pulley and timing case – Twin Cam engines (Sec 10)

11 Sparking plugs and leads

1 The correct functioning of the sparking plugs is vital for the correct running and efficiency of the engine.

2 At intervals of 6000 miles (9500 km) the plugs should be removed, examined, cleaned, and if worn excessively, renewed. The condition of the sparking plug will also tell much about the overall condition of the engine.

3 The spark plugs fitted as standard are listed in the Specifications at the start of this Chapter, although of course a set of equivalent alternatives may be fitted. Remove each plug in turn and inspect it as follows.

4 If the insulator nose of the sparking plug is clean and white, with no deposits, this is indicative of a weak mixture, or too hot a plug. (A hot plug transfers heat away from the electrode slowly – a cold plug transfers it away quickly).

5 If the tip and insulator nose is covered with hard black-looking deposits, then this is indicative that the mixture is too rich. Should the plug be black and oily, then it is likely that the engine is fairly worn, as well as the mixture being too rich.

6 If the insulator nose is covered with light tan to greyish brown deposits, then the mixture is correct and it is likely that the engine is in good condition.

7 If there are any traces of long brown tapering stains on the outside of the white portion of the plug, then the plug will have to be renewed, as this shows that there is a faulty joint between the plug body and the insulator, and compression is being allowed to leak away.

8 Plugs should be cleaned by a sand blasting machine, which will free them from carbon more thoroughly than cleaning by hand. The machine will also test the condition of the plugs under compression. Any plug that fails to spark at the recommended pressure should be renewed.

9 The sparking plug gap is of considerable importance, as, if it is too large or too small, the size of the spark and its efficiency will be seriously impaired. The sparking plug gap should be set to the measurement given in the Specifications for the best results.

10 To set it, measure the gap with a feeler gauge, and then bend open, or close, the outer plug electrode until the correct gap is achieved. The centre electrode should never be bent as this may crack the insulation and cause plug failure of nothing worse.

11 Replace the leads from the distributor in the correct firing order, which is 1, 3, 4, 2, No. 1 cylinder being the one nearest the radiator.

12 The plug leads require no routine attention other than being kept clean and wiped over regularly. At intervals of 6000 miles (9500 km), however, pull each lead off the plug in turn and remove them from the distributor by unscrewing the knurled moulded terminal knobs. Water can seep down into these joints giving rise to a white corrosive deposit which must be carefully removed from the brass washer at the end of each cable, through which the ignition wires pass. Note that later distributor caps do not incorporate moulded terminal knobs.

12 Ignition system – faults diagnosis

1 By far the majority of breakdown and running troubles are caused by faults in the ignition system either in the low tension or high tension circuits.

2 There are two main symptoms indicating ignition faults. Either the engine will not start or fire, or the engine is difficult to start and misfires. If it is a regular misfire, ie, the engine is only running on two or three cylinders the fault is almost sure to be in the secondary, or high tension, circuit. If the misfiring is intermittant, the fault could be in either the high or low tension circuits. If the car stops suddenly, or will not start at all, it is likely that the fault is in the low tension circuit. Loss of power and overheating, apart from faulty carburation settings, are normally due to faults in the distributor or incorrect ignition timing.

Engine fails to start

3 If the engine fails to start it is likely that the fault is in the low tension circuit. The way the starter motor spins over will indicate whether there is a good charge in the battery. If the battery is evidently in good condition, then check the distributor.

4 Remove the distributor cap and rotor arm, and check that the contact points are not burnt, pitted or dirty. If the points are badly pitted, burnt or dirty, clean and reset them as described in Section 3.

5 If the engine still refuses to fire check the low tension circuit further. Check the condition of the condenser as described in Section 4.

6 Switch on the ignition and turn the crankshaft until the contact breaker points have fully opened. With either a voltmeter, or bulb and length of wire, connect the contact breaker plate terminal to earth on the engine.

7 If the bulb lights, the low tension circuit is in order, and the fault is in the points. If the points have been cleaned and reset, and the bulb still lights, then the fault is in the high tension circuit.

8 If the bulb fails to light, connect it to the ignition coil terminal CB and earth. If it lights, it points to a damaged wire or loose connection in the cable from the CB terminal to the terminal on the contact breaker plate.

9 If the bulb fails to light, connect it between the ignition coil terminal SW and earth. If the bulb lights it indicates a fault in the primary winding of the coil, and it will be necessary to fit a new unit.

10 Should the bulb not light at this stage, then check the cable to SW for faults or a loose connection. Connect the bulb from the negative terminal of the battery to the SW terminal of the coil. If the bulb lights, with the contact points closed, then the fault is somewhere in the switch, or wiring and control box. Check further as follows:-

(a) Check the cable leading from the control box terminal to the ignition switch. If the bulb fails to light, then this indicates that the cable is damaged, or one of the connections loose, or that there is a fault in the switch
(b) Connect the bulb between the ignition switch white terminal cable with the red tracer and earth. If the bulb fails to light, this indicates a fault in the switch or in the wiring leading from the control box
(c) Connect the bulb to the other ignition switch terminal and then to earth. If the bulb fails to light, this indicates a fault or loose connection in the wiring leading from the control box
(d) Connect the bulb between the lighting and ignition terminal in the control box, and then to earth. If the bulb fails to light this indicates a faulty control box
(e) Connect the bulb from the control box 'A' terminal to earth. If the bulb fails to light this indicates a fault or loose connection in the wire leading from the starter switch to the control box
(f) Connect the bulb from the input terminal of the starter switch to earth. If the bulb fails to light then there is a fault in the cable from the battery to the starter switch, or the earth lead of the battery is not properly earthed, and the whole circuit is dead

11 If the fault is not in the low tension circuit check the high tension circuit. Disconnect each plug lead in turn at the sparking plug end, and hold the end of the cable about 0.2 in (5 mm) away from the cylinder block. Spin the engine over with (the ignition switched on).

12 Sparking between the end of the cable and the block should be fairly strong with a regular blue spark. (Hold the lead with rubber to avoid electric shocks).

13 Should there be no spark at the end of the plug leads, disconnect the coil lead at the distributor cap, and hold the end of the lead about 0.25 in (6 mm) from the block.

14 Spin the engine as before, when a rapid succession of blue sparks between the end of the lead and the block, indicates that the coil is in order, and that either the distributor cap is cracked, or the carbon brush is stuck or worn, or the rotor arm is faulty.

15 Check the cap for cracks and tracking, and the rotor arm for cracks or looseness of the metal portion and renew as necessary.

16 If there are no sparks from the end of the lead from the coil, then check the connections of the LT lead to the coil and distributor, and if they are in order, and the low tension side is without fault, then it will be necessary to fit a new coil.

Engine starts but misfires

17 If the engine misfires regularly, run it at a fast idling speed, and short out each of the plugs in turn by placing a short screwdriver across from the plug terminal to the cylinder. Ensure that the screwdriver has a wooden or plastic insulated handle.

18 No difference in engine running will be noticed when the plug in the defective cylinder is short circuited. Short circuiting the working plugs will accentuate the misfire. Remove the plug lead from the end of the defective plug and hold it about 0.2 in (5 mm) away from the block. Restart the engine. If the sparking is fairly strong and regular the fault must lie in the sparking plug.

19 The plug may be loose, the insulation may be cracked, or the points may have burnt away giving too wide a gap for the spark to jump. Worse still, one of the points may have broken off. Either renew the plug, or clean it, reset the gap, and then test it.

20 If there is no spark at the end of the plug lead, or if it is weak and intermittent, check the lead for a broken core.

21 If there is still no spark, examine the distributor cap carefully for tracking. This can be recognised by a very thin black line running between two or more electrodes, or between an electrode and some other part of the distributor. These lines are paths which now conduct electricity across the cap thus letting it run to earth. The only answer is a new distributor cap.

22 Apart from the ignition timing being incorrect, other causes of misfiring have already been dealt with under the section dealing with the failure of the engine to start.

23 If the ignition timing is too far retarded, it should be noted that the engine will tend to overheat, and there will be a quite noticeable drop in power. If the engine is overheating and the power is down, and the ignition timing is correct, then the carburettors should be checked, as it is likely that this is where the fault lies. See Chapter 3 for details on this.

Chapter 5 Clutch

Contents

Clutch and brake pedals – removal and refitting	11
Clutch hydraulic system – bleeding	3
Clutch – maintenance and adjustment	2
Clutch master cylinder (dual type) – removal, dismantling, inspection, reassembly and refitting	8
Clutch master cylinder (separate type) – removal, dismantling, examination, reassembly and refitting	9
Clutch – reassembly	6
Clutch release bearing unit – removal and refitting	10
Clutch slave cylinder – removal, dismantling, inspection, reassembly and refitting	7
Clutch unit – dismantling and inspection	5
Clutch unit – removal and refitting	4
Fault diagnosis – clutch	12
General description	1

Specifications

Make	Borg and Beck
Type	Single dry plate
Type number	A6-G (overhead valve engines) 8ARG (Twin Cam engine)
Diameter	8 in (203 mm)
Number of pressure springs	6
Colour of pressure springs	
1500 and 1600 Mk I	Black/yellow (Cream and light green from engine No. 16225)
1600 Mk II	Light grey
Twin Cam	Light grey
Number of damper springs	6
Colour of damper springs	
1500 and 1600 Mk I	White/Light green stripes
1600 Mk II	Maroon/light green
Twin Cam	Maroon/light green
Clutch cylinder piston to pushrod clearance (pedal released)	0·03 in (0·8 mm)

Torque wrench settings	lbf ft	kgf m
Clutch to flywheel bolts	35 to 40	4·8 to 5·5

1 General description

All models are fitted with a Borg & Beck single dry plate clutch of 8 in (203 mm) diameter which is hydraulically actuated and adjusts automatically for wear.

The clutch assembly comprises a steel cover which is bolted and dowelled to the rear face of the flywheel and contains the pressure plate, pressure plate springs, release levers, and clutch disc or driven plate.

The pressure plate, pressure springs, and release levers are all attached to the clutch assembly cover. The clutch disc is free to slide along the splined first motion shaft and is held in position between the flywheel and the pressure plate by the pressure of the pressure plate springs.

Friction lining material is riveted to the clutch disc and it has a spring cushioned hub to absorb transmission shocks and to help ensure a smooth take off.

The clutch is actuated hydraulically. The pendant clutch pedal is connected to the clutch master cylinder and hydraulic fluid reservoir by a short pushrod. The master cylinder and hydraulic reservoir are mounted on the engine side of the bulkhead in front of the driver.

On some models the master cylinder for the brake and clutch hydraulic systems are separate whilst on others they share a common reservoir unit.

Depressing the clutch pedal moves the piston in the master

cylinder forwards, so forcing hydraulic fluid through the clutch hydraulic pipe to the slave cylinder.

The piston in the slave cylinder moves backwards on the entry of the fluid and actuates the clutch release arm by means of a short pushrod. The opposite end of the release arm is forked and is located behind the release bearing.

As this pivoted clutch release arm moves backwards it bears against the release bearing pushing it forwards to bear against the release bearing thrust plate and three clutch release levers. These levers are also pivoted so as to move the pressure plate backwards against the pressure of the pressure plate springs, in this way disengaging the pressure plate from the clutch disc.

When the clutch pedal is released, the pressure plate springs force the pressure plate into contact with the high friction linings on the clutch disc, at the same time forcing the clutch disc against the flywheel and so taking the drive up.

As the friction linings on the clutch disc wear, the pressure plate automatically moves closer to the disc to compensate. This makes the inner ends of the release levers travel further towards the gearbox which decreases the release bearing clearance but not the clutch free pedal travel, as unless the master cylinder has been disturbed this is automatically compensated for.

2 Clutch – maintenance and adjustment

1   Routine maintenance of the clutch is minimal and consists of checking the hydraulic fluid level in the master cylinder every 1000 miles (1600 km) and if necessary topping it up.
2   If the level of the hydraulic fluid has dropped then an immediate check must be made to trace the source of leakage in the circuit.
3   Whenever a check is to be made on the fluid level, wipe the master cylinder reservoir clean externally so that when the cap is removed no dirt particles can enter the system – this is most important. Do not however clean the reservoir with a solvent or any other similar cleaning liquid since it may enter the system and contaminate it.
4   The level of fluid in the reservoir must be to within 0.25 in (6 mm) of the filler neck. Make sure that the vent hole in the filler cap is clear.

Adjustment
5   When the clutch pedal is in the released position there must be a clearance of 0.03 in (0.8 mm) between the master cylinder pushrod and piston.
6   Any adjustment that may be necessary is made by loosening off the pushrod locknut and screwing the pushrod in the desired direction to increase or decrease the adjustment as necessary, but make sure that the pedal is releasing fully and isn't getting caught against the toeboard or carpeting. Always check the hydraulic fluid level before making any adjustment and top-up the reservoir if required. Retighten the locknut to complete.

3 Clutch hydraulic system – bleeding

1   Gather together a clean jam jar, a length of rubber tubing which fits tightly over the bleed nipple in the slave cylinder, a tin of hydraulic brake fluid, and a friend to help.
2   Check that the master cylinder is full and if not fill it, and cover the bottom two inches of the jar with hydraulic fluid.
3   Remove the rubber dust cap from the bleed nipple on the slave cylinder and with a suitable spanner open the bleed nipple one turn.
4   Place one end of the tube securely over the nipple and insert the other end in the jam jar so that the tube orifice is below the level of the fluid.
5   The assistant should now pump the clutch pedal up and down slowly until air bubbles cease to emerge from the end of the tubing. He should also check the reservoir frequently to ensure that the hydraulic fluid does not disappear so letting air into the system.
6   When no more air bubbles appear, tighten the bleed nipple on the downstroke.
7   Refit the rubber dust cap over the bleed nipple. Allow the hydraulic fluid in the jar to stand for at least 24 hours before using it, to allow all the minute air bubbles to escape.
8   Top-up the fluid level in the reservoir to complete the operation.

4 Clutch unit – removal and refitting

1   Encased as it is between the engine and gearbox the clutch unit can only be detached from the flywheel when the engine is withdrawn from the car. Therefore refer to Chapter 1 and remove the engine or engine and gearbox as applicable.
2   If the engine and gearbox are to be removed as a unit, they will have to be separated for access to the clutch. Both units will have to be suitably supported whilst the clutch housing bolts are withdrawn.
3   Once the bolts are removed carefully withdraw the gearbox from the engine and support it so that the weight of the box is not resting on the gearbox input shaft. When the shaft is clear of the clutch the gearbox can be lifted out of the way.
4   To remove the clutch assembly, unscrew the six bolts retaining the unit to the flywheel. Unscrew each bolt half a turn at a time in a diagonally opposed sequence until all are loose and can be removed with their spring washers.
5   Withdraw the clutch unit from the location dowels on the flywheel. The clutch disc (driven plate) will probably fall out on removal as it is

4.9 Refitting the clutch unit using an old input shaft unit to centralise the disc. Note dowel (arrowed)

7.3 The clutch slave cylinder unit

Chapter 5 Clutch

not attached to the clutch cover unit or the flywheel.
6 Refitting the clutch unit is a reversal of the removal procedure but the following points must be noted.
7 It is important that no oil or grease gets on the clutch disc friction linings, or the pressure plate and flywheel faces. It is advisable to refit the clutch with clean hands and to wipe down the pressure plate and flywheel faces with a clean dry rag before assembly begins.
8 Place the clutch disc against the flywheel with the shorter end of the hub, which is the end with the chamfered splines, facing the flywheel. On no account should the clutch disc be fitted with the longer end of the centre hub facing the flywheel as on reassembly it will be found quite impossible to operate the clutch in this position.
9 Refit the clutch cover assembly loosely on the dowels. (One of the dowels is shown in the photo). Refit the six bolts and spring washers and tighten them finger tight so that the clutch disc is gripped but can still be moved.
10 The clutch disc must now be centralised so that when the engine and gearbox are mated, the gearbox input shaft splines will pass through the splines in the centre of the driven plate hub.
11 Centralisation can be carried out quite easily by inserting a round bar or long screwdriver through the hole in the centre of the clutch, so that the end of the bar rests in the small hole in the end of the crankshaft containing the input shaft bearing bush. Ideally an old input shaft should be used.
12 Using the input shaft bearing bush as a fulcrum, moving the bar sideways or up and down will move the clutch disc in whichever direction is necessary to achieve centralisation.

13 Remove the bar and view the driven plate (clutch disc) in relation to the hole in the release bearing. When the hub appears exactly central with the release bearing it is correct.
14 Leave the centralising tool in position whilst the clutch bolts are tightened to the specific torque. Tighten the bolts in a diagonal sequence to avoid any distortion of the cover. Remove the centralising tool on completion.
15 Refit the engine to the gearbox and check the operation of the clutch.

5 Clutch unit – dismantling and inspection

1 It is not very often that it is necessary to dismantle the clutch cover assembly, and in the normal course of events clutch replacement is the term used for simply fitting a new clutch disc.
2 If a new clutch disc is being fitted it is a false economy not to renew the release bearing at the same time. This will preclude having to renew it at a later date when wear on the clutch linings is still very small.
3 It should be noted here that it is preferable to purchase an exchange clutch cover assembly unit, which will have been properly balanced rather than to dismantle and repair the existing cover.
4 Before beginning work ensure that either the clutch assembly gauging tool 18G 99A (and 18G 99B – Twin Cam models) or a press and a block of wood is available for compressing the clutch springs so that the three adjusting nuts can be freed.

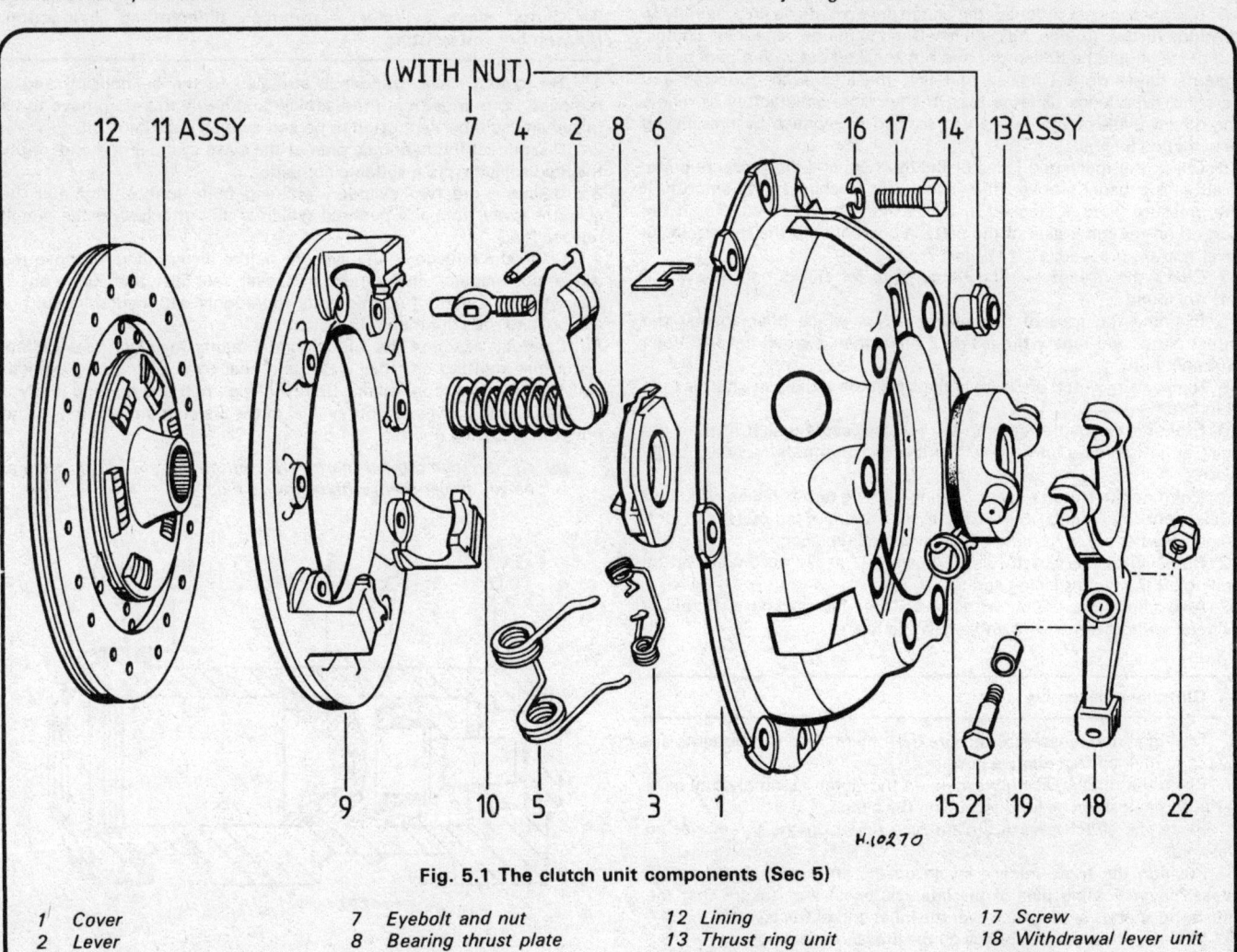

Fig. 5.1 The clutch unit components (Sec 5)

1 Cover	7 Eyebolt and nut	12 Lining
2 Lever	8 Bearing thrust plate	13 Thrust ring unit
3 Retainer	9 Pressure plate	14 Carbon ring
4 Pin	10 Pressure plate spring	15 Retainer spring
5 Spring (anti-rattle)	11 Driven plate unit	16 Spring washer
6 Strut		

17 Screw	21 Bolt
18 Withdrawal lever unit	22 Nut
19 Bush	

5   Presuming that it is possible to borrow from your local Leyland agent, clutch assembly tool 18G 99B proceed as follows:-
6   Mark the clutch cover, release levers, and pressure plate lugs so that they can be refitted in the same relative positions.
7   Unhook the springs from the release bearing thrust plate and remove the plate and spring.
8   Place the three correctly sized spacing washers provided with the clutch assembly tool on the tool base plate in the positions indicated by the chart (found inside the lid of the assembly tool container).
9   Place the clutch face down on the three spacing washers so that the washers are as close as possible to the release levers, with the six holes in the cover flange in line with the six holes in the base plate.
10 Insert the six bolts provided with the assembly tool through the six holes in the cover flange, and tighten the cover down diagonally onto the base plate.
11 With a suitable punch, tap back the three tab washers and then remove the three adjusting nuts and bearing plates from the pressure plate bolts on early models, and just unscrew the three adjusting nuts on later models.
12 Unscrew the six bolts holding the clutch cover to the base plate, diagonally, and a turn at a time, so as to release the cover evenly. Lift the cover off and extract the six pressure springs and the spring retaining cups.
13 Clean the respective components for inspection.
14 Examine the clutch disc friction linings for wear and loose rivets and the disc for rim distortion, cracks, broken hub springs, and worn splines.
15 It is always best to renew the clutch driven plate as an assembly to preclude further trouble, but, if it is wished to merely renew the linings, the rivets should be drilled out and not knocked out with a punch. The manufacturers do not advise that only the linings are renewed and personal experience dictates that it is far more satisfactory to renew the driven plate complete than to try and economise by only fitting new friction linings.
16 Check the machined faces of the flywheel and the pressure plate. If either are badly grooved they should be machined until smooth. If the pressure plate is cracked or split it must be renewed, also if the portion on the other side of the plate in contact with the three release lever tips are grooved.
17 Check the release bearing thrust plate for cracks and renew it if any are found.
18 Examine the tops of the release levers which bear against the thrust plate, and renew the levers if more than a small flat has been worn on them.
19 Renew any clutch pressure springs that are broken or shorter than standard.
20 Examine the depressions in the release levers which fit over the knife edge fulcrums and renew the levers if the metal appears badly worn.
21 Examine the clutch release bearing in the gearbox bellhousing and if it is worn to within 0.06 in (1.6 mm) of the rim of the metal cup, or if it is cracked or pitted, it must be removed and replaced.
22 Removal of the clutch release bearing is easily accomplished by pulling off the two retaining springs.
23 Also check the clutch withdrawal lever for slackness. If this is evident, withdraw the lever and renew the bush.

6 Clutch – reassembly

1   During clutch reassembly ensure that the marked components are placed in their correct relative positions.
2   Place the three spacing washers on the clutch assembly tool base in the same position as for dismantling the clutch.
3   Place the clutch pressure plate face down on the three spacing washers.
4   Position the three release levers on the knife edge fulcrums (or release lever floating pins in the later clutches) and ensure that the anti-rattle springs are in place over the inner end of the levers.
5   Position the pressure springs on the pressure plate bosses.
6   Fit the flanged cups to the clutch cover and fit the cover over the pressure plate in the same relative positions as it was originally.
7   Insert the six assembly tool bolts through the six holes in the clutch cover flange and tighten the cover down, diagonally, a turn at a time.
8   Refit the three bearing plates, tag washers, and adjusting nuts

over the pressure plate studs in the early units, and just screw the adjusting nuts into the eyebolts in the later models.
9   To correctly adjust the clutch release levers use the clutch assembly tool as detailed below:-

(a) Screw the actuator into the base plate and settle the clutch mechanism by pumping the actuator handle up and down a dozen times. Unscrew the actuator
(b) Screw the tool pillar into the base plate and slide the correctly sized distance piece (as indicated in the chart in the tool's box) recessed side downwards, over the pillar
(c) Slip the height finger over the centre pillar and turn the release lever adjusting nuts, until the height fingers, when rotated and held firmly down, just contact the highest part of the clutch release lever tips
(d) Remover the pillar, replace the actuator, and settle the clutch mechanism as in (a)
(e) Refit the centre pillar and height finger and recheck the clutch release lever clearance, and adjust if not correct.

10 With the centre pillar removed, lock the adjusting nuts (early clutches) by bending up the tab washers.
11 Refit the release bearing thrust plate and fit the retaining springs over the thrust plate hooks.
12 Unscrew the six bolts holding the clutch cover to the base plate, diagonally, a turn at a time and assembly is now complete.

7 Clutch slave cylinder – removal, dismantling, inspection, reassembly and refitting

1   The clutch slave cylinder is attached to the bellhousing and is removed from underneath the vehicle and it will therefore have to be raised and suitably supported or parked over an inspection pit.
2   Disconnect the hydraulic pipe at the slave cylinder end and empty the fluid spillage into a suitable container.
3   Unscrew the two cylinder retaining bolts (photo) and pull the cylinder away from the pushrod which is still attached to the clutch release fork.
4   Clean the outside of the cylinder before dismantling. Remove the rubber dust cap and shake the piston, seal, seal filler, and spring out of the cylinder. Clean all components thoroughly with hydraulic fluid or alcohol and then dry them off.
5   Carefully examine the rubber components for signs of swelling, distortion, splitting or other wear, and check the piston and cylinder wall for wear and score marks. Renew any parts that are found faulty.
6   Reassembly is a straight reversal of the dismantling procedure, but note the following points:-

(a) As the component parts are refitted to the slave cylinder barrel, smear them with hydraulic fluid

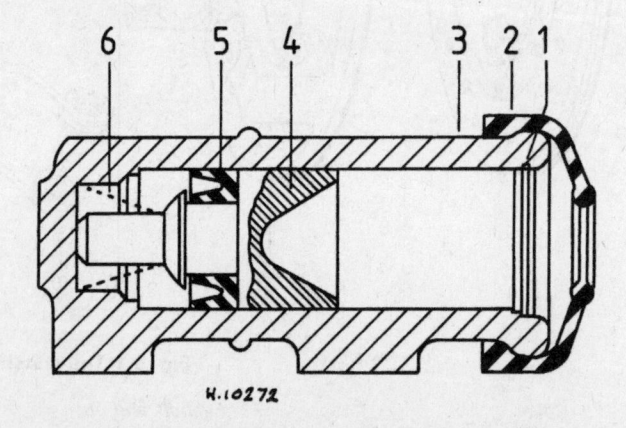

Fig. 5.2 The clutch slave cylinder components – cross-section view (Sec 7)

1 Circlip	4 Piston
2 Dust cover	5 Seal
3 Housing	6 Spring

Chapter 5 Clutch

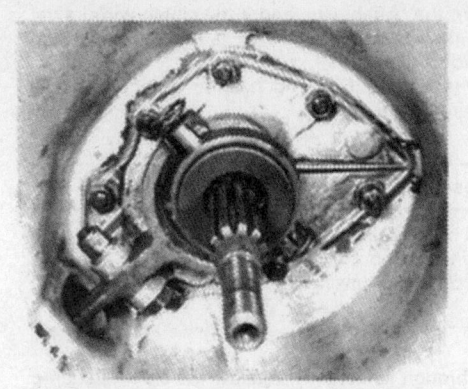

93

10.5 The clutch operating lever and release bearing assembly in position

10.6 Check the bearing A and pivot bush B for wear

11.1 The clutch and brake pedals pivot bracket

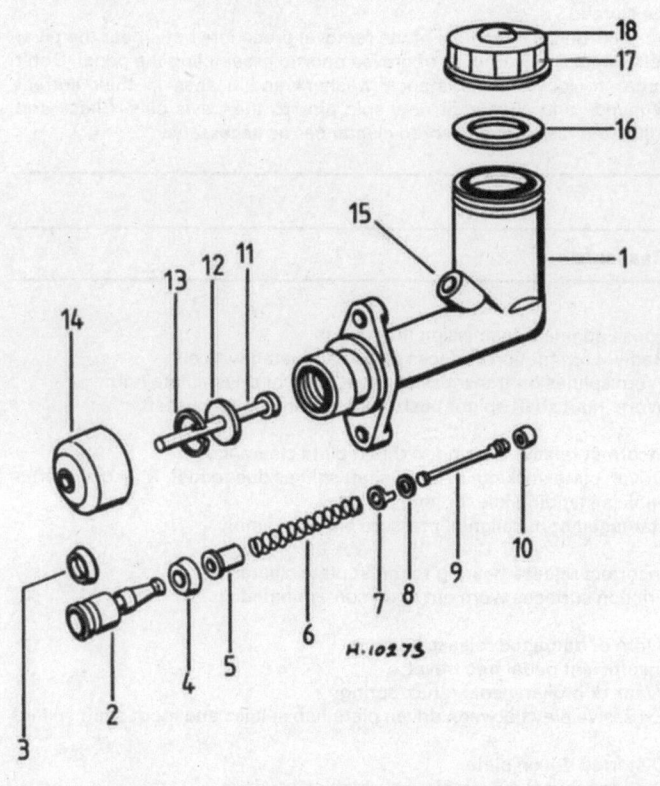

Fig. 5.3 Exploded view of the clutch master cylinder unit (single type) (Sec 8)

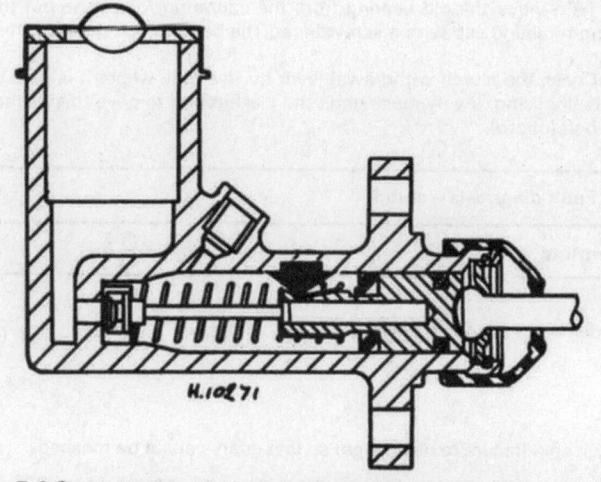

1 Cylinder body
2 Plunger
3 End seal
4 Plunger seal
5 Spring thimble
6 Spring
7 Valve spacer
8 Spring washer
9 Valve stem
10 Seal
11 Push-rod
12 Washer
13 Circlip
14 Dust cover
15 Outlet
16 Cap washer
17 Filler cap
18 Air vent

Fig. 5.4 Cross-section view of clutch master cylinder (single type). The thimble leaf location is arrowed (Sec 9)

unit, and the removal, overhaul, and refitting procedures are given in Chapter 9.

9 Clutch master cylinder (separate type) – removal, dismantling, examination, reassembly and refitting

1 Extract the clevis pin from the pedal to pushrod joint just forward of the cylinder. Detach and remove the pushrod clevis.
2 Unscrew the hydraulic union nut from the cylinder and plug the pipe to prevent the ingress of dirt.
3 Unscrew and remove the two cylinder to mounting bracket retaining bolts and carefully lift the unit clear.
4 Empty out any remaining fluid from the cylinder and wipe it clean externally before dismantling.
5 Pull the dust cover from the end of the cylinder and extract the retaining clip from its groove in the bore. Long nosed pliers are probably most suitable here.
6 Withdraw the pushrod and retaining washer. The plunger unit can now be extracted and dismantled for inspection. Lift the thimble leaf shown in Fig. 5.4 to clear the plunger shoulder, depress the return spring and let the valve stem slide through the thimble. Remove the spring, thimble and valve unit.
7 When removing the spacer observe how the spring washer is located with its side to the valve head under face.
8 Clean all parts thoroughly before reassembly, and renew the seals plus any other defective or suspect items. Lubricate all parts with hydraulic fluid as they are assembled.
9 Assembly of the piston and valve unit is a reversal of the dismantling procedure. When the valve stem is refitted ensure that it is centrally located in the thimble and that the spring is central on the spacer. The new seal is fitted so that its flat face abutts the plunger.
10 On completion ensure that the circlip is securely located and fit a

(b) When reassembling the operating cylinder, locate the piston seal at the end of the piston so that the sealing lip is away from the body of the piston
(c) On completion of reassembly, top up the reservoir tank with the correct grade of hydraulic fluid and bleed the system

8 Clutch master cylinder (dual type) – removal, dismantling, examination, reassembly and refitting

1 The clutch and brake master cylinders are combined in a single

new dust cover onto the end of the cylinder.
11 Refit the cylinder into position in the bracket and secure with bolts and spring washers. Use a new split pin to secure the clevis pin when reinserted.
12 Top-up the cylinder on completion with some hydraulic fluid. Operate the cylinder as you top-up and then bleed the circuit (see Section 3).

10 Clutch release bearing unit – removal and refitting

1 To inspect and possibly replace the clutch release bearing and its associate parts it is necessary to remove the engine as given in Chapter 1.
2 With the engine removed from the gearbox the release bearing and operating fork are readily accessible.
3 The carbon release bearing is a relatively inexpensive but important component and unless it is nearly new it is a mistake not to renew it during an overhaul of the clutch.
4 To remove the old bearing from the operating fork, prise out the spring retaining clip with a screwdriver. The bearing can then be lifted clear.
5 Check the clutch withdrawal lever for free play where it is held to the bellhousing. If very loose undo the locknut and remove the washer and bolt (photo).
6 Tackle the lever from the bellhousing and if the clutch withdrawal lever bushes are worn they must be renewed at your local Leyland garage or engineering works (photo).
7 Refitting of both the release fork and bearing assemblies is a reversal of the removal procedure.

11 Clutch and brake pedals – removal and refitting

1 Both the clutch and brake pedals pivot from a common bolt which is secured to the pedal bracket (photo).
2 To remove the clutch pedal, unscrew and remove the pivot bolt nut.
3 Extract the split pin from the clutch pushrod clevis and withdraw the clevis pin.
4 Pull the pivot bolt through sufficiently to allow the clutch pedal to be lowered and withdrawn from the support bracket.
5 If the brake pedal is to be removed, withdraw the bolt completely and disconnect the brake pushrod clevis in the same manner as that of the clutch.
6 Refitting is a reversal of the removal procedure but smear the pivot bolt with a small amount of grease prior to assembling the pedal. Don't forget to locate the distance washers and bushes in their correct sequence and always fit new split pins to the clevis pins. Check and adjust the respective pushrod clearances as necessary.

12 Fault diagnosis – clutch

Symptom	Reason/s
Judder when taking up drive	Loose engine transmission mountings Badly worn friction surfaces or contaminated with oil Worn splines on transmission input shaft or driven plate hub Worn input shaft spigot bush (pilot bearing) in crankshaft
Clutch spin (failure to disengage) so that gears cannot be meshed	Incorrect release bearing to thrust plate clearance Driven plate sticking on input shaft splines due to rust. May occur after vehicle standing idle for long period Damaged or misaligned pressure plate assembly
Clutch slip (increase in engine speed does not result in increase in vehicle road speed – particularly on gradients)	Incorrect release bearing to thrust plate clearance Friction surfaces worn out or oil contaminated
Noise evident on depressing clutch pedal	Worn or damaged release bearing Insufficient pedal free travel Weak or broken pedal return spring Excessive play between driven plate hub splines and input shaft splines
Noise evident as clutch pedal released	Distorted driven plate Broken or weak driven plate cushion coil springs Insufficient pedal free travel Weak or broken clutch pedal return spring Distorted or worn input shaft

Chapter 6 Gearbox

Contents

Fault diagnosis – gearbox ... 7	Gearbox – removal and installation ... 2
Gearbox – dismantling general ... 3	General description ... 1
Gearbox – dismantling ... 4	Mainshaft and gearbox – reassembly ... 6
Gearbox – examination and renovation ... 5	

Specifications

Overhead valve engine models

Gearbox type .... 4 forward and 1 reverse gear with synchromesh on 2nd, 3rd and 4th gears

Gear ratios
4th .... 1·0 : 1
3rd .... 1·374 : 1
2nd .... 2·214 : 1
1st .... 3·64 : 1
Reverse .... 4·76 : 1

Overall ratios

Axle ratio	**10·43 (standard)***	**10·41 (1600 Mk II)**
4th	4·3 : 1	4·1 : 1
3rd	5·908 : 1	5·633 : 1
2nd	9·520 : 1	9·077 : 1
1st	15·652 : 1	14·924 : 1
Reverse	20·468 : 1	19·516 : 1

*Optional axle ratio available 9.41 : 1

Speedometer gear ratio .... 5 : 12

Twin Cam models

Standard gearbox .... As for the overhead valve models

Close ratio gearbox

Gear ratios
4th .... 1·0 : 1
3rd .... 1·267 : 1
2nd .... 1·62 : 1
1st .... 2·445 : 1
Reverse .... 3·199 : 1

Overall ratios
4th .... 4·3 : 1
3rd .... 5·449 : 1
2nd .... 6·966 : 1
1st .... 10·52 : 1
Reverse .... 13·75 : 1

Chapter 6 Gearbox

1 General description

The gearbox fitted to all models contains four forward and one reverse gear. Synchromesh is fitted to 2nd, 3rd, and 4th gears. The aluminium alloy bellhousing and gearbox casing are a combined casting (photo). Attached to the rear of the gearbox casing is an extension which houses the selector mechanism (Fig. 6.1).

The input shaft (1st motion shaft) relays the drive from the power unit and its drive gear is in constant mesh with the laygear (2nd motion shaft) which is located in the lower half of the gearcase and runs in needle roller bearings. The mainshaft (3rd motion shaft) runs concentric with the input shaft and contains the respective drive gears and synchromesh assemblies. The synchromesh units are basically cone clutches, which when operated provide the means to equalize the speeds of the gears to be engaged and thus provide a smooth change.

The gearboxes fitted to all models are basically the same the main difference being different ratios (see Specifications). The speedometer drive gear on the later models have a distance collar fitted between the gear and locknut and washer on the tail end of the mainshaft. The later models also have a flanged hub located on the rear of the mainshaft to which the later type propeller shaft is bolted. On earlier models the propeller shaft was splined at the front and engaged direct into the mainshaft splines.

The gearbox casing was modified with the introduction of the GD series engine, the starter motor location being higher. The rear extension was also modified at the same time to enable the later type of propeller shaft flange (see paragraph 5) to be fitted. To prevent the 3rd gear from jumping out of engagement the detent notch depth in the selector fork rods was increased, phosphor bronze bushes were fitted to the 3rd gear in place of the sintered bronze bushes previously used and the depth of bore in the fork rod location block for the detent springs was decreased to 2.094 in (53.18 mm).

2 Gearbox – removal and refitting

1 The gearbox can be removed together with the engine as a complete unit as described in Section 5 of Chapter 1, or separate from the engine.
2 Whichever method is employed the gearbox must be removed forwards and upwards through the engine compartment. It is not possible to remove the gearbox from underneath with the engine still in situ.
3 To remove the gearbox separately from the engine, first refer to Section 6 in Chapter 1 and remove the engine.
4 Refer to Section 5, Chapter 1 and follow the instructions given in paragraphs 13 to 17 inclusive. Drain the oil from the gearbox.
5 Unscrew and remove the gearbox mounting bracket retaining nut bolt and spring washer whilst supporting the gearbox (photo).
6 Having checked that all other components and attachments to the gearbox are free, lower and withdraw the gearbox forwards through the engine compartment.
7 Refitting is a reversal of the removal procedure. Be sure to align the relative markings on the propeller shaft and rear axle flanges and check that the drain plug is secure in the gearbox before topping it up to the specified amount. To assist in lifting and pulling the gearbox into position when fitting it into the car with the engine, get an assistant to loop a piece of rope around the gearbox rear extension. Pass the rope down through the aperture in the transmission tunnel as shown (photo). When lowering and pushing the power unit into position at the front, simultaneously get the assistant to lift the rear extension up over the crossmember within the transmission tunnel so that the unit can be fully located. Although this method was a bit difficult and a certain amount of assistance was required, it did prevent the need to remove the floor boards and associate fittings as originally suggested by MG.
8 Refer to paragraph 44 in Section 6 when refitting the extension unit lever turret.

3 Gearbox dismantling – general

1 With the gearbox removed and ready for dismantling the first thing to do is clean down the exterior surfaces of the casing.
2 Prior to dismantling, thought should be given to the cause necessitating such action. The most common reason is to renew the synchromesh units (2nd gear being most susceptible) and in this instance, the effort involved in dismantling and reassembling the gearbox is worthwhile. If however the gears are suspected of breaking up or serious damage has taken place, consideration should be given to exchanging the complete unit for a rebuilt one, thus saving time, effort and dependent on the extent of damage, possibly even money!
3 A brief inspection can be made of the internals by removing the side cover.

4 Gearbox – dismantling

1 Withdraw the dipstick and unscrew the speedometer drive unit.
2 Unscrew the clutch operating lever pivot bolt and remove it with the lever and clutch thrust assembly (photo).
3 If still attached, unbolt and remove the extension lever remote control turret (photo). Lift the control turret up and away from the rear extension together with its gaskets and spacer plate.
4 On gearboxes fitted to and including GD engine and Twin Cam engine models onwards, unscrew the propeller shaft drive flange retaining nut and remove with the spring washer. Pull the flange free from the shaft (see Fig. 6.2).
5 Unscrew the bolts from the rear extension cover and prise the cover free with its gasket. Extract the interlock arm and bracket (photo).
6 Unscrew and remove the nuts and setscrews securing the rear extension to the gearbox and carefully withdraw the exterior. As the extension unit is pulled rearwards, disengage the remote control shaft selector lever from the selectors.
7 If it hasn't already been removed for inspecting, unscrew and remove the gearbox side cover retaining screws and prise the cover free.
8 To remove the selector forks the rods must be withdrawn. If the rods and selector units at the rear of the location block are to be dismantled, remove the lock wire and unscrew the respective selector setscrews. Alternatively they can be left assembled and withdrawn with the shafts as a unit.
9 Unscrew the location block retaining setscrews. If the rear selectors are to be dismantled, note their relative positions and withdraw them from the shafts. The location block can now be withdrawn if required. As it is removed, catch the three selector balls and springs as they exit from their apertures. Note the location dowels for the block in the rear of the gearcase.
10 Unscrew the selector fork retaining bolts and withdraw the fork rods to the rear, either in unit with the location block and rear selectors or separately as necessary.
11 Extract each selector fork from the gearbox and slide into position onto the respective shafts. The forks are removed in the order: reverse, 3rd/4th and then 2nd and 1st.
12 The gearbox front cover can now be removed. Unscrew the retaining nuts and withdraw it through the clutch housing.
13 Take a note of the shims and remove them from the front of the input shaft bearing. Put them with the cover or keep in a safe place.
14 Use a suitable brass or aluminium drift and drive the layshaft out. The laygear assembly will drop into the base of the gearbox and can stay there until the mainshaft assembly is withdrawn. If turning the gearbox on its side during subsequent operations be careful not to lose the rollers or thrust washers of the layshaft should they drop out.
15 Unscrew the setscrew retaining the reverse gear idler shaft in position. Extract the shaft and gear noting which way round it is fitted.
16 The mainshaft gear assembly can now be withdrawn through the rear of the gearbox. It may be necessary to tap the assembly out with a soft drift from the inside.
17 Withdraw the input (1st motion) shaft forwards through the front of the housing, tapping lightly with a soft drift if it is reluctant to emerge. Take care not to lose any of the 18 spigot needle rollers.
18 The layshaft gear assembly and thrust washers can now be lifted out from the bottom of the gearbox.
19 The gearbox is now dismantled into its principle sub-assemblies and these can be further dismantled as necessary for more detailed inspection and/or renewal.
20 The mainshaft can be dismantled as follows.
21 Withdraw the 3rd/4th gear synchromesh unit comprising the sliding coupling, the synchroniser and the respective baulk rings, (one each side). Keep the respective parts in order of appearance and if dismantling the synchro hub unit pull the coupling free from the synchroniser but collect the interlocking springs and balls which will eject

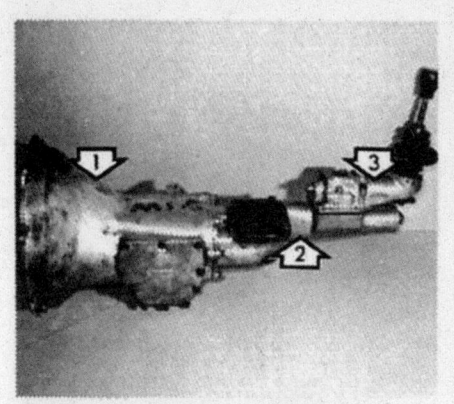

1.1 The main gearbox assemblies (1) main housing (2) extension and (3) lever turret

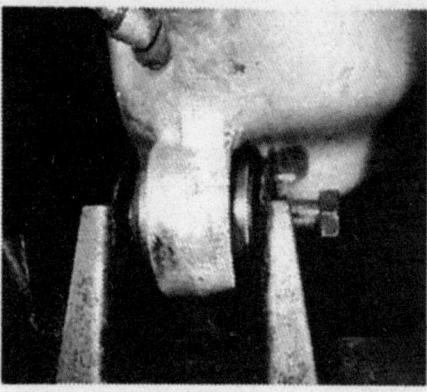

2.5 Disconnect the gearbox mounting and withdraw the through bolt

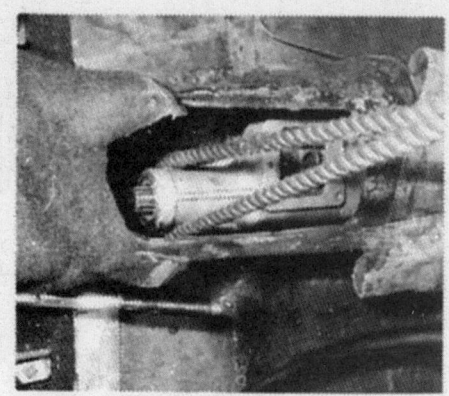

2.7 Manoeuvreing the extension over the support bracket with the aid of a lifting rope

4.2 Remove the clutch thrust assembly and operating lever from the clutch housing

4.3 Removing the extension lever turret – note spacer and gaskets

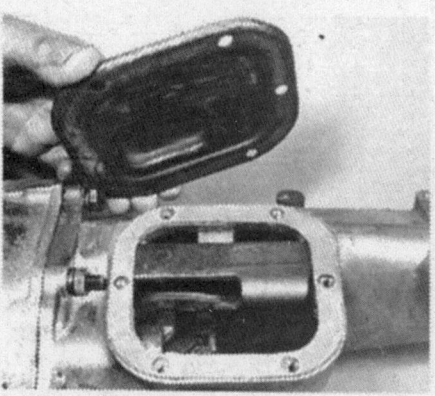

4.5 Remove the extension cover and extract the interlock arm and bracket

4.30 The input shaft nut washer and bearing

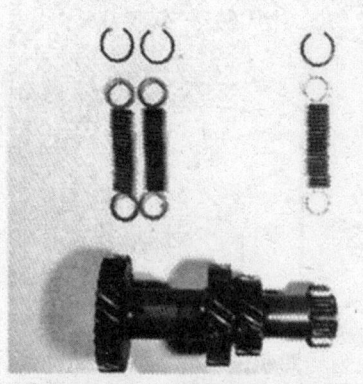

5.3 The laygear and bearing assemblies laid out for inspection (earlier type shown)

5.7a Check the 3rd gear endfloat

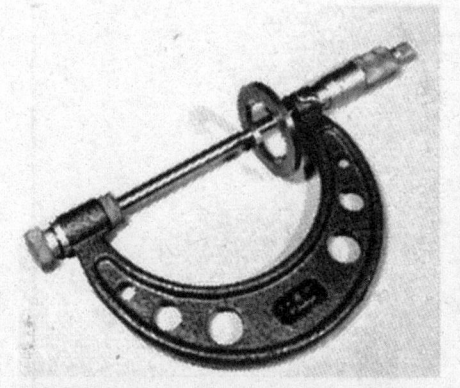

5.7b Check the interlock ring thickness with a micrometer

5.10 Renew the rear extension oil seal

5.14 Renew the rear mounting rubber bush if necessary

98

Fig. 6.1 The gearbox components layout (Sec 1)

1 Gearbox casing
2 Front cover stud
3 Drain plug
4 Dowel
5 Stud
6 Blanking plug
7 Joint washer
8 Dust cover
9 Dipstick
10 Felt
11 Front cover
12 Front cover gasket
13 Nut
14 Spring washer
15 Side cover
16 Side cover gasket
17 Set screw
18 Spring washer
19 Countersunk screw
20 Shakeproof washer
21 Gearbox extension
22 Bush
23 Oil seal
24 Joint washer
25 Gasket
26 Nut
27 Set screw
28 Spring washer
29 Plug
30 Cover – extension side
31 Extension side cover gasket
32 Set screw
33 Spring washer
34 Breather
35 Remote control shaft
36 Front selector lever
37 Set screw
38 Spring washer
39 Selector lever key
40 Rear selector lever
41 Bush (rear selector lever)
42 Circlip (lever bush)
43 Set screw
44 Spring washer
45 Selector lever key
46 1st and 2nd speed fork
47 Screw
48 1st and 2nd speed fork shaft
49 Ball (shaft)
50 Spring
51 3rd and 4th speed fork
52 Fork locating screw
53 3rd and 4th speed fork shaft
54 Reverse fork
55 Fork locating screw
56 Reverse fork shaft
57 Shaft locating block
58 Set screw (block to casing)
59 Spring washer
60 1st and 2nd gear selector
61 Selector locating screw
62 3rd and 4th gear selector
63 Selector locating screw
64 Reverse gear selector
65 Reverse gear selector screw
66 Interlock arm (complete)
67 1st pinion shaft
68 Nut
69 Lockwasher
70 Bearing
71 Spring ring
72 Shim (bearing)
73 Rollers
74 3rd motion shaft
75 Oil restrictor
76 Front thrust washer
77 Rear thrust washer
78 Peg
79 Spring
80 Bearing (rear) 3rd motion shaft
81 Bearing housing
82 Peg
83 Distance piece speedometer gear)
84 Nut
85 Lockwasher
86 Gear (speedometer drive)
87 Key
88 Speedometer drive pinion
89 Pinion bush
90 Oil seal
91 Oil seal retaining ring
92 Bush to rear cover gasket
93 Gear (1st)
94 Gear (2nd)
95 Synchroniser (2nd)
96 Ball (synchroniser)
97 Spring
98 Baulk ring (2nd gear)
99 Bush (2nd) gear
100 Gear (3rd)
101 Baulk ring 3rd and 4th gear
102 Bush 3rd gear
103 Ring (interlock) (2nd and 3rd) bushes
104 Coupling (3rd and 4th)
105 Synchroniser (3rd and 4th)
106 Ball – synchroniser
107 Spring
108 Layshaft
109 Gear unit (layshaft)
110 Bearing (needle roller) layshaft – outer
111 Bearing (needle roller) layshaft – inner
112 Spring ring
113 Distance piece
114 Front thrust washer
115 Rear thrust washer
116 Reverse shaft
117 Screw
118 Lockwasher
119 Reverse gear
120 Bush
121 Bolt (gearbox to mounting plate)
122 Spring washer
123 Nut
124 Remote control tower
125 Dowel
126 Core plug
127 Lever
128 Knob
129 Locknut
130 Stop plate
131 Snug
132 Spring
133 Cover (ball spring)
134 Circlip (ball spring cover)
135 Plunger (reverse selector)
136 Spring
137 Plug (reverse plunger)
138 Dowel (reverse plunger)
139 Ball (reverse plunger)
140 Spring (reverse plunger detent)
141 Gasket
142 Bolt (short)
143 Bolt (long)
144 Spring washer
145 Plug (ball retaining)
146 Washer
147 Plunger
148 Spring
149 Ball (selector lever)
150 Remote control shaft
151 Selector lever (front)
152 Selector lever (rear)
153 Set screw
154 Spring washer
155 Key
156 Draught excluder (rubber)
157 Ring (lever draught excluder)
158 Flexible bush
159 Bolt (rear mounting bush)
160 Spring washer
161 Nut

100 Chapter 6 Gearbox

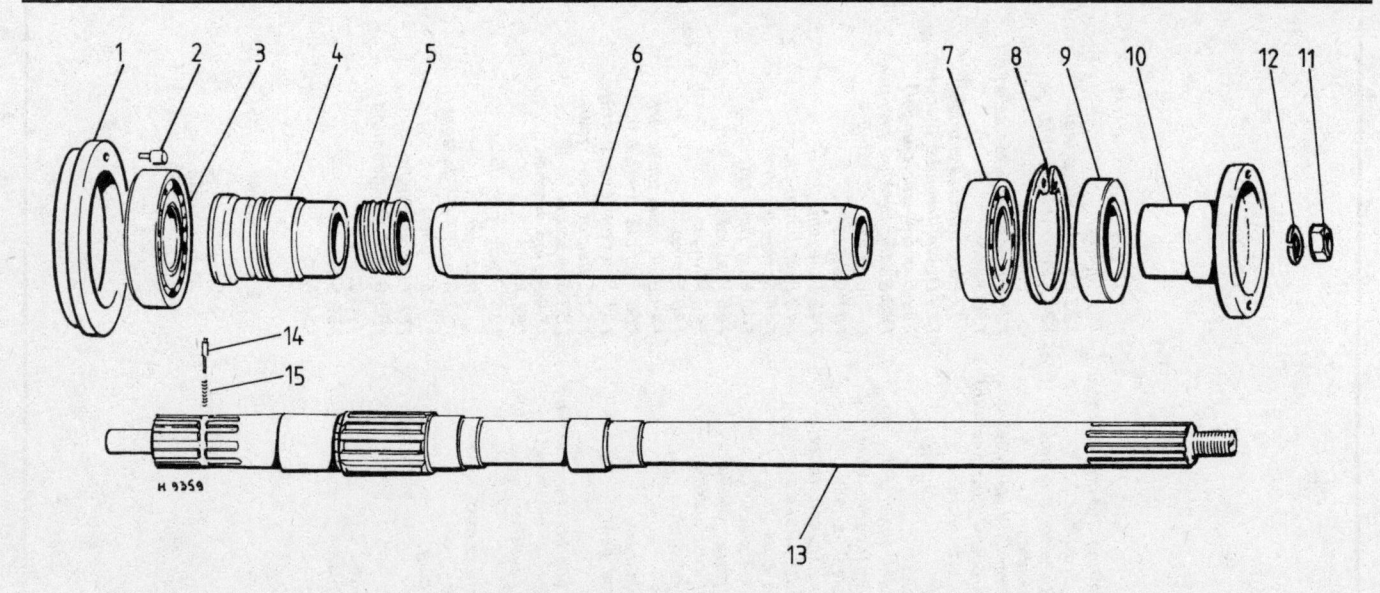

Fig. 6.2 The gearbox 3rd motion (mainshaft) rear bearing and seal assembly differences on the later models to facilitate fitting the modified propeller shaft front joint (Sec 4)

1 Bearing housing
2 Locating peg
3 Bearing
4 Distance piece
5 Speedometer drive pinion
6 Distance piece
7 Rear extension bearing
8 Circlip
9 Seal
10 Rear flange
11 Nut
12 Spring washer
13 3rd motion shaft (mainshaft)
14 Front thrust washer peg
15 Spring

on removing the coupling from the hub.
22 Compress the 3rd gear cone thrust washer plunger, rotate the washer round its groove to align the washer splines with those of the shaft and withdraw the washer.
23 Remove the 3rd gear and bush noting their direction of fitting.
24 Remove the bush interlock washer and withdraw the 2nd gear together with bush and baulk ring.
25 Withdraw the thrust washer from the shaft and then remove 1st/2nd speed synchromesh hub and gear unit. Dismantling the 1st/2nd gear synchromesh hub is similar to that of 3rd/4th hub unit.
26 On pre GD engine models, bend back the lockwasher tab and unscrew the nut retaining the speedometer drive gear and distance sleeve in position on the rear of the shaft. Withdraw the distance sleeve and speedometer drive gear (which is located on a Woodruff key). The rear bearing and flanged housing can now be pressed from the shaft if necessary.
27 On GD engine models (and Twin Cam) engine models, withdraw the distance sleeve, speedometer drive gear and its distance piece from the rear end of the mainshaft. The rear bearing and flanged housing can be pressed free if they are to be removed.
28 The input or 1st motion shaft can be dismantled if necessary as follows. Extract the needle rollers from the mainshaft aperture.
29 Support the shaft in a vice with soft jaws to protect the splines. Bend over the lockwasher tab and unscrew the retaining nut (left-hand thread).
30 Remove the nut, lockwasher and shim (photo).
31 The ball bearing can be removed using a suitable puller but remove the location ring from the outer race of the bearing to avoid damaging it.

5 Gearbox – examination and renovation

1 Carefully clean and then examine all the component parts starting with the baulk ring synchronisers, for general wear, distortion, and damage to machined faces and threads.
2 Examine the gearwheels for excessive wear and chipping of the teeth and renew them as necessary, If the laygear endfloat is above the permitted tolerance of 0.002 to 0.003 in (0.005 to 0.08 mm) the thrust washers must be renewed. These are available from your local Leyland agent in varying thicknesses to compensate for laygear wear.

Compare the old thrust washers with new standard units as the wear may be in the thrust washers. New thrust washers are available in the following thicknesses:- 0.154 to 0.156 in (3.81 to 3.96 mm), 0.157 to 0.159 in (3.95 to 4.03 mm), 0.160 to 0.161 in (4.06 to 4.08 mm), 0.163 to 0.164 in (4.13 to 4.16 mm). Measure their thicknesses with a micrometer.
3 Needle roller bearings are fitted at each end of the laygear. Unless the car has only done a very small mileage they invariably need renewing. To examine them pull out the spring rings and with a finger pull out the rollers and the distance tube. Renew the roller bearings and races if worn. On early cars the rollers are loose (photo) but on later models they are caged. The later type are very much easier to deal with.
4 To reassemble the roller bearings inside the laygear, start by assembling them to the layshaft. Fit the stepped end of the layshaft in a vice, grease the shaft generously and fit the bottom two sets of rollers, distance tube and top rollers to the shaft. Slip the spring retaining ring into its groove in the rear end of the laygear and carefully slide the laygear over the layshaft, taking great care not to dislodge any of the rollers. Remove the laygear and layshaft from the vice and fit the remaining spring retaining ring. Some early models have circlips fitted each side of the front roller bearings in which case the innermost circlip should be fitted first followed by the inner bearing, middle circlip, and outer bearing.
5 Examine the condition of the main ball bearings, one on the first motion shaft, and the other on the main shaft. If there is looseness between the inner and outer races the bearings must be pulled off and renewed.
6 On the first motion shaft it is necessary to remove the retaining nut and lockwasher before the bearing is pulled. **Note.** *The locknut has a left-hand thread, and note the position of the spring ring.* On refitting a new bearing to the first motion shaft position the tag on the lockwasher in the shaft keyway so that it faces towards the nut.
7 On the mainshaft first check the endfloat on third gear (photo) and note the measurement so the correct thrust washer can be fitted on reassembly. Then place the shaft in a vice with padded jaws, release the speedometer gear, the half-moon shaped Woodruff key, and distance piece, if this has not already been done, and then pull the bearing housing and bearing off the shaft. The bearing can then be driven away from its housing.
8 Examine the first motion shaft needle roller bearings and renew them if worn.
9 Having dismantled the mainshaft as previously described, examine

Chapter 6 Gearbox

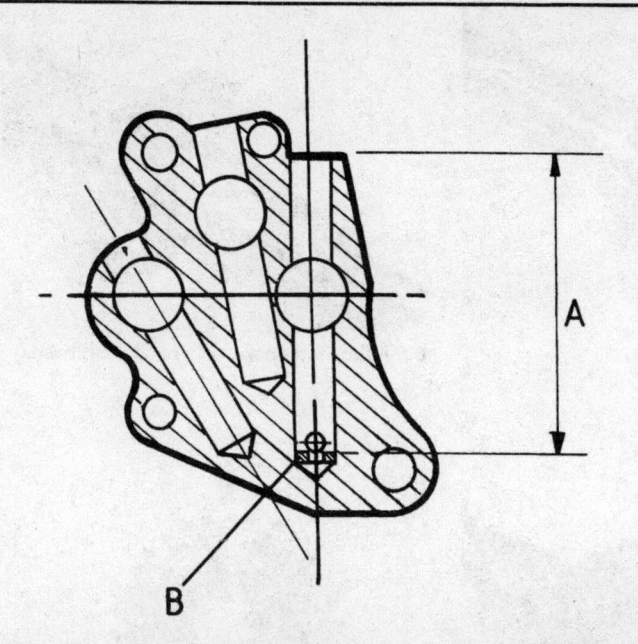

Fig. 6.3 End view of modified fork location block (Sec 5). Washer 'B' is 0.063 in (1.59 mm) thick to give bore depth 'A' of 2.094 in (53.18 mm) (Sec 4)

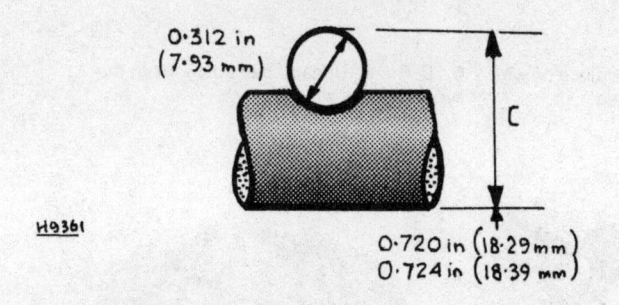

Fig. 6.4 3rd/4th selector fork rod and detent ball on modified types to measure as shown (Sec 5)

the second and third gear bushes and the reverse gear internal bush for wear, and renew them if suspect. When fitting a new bush to the reverse gear press it in from the small end of the gear until the end of the bush is flush with the end face of the gear.
10 To exclude the possibility of oil leaks developing at the front or the rear of the gearbox the first motion shaft and mainshaft rear extension oil seals should be renewed as a matter of course. The seal in the rear extension can be extracted by carefully prising free using a large screwdriver or similar tool for leverage but take care not to damage the housing in any way. The new seal can be driven into position using a tube of suitable diameter (photo).
11 The front cover seal can be fitted in a similar fashion but ensure that the lip faces towards the gearbox. **Note.** *This seal was only fitted from Engine No. 7981.*
12 Check the free length of the synchromesh hub springs with new ones. Renew any springs which do not meet the required standard and reassemble the first speed gear and synchroniser, and the third and fourth gear synchroniser and coupling sleeve using Service Tools 18G222 and 18G 223 if available to facilitate the rapid fitting of the springs and bolts.
13 Renew the clutch release fork and gearlever rubber gaiters if they are split or have deteriorated. Examine the split nylon bush on the selector lever and renew it if it is damaged or worn. Thoroughly clean out the gearbox casing lubrication channels and oilways. The gearbox should be spotlessly clean before reassembly.
14 Renew the rubber mounting bush (photo) if perished or defective.
15 Inspect the general condition of the shift fork location block, the shifts and forks. Check these items together with the detent springs and balls for wear and renew where necessary.
16 On earlier models third gear will sometimes 'jump out of gear'. To overcome this fault, the location block was modified slightly by having the depth of the detent spring bore reduced and the engagement notch in the 3rd/4th speed selector shaft increased in depth.
17 The free length of the detent spring should be 1.187 in (30.16 mm). If less than this renew it.
18 On earlier gearboxes the detent spring hole depth in the location block was 2.157 in (54.77 mm) whilst in the modified types this was reduced to 2.094 in (53.18 mm). To reduce the depth of bore in the earlier type location plate a packing washer, 0.063 in (1.59 mm) in depth can be fitted (Fig. 6.3).
19 The later type selector shaft can be fitted to the earlier gearbox if required the advantage being the greater depth of detent notch (Fig. 6.4).

6 Mainshaft and gearbox – reassembly

1 If the mainshaft has been dismantled, gearbox reassembly starts by rebuilding the former. Use new washers, gaskets and joint washers throughout reassembly.
2 Generously lubricate all the gears, bushes, and bearings with oil as they are assembled. Commence by reassembling the mainshaft.

Mainshaft assembly
3 Slide the rear thrust washer into position on the shaft splines at the front (photo).
4 The 2nd gear bronze bush is now assembled onto the shaft with its 'dog' end section towards the front of the shaft. Ensure that the oil hole in the bush and shaft are aligned. In addition check that when the 3rd speed splined bush is fitted that it's cutaway section will engage over the location peg hole as the respective bush dogs are engaged with the bush interlock washer.
5 Now locate the baulk ring into position on the 2nd gear and fit the gear onto the bush. The gear must have the plain shouldered side facing front (photo).
6 Slide the interlock ring washer down the shaft splines followed by the shorter splined bush. Engage the short and long bush in the interlock ring. Align the bush with the oil hole in the shaft (photo).
7 Locate the spring and its location peg into the hole in the shaft.
8 Slide 3rd speed gear into position on the bush, (the coned face to the front) (photo).
9 Now fit the front thrust washer into position so that its machined face is to the gear. As the washer is pushed onto the shaft, insert a small punch through the hole in the gear cone and compress the location peg to enable the thrust washer to be fully fitted within the coned section of the gear and over the peg. Rotate the washer to engage the peg in a spline (photo).
10 Reassemble the 1st/2nd and 3rd/4th synchromesh units respectively. On each unit the three springs and balls must be located into the synchro hub, be simultaneously compressed and the sliding coupling pushed into position (photo). This can be tricky and much care and patience are required – take care not to lose the springs and balls should they fly apart during assembly.
11 Fit the 1st/2nd synchromesh unit into position over the rear end of the shaft (photo) together with its baulk ring.
12 If fitting a new rear bearing, press it into its housing and locate the unit onto the shaft with the vertical flange rearwards (photo).
13 Slide the speedometer gear distance piece into position on the shaft butting it against the bearing, followed by the speedometer drive gear. The speedometer gear is located over a Woodruff key. The oil hole in the shaft aligns with the distance piece oil hole when fitted. Use a long piece of tube to drift the speedometer drive gear home (photos).
14 On the earlier type gearbox, fit the nut and lockwasher to retain the speedometer drive gear and bearing in position (photo).
15 On later models slide the distance piece onto the shaft followed by the rear flange hub and nut to temporarily retain the assembly in position until ready for fitting into the gearbox rear extension.
16 If not already fitted, assemble the rear extension ball bearing and/or oil seal (as applicable) into position and retain with the circlip.
17 Now assemble the 3rd/4th gear synchromsh hub unit together with the baulk rings into position on the front end of the mainshaft (photo).
18 The mainshaft is now ready for fitting into the gearbox. Place it to

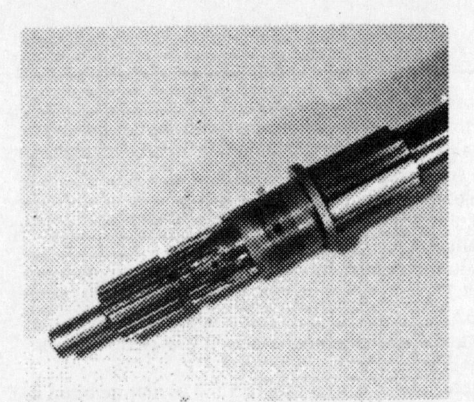

6.3 Locate the thrust washer followed by the bronze bush. Note bush fitted with oil holes aligned and dog section forward

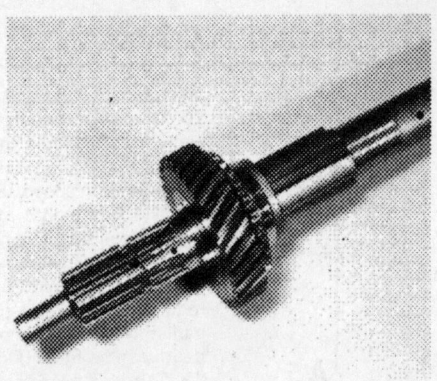

6.5 Locate 2nd gear

6.6 Fit the interlock washer and short bush

6.8 Slide 3rd gear onto the bush

6.9 Locate thrust washer and use piece of wire as shown to compress location peg

6.10 The spring and ball positions in the synchro hubs

6.11a Fit the baulk ring and then ...

6.11b ... locate the 1st/2nd synchro unit

6.12a New rear bearing fitted into flange

6.12b Fit rear bearing onto shaft

6.13a Locate the distance collar ...

6.13b ... and speedometer drive pinion – note Woodruff key

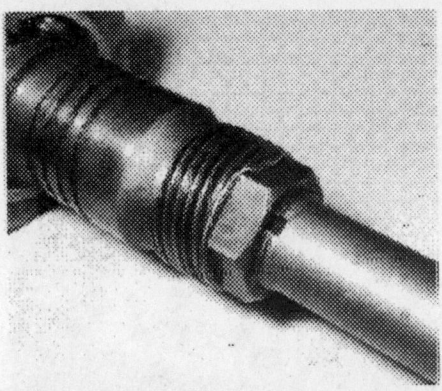

6.14 Secure with nut and tab washer (early type)

6.17 Assemble and fit 3rd/4th synchro hub unit and baulk ring

6.21 Locate the laygear into the bottom of the gearbox

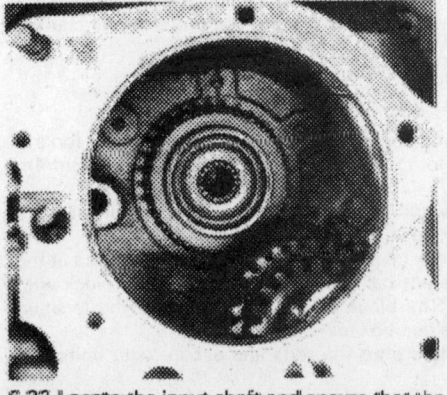

6.22 Locate the input shaft and ensure that the bearing rollers are all exactly in position before fitting the mainshaft

6.29 Reposition reverse gear

6.30a Locate the shims into the front cover ...

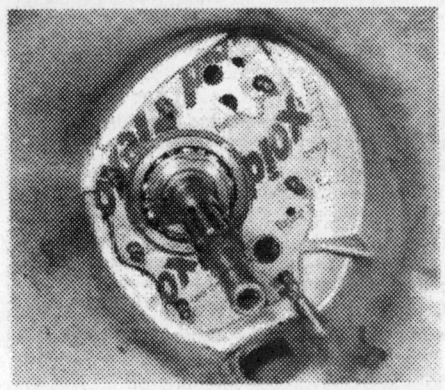

6.30b ... and the gasket to the gearbox front face

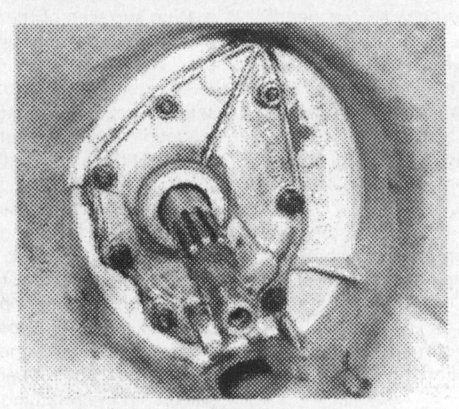

6.30c Refit the front cover

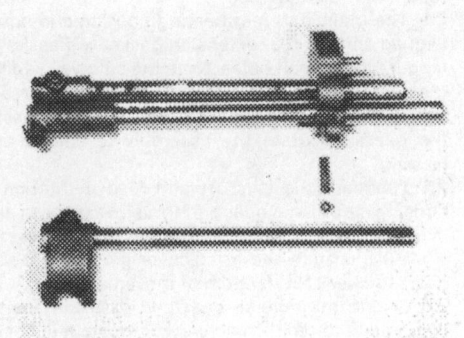

6.32a Assemble the selectors with interlock balls and springs

6.32b Insert the selector shafts passing through the forks. Note the 3rd/4th selector shaft distance tube

6.35 Lockwire the retaining bolts where applicable

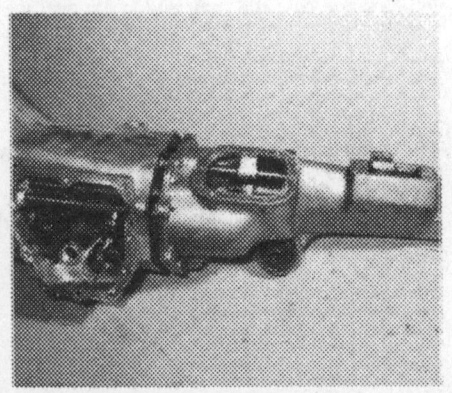

6.38 Refit the rear extension

Chapter 6 Gearbox

6.41 Locate the gasket and refit the side cover

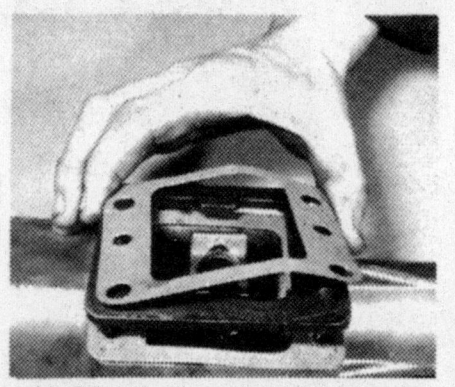

6.44a Relocating the gaskets and spacer plate to the extension

6.44b Relocate the turret and secure with four bolts (shown assembled out of car for clarity)

one side for the time being.

19 Prepare the layshaft gear for assembly into the gearbox. If not already assembled relocate the needle bearing and distance tube with circlips, as detailed in paragraph 4 of Section 5.

20 Smear the ends of the layshaft gears with grease and locate the thrust washers so that they adhere to the grease.

21 Carefully place the laygear assembly into the bottom of the gearcase. The shaft is not fitted just yet (photo).

22 Insert the input shaft (1st motion) into the front of the gearbox. Grease the needle roller bearings and their aperture in the shaft and carefully assemble them into position. There are 18 in all and they will stick to the grease enabling them all to be located (photo).

23 The mainshaft can now be inserted through the rear of the gearbox, but take care as it is fed through the box, especially when locating it s front journal into the input shaft otherwise the needle rollers may be disturbed.

24 The mainshaft rear bearing housing and dowels must be correctly aligned and the rear extension gasket will assist in this respect by aligning it with its bolt holes. Note the cutaway section on the front face of the bearing housing. Position to clear the reverse gear.

25 When the mainshaft and its bearing housing are fully located in the gearbox, rotate the assembly to ensure that it is free and not binding.

26 Lubricate the layshaft and feed it through the end of the gear housing. Lift the laygear and thrust washers to align with the shaft and push the shaft through so that the cutaway section at the front of the shaft aligns with the front cover groove. Once in position rotate the gears to check for freedom of movement.

27 Locate the reverse gear and pass the shaft through to locate it. Insert and tighten the setscrew to locate it in position (photo) and bend over the lockwasher.

28 The gearbox front end cover can now be fitted. Locate the front bearing shims into the cover recess (photo). Lubricate the lips of the oil seal in the front cover before assembly and push the cover carefully into position over the shaft and locate over the front face studs. Hand tighten the nuts (with spring washers) and then use a box wrench or socket and extension and progressively tighten the nuts in a diagonal sequence, a $\frac{1}{2}$ turn at a time until fully tight. This method is employed so that the cover and seal are centralized on the shaft and are not distorted in any way.

29 Locate the reverse, 1st/2nd and 3rd/4th gear selector forks into position in the gearbox (in that sequence).

30 Insert the respective selector shafts with springs and balls into the location block (photo) and pass the shafts into their respective holes in the rear of the gearbox and engage with the respective selector forks in the box. Don't forget to locate the distance tube on the 3rd/4th selector rod (photo).

31 Refit the setscrews and locknuts and tighten to secure. Locate with new lockwire if applicable.

32 Slide the location block up against the gearbox rear face and at the same time insert the detent balls and springs. Retain the block with the bolts and washers. The block is exactly aligned via the location pegs protruding from the gearbox rear face.

33 Refit the rear selectors onto the rods and secure with bolts and lockwire (photo).

34 Before refitting the rear extension remove the nut and flange from the rear of the mainshaft (later models only).

35 Lubricate the oil seal lips in the rear extension. Wipe clean the mating surfaces of the rear face of the gearbox and the rear extension front face and smear with some sealant.

36 Locate the gasket onto one of the faces and then carefully refit the rear extension (photo). Make sure that the remote control shaft selector lever is engaged with the selectors. Insert and tighten the respective retaining nuts and bolts with the washers to secure.

37 Refit the extension side cover with overshoot assembly and bolt in position using a new gasket.

38 Before refitting the side inspection cover and gasket, temporarily refit the gear lever turret to the rear cover and check the respective gears for engagement. The change should be firm with not too much drag or effort required to engage or disengage the respective gears. On the other hand they shouldn't slip in and out too easily.

39 If selection is in order, remove the lever and turret from the rear extension and then smear the mating faces of the side inspection cover and the gearbox mating flange with sealant and locate the cover with gasket. Fit the retaining bolts and screws to secure (photo).

40 Refit the speedometer driven gear unit.

41 Refit the clutch operating fork and thrust bearing assembly (see Chapter 5) to complete.

42 When the gearbox unit is relocated into the car, the extension gear lever turret unit can be refitted. New gaskets must be fitted each side of the spacer plate (photos). To simplify the location of the two front turret to extension retaining bolts, we cut a slot in the head of each bolt to enable them to initially tightened with a screwdriver. Once the bolts are screwed down a small socket and extension can be used to tighten them. To cut the slots in the bolt heads, locate the bolts in a vice so that the thread section will not be damaged, then cut the slots centrally using a hacksaw but only cut sufficiently enough to enable a screwdriver blade tip to be engaged.

7 Faults diagnosis – gearbox

Symptom	Reason/s
Trouble changing gear	Worn/damaged synchromesh Selector/s worn/damaged Clutch needs adjustment or renewal
Jumps out of gear	Broken gearchange fork rod spring Gearbox coupling dogs badly worn Selector fork rod groove badly worn Selector fork rod securing screw and locknut loose
Excessive noise	Incorrect grade of oil in gearbox or oil level too low Bush or needle roller bearings worn or damaged Gearteeth excessively worn or damaged Laygear thrust washers worn allowing excessive endplay

Chapter 7 Propeller shaft

Contents

General description ... 1	Universal joints – inspection and repair ... 3
Propeller shaft – removal and refitting ... 2	Universal joints – reassembly ... 5
Universal joints – dismantling ... 4	

Specifications

Type
GB engine models	Tubular – reverse spline with Hardy Spicer universal joints
GA, GC, GD and Twin Cam engine models	Tubular – flanged with sliding spline joint and Hardy Spicer universal joints

Overall length
GB engine models	38·4 in (97·55 cm)
GA, GC, GD and Twin Cam engine models	32·6 in (83·03 cm) – fully extended

Diameter of tube
2 in (50·8 mm)

Length between joint centres
GB engine models	31·4 in (79·69 cm)
GA, GC, GD and Twin Cam engine models	30·3 in (77 cm) fully extended, 29·4 in (74·65 cm) fully compressed

1 General description

To transmit the drive from the gearbox to the rear axle a tubular propeller shaft is employed. Hardy Spicer universal joints are fitted to each end of the shaft, which is fully balanced to prevent any oscillations causing vibrations through the transmission and body. The universal joints allow for the rear axle movements over the varying road surface conditions. The universal joints comprise of a four legged centre spider, four needle roller bearing sets and two yokes.

On earlier models, the fore and aft movement of the rear axle is absorbed by a sliding spline joint of the front of the propeller shaft and this mates over the splined rear section of the gearbox main shaft. An oil seal in the tail section of the rear gearbox housing prevents leakage of oil from the gearbox past the sliding joint.

On later models a modified shaft assembly was fitted and this incorporates its own sliding joint section at the front end, just to the rear of the front universal joint. The front universal joint is joined to the gearbox via four bolts through flanges in a similar fashion to the rear joint connection to the rear axle (photo).

Each universal joint assembly is provided with a grease nipple and the joints must be lubricated every 3000 miles (5000 km). Later models also have a grease nipple adjacent to the sliding joint and this too must be lubricated at the same mileage intervals.

2 Propeller shaft – removal and refitting

1 Raise the rear of the car and make secure with axle-stands or blocks. If a pit or ramps are available then obviously these are preferable.

2 If the rear wheels are clear of the ground place chocks each side of the front wheels. Apply the handbrake to prevent the propeller shaft turning when the flange nuts are removed from the joints.

3 The propeller shaft is carefully balanced to fine limits and it is important that it is replaced in exactly the same position it was in prior to its removal. Scratch a mark on the propeller shaft and rear axle flanges to ensure accurate mating when the time comes for reassembly. On the later models, the front universal joint flange will have to be detached from the gearbox third motion shaft (mainshaft) flange and these flanges must also be marked for correct alignment on reassembly (photo).

4 Unscrew and remove the self locking nuts and withdraw the bolts from the flanges at the rear. The shaft will have to be turned for access to all of the bolts and the handbrake can be temporarily released to achieve this.

5 On earlier models support the shaft at the rear and pull it free from the gearbox mainshaft splines and then lower it for removal. Tie a polythene bag or piece of cloth around the rear of the gearbox to catch any escaping oil.

6 On later (GD models on) disconnect the front joint flange in the same manner as for the rear whilst supporting the shaft at the rear with a single bolt. When the front joint is uncoupled, support the shaft, remove the rear bolt and remove the shaft assemblies.

7 Refitting the propeller shaft is a reversal of the removal procedure. Ensure that the mating marks on the flanges are realigned before inserting the bolts. Check and top-up the gearbox oil if necessary.

3 Universal joints – inspection and repair

1 Wear in the needle roller bearings is characterised by vibration in

1.0 The front universal joint nuts of the later models

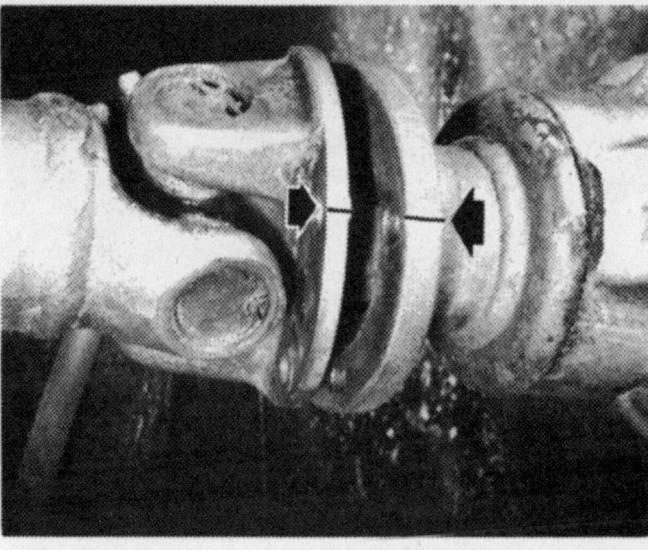

2.3 Make an alignment mark between the propeller shaft and rear axle pinion shaft flange as shown. Similarly mark the front joint flanges

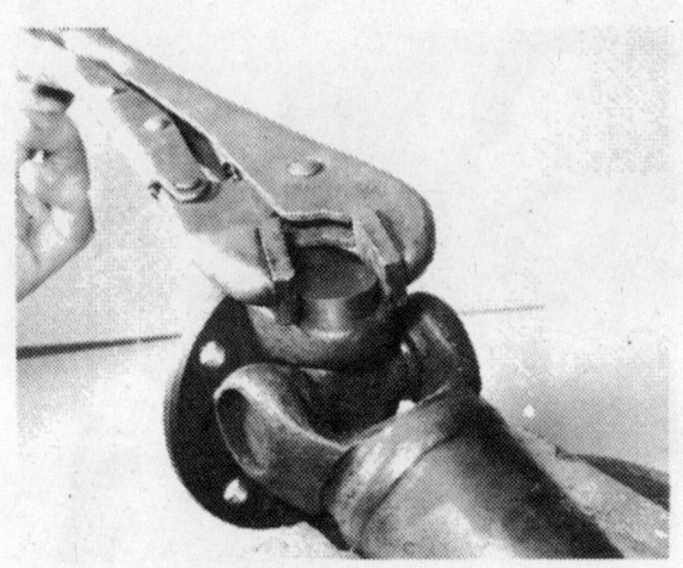

4.2 Remove the bearing cup with a pair of grips

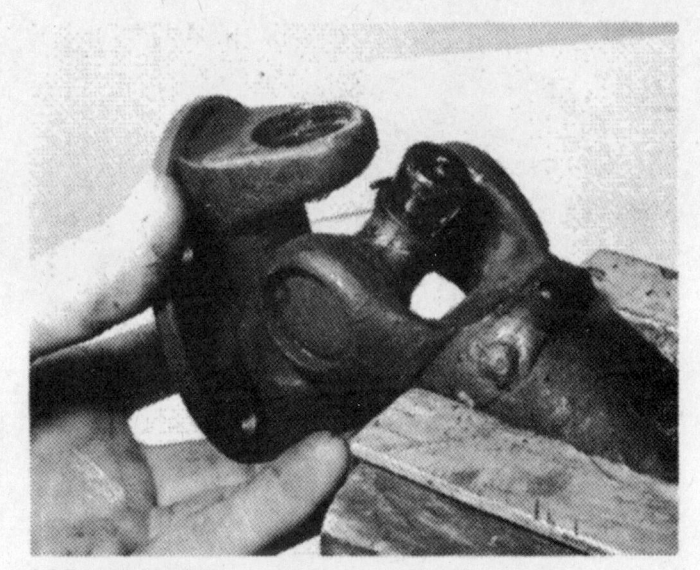

4.3 Remove the flanged yoke. Repeat the procedure with the shaft yoke to remove the spider

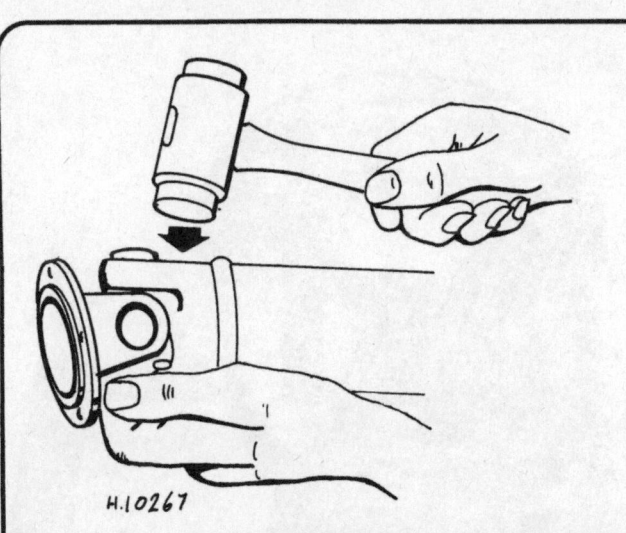

Fig. 7.1 Tap the yoke lightly as shown after removing the retaining circlip to free the bearing (Sec 4)

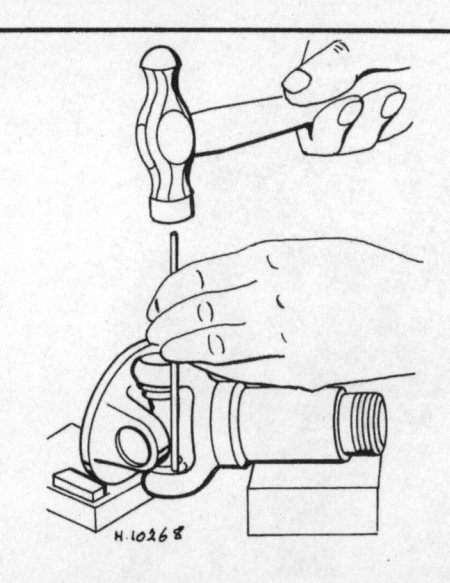

Fig. 7.2 When reluctant to move, tap the bearings out from the inside using a thin drift as shown (circlip removed) (Sec 4)

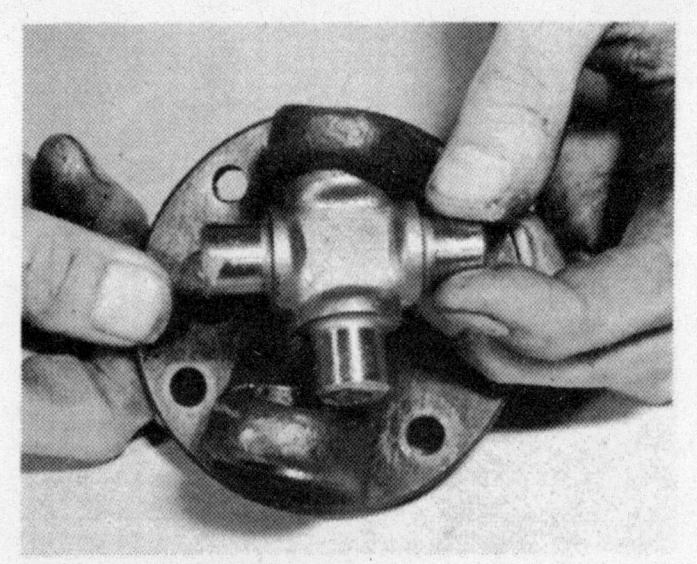

5.2 Fit spider into the yoke

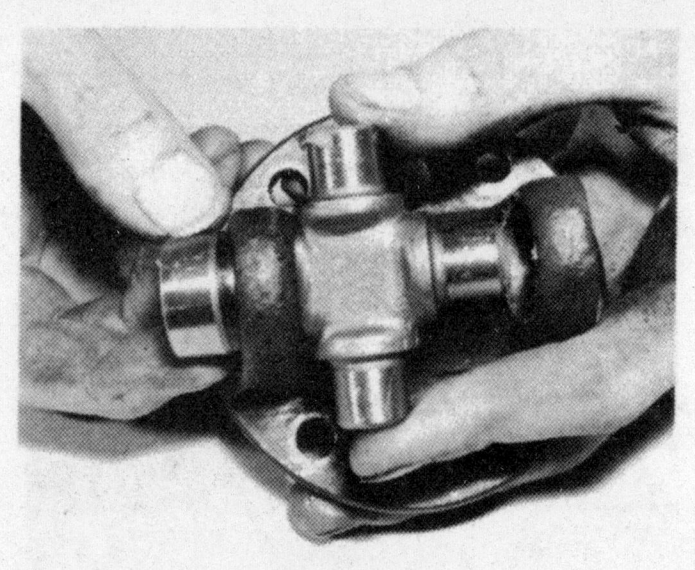

5.3a Engage the yoke and bearing and then ...

5.3b ... carefully press first bearing into position

5.5 Locate the spider into the bearing and drive the bearing into the shaft yoke whilst supporting the flange

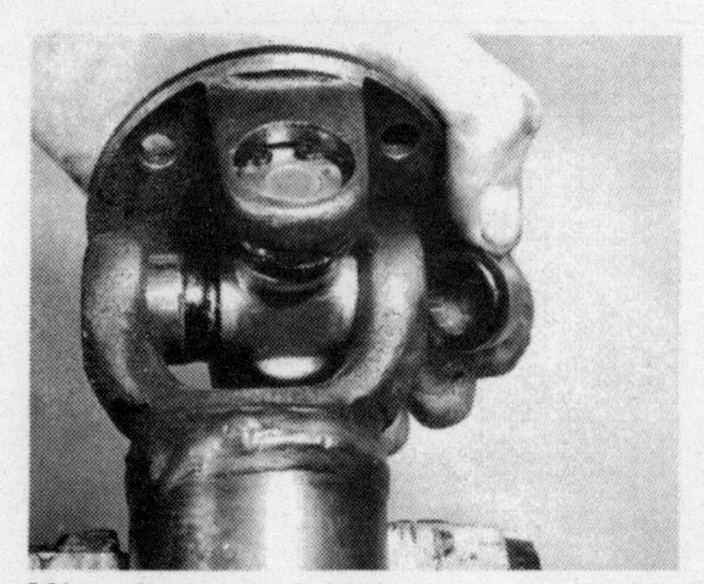

5.6 Locate the opposing bearing into the yoke

5.7 Press the bearing home in vice jaws

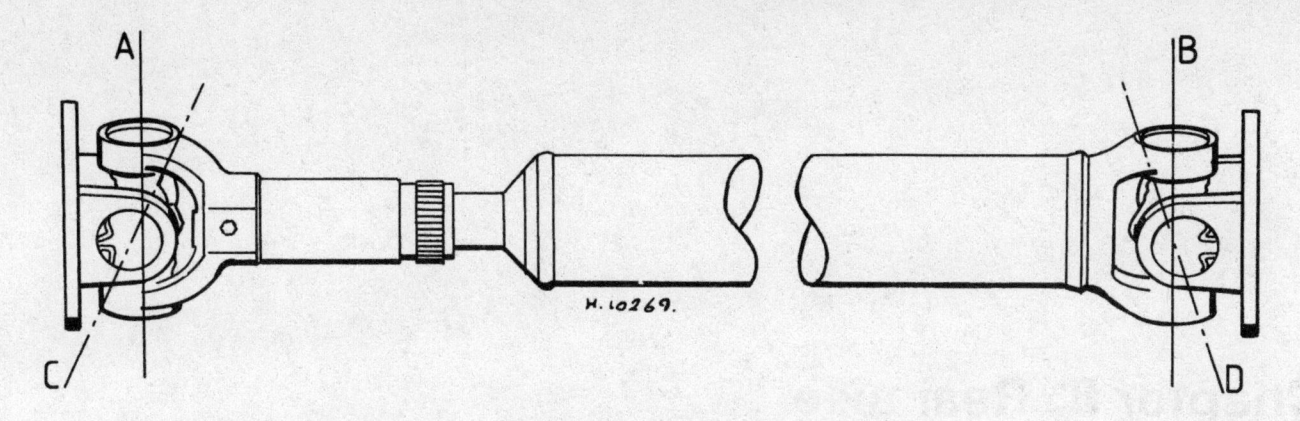

Fig. 7.3 When reassembling the propeller shaft it is essential to ensure that the yoke 'A' is in alignment with yoke 'B', and that the flange yoke 'C' is in alignment with flange yoke 'D' (Sec 5)

the transmission, 'clonks' on taking up the drive, and in extreme cases of lack of lubrication, metallic squeaking, and ultimately grating and shrieking sounds as the bearings break up.

2   It is easy to check if the needle roller bearings are worn with the propeller shaft in position, by trying to turn the shaft with one hand, the other hand holding the rear axle flange when the rear universal joint is being checked, and the front gearbox coupling when the front universal joint is being checked. Any movement between the propeller shaft and the front and rear half couplings is indicative of considerable wear.

3   If worn, the old bearings and spiders will have to be discarded and a repair kit, comprising new universal joint spiders, bearings, oil seals, and retainers purchased. Check also be trying to lift the shaft and noticing any movement in the joints.

4   Examine the propeller shaft splines for wear. If worn it will be necessary to purchase a new front half coupling, or if the yokes are badly worn, an exchange propeller shaft.

5   It is not possible to fit oversize bearings and journals to the trunnion bearing holes.

4   Universal joints – dismantling

1   Clean away all traces of dirt and grease from the circlips located on the ends of the spiders. Remove the clips by pressing their open ends together with a pair of pliers and lever them out with a screwdriver. If they are difficult to remove tap the bearing face resting on top of the spider with a mallet which will ease the pressure on the circlip.

2   Hold the propeller shaft in hand and remove the bearing cups and needle rollers by tapping the yoke at each bearing with a copper or hide faced hammer. As soon as the bearings start to emerge they can be drawn out with your fingers. If the bearing cup refuses to move, support the shaft in the vice and using a suitable tubular drift (a socket will do) drive the bearing through to partially expose the opposing bearing which can then be gripped in a pair of pliers and extracted (photo). If the bearing is seized, refer to Fig. 7.2.

3   The flanged yoke can now be removed (photo) and the procedure repeated to disengage the shaft yoke and remove the spider.

4   Once removed, the respective spider journals and bearing assemblies can be cleaned and laid out for inspection. Keep each bearing set with its relative spider journal so that they don't get mixed up if the old ones are to be reused.

5   If the bearings and spider journals are thought to be badly worn this can easily be ascertained visually with the universal joints dismantled.

5   Universal joints – reassembly

1   Ensure prior to assembly that all parts are perfectly clean. Ensure that the lubrication passages are perfectly clear (if applicable).

2   Insert the spider into the yoke flange and where a grease nipple is fitted, remember to fit it so that the nipple faces the propeller shaft and that it is fully accessible when in position in the car (photo). Locate the bearing seals over the spider journals.

3   Hold the spider offset in the yoke and engage a bearing over the yoke journal taking care not to disturb the needle rollers. With the bearing aligned with the yoke housing located in the jaws of a vice and using a tube drift, press into the yoke (photo).

4   Repeat the procedure with the opposing bearing of the yoke and then press both bearings fully home so that they are clear of the circlip groove (photo). Insert the new circlips to secure. Ensure that the circlips are fully engaged in their grooves.

5   Hold the propeller shaft in the vice as shown and insert the spider between the yokes. Locate the spider journal one side with bearing and carefully tap the bearing into position (photo).

6   Locate the opposing bearing and press home with a tube drift (photo).

7   Press both bearings beyond their circlip grooves and insert the new clips. Check that they are fully engaged in their grooves (photo).

8   On completion, rotate the flange to ensure that the joint can pivot and swivel without binding or stiffness. The joint will have to be stripped again if there is any sign of binding as it is likely that a bearing roller became dislodged during assembly and will have to be renewed.

Chapter 8 Rear axle

Contents

Differential unit – dismantling and examination	8
Differential unit – reassembly	9
Differential unit – removal and refitting	7
Faults diagnosis – rear axle	10
General description	1
Half shaft (drum brake models) – removal and refitting	3
Half shaft (rear disc brake models) – removal and refitting	4
Pinion oil seal – removal and refitting	6
Rear axle unit – removal and refitting	2
Rear hub – removal and refitting	5

Specifications

Type .... Hypoid-three quarter floating

Ratio
1500 and 1600 Mk I .... 4·3 : 1 (standard) or 4·56 : 1 (optional)
1600 Mk II .... 4·1 : 1
Twin Cam .... 4·3 : 1

Pinion bearing preload
Without oil seal .... 10 to 12 lbf in (0·12 to 0·14 kgf m)
With oil seal .... 13 to 15 lbf in (0·150 to 0·173 kgf m)

Crownwheel and pinion backlash .... Etched on crownwheel rear face

Torque wrench settings

	lbf ft	kgf m
Crownwheel bearing cap to differential carrier	65	8·99
Pinion drive flange nut	140	19·4
Crownwheel to differential cage bolts	60	8·3

1 General description

The rear axle unit is of the three-quarter-floating type, and is held in place by semi-elliptic springs which are constructed from a number of individual leaves, of different lengths and are held together by a long bolt and clips. The semi-elliptic springs provide all the necessary lateral and longitudinal location of the axle.

The differential assembly incorporates a hypoid crownwheel and pinion The crownwheel and pinion together with the differential gears are mounted in the differential unit which is bolted to the front face of the banjo-type axle casing.

Adjustments are provided for the crownwheel and pinion backlash; pinion depth of mesh; pinion shaft bearing preload; and backlash between the differential gears. All these adjustments may be made by varying the thickness of the various shims and thrust washers.

The axle or half shafts are easily withdrawn and are splined at their inner ends to fit into the splines in the differential wheels. The inner wheel bearing races are mounted on the outer ends of the axle casing and are secured by nuts and lockwashers. The rear wheel bearing outer races are located in the hubs.

The hub bearings are lubricated via the axle oil and it is essential that the correct grade and amount of lubricant be used and changed at the specified intervals (see Maintenance Section at front of this manual).

2 Rear axle unit – removal and refitting

1 Loosen the rear wheel nuts.
2 Raise and support the rear of the body and the differential casing with chocks or jacks so that the rear wheels are clear of the ground. This is most easily done by placing a jack under the centre of the differential, jacking-up the axle and fitting suitable chocks to support the body under the chassis frame just in front of the rear springs.
3 Remove both rear wheels.
4 Release the handbrake lever to the off position and then disconnect the cable assembly from its axle location point on the right-hand side, the fulcrum unit on the left-hand side and from the clevis location on the inside face of each rear hub backplate (photo).
5 Detach the flexible hydraulic brake hose connection at the T-junction on the axle (photo). Clamp or plug the flexible hose to prevent leakage and the ingress of dirt.
6 Make an alignment mark across the propeller shaft to pinion shaft flanges, unscrew the nuts and remove the bolts to disconnect the propeller shaft at the rear end.
7 Disconnect the exhaust pipe rear section.
8 Undo the nuts and locknuts from the four U-bolts and remove the spring clamp and damper bracket plates.
9 Free the rear ends of the semi-elliptic springs by removing the rear shackle nuts and plates, and then lower the ends of the springs to the ground. Disconnect the rebound straps if fitted.

Chapter 8 Rear axle

2.4 Detach the handbrake cable fulcrum – left side of axle

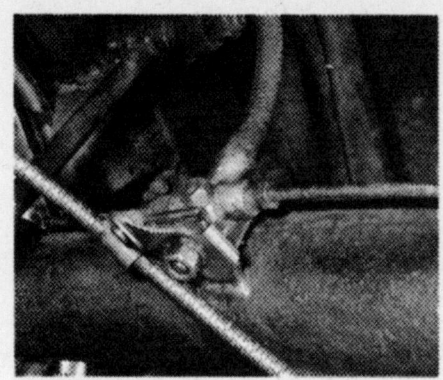

2.5 Detach the handbrake cable and hydraulic T Section – right side of axle

3.5 Refitting a half shaft – use a new gasket seal and align retaining screw hole

10 The axle will now be resting on the jack and can be lowered and removed from under the car.
11 Refitting is a straightforward reversal of the removal sequence.
12 Top-up the brake hydraulic master cylinder fluid and bleed the brakes. Reconnect the handbrake cable and check the brake adjustments as given in Chapter 9.
13 When reconnecting the propeller shaft to the pinion flange ensure that the alignment marks made on removal correspond.
14 Top-up the axle oil level.

3 Half shaft (drum brake models) – removal and refitting

1 Refer to the previous Section and follow paragraphs 1, 2 and 3. Note that if the axle shaft is removed with the car on an even keel it is likely that oil will run out from the differential and contaminate the brake linings. If only one shaft is being removed then jack-up that side of the car only. If both shafts are being removed drain the oil from the differential before proceeding further.
2 Release the handbrake and slacken the brake adjusters right off.
3 Unscrew the two cross-headed countersunk brake drum retaining screws and pull off the brake drum. If necessary tap the brake drums off with a wooden or hide hammer. Under no circumstances use a steel headed hammer directly on the drum. If using a steel headed hammer then interpose a piece of wood between the hammer head and the drum.
4 Unscrew the single shaft flange locating screw and pull the half shaft by its flange out from the axle casing. If the shaft appears to be stuck a little judicious levering with a tyre wrench will start the shaft moving. Once loose it will pull out quite easily.
5 Refitting of the half shafts is a reversal of the above process. Always renew the paper washers to ensure that no oil leaks will develop and ensure that all mating surfaces are clean (photo). Top-up the axle oil level if the level has dropped due to spillage. Refer to Chapter 9 and adjust the brakes.

4 Half shafts (rear disc brake models) – removal and installation

1 Refer to Section 2 and follow the procedures given in paragraphs 1 to 3 inclusive. Note that if the axle shaft is removed with the car on an even keel it is likely that oil will run out from the differential and contaminate the brake linings. If only one shaft is being removed then jack-up that side of the car only. If both shafts are being removed drain the oil from the differential before proceeding further (refer to Fig. 8.2).
2 Release the handbrake right off.
3 Unscrew the four locknuts that retain the hub extension drive flange to the hub.
4 The axle shaft and hub extension can now be withdrawn from the axle. If the shaft is reluctant to be withdrawn, refit the winged centre lock wheel nut and tap the 'ears' of the nut with a soft head mallet to extract the shaft.
5 If the hub extension and shaft are to be separated, extract the welch plug and press or drive the shaft out of the hub.
6 Refitting is a reversal of the removal sequence. Be sure to fit a new joint washer between the hub and bearing housing joint faces. If the shaft and hub were separated fit a new welch plug.

5 Rear hub – removal and refitting

1 Remove the axle half shafts as described in Sections 3 or 4 as applicable.
2 On drum brake models remove the bearing spacer.
3 On disc brake models refer to Chapter 9 and remove the brake caliper unit.
4 Knock back the tab of the locking washer and unscrew the hub retaining nut. Note that the left-hand hub bearing nut has a left-hand thread on later models, so must be turned clockwise to unscrew. The right-hand hub nut has a right-hand thread.
5 Remove the lockwasher from the axle casing end by lifting the washer so its key is freed from the locating groove.
6 With a hub puller pull off the hub complete with bearing and oil seal.
7 Refitting is a reversal of the removal procedure but the following points should be noted:

(a) When fitting the new oil seal carefully drive it into position before the bearing and ensure that it is placed with the lip facing outwards towards the wheel. On later models a modified hub was fitted having an additional oil seal ring fitted into a groove in between the hub and axle shafts to hub joint. This seal must also be renewed
(b) Before refitting the rear bearings lubricate them with high-melting point grease
(c) Always renew the washer between the hub assembly and the half shaft flange and if making one up ensure that it is cut from paper at least 0.008 in (0.2 mm) thick
(d) On drum brake models, ensure that the outer face of the bearing spacer protrudes between 0.001 in and 0.004 in (0.03 and 0.1 mm) from the outer face of the hub after the bearing has been pressed into place. This is because the bearing must be held by the axle shaft driving flange and the abutment shoulder in the hub
(e) Remember to knock back the locking tab of the locking washer
(f) When refitting the brake caliper unit on disc brake models, don't forget to refit the exact amount of shims at the rear of the caliper body mounting lugs

6 Pinion oil seal – removal and refitting

1 If oil is leaking from the front of the differential nose piece it will be necessary to renew the pinion oil seal. If a pit is not available, jack and chock up the rear of the car. It is much easier to do this job over a pit or with the car on a ramp.
2 Mark the propeller shaft and pinion drive flanges to ensure that they are refitted in the same relative positions.
3 Unscrew the nuts from the four bolts holding the flanges together, remove the bolts and separate the flanges.

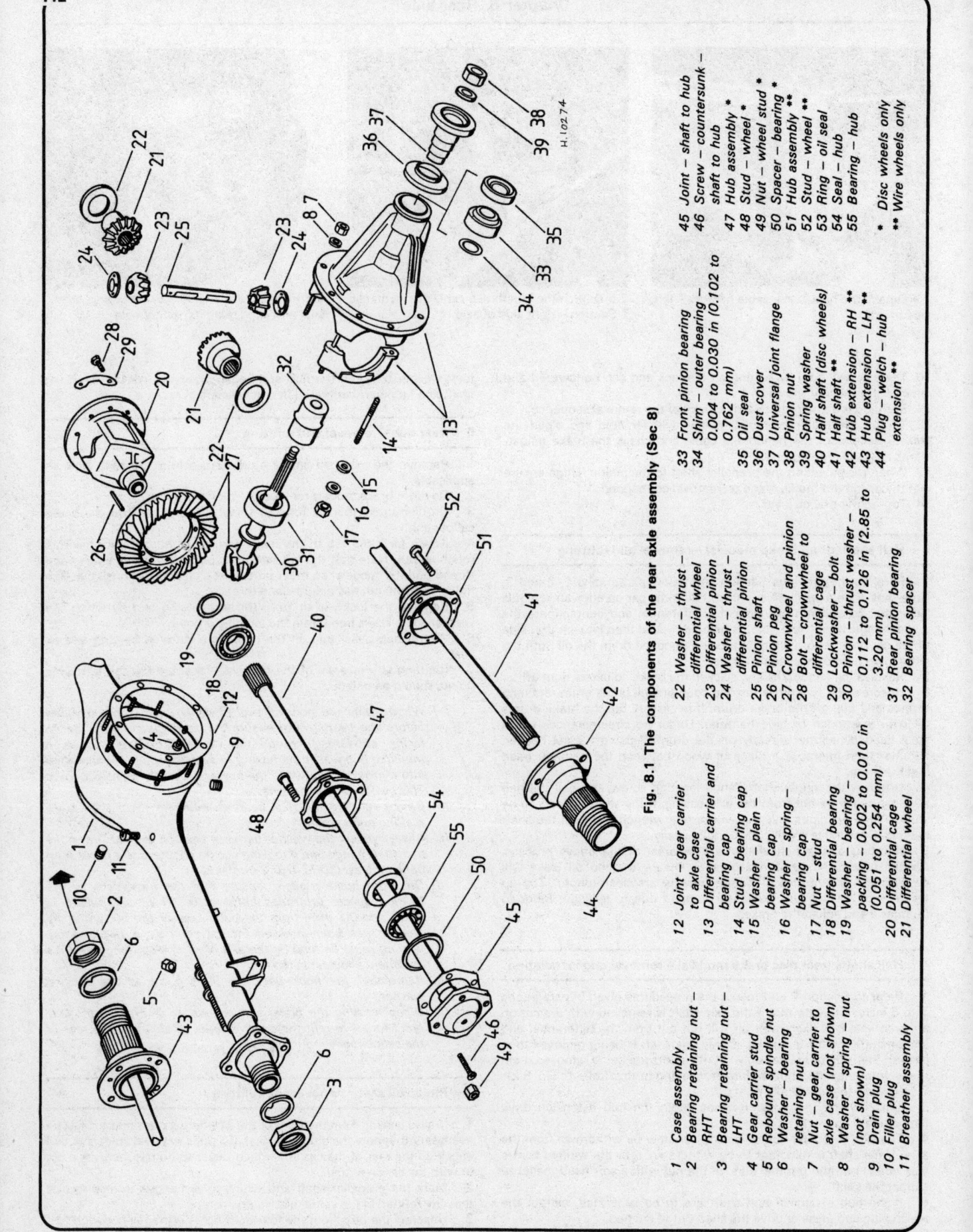

Fig. 8.1 The components of the rear axle assembly (Sec 8)

1 Case assembly
2 Bearing retaining nut – RHT
3 Bearing retaining nut – LHT
4 Gear carrier stud
5 Rebound spindle nut
6 Washer – bearing retaining nut
7 Nut – gear carrier to axle case (not shown)
8 Washer – spring – nut (not shown)
9 Drain plug
10 Filler plug
11 Breather assembly
12 Joint – gear carrier to axle case
13 Differential carrier and bearing cap
14 Stud – bearing cap
15 Washer – plain – bearing cap
16 Washer – spring – bearing cap
17 Nut – stud
18 Differential bearing
19 Washer – packing – 0.002 to 0.010 in (0.051 to 0.254 mm)
20 Differential cage
21 Differential wheel
22 Washer – thrust – differential wheel
23 Differential pinion
24 Washer – thrust – differential pinion
25 Pinion shaft
26 Pinion peg
27 Crownwheel and pinion
28 Bolt – crownwheel to differential cage
29 Lockwasher – bolt
30 Pinion – thrust washer – 0.112 to 0.126 in (2.85 to 3.20 mm)
31 Rear pinion bearing
32 Bearing spacer
33 Front pinion bearing
34 Shim – outer bearing – 0.004 to 0.030 in (0.102 to 0.762 mm)
35 Oil seal
36 Dust cover
37 Universal joint flange
38 Pinion nut
39 Spring washer
40 Half shaft (disc wheels)
41 Half shaft **
42 Hub extension – RH **
43 Hub extension – LH **
44 Plug – welch – hub extension **
45 Joint – shaft to hub
46 Screw – countersunk – shaft to hub
47 Hub assembly *
48 Stud – wheel *
49 Nut – wheel stud *
50 Spacer – bearing *
51 Hub assembly **
52 Stud – wheel **
53 Ring – oil seal
54 Seal – hub
55 Bearing – hub

* Disc wheels only
** Wire wheels only

Chapter 8 Rear axle

4 If the oil seal is being renewed with the differential nose piece in position, drain the oil and check that the handbrake is firmly on to prevent the pinion flange moving.
5 Unscrew the nut in the centre of the pinion drive flange. Remove the nut and spring washer.
6 Pull off the splined drive flange, which may be a little stubborn, the pressed steel end cover; and prise out the oil seal with a screwdriver taking care not to damage the lip of its seating.
7 Refitting is a reversal of the removal procedure. Note that the new seal must be pushed into the differential nose piece with the edge of the sealing ring facing inwards, and take great care not to damage the edge of the oil seal when refitting the end cover and drive flange. Smear the face of the flange which bears against the oil seal lightly with oil before driving the flange onto its splines. Tighten the nut to the torque wrench settings given in the Specifications.
8 Ensure that the propeller shaft and pinion flange alignment marks correspond when reassembling.
9 Check and top-up the rear axle oil as necessary.

7 Differential unit – removal and refitting

1 If the differential unit is to be removed, first refer to Section 3 or 4 as applicable, and withdraw each half shaft sufficiently so that they are disengaged from the differential wheels. Drain the oil from the axle housing.
2 Mark the propeller shaft and pinion flanges to ensure that they are refitted in the same relative position.
3 Unscrew the nuts from the four bolts holding the flanges together, remove the bolts and separate the flanges.
4 Remove the ring of nuts and spring washers which join the differential nose piece to the axle casing, and pull the nose piece complete with differential assembly out of the casing.
5 Carefully clean down the inside of the axle casing, fit a new nose piece to casing joint, and then fit the exchange or rebuilt differential assembly. Refitting is a reversal of the removal procedure.
6 Refill the differential with the correct grade of oil and run the axle in slowly for the first 500 miles (800 km), and then change the oil when it is hot.

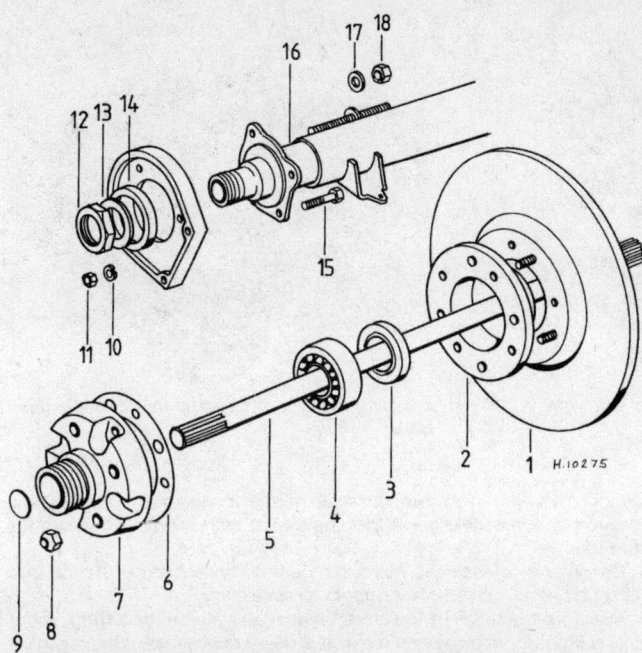

Fig. 8.2 The half shaft and hub unit on the rear disc brake axle (Sec 4)

1 Brake disc
2 Wheel bearing housing
3 Seal
4 Bearing
5 Half shaft
6 Gasket
7 Hub extension
8 Nut
9 Welch plug
10 Spring washer
11 Nut
12 Locknut
13 Tab washer
14 Dust cover
15 Adaptor plate
16 Axle housing
17 Washer
18 Nut

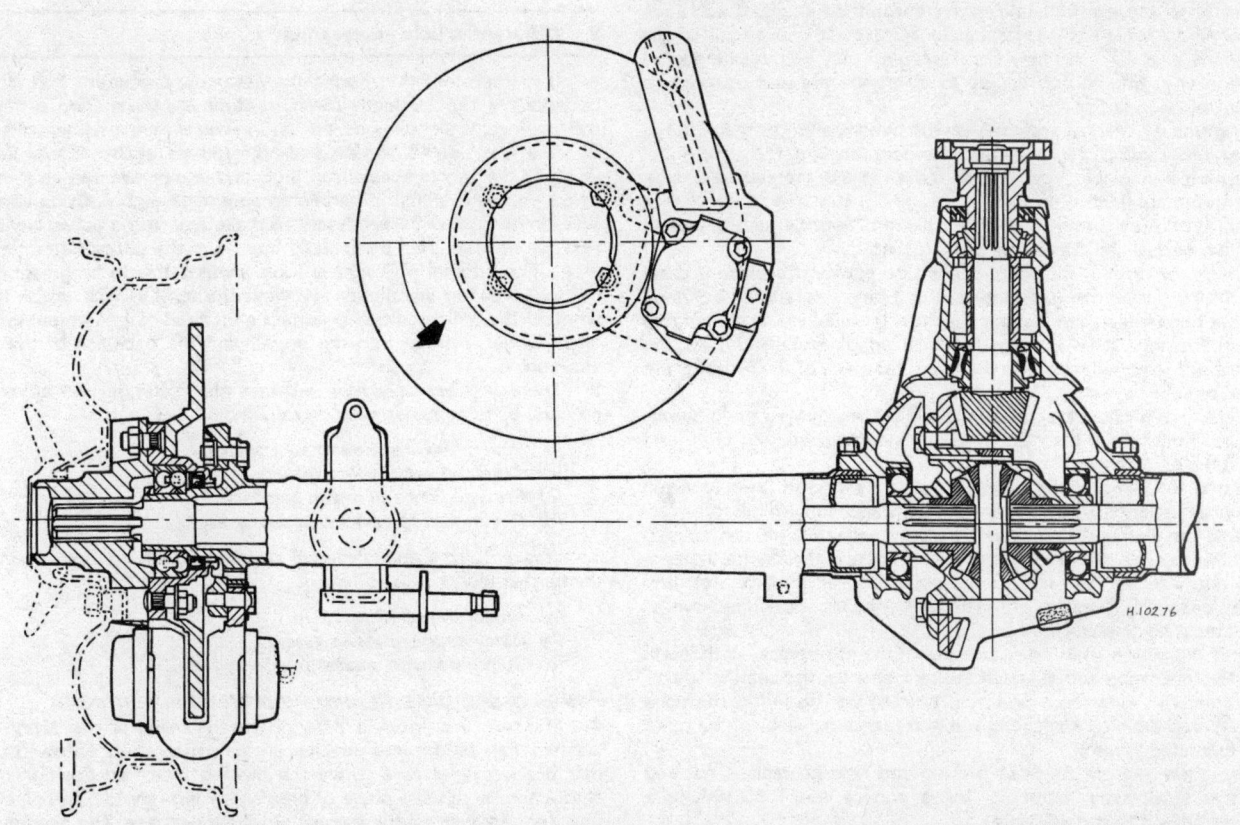

Fig. 8.3 The rear axle assembly of the Twin Cam model showing the cross section view of the differential unit and the hub/disc assembly (Sec 4)

8.4 Remove the bearing cap nuts and washers

8.5 Remove the crownwheel unit

8.7 Unscrew the differential unit/crownwheel bolts

8 Differential unit – dismantling and examination

1 Having removed the differential unit, it can be cleaned off and initially examined for obvious signs of excessive wear and possibly damage. If extensive wear and/or damage are readily apparent to the main components, ie crownwheel and/or pinion assemblies, serious consideration must be given to renewing the complete differential carrier assembly as a unit, rather than to dismantle and renew the items concerned. The crownwheel and pinion are a matched pair and to renew one or the other is not generally recommended as, apart from being bad engineering practice, the noise created when matching new with old gears can be intolerable.

2 Another point to consider before dismantling is that special tools are required to accurately set up the differential unit when assembling it. Not too many professional garages have these tools or indeed in some cases the staff sufficiently qualified to use them and for this reason, (apart from the time and cost aspect), they will usually prefer to fit a new or factory reconditioned unit.

3 In view of these points, unless you feel suitably qualified, and have the necessary tools and equipment to complete the overhaul of the differential unit, it is strongly recommended that you exchange the complete unit. Should you decide to dismantle the unit proceed as follows, referring to Fig. 8.1.

4 With the differential assembly on the bench begin dismantling the unit by unscrewing the nuts and washers holding the differential bearing caps in place. Ensure that the caps are marked to ensure correct refitment (photo).

5 Pull off the caps and then lever out the differential unit complete with crownwheel and differential gears (photo).

6 Check the differential bearings for side play and if present draw them off the differential cage together with any shims fitted between the inner ring of each bearing and the cage. If available use the bearing removal tool no. 18G47C together with adaptors 18G47T. As the bearings are removed note that the thrust face side of the bearings are marked as such.

7 Eight high tensile steel bolts hold the crownwheel to the differential cage. Knock back the tabs of the locking washers and undo and remove the bolts (photo).

8 Clamp the pinion flange in a vice fitted with soft jaws to avoid damaging the flange when undoing the central pinion nut (photo).

9 With the nut and spring washer removed, pull off the splined pinion flange, (tap the end of the pinion shaft if the flange appears stuck) and remove the pressed end cover and oil seal (photo). Any damage caused to the edge of the flange by the vice during removal of the nut must be carefully filed smooth.

10 Drift the pinion shaft rearwards out of the nose piece. With it will come the inner race and rollers of the rear bearing, the bearing spacer and shims. The outer race and front bearing will be left in the nose piece. With the pinion shaft removed, the rear outer race can be quite easily extracted (photo).

11 The inner race of the front bearing can now be tapped out and then the outer race extracted, using service tool 18G264 with adaptors 18G264E and 18G264F.

12 The inner race of the rear bearing is a press fit on the pinion shaft, and must be drifted off carefully. If the MG special tool 18G285 is available this will help the removal of the inner race considerably. Remove the thrust washer under the pinion gear head, and retain for future use.

13 Check the rollers and races for general wear, score marks, and pitting and renew these components as necessary.

14 Examine the teeth of the crown wheel and pinion for pitting, score marks, chipping, and general wear. If a new crownwheel and/or pinion are required, a new matched pair must be fitted (photo).

15 Tap out the pinion peg from the crownwheel side of the differential cage to free the pinion shaft which is then driven out. Note that the hole into which the peg fits is slightly tapered, and the opposite end may be lightly peened over and should be cleared with a 0.19 in (4.8 mm) drill.

16 Extract the pinions, wheels, and thrust washers from the differential cage. Check them for wear and renew as necessary. Refitting the pinions is a reversal of the removal procedure. Note that after the peg has been inserted, the larger end of the hole should be lightly peened over to retain the pin in position.

9 Differential unit – reassembly

1 It is important that during the assembly procedure that all components are kept perfectly clean, in particular the mating surfaces of the bearings, their housings, the setting washer and preload shims.

2 The original MG setting and adjustments of the differential unit involved the use of specialised tools and equipment and as these are unlikely to be available, a certain amount of assembly, dismantling and reassembling may be necessary to make any of the adjustments and settings needed. This particularly applies to the pinion setting adjustment. The original MG special tools enabled this to be preset during the initial pinion installation. Without the tools it will not be known whether the pinion setting is correct or in need of adjustment until the crownwheel is fitted into the carrier and the backlash of the gears checked.

3 There are basically four sub-assembly settings and adjustment procedures to be undertaken these being:

(a) Pinion bearing preload adjustment
(b) Crownwheel position setting
(c) Crownwheel and pinion backlash
(d) Pinion position setting (if necessary)

To achieve these settings you will need the following items apart from the normal tools:

(a) A micrometer (0 to 1.0 in)
(b) Clock gauge or feeler gauges
(c) Spring balance tension gauge

Pinion assembly and bearing preload adjustment

4 Measure and make a note of the thickness of the pinion head washer then slide it into position on the pinion shaft, followed by the rear bearing inner race. Drive the bearing race into position on the shaft using a suitable piece of pipe as shown (photo). The pipe must only bear against the inner cone, not the roller cage. The bearing must butt up against the washer.

5 Slide the bearing spacer into position on the pinion shaft, followed

8.8 Unscrew the central pinion nut

8.9 Remove the pinion flange

8.10 Remove the pinion shaft from the nose piece

8.14 Check the teeth of both crownwheel and pinion

9.4 Carefully locate the bearing onto the pinion shaft

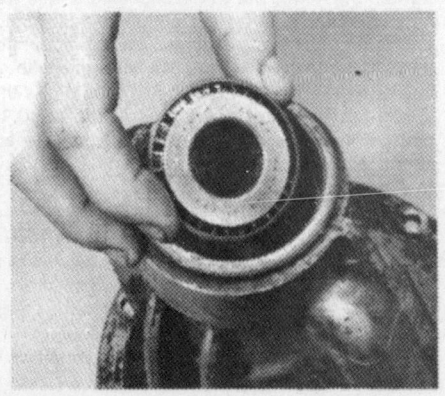

9.7 Locate the bearing cones into the nose piece

9.8 Tap the seal into position using wood block for protection

9.9 Fit dust cover and flange

9.10 Torque tighten the flange nut

9.11 Pinion bearing pre-load check method

9.15 Bend over the lock tabs to secure

9.16 Check the gear backlash using engineers blue

by a nominal amount of preload adjustment shims to the value of about 0.008 to 0.011 in (0.2 to 0.28 mm) in thickness.
6   Support the differential nose piece and fit the bearing (front and rear) outer races into position in their respective housings. Press or drive them into position with a pipe of suitable diameter and ensure that the housings are perfectly clean before fitting.
7   Insert the pinion shaft forwards into the differential nose piece from inside the casing and locate the front inner bearing race and rollers into place (photo).
8   Lubricate the bearings with the correct grade of rear axle oil. Fit a new oil seal with the edge of the sealing ring facing inwards. A block of wood is useful for ensuring the seal is driven on squarely (photo).
9   With the seal in position, refit the dust cover, lubricate the pinion flange shoulder which bears against the oil seal and drive the flange onto the splines with a hammer and block of wood (photo).
10 Refit the spring washer and with the flange held securely in a vice tighten the flange nut to the specified torque wrench setting (photo).
11 To obtain the correct pinion bearing preload, slowly tighten the nut, taking frequent readings. The correct preload should be 13 to 15 lbf in (0.15 to 0.17 kgf m). Measure this with a spring balance hooked into one of the drive flange holes (photo). As these holes are 1.5 in (38 mm) from the shaft axis a pull of 9 lbf in (0.11 kgf m) is the correct preload figure using this method. If the preload is too great add more shims accordingly. If the preload is insufficient subtract the shim thickness as required.

Crownwheel assembly and adjustment
12 Refit the shims and differential bearings to the differential cage.
13 Ensure that the crownwheel and cage are scrupulously clean and then bolt the crownwheel to the differential cage flange, tightening the bolts to the specified torque wrench setting.
14 Position the crownwheel unit in a pair of V-blocks and check the run out using the clock gauge. The run out must not exceed 0.002 in (0.05 mm). Provided the surfaces of the crownwheel and the flange of differential cage are perfectly clean the crownwheel should run true.
15 With the crownwheel retaining bolts tightened to the specified torque, bend over the lock tab ears to secure (photo).
16 Locate the differential unit into the gear carrier and refit the bearing caps to their original positions as marked. Tighten the retaining nuts to the specified torque wrench setting.

Crownwheel and pinion backlash check and adjustment
17 Check the crownwheel to pinion backlash figure using a clock gauge. The backlash of the two gears must be to within 0.005 to 0.007 in (0.127 to 0.178 mm). As they are a matched pair, their particular backlash requirement will be etched into the rear face of the crownwheel. An adjustment of 0.002 in (0.05 mm) can be made by transferring the bearing shim to the opposing side of the differential but the bearings should only be removed once to make this adjustment.
18 To check the crownwheel and pinion mesh, smear some engineers blue on the teeth of the crownwheel and then rotate the pinion. The contact mark of the respective gear teeth should be indicated in the middle of the crownwheel teeth (photo).
19 If the pinion setting position is in need of adjustment an alternative pinion head washer must be fitted as required. Variations in the washer thickness are available within the range of 0.112 to 0.126 in (2.84 to 3.20 mm) in steps of 0.002 in (0.05 mm). Should it be necessary to fit an alternative washer, it will then be necessary to dismantle and reassemble the pinion unit and consequently the pinion bearing preload setting must be rechecked and if necessary adjusted accordingly by adding or subtracting the preload bearing shims as necessary. This was described in paragraphs 1 to 8. Recheck the crownwheel and pinion backlash on completion.

10 Fault diagnosis – rear axle

Symptom	Reason/s
Noise on drive, coasting or overrun	Shortage of oil Incorrect crownwheel to pinion mesh Worn pinion bearings Worn side bearings Loose bearing cap bolts
Noise on turn	Differential side gears worn, damaged or tight
Knock on taking up drive or during gearchange	Excessive crownwheel to pinion backlash Worn gears Worn axle-shaft splines Pinion bearing preload too low Loose drive coupling nut Loose securing bolts or nuts within unit Loose roadwheel nuts or elongated wheel nut holes Loose wheel spokes Worn hub splines (spoke wheels)
Oil leakage	Defective gaskets or oil seals possibly caused by clogged breather or oil level too high

Chapter 9 Braking system

Contents

Bleeding the hydraulic system 4	Handbrake adjustment 3
Brake master cylinder unit (Dunlop brakes) – removal and refitting 15	Handbrake cable – removal and refitting 17
Brake pedal – adjustment 18	Handbrake friction pads (Dunlop system) – removal, inspection and refitting 7
Disc brake pads – inspection, removal and refitting 6	Hydraulic pipes and hoses – inspection, removal and refitting ... 12
Drum brakes – adjustment 2	Lockheed brake calliper and disc units – removal and dismantling . 8
Drum brake shoes – removal, inspection and refitting 5	Lockheed brake calliper and disc units – reassembly and refitting . 9
Dunlop brake calliper – dismantling and assembly 11	Lockheed brake/clutch master cylinder – removal and refitting .. 14
Dunlop disc and calliper nuts – removal and refitting 10	Master cylinder – dismantling and overhaul 16
Fault diagnosis – brake system 19	Wheel cylinder – removal, overhaul and refitting 13
General description 1	

Specifications

Make and type
1500	Lockheed drum brakes front and rear
1600 and 1600 Mk II	Lockheed disc brakes front and drum brakes rear or Dunlop disc brakes front and rear
Twin Cam	Dunlop disc brakes front and rear
Footbrake	Hydraulic to all four wheels
Handbrake	Mechanical to rear wheels only

Front drums
Type	Twin leading shoe
Diameter/width	10·00 in (254 mm)/1·750 in (44·4 mm)
Lining area	67·2 in^2 (433·55 cm^2)

Rear drums (1500 and 1600 with drums brakes at front)
Type	Single leading shoe
Diameter/width	10·00 in (254 mm)/1·750 in (44·4 mm)
Lining area	67·2 in^2 (433·55 cm^2)

Rear drum brakes (1600 with disc brakes at front)
Diameter/width	9·63 in x 1·7 in (244·6 mm x 43·2 mm)
Lining area	65·48 in^2 (422·36 cm^2)

Disc brakes (Lockheed type)
Disc diameter	11·0 in (279 mm)

Disc brakes (Dunlop type)
Disc diameter	11·0 in (279 mm)
Minimum disc thickness allowable	0·340 to 0·330 in (8·64 to 8·38 mm)
Maximum allowable disc run out	0·006 in (0·152 mm)

Torque wrench settings
	lbf ft	kgf m
Brake calliper securing bolts	45 to 50	6·22 to 6·91
Calliper half section bolts (Lockheed) – large	65	8·99
Calliper half section bolts (Lockheed) – small	10	1·38

Chapter 9 Braking system

1 General description

The braking system employed varied according to the model but basically there were three types, being drum brakes front and rear (Lockheed), fitted to all 1500 models, disc brakes front and drums rear (Lockheed), fitted to all 1600 and 1600 MK II models, disc brakes front and rear (Dunlop), fitted to all Twin Cam models and a small number of 1600 De Luxe models employing the Twin Cam chassis. All types have hydraulically operated foot brakes all round with a mechanical (cable) operated handbrake.

On the all drum brake type system, the front brakes are of the two leading shoe type with a separate cylinder for each shoe. Both cylinders are fixed to the backplate and the trailing end of each shoe is free to slide laterally in a small groove in the closed end of the brake cylinders, so ensuring automatic centralisation when the brakes are applied.

The rear brakes are of the single leading shoe type, with one brake cylinder per wheel for both shoes. The cylinder is free to float on the backplate. Attached to each of the rear wheel operating cylinders is a mechanical expander operated by the handbrake lever through a cable which runs from the brake lever to a compensator on the rear axle and thence to the wheel operating levers.

Drum brakes have to be adjusted periodically to compensate for wear in the linings. It unusual to have to adjust the handbrake system as the efficiency of this system is largely dependent on the condition of the brake linings and the adjustment of the brake shoes. The handbrake can, however, be adjusted separately to the footbrake operated hydraulic system.

On the disc brake, drum brake type system the brakes fitted to the front two wheels are of the rotating disc and static caliper type, with one caliper per disc, each caliper containing two piston operated friction pads, which on application of the footbrake pinch the disc rotating between them.

Application of the foot brake creates hydraulic pressure in the master cylinder and fluid from the cylinder travels via steel and flexible pipes to the cylinders in each half of the callipers, the fluid so pushing the pistons, to which are attached the friction pads, into contact with either side of each disc.

As the friction pad wears so the pistons move further out of the cylinders and the level of the fluid in the hydraulic reservoir drops, but disc pad wear is thus taken up automatically and eliminates the need for periodic adjustments by the owner.

On the all disc brake type system Dunlop disc brakes are fitted to the front and rear wheels. Whilst the disc brakes are of a different manufacture, the operating features are similar to that of the Lockheed type previously described. The handbrake layout to the rear differs somewhat in that a separate handbrake carrier unit is attached to each rear caliper unit. This carrier unit is shown in Fig. 9.5 and as can be seen, it contains its own friction pads. This unit is operated independently via the handbrake cable/lever assembly and an adjustment is available at the carrier when the friction pads wear down.

The hydraulic master cylinder type also differs according to model. On earlier types the brake master cylinder also incorporates the clutch master cylinder components, both systems operating in a joint housing. On later types seperate cylinders were fitted, being mounted side by side on the bulkhead, directly above the pedals.

The hydraulic brake system functions for the drum brakes in exactly the same way as for the disc brakes, ie on application of the brake pedal, hydraulic fluid under pressure is pushed from the master cylinder to the brake operating cylinders at each of the wheels, by means of a four way union and steel pipe lines and flexible hoses.

The hydraulic fluid moves the pistons out so pushing the brake shoes into contact with the brake drums. This provides an equal degree of retardation between the front and rear wheels in direct proportion to the pressure applied to the brake pedal. Return springs between each pair of brake shoes draw the shoes together when the brake pedal is released.

Drum brakes have to be adjusted periodically to compensate for wear in the linings. It is unusual to have to adjust the handbrake system as the efficiency of this system is largely dependent on the condition of the brake linings and the adjustment of the brake shoes. The handbrake can, however, be adjusted separately to the foot brake operated hydraulic system.

Apart from periodic adjustment where necessary the master cylinder hydraulic fluid level must be kept topped up to the required level. Another regular maintenance task is to pump grease into the handbrake cable. A nipple is fitted in the outer cable for this purpose and is located just forward of the rear wheels on the right-hand side (photo). If neglected the cable will stick on, as will the brakes, causing increased lining wear, overheating in the rear hub/s and a consequent loss in power.

2 Drum brakes – adjustment

1 When the periodic adjustment of the brakes becomes necessary to take up the wear of the brake linings, it is not necessary to remove either the roadwheels or brake drums. An adjuster access hole is located in both the roadwheels and brake drums and providing that the wheel was last fitted correctly these holes should align. Adjust as follows.
2 Jack-up the car on the side concerned so that the wheel/s are clear of the ground. Chock the opposing side wheels then release the handbrake.
3 Remove the hub cap from the wheel (if fitted).
4 Prise the rubber or neoprene plug/s free from the adjuster hole/s in the roadwheel concerned. On the rear wheels there is just one adjuster point whilst the front wheels have two at diagonally opposing points.
5 Rotate the wheel so that the adjuster hole is in alignment with the adjuster screw/s. Use a screwdriver and turn the adjuster clockwise until the wheel is locked (photo).
6 Now unscrew the adjuster by one notch and spin the wheel. It should be free to rotate although a slight binding may occur and is acceptable especially where new linings have been fitted.
7 On front brakes repeat this procedure on the second adjuster.
8 When adjusted spin the wheel and apply the brakes hard to centralise the shoes and recheck the adjustment.
9 Repeat the procedure on the wheels on the other side of the car.
10 A rubbing noise when the drum is rotated is usually due to dust in the brake drum. If there is no obvious slowing of the drum due to brake binding, there is no need to slacken off the adjusters until the noise disappears. However, it is advisable to remove the drum and clean the dust out (but don't inhale it as it is most detrimental to the health).
11 Whenever the drum is removed from a brake unit, it is advisable to paint the end of the adjuster white, to enable future adjustments to be made easier since it will be more clearly seen within the drum housing.
12 If after the brakes have been adjusted there is little improvement to the braking and excessive pedal clearance is still apparent, then it is likely that the linings are worn down beyond the minimum wear limits in which case they must be renewed.

3 Handbrake – adjustment

Drum brakes
1 On drum brake models, the handbrake adjustment is normally

Fig. 9.1 The handbrake carrier pad adjuster on Dunlop brakes (Sec 3)

Chapter 9 Braking system

taken up when the rear brakes are adjusted as described in the previous Section. However after high mileages it is possible that the handbrake cables will have stretched and will need to be adjusted.

2 First adjust the rear brakes as described in Section 2.

3 With the rear wheels free off the ground and chocks under the front wheels to prevent any forward movement pull the handbrake on three notches.

4 Turn the brass adjusting nut on the front end of the rear longitudinal cable at the operating lever in a clockwise direction until the rear brakes are firmly on, and then release the handbrake. Check that the rear wheels turn freely when the handbrake is off (photo).

Disc brake models

5 Should the handbrake lever travel become excessive when applying the handbrake, adjustment is possible but at the brake units, not at the relay lever. Proceed as follows.

6 Raise the car at the rear so that the rear wheels are clear of the ground. Chock the front wheels and fully release the handbrake lever.

7 Working under the car, loosen off the brass adjuster nut at the relay lever (near the propeller shaft front universal joint) so that the cable is free to hang loose.

8 Now tighten the respective pad adjuster bolts at the brake units, screwing up so that the pads are just touching the brake disc (Fig. 9.1).

9 Returning to the adjuster nut at the relay lever, tighten it to take up any slack in the cable, but ensure that it is not under load.

10 Now unscrew each pad adjuster bolt about $\frac{1}{3}$rd of a turn and spin each disc to ensure that it rotates freely.

4 Bleeding the hydraulic system

1 Removal of all the air from the hydraulic system is essential to the working of the braking system, and before undertaking this examine the fluid reservoir cap to ensure that both vent holes, one on top and the second underneath but not in line, are clear; check the level of fluid and top up if required.

2 Check all brake line unions and connections for possible seepage, and at the same time check the condition of the rubber hoses, which may be perished.

3 If the condition of the wheel cylinders is in doubt, check for possible signs of fluid leakage.

4 If there is any possibility of incorrect fluid having been put into the system, drain all the fluid out and flush through with methylated spirits. Renew all piston seals and cups since these will be affected and could possibly fail under pressure.

5 Gather together a clean jam jar, a 9 in length of tubing which fits tightly over the bleed nipples, and a tin of the specified brake fluid.

6 To bleed the system clean the areas around the bleed valves, and start on the rear brakes first by removing the rubber cup over the bleed valve and fitting a rubber tube in position (photo).

7 Place the end of the tube in a clean glass jar containing sufficient fluid to keep the end of the tube underneath during the operation.

8 Open the bleed valve with a spanner and quickly press down the brake pedal. After slowly releasing the pedal, pause for a moment to allow the fluid to recoup in the master cylinder and then depress again. This will force air from the system, and should continue until no more air bubbles can be seen coming from the tube. Tighten the bleed valve on a down stroke. At intervals make certain that the reservoir is kept topped-up, otherwise air will enter at this point again.

9 Repeat this operation on all four brakes, and when completed, check the level of the fluid in the reservoir and then check the feel of the brake pedal, which should be firm and free from any 'spongy' action, which is normally associated with air in the system.

5 Drum brake shoes – removal, inspection and refitting

After high mileages it will be necessary to fit replacement brake shoes with new linings. Refitting new brake linings to old shoes is not always satisfactory, but if the services of a local garage or workshop with brake lining equipment are available, then there is no reason why your own shoes should not be successfully relined. Refer to Figs. 9.2 and 9.3 as applicable

1 Remove the hub cap, loosen off the wheel nuts, securely jack-up the car, and remove the roadwheel.

2 Completely slacken off the brake adjustment and take out the two set screws, which hold the drum in place. Remove the brake drum. If it proves obstinate tap the rim gently with a soft-headed hammer.

3 The brake linings should be renewed if they are so worn that the rivet heads are flush with the surface of the lining. If bonded linings are fitted they must be removed when the material has worn down to 0.03 in (0.8 mm).

4 Use a pair of pliers to turn the steady spring 90° and release the washers (if fitted) and springs. These are only fitted to the rear wheels (photo).

5 Before detaching the shoe pull off and tension springs note their respective positions and how they are located (photo). Prise them free from the shoes using a large screwdriver.

6 Detach the shoes from the wheel cylinders/adjuster pivot.

7 Thoroughly clean all traces of dust from the shoes, backplates, and brake drums with a dry paint brush. Brake dust can cause squeal and judder and it is therefore important to clean out the brakes thoroughly.

8 Check that the pistons are free in their cylinders and that the rubber dust covers are undamaged and in position and that there are no hydraulic fluid leaks. Secure the pistons with wire or string.

9 Prior to reassembly smear a trace of white brake grease to all sliding surfaces. The shoes should be quite free to slide on the closed end of the cylinder and the piston anchorage point. It is vital that no grease or oil comes in contact with the brake drums or the brake linings.

10 Refitting is a straightforward reversal of the removal procedure, but note the following points:-

(a) Check that when the adjusters are refitted they are backed right off
(b) Ensure that the return springs are in their correct holes in the shoes and lie between them and the backplate
(c) The recessed ends of the shoes engage to the adjusters

6 Disc brake pads – inspection, removal and refitting

Lockheed disc brakes

1 Apply the handbrake, loosen the front wheel nuts, jack-up the front of the car, and remove the road wheels.

2 Inspect the amount of friction material left on the friction pads. The pads must be renewed when the thickness of the material has worn down to 0.06 in (1.6 mm).

3 Press down on the pad retaining spring and extract the pad retaining pins.

4 Take off the spring clip and with a slight rotational movement, remove the friction pads using a pair of sharp-nosed pliers if necessary.

5 Carefully clean the recesses in the calliper in which the friction pad assemblies lie, and the exposed face of each piston from all traces of dirt and rust.

6 Remove the cap from the hydraulic fluid reservoir and place a large rag underneath the unit. Press the pistons in each half of the calliper right in – this will cause the fluid level in the reservoir to rise and possibly to spill over the brim onto the protective rag.

7 After checking that the relieved face of each piston is positioned at the lower end of the caliper (Fig. 9.8), fit the new friction pads into the callipers.

8 Check that the new friction pad assemblies move freely in the calliper recesses and remove any high spots on the edge of the pressure plate by careful filing.

9 Check that the retaining spring clips show no sign of damage or loss of tension and then, if sound, refit them, press them down and insert the split pins.

10 Refit the roadwheels and remove the jacks. Press the brake pedal several times to adjust the brakes. Top-up the master cylinder as required.

Dunlop disc brakes

11 On the Dunlop disc brake unit the pads are retained in position via a keep plate (see Fig. 9.9) and this is located by a bolt through the calliper.

12 The minimum permissible pad thickness on this type of brake unit is 0.25 in (6.35 mm) and therefore if they are worn down to this thickness or beyond they must be renewed.

13 To remove the pads, unscrew the nut from the bolt retaining the keep plate in position and withdraw the bolt. Remove the plate and

1.8 Lubricate the handbrake cable via the nipple

2.5 Adjusting a drum brake (wheel removed for clarity)

3.4 The handbrake cable adjuster nut

4.6 Clean the bleed nipple (arrowed) before attempting to bleed brakes

5.4 Remove the steady springs

5.5 When removing the brake shoes, note tension spring positions

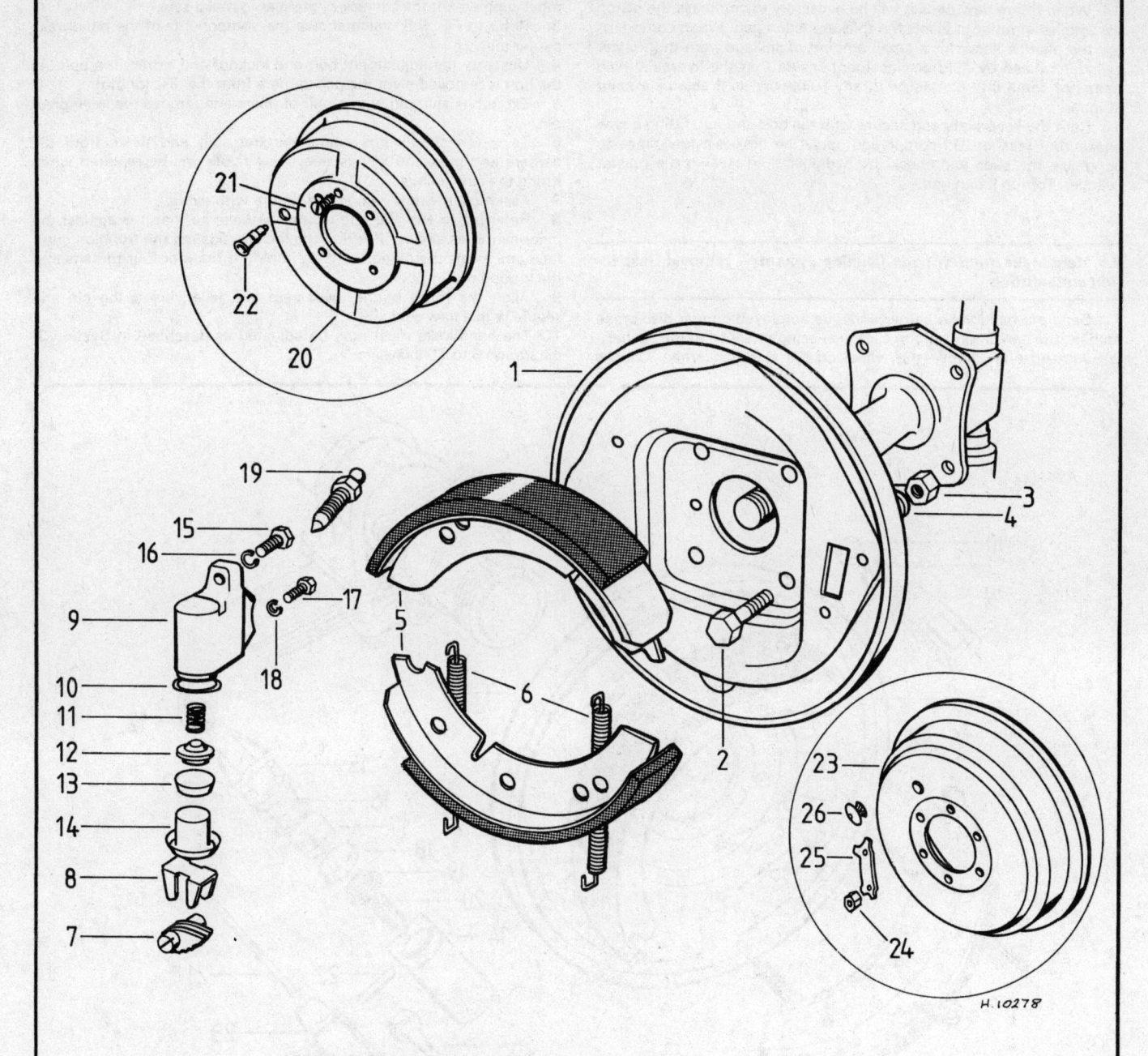

Fig. 9.2 The front drum brake components (Sec 5)

1 Backplate	10 Sealing ring	19 Bleed nipple
2 Bolt	11 Spring	20 Brake drum
3 Nut	12 Piston cup filler	21 Plug
4 Washer	13 Cup	22 Screw
5 Shoes and linings	14 Piston and dust cover	23 Brake drum
6 Tension springs	15 Bolt	24 Nut
7 Adjuster	16 Spring washer	25 Lock tab washer
8 Mask	17 Bolt	26 Plug
9 Wheel cylinder	18 Spring washer	

{ Wire wheels (brace for 23, 24, 25, 26)

Chapter 9 Braking system

extract the pads.

14 When fitting new pads it will be necessary to compress the piston assemblies in order to insert the thicker friction pad. When compressing the pistons allow for a small amount of spillage from the master cylinder caused by fluid displacement. Ensure that the hydraulic fluid does not come into contact with any paintwork as it acts as a paint stripper.

15 Refit the keep plate and secure with the bolt and nut, fitting a new shakeproof washer. On completion apply the brakes a few times to centralise the pads and check the hydraulic fluid level in the master cylinder. Top-up if required.

7 Handbrake friction pads (Dunlop system) – removal, inspection and refitting

1 Separate handbrake carrier units are employed on rear disc brake models, the handbrake unit on each side being attached to the caliper.
2 Jack-up and remove the wheel on the side concerned. Chocks must be positioned against the front wheels and axle-stands or blocks must supplement the car jack at the rear to make safe.
3 Refer to Fig. 9.5 which shows the components of the handbrake carrier unit.
4 Unscrew the adjustment bolt and locknut and extract the bolt. As the bolt is removed pivot the pad carriers from the disc (photo).
5 Extract its split pin with a pair of pliers and remove the lever pivot pin.
6 To renew the linings, compress the split end rivets from the carriers and prise the linings free. New rivets will be required when fitting the new linings.
7 Assemble the new linings and secure with rivets.
8 Referring to Fig. 9.6 and locate the lever so that it is against the inner carrier as shown. Position the locknut against the trunnion outer face and insert the carrier bolt, tightening it three or four threads into the locking nut.
9 Align the holes of the pivot seat and lever, insert the pin and secure with a new split pin.
10 The handbrake must now be adjusted as described in Section 3, paragraph 5 to 10 inclusive.

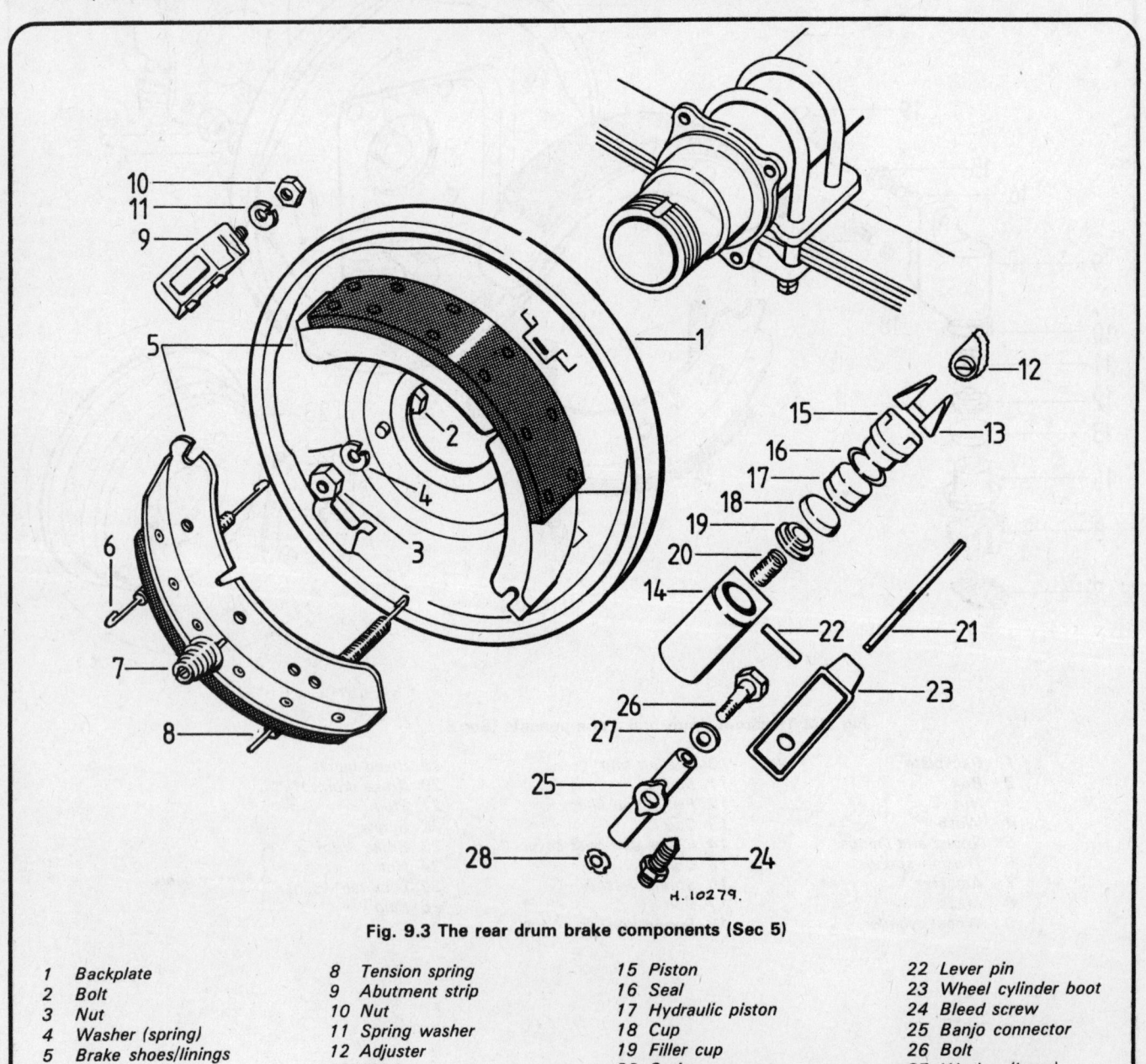

Fig. 9.3 The rear drum brake components (Sec 5)

1 Backplate	8 Tension spring	15 Piston	22 Lever pin
2 Bolt	9 Abutment strip	16 Seal	23 Wheel cylinder boot
3 Nut	10 Nut	17 Hydraulic piston	24 Bleed screw
4 Washer (spring)	11 Spring washer	18 Cup	25 Banjo connector
5 Brake shoes/linings	12 Adjuster	19 Filler cup	26 Bolt
6 Tension spring	13 Mask	20 Spring	27 Washer (large)
7 Steady spring	14 Wheel cylinder	21 Handbrake lever	28 Washer (small)

Chapter 9 Braking system

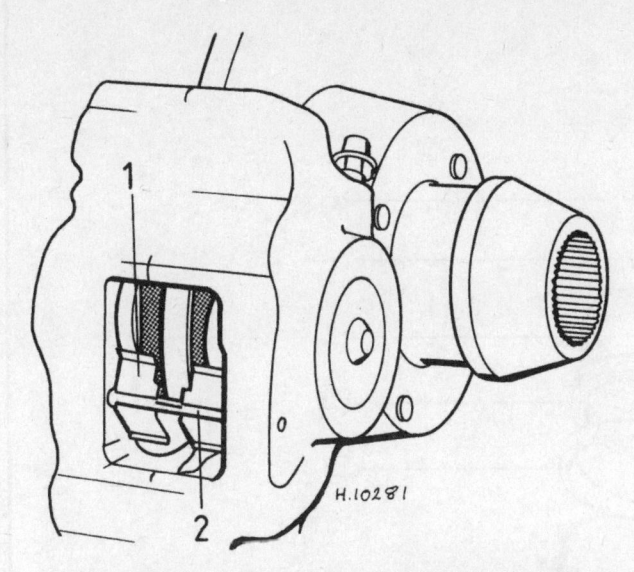

Fig. 9.4 General view of the brake calliper (Sec 6)

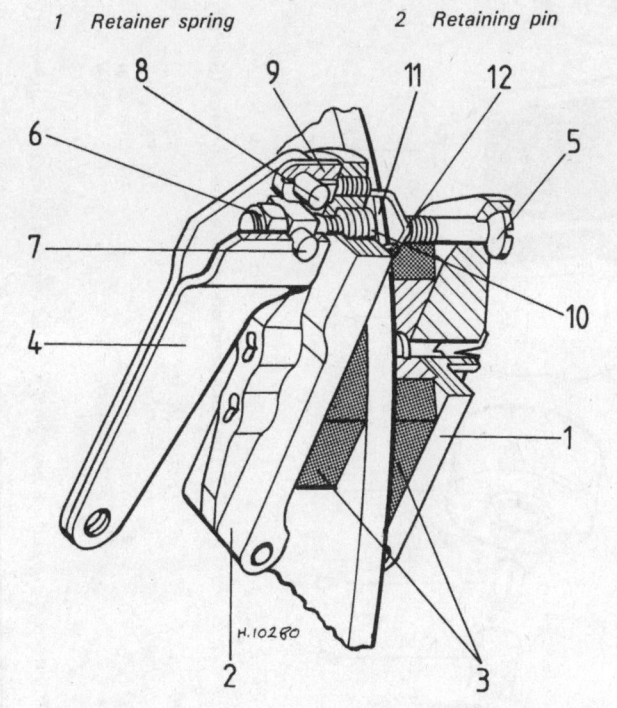

1 Retainer spring
2 Retaining pin

Fig. 9.5 The handbrake carrier components – Dunlop system (Sec 7)

1 Outer pad carrier
2 Inner pad carrier
3 Pads
4 Lever
5 Adjuster bolt
6 Locknut
7 Trunnion
8 Pivot pin
9 Pivot seat
10 Spring
11 Retaining nut
12 Spring plate

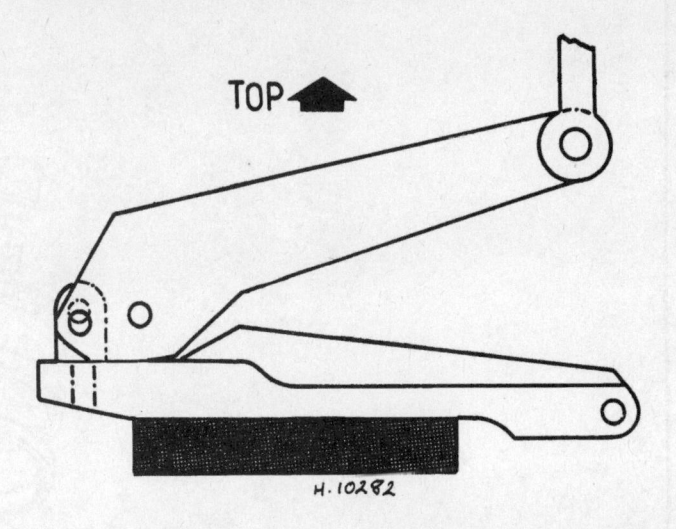

Fig. 9.6 Locate the lever against the inner carrier as shown (Sec 7)

8 Lockheed brake calliper and disc units – removal and dismantling

1 Ensure the handbrake is on, loosen the wheel securing nuts, jack-up the car, and remove the wheel.
2 Remove the disc brake friction pads as described in Section 6.
3 Where the calliper is not being dismantled, the hydraulic pipe can be left connected. Remove the brake hose support bracket nuts and spring washers and detach the bracket. When the caliper unit is removed, it can be tied up and hung out of the way until ready for refitting. Do not allow the calliper to hang free as the full weight will be taken by the hose which could well distort and damage it.
4 If the calliper is to be removed completely, unscrew the nuts which hold the flexible hose in place as described in Section 12 and catch the hydraulic fluid in a suitable container. Remove the hose from the calliper. The flexible hose section can be temporarily clamped to prevent excessive fluid spillage but take care not to damage the hose. Plug the open ends of the brake pipe and the hose to prevent the entry of any foreign matter.
5 Lever back the ears of the lockwasher and undo the two bolts which hold the calliper to the stub axle. Remove the calliper from the car, noting any shims that may be fitted behind the calliper mounting lugs.
6 To dismantle the caliper, the pistons must be extracted. If still attached to the hydraulic line place the calliper on a block or similar support, or ask a friend to hold it to avoid it hanging on the hydraulic hose which could damage the latter.
7 Clamp the piston in either the mounting half or the rim half of the calliper with wire or a suitable clamp, depending on which side of the calliper the piston is to be removed from first.
8 Gently apply the footbrake so forcing the unclamped piston out of the calliper unit until it is in a position where it can be removed by hand.
9 Where the caliper unit has been removed completely, apply a jet of compressed air into the hydraulic pipe connection in the caliper to force the pistons out. Take care using this method as too much pressure will eject the pistons too quickly.
10 Gently prise the dust seal retainer from the cylinder by carefully inserting a penknife blade between the dust seal retainer and the dust seal, and then extract the seal.
11 Remove the inner hydraulic fluid seal from its groove in the calliper cylinder with a blunt nosed tool. Great care should be taken not to damage or scratch the cylinder bore or fluid seal groove.
12 After the piston and rubber seals in one side of the calliper have been checked and replaced as necessary, and the piston reassembled to the calliper as detailed in the following section, the piston in the other half of the calliper can be removed by clamping the rebuilt piston assembly in place and then repeating the process used to remove the first piston.
13 To remove the hub and disc, refer to Chapter 11. To separate the hub from the disc, unscrew the four set bolts and lockwashers and lift the disc away from the hub. **Note:** *Do not dismantle the calliper further than described, as the manufacturer specifies that the calliper halves must not be split.*

9 Lockheed brake calliper and disc units – reassembly and refitting

1 Fit the disc to the hub casing and refit the hub assembly as described in Chapter 11.

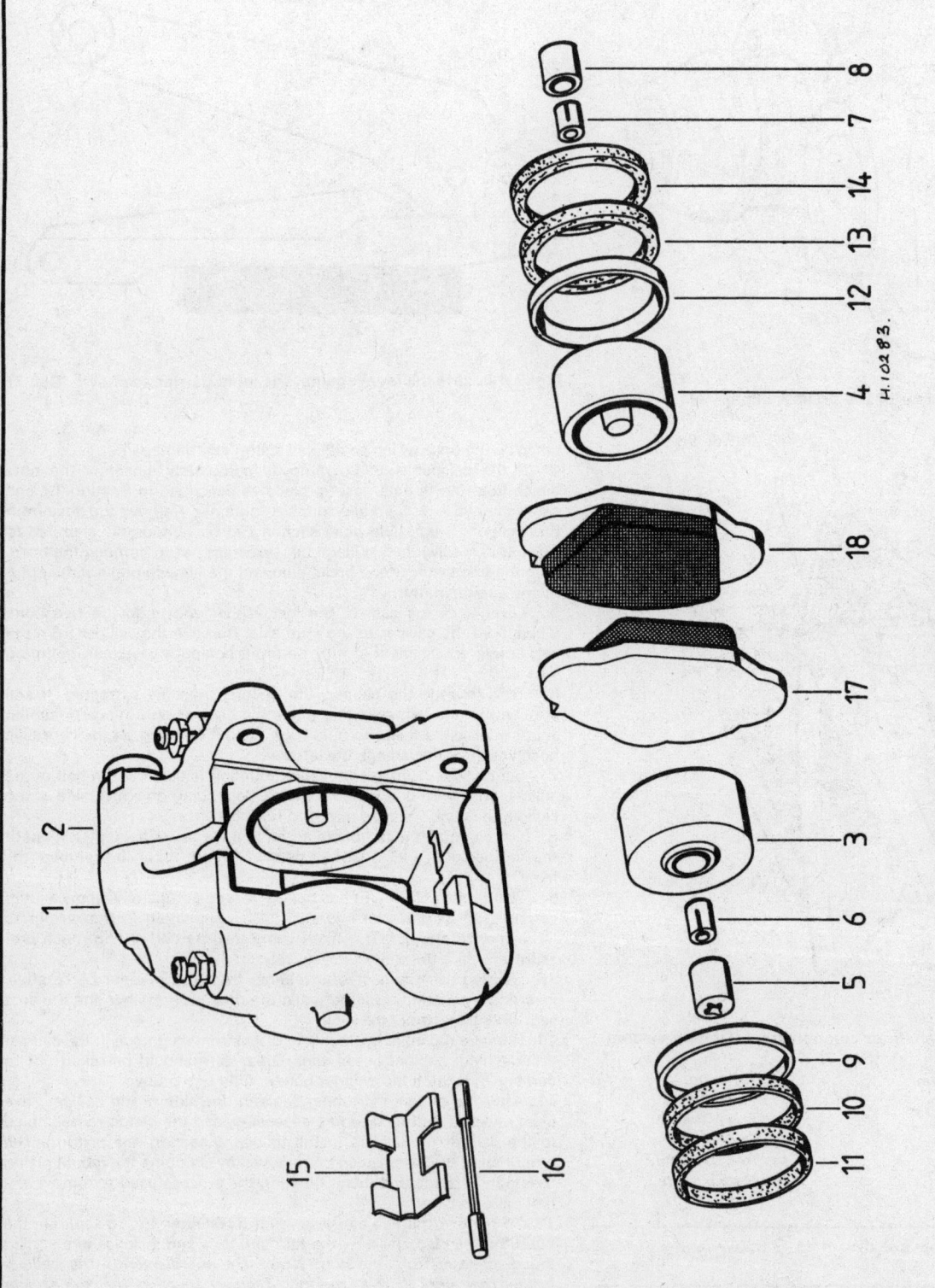

Fig. 9.7 The Lockheed disc brake components (Sec 8)

1 Calliper (rim half)
2 Calliper (mounting half)
3 Hydraulic piston
4 Hydraulic piston
5 Sleeve*
6 Friction stop*
7 Friction stop*
8 Sleeve*
9 Seal retainer
10 Dust seal
11 Fluid seal
12 Seal retainer
13 Dust seal
14 Fluid seal
15 Retainer spring
16 Retainer pin
17 Friction pad
18 Friction pad

*Items thus marked are positionally locked when manufactured and must not be dismantled

7.4 Dunlop handbrake components
1 Adjustment bolt
2 Lever
3 Pads
4 Bleed nipple for calliper

10.1 General view of the front hub and Dunlop disc brake

10.8 General view of the rear hub, Dunlop disc calliper and handbrake unit

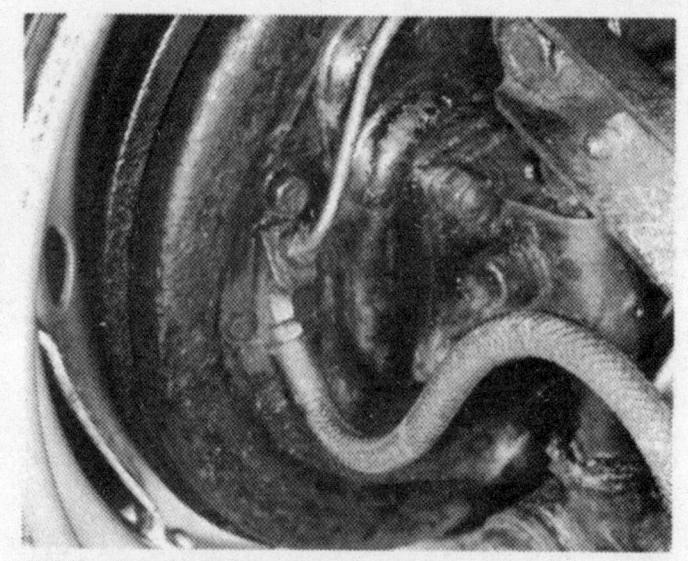

12.1 Check the flexible hoses for signs of leaks and deterioration. Also check the interconnecting front wheel cylinder hydraulic pipe shown

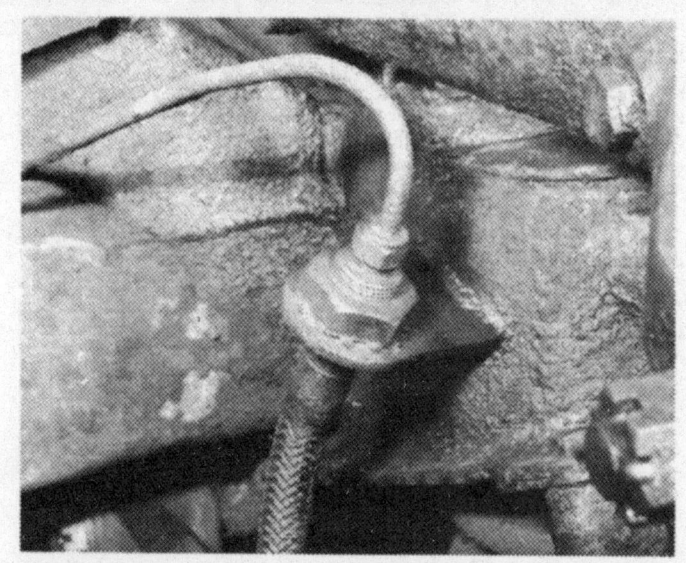

12.4 Typical flexible pipe to steel pipe connection with chassis mounted steady bracket

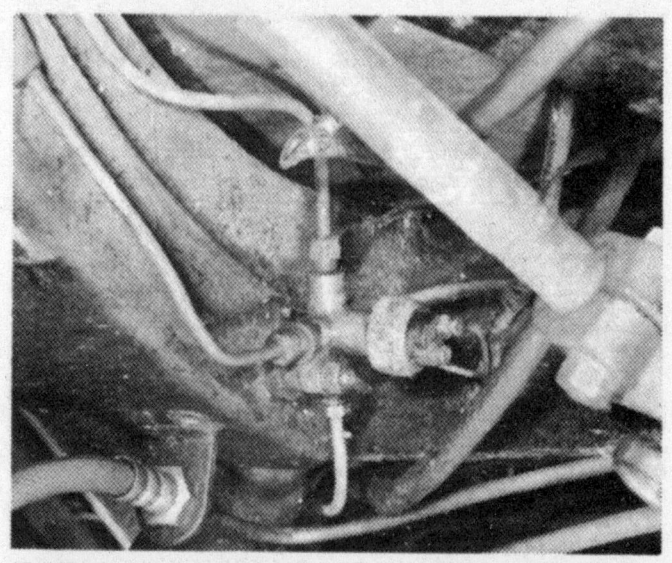

12.6 The four-way pipe connection and brake light switch on the right-hand chassis member

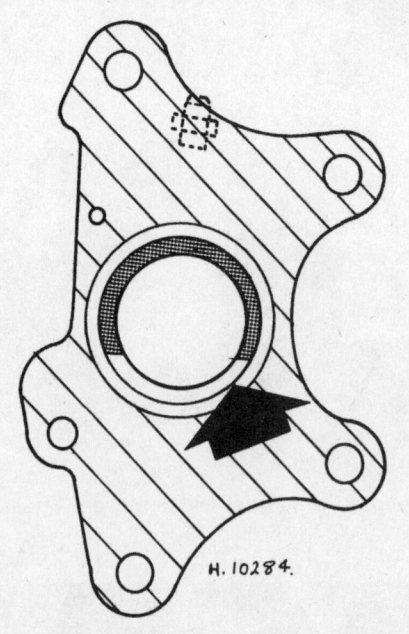

Fig. 9.8 The undercut piston section must face the calliper lower end (opposite the bleeder screw) (Sec 9)

2 Check the run out at the outer periphery of the disc. If it exceeds 0.003 in (0.076 mm) remove the disc and reposition it on the hub casing.
3 Coat a new rubber fluid seal with a rubber grease and fit the seal to the inner groove in the cylinder.
4 Slacken the bleed screw in the calliper one turn.
5 Lubricate the piston with disc brake lubricant and press the piston into the cylinder carefully, with the undercut portion facing towards the calliper lower section (away from the bleed nipple) (Fig. 9.8). Press the piston in squarely until approximately 0.25 in (6 mm) protrudes from the cylinder and take great care to ensure the piston does not tilt in its bore.
6 Smear a new dust seal with hydraulic fluid and fit it to its retainer (early type callipers). On the later type, press the seal into the bore mouth then fit the retainer (recessed face out). The two types of seal are interchangeable.
7 Place the dust seal assembly with the seal resting on the raised portion of the piston and press the piston and seal home with a suitable clamp. Tighten the bleed screw. Repeat this procedure with the remaining cylinder in the other half of the calliper.
8 Refit the calliper to the disc and stub axle and tighten the securing bolts to the torque wrench setting given in the Specifications. Knock over the tabs on the lock nuts.
9 Fit the disc brake friction pads as previously detailed and bleed the hydraulic system. Assembly is now complete.

10 Dunlop disc and calliper units – removal and refitting

Front brakes
1 Raise and support the front of the car, remove the roadwheel/s (photo).
2 Disconnect the hydraulic supply pipe at the calliper and plug the pipe to prevent excess leakage and the ingress of dirt.
3 Disconnect the brake hose support bracket.
4 Unscrew and remove the calliper retaining bolts. Remove the calliper and cylinders, noting any shims fitted between the calliper and the mounting lugs. The exact number of shims must be refitted to their original locations on reassembly.
5 Refer to Chapter 11 for removal of the hub and disc unit.
6 Refitting is a reversal of the removal procedure. When assembly is complete check the clearance each side of the disc and calliper. The distance each side should be within 0.010 in (0.254 mm). Any adjustment that may be necessary is made by adding or subtracting shims accordingly.
7 Bleed the hydraulic system and top-up the fluid reservoir.

Rear brakes
8 Raise and support the rear of the car and remove the roadwheels (photo).
9 Detach the hydraulic supply pipe at the union below the inner cylinder block. Blank off the pipe to prevent fluid leakage and the ingress of dirt.
10 Extract the split pin from the clevis pin retaining the handbrake cable yoke. Withdraw the clevis pin and detach the cable from the calliper lever.
11 Peen back the lockwasher tabs of the calliper retaining bolts. Unscrew the bolts retaining the calliper to the mounting flange and then remove the calliper together with the parking brake mechanism. Take a note of any shims fitted between the calliper and flange as they must be refitted exactly on assembly.
12 Renew any defective components as necessary. Refer to Section 11 to service the calliper unit.
13 Refer to Chapter 11 should it be necessary to remove the disc.
14 Refitting is a reversal of the removal procedure. When reassembly is complete check the clearance each side between the disc and calliper. The distance each side must be within 0.010 in (0.254 mm). If necessary adjust by adding or subtracting shims as necessary between the caliper and mounting lugs.
15 Apply the brake pedal a few times on completion to centralise the pads once the hydraulic system has been bled and ensure that the hydraulic fluid level in the master cylinder is up to the required level.
16 Check the adjustment of the handbrake as described in Section 3.

11 Dunlop brake calliper – dismantling and assembly

1 Refer to Section 6 paragraphs 11 to 13 and remove the friction pads (if not already removed). Refer to Fig. 9.9.
2 Unscrew and disconnect the bridge pipe connections at each end and remove the pipe noting its location position.
3 Unscrew and remove the cylinder block retaining bolts (to the calliper) and detach the blocks.
4 Extract the dust seal from the cylinder block face lip and then apply a controlled amount of compressed air through the hydraulic intake connection in the cylinder unit to eject the piston. Alternatively reconnect the cylinder to the hydraulic hose and gently pump the brake pedal to eject the cylinder under hydraulic pressure.
5 Unscrew the plate to piston retaining screw and remove the plate with the piston seal.
6 Remove the retractor bush from the bore of the piston and then carefully cut out and remove the dust seal.
7 Locate the back plate on a bush of suitable diameter to hold the piston and then using a suitable piece of tubing press out the piston by applying the tube to the end of the piston spigot. As the piston is being pressed out by the tube take care not to damage the piston.
8 All parts can now be cleaned in hydraulic fluid and inspected for defects. Renew any items that are in any way defective.
9 Wash the respective parts in methylated spirits.
10 Prior to assembly of the calliper ensure that all parts are perfectly clean and dry. Blow dry with compressed air if available.
11 The hub and disc are refitted and adjusted as described in Chapter 11.
12 Fit the new dust seal collar with its lip on the back plate onto the piston spigot. Support the piston and press home the backing plate.
13 The retractor bush is now inserted into the bore of the piston. The new piston seal must be smeared with hydraulic fluid and then fitted to the piston. Locate the piston plate and retain with screws. When each screw is tightened, peen lock using a centre punch to secure.
14 Engage the piston onto the retractor pin and using a hand press if available slowly press on the back plate to locate the assembly into the cylinder bore. As the piston assembly is being fitted check that it is kept square to the bore and that the seal is not allowed to twist or distort, especially during the initial entry.
15 Fit the dust seal lip with the corresponding section on the cylinder block.
16 Refit the cylinder blocks to the calliper and locate the bridge pipe unit. The pipe is fitted with its near vertical section at the furthest point from the wheel. Refit the brake unit as described in the previous Section.

Chapter 9 Braking system

12 Hydraulic pipes and hoses – inspection, removal and replacement

1 Inspect the condition of the flexible hydraulic hoses leading from the chassis mounted metal pipes to the brake backplates (photo). If any are damaged, cut or chafed, they must be renewed.
2 Unscrew the metal pipe union nuts from its connection to the hose, and then holding the hexagon on the hose with a spanner, unscrew the attachment nut and washer.
3 The chassis end of the hose can now be pulled from the chassis mounting bracket and will be quite free.
4 Disconnect the flexible hydraulic hose at the backplate by unscrewing it from the brake cylinder (photo). When releasing the hose from the backplate, the chassis end must always be freed first.
5 Refitting is a straight reversal of the removal procedure.
6 The metal pipes should also be inspected periodically for signs of leakage, corrosion or damage (photo). Where such defects are found the pipes must be renewed.
7 The pipe section concerned is removed in a similar manner to that of the flexible type mentioned above but take care not to distort the shape since if a new pipe is to be made up the old one will be used as a pattern.
8 The new pipe will have to be made up at your local garage or brake specialist who will have the necessary tools and equipment for the job.
9 Refitting is the reverse of the removal sequence and bleed the system (Section 4) on completion.

13 Wheel cylinder – removal, overhaul and refitting

1 Refer to Section 5 and remove the brake drum and brake shoes from the wheel assembly concerned.
2 Ensure that all the other wheels and drums are in place and where two brake operating cylinders are fitted to one backplate, as on the front wheels, securely wire the piston in the cylinder which is not to be dismantled. Remove the piston, piston rubber and seal from the cylinder being dismantled by applying gentle pressure to the footbrake. Place a quantity of rag under the backplate or a tray to catch the hydraulic fluid as it pours out of the cylinder.
3 Inspect the inside of the cylinder for score marks caused by

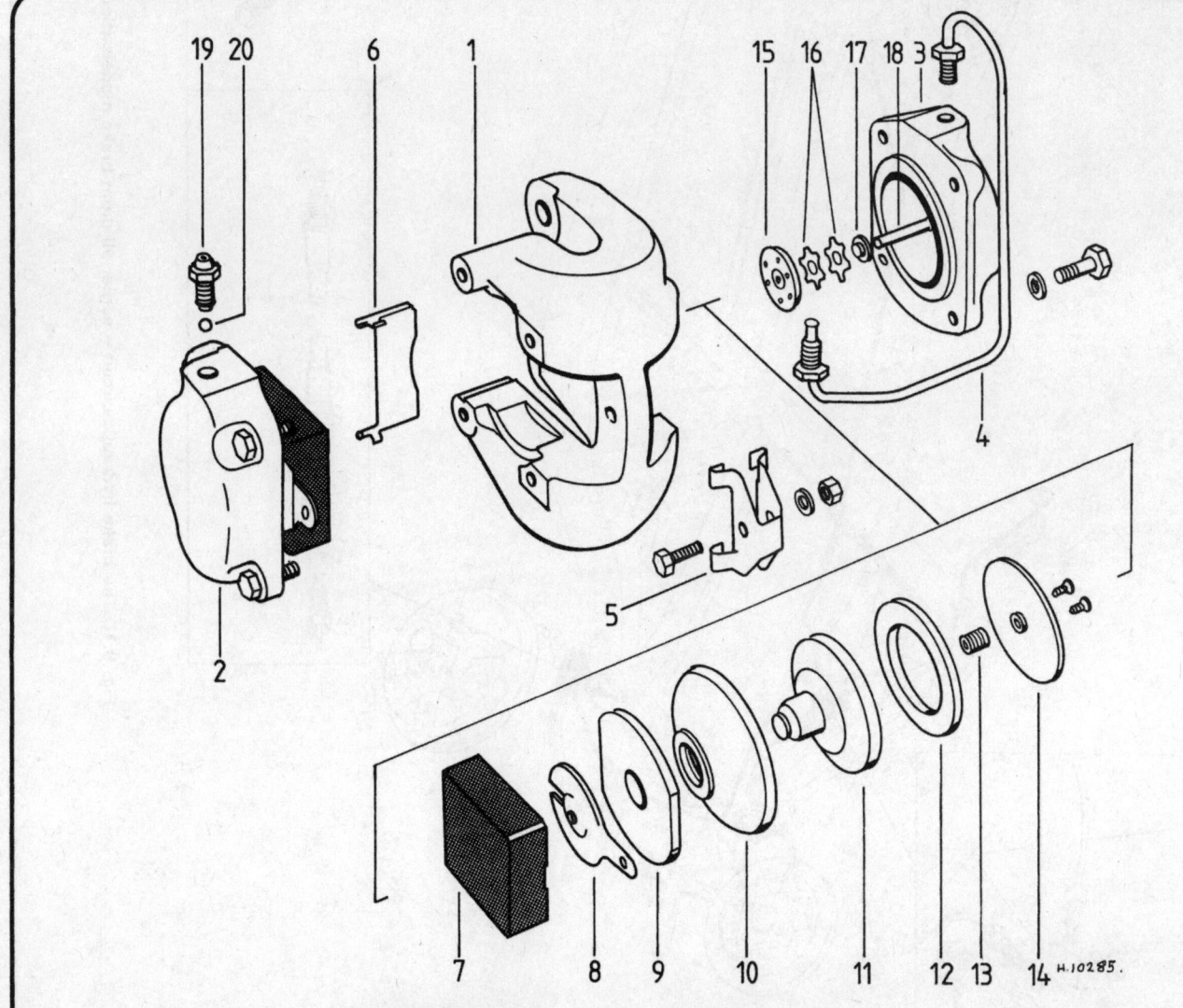

Fig. 9.9 The Dunlop disc brake unit components (Sec 11)

1 Calliper	6 Support plate	11 Piston	16 Spring washer
2 Cylinder block	7 Friction pad	12 Piston seal	17 Retractor stop bush
3 Cylinder block	8 Securing plate	13 Retractor bush	18 Retractor pin
4 Bridge pipe	9 Backing plate	14 Plate	19 Bleed screw
5 Keep plate	10 Dust seal	15 Cap	20 Bleed screw ball

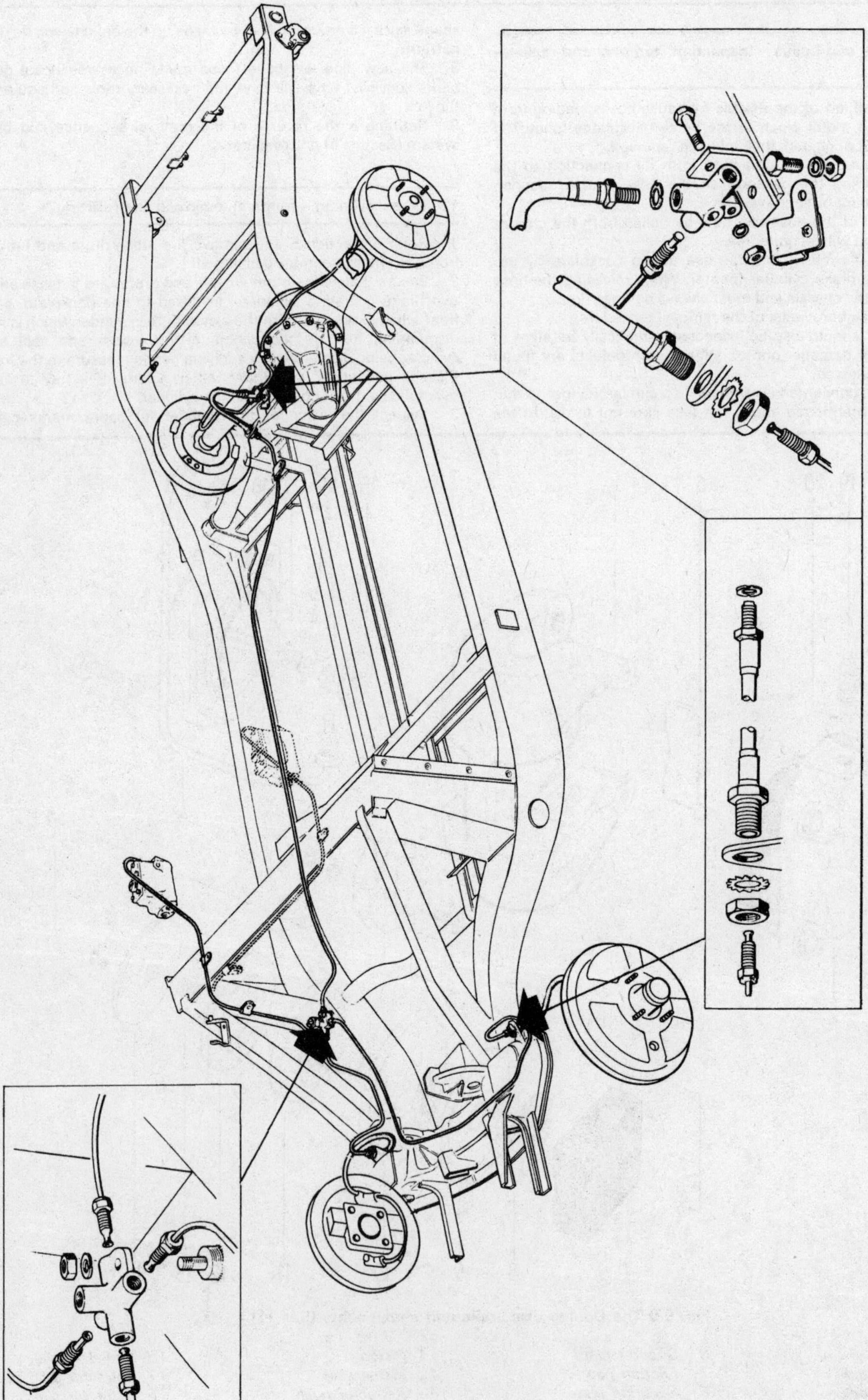

Fig. 9.10 The brake hydraulic circuit – earlier all drum brake models (Sec 12)

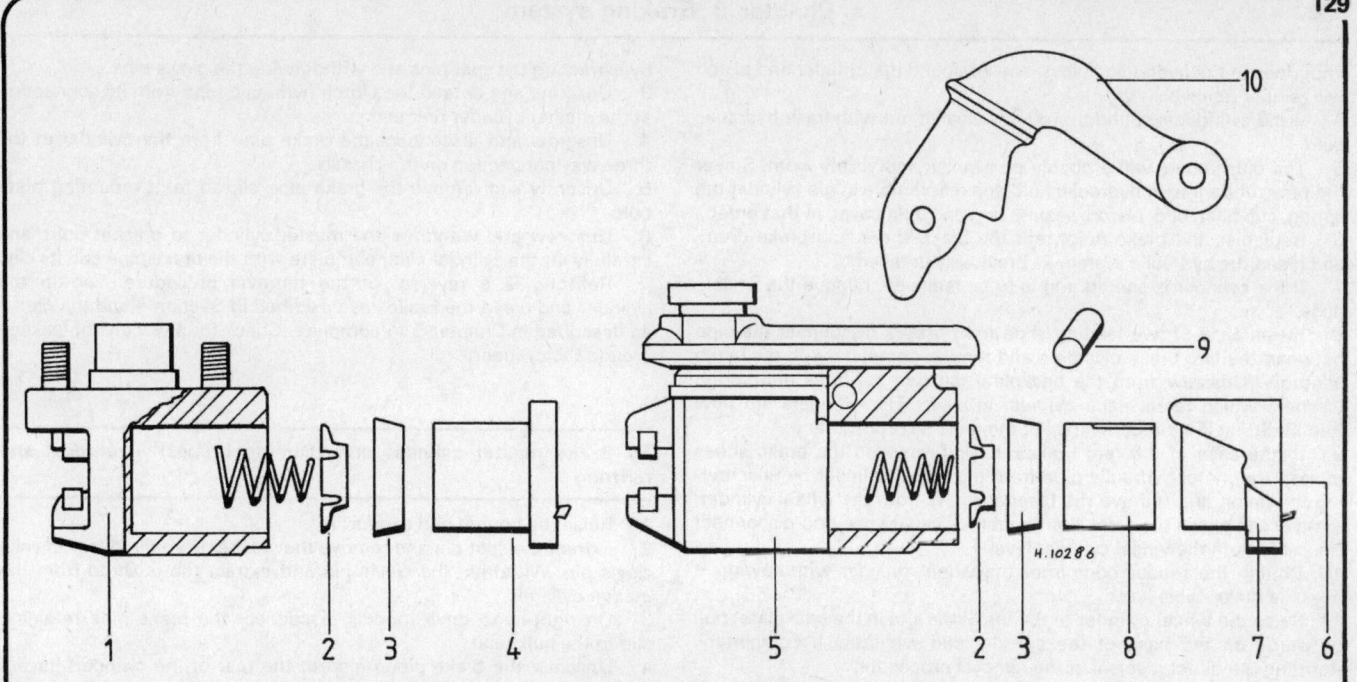

Fig. 9.11 Wheel cylinder components (Sec 13)

1	Front wheel cylinder	4	Piston and dust cover	7	Piston seal
2	Cup filler	5	Rear wheel cylinder	8	Piston
3	Piston cup	6	Piston and dust cover	9	Pivot pin
				10	Handbrake lever

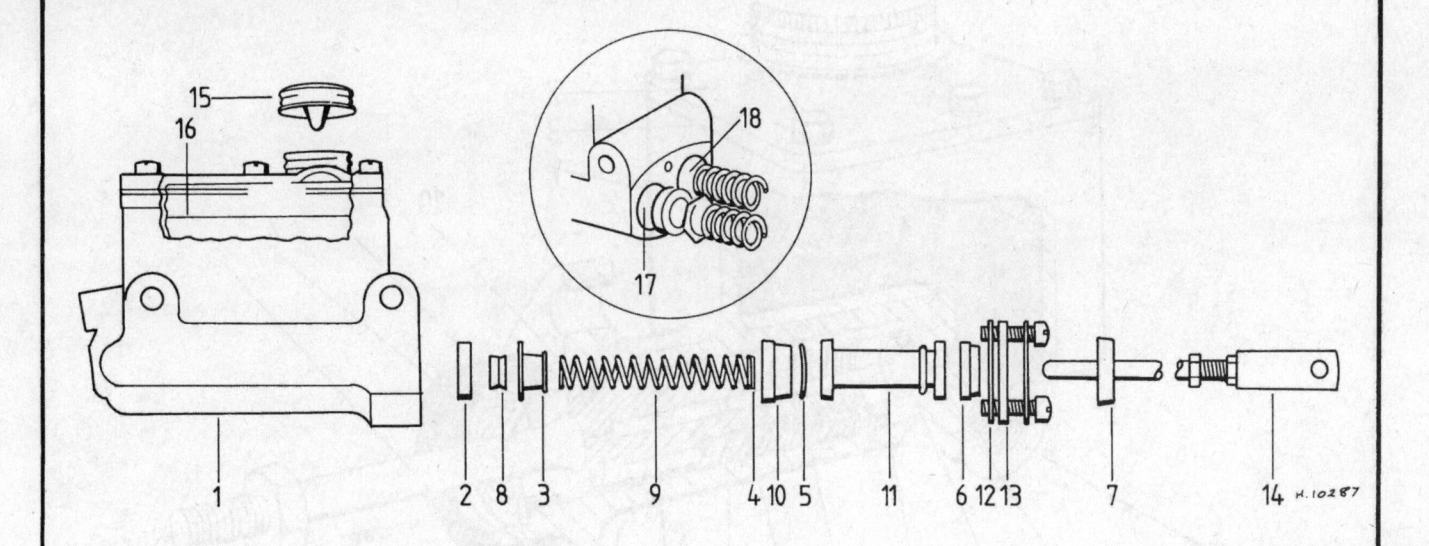

Fig. 9.12 Lockheed brake and clutch master cylinder unit (Sec 16)

1	Master cylinder	6	Secondary cup	11	Piston	15	Filler cap
2	Valve washer	7	Rubber boot	12	Gasket	16	Fluid level
3	Valve body	8	Valve cup	13	Cover plate	17	Brake cylinder
4	Spring seal	9	Piston return spring	14	Pushrod assembly	18	Clutch cylinder
5	Dished washer	10	Master cup				

130 Chapter 9 Braking system

impurities in the hydraulic fluid. If any are found the cylinder and piston will require renewal.
4 If the cylinder is sound thoroughly clean it out with fresh hydraulic fluid.
5 The old rubbers will probably be swollen and visibly worn. Smear the new rubbers with hydraulic fluid and reassemble in the cylinder the spring, cup filler, cup, piston, sealing ring and dust cover, in that order.
6 Replenish the brake fluid, refit the brake shoes and brake drum, and bleed the hydraulic system as previously detailed.
7 If the cylinder is scored and is to be renewed, remove the flexible hose.
8 In the case of two leading shoe front brakes disconnect the pipe between the two brake cylinders and remove complete with the banjo adaptors. Unscrew from the backplate the two set bolts and spring washers which retain each cylinder in place. The cylinders are now free. Refitting is a direct reversal of the removal procedure.
9 In the case of the rear brakes; having removed the brake shoes release the metal hydraulic pipe from the wheel cylinder by unscrewing the union nut, remove the bleeder screw from the wheel cylinder, remove the clevis pin from the handbrake cable yoke and disconnect the cable from the wheel cylinder lever.
10 Detach the rubber boot from the wheel cylinder withdrawing it over the brake cable lever.
11 Raise the wheel cylinder to the top of the slot in the backplate, pull outwards on the base of the cylinder and withdraw it completely. Refitting is a direct reversal of the removal procedure.

14 Lockheed brake/clutch master cylinder – removal and refitting

1 Raise and support the bonnet.
2 Disconnect the clutch and brake pushrod to pedal arm clevis joints by extracting the split pins and withdrawing the clevis pins.
3 Unscrew and detach the clutch hydraulic pipe from its connection at the master cylinder rear end.
4 Unscrew and disconnect the brake pipe from the cylinder at the three way connection on the chassis.
5 Unscrew and remove the brake pipe clip to front mounting plate bolt.
6 Unscrew and withdraw the master cylinder to bracket bolts and carefully lift the cylinder clear complete with the brake pipe and its clip.
7 Refitting is a reversal of the removal procedure. Top-up the cylinder and bleed the brakes as described in Section 4 and the clutch as described in Chapter 5 to complete. Check for any signs of leakage around the cylinder.

15 Brake master cylinder unit (Dunlop brakes) – removal and refitting

1 Raise the bonnet and support it.
2 Extract the split pin and remove the washer from the pushrod yoke clevis pin. Withdraw the clevis pin and extract the pushrod from the master cylinder.
3 On right-hand drive models disconnect the brake pipe retaining clip to the bulkhead.
4 Unscrew the brake pipe union at the rear of the cylinder, have a rag handy to soak up the fluid spillage.
5 Unscrew and remove the master cylinder to bracket retaining bolts/nuts and washers. Carefully lift the cylinder clear.
6 Refitting is a reversal of the removal procedure. Once fitted, top-up the reservoir and bleed the brakes as given in Section 4. Check for any signs of hydraulic leakage around the cylinder.

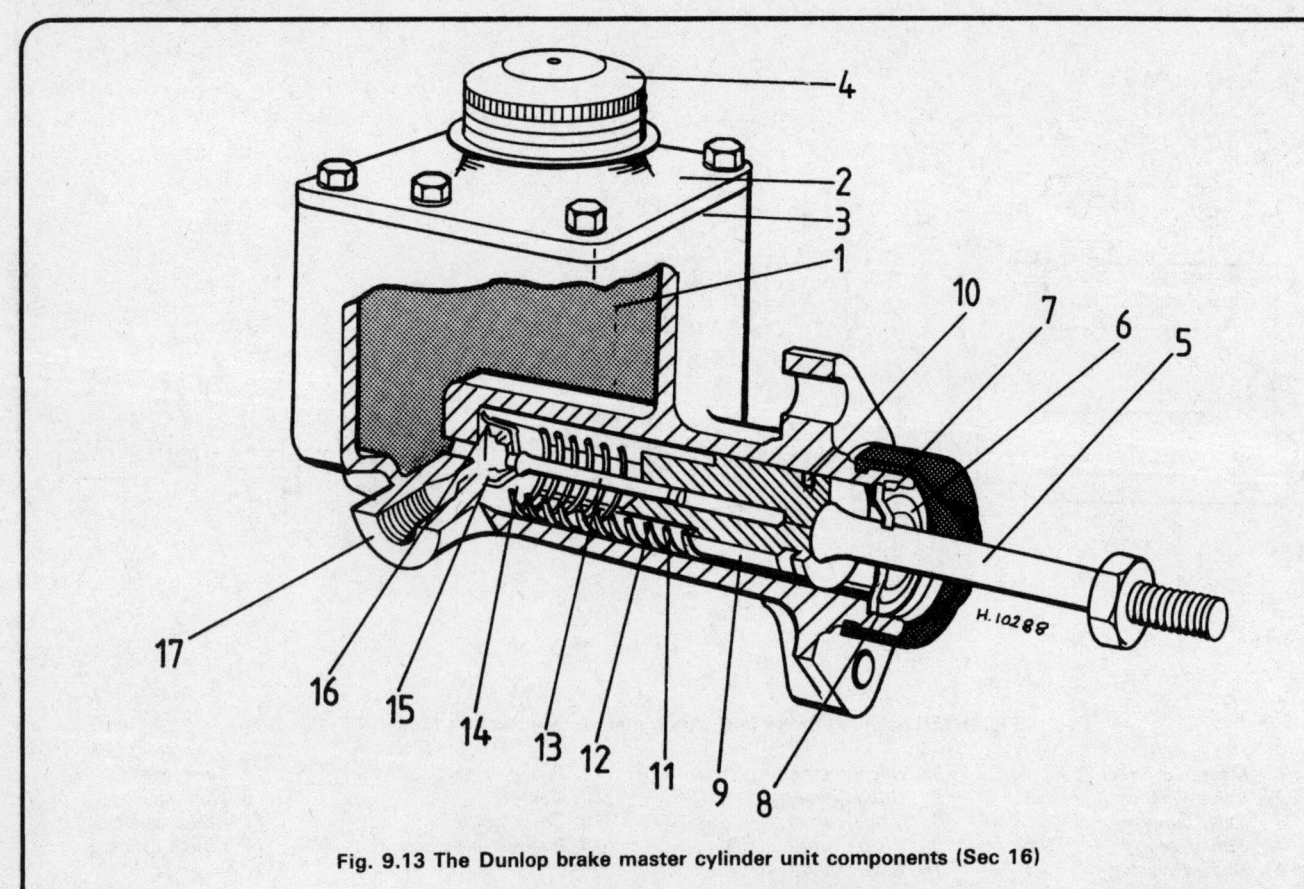

Fig. 9.13 The Dunlop brake master cylinder unit components (Sec 16)

1 Reservoir	6 Washer (dished)	10 O-ring	14 Spring support
2 Cover	7 Dust seal	11 Return spring	15 Valve spring
3 Cork gasket	8 Circlip	12 Spring support	16 Seal
4 Filler cap	9 Piston	13 Valve	17 Outlet connection
5 Pushrod			

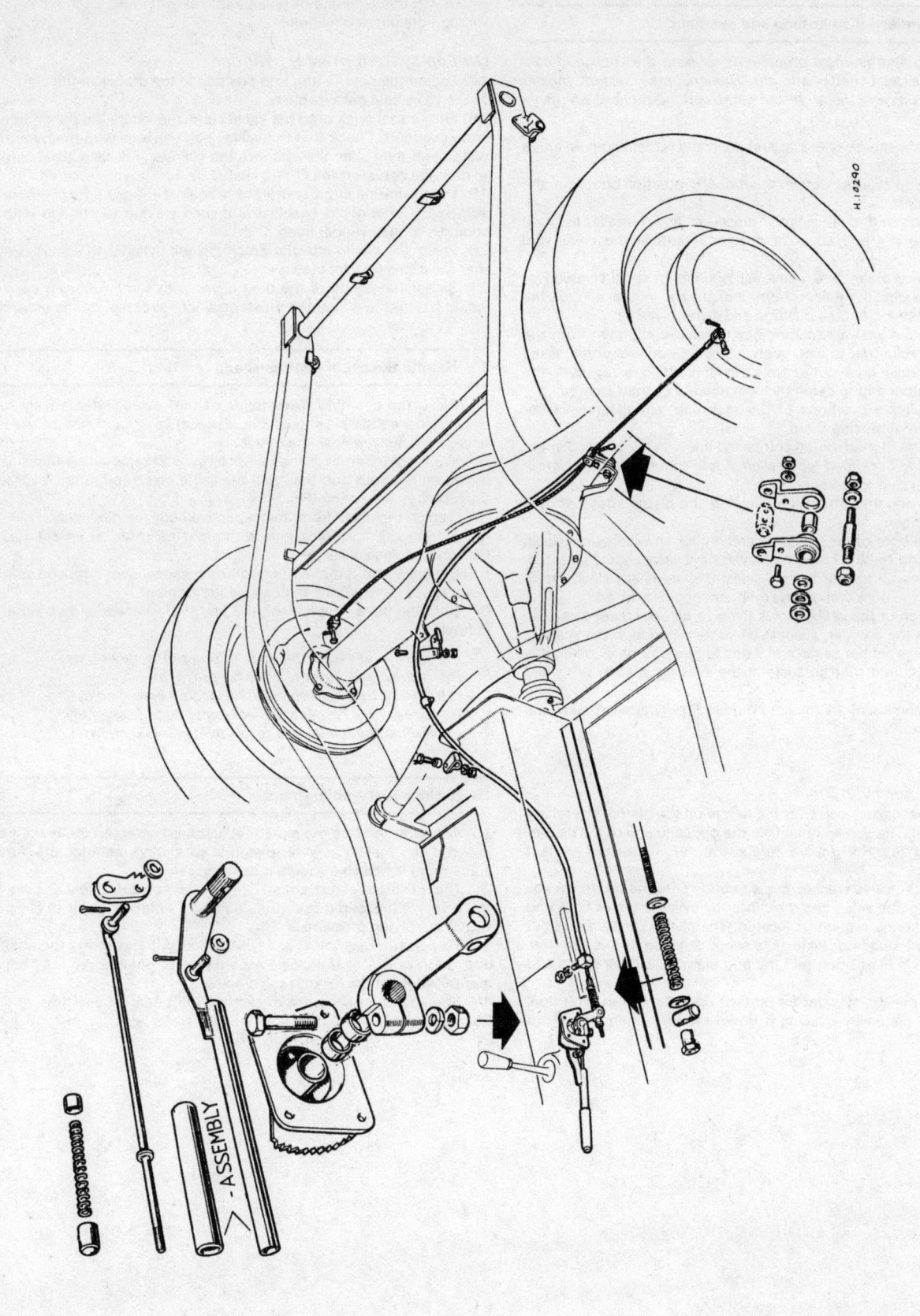

Fig. 9.14 The handbrake cable system components and layout (rear drum brake models) (Sec 17)

16 Master cylinder – dismantling and overhaul

The dismantling and overhaul procedures for both the Lockheed dual brake/clutch master cylinder and the Dunlop brake system master cylinder are similar and therefore the combined instructions are given below.

1   Remove the reservoir filler cap and drain any remaining fluid into a container for disposal.
2   On the Dunlop cylinder detach the rubber protection boot from the end of the cylinder.
3   On the Lockheed dual cylinder unscrew and remove the two screws retaining the end cover in position. Remove the cover and gasket.
4   On the Dunlop brake type, use a pair of pliers or small screwdriver and extract the circlip retainer from the groove in the end of the cylinder bore, then extract the pushrod and dished washer.
5   The piston and seal assemblies can now be withdrawn from the cylinder bore. If reluctant to exit, apply a small amount of compressed air to the hydraulic fluid outlet hole whilst holding a rag over the cylinder at the other end to catch the components as they emerge.
6   Note the relative positions of the seal, cup, spring and washer assemblies before removing them.
7   Wash all parts in methylated spirits and allow to dry off for inspection. **Note**: *On the Lockheed type cylinder note that the clutch cylinder does not have a valve assembly*
8   When removing and fitting the cup over the piston stretch it over using only the fingers.
9   Examine the bore of the cylinder carefully for any scores or ridges, and if this is found to be a smooth all over, new seals should be fitted. It is a false economy to refit the old seals. If there is any doubt as to the condition of the bore then a new cylinder should be fitted.
10   If examination of the seals shows them to be apparently oversize, or very loose on the plunger, suspect oil contamination in the system. Oil will swell these rubber seals, and if one is found to be swollen, it is reasonable to assume that all seals in the braking system will need attention.
11   Before reassembly of the master cylinder dip all parts in brake fluid and assemble them wet.

Lockheed master cylinder

12   Locate the secondary cup over the flange on the piston (stretching with fingers only). The cup lip must face the opposite end of the piston.
13   When fitted into its groove rotate the cup to ensure correct seating.
14   Now locate the valve washer, cup and body onto the return spring.
15   Fit the spring and valve assembly into the cylinder (valve first) and ensure that the spring retainer is located. The piston is now fitted but be careful not to damage or distort the secondary cup as it is inserted. When the piston is in position refit the end plate the rubber boots and pushrods.
16   To test the master cylinder for correct operation, fill it with fluid and operate the piston by pushing it down the bore then allow it to return. Do this a couple of times and if in order fluid should be ejected through the outlet pipe hole.

Dunlop system master cylinder

17   Locate the new O-ring into position in the groove in the piston and fit the valve seal onto its bush.
18   Fit the seal bush onto the valve stem and locate the piston into the spring support. Check that the valve head engages with the bore of the piston and then slide the unit into the cylinder, but take great care not to damage or distort the O-ring seal.
19   Locate the pushrod and press it against the piston to compress it sufficiently enough to enable the dished washer to engage with the shoulder at the cylinder head.
20   Insert the circlip into the groove in the cylinder to secure. Ensure that the clip is fully located.
21   Smear the inside of the dust cover with some rubber grease and locate it onto the end of the master cylinder to complete the assembly.

17 Handbrake cable – removal and refitting

1   Raise the car onto axle-stands at the rear or alternatively run it over an inspection pit if available. Place chocks each side of the front wheels and fully release the handbrake.
2   Working underneath the car unscrew and remove the brass handbrake adjuster nut and then pull the cable end through the lever location and free the spring (Fig. 9.14).
3   Detach the cable from the respective body location clips.
4   Extract the split pins and withdraw the cable to wheel cylinder lever clevis pins each side.
5   Unscrew and remove the two axle balance lever nuts and split the lever halves to withdraw the cable and trunnion.
6   Refitting is a reversal of the removal procedure but note the following:

   (a) Always use new split pins to secure the clevis pins
   (b) If the clevis pins are worn renew them
   (c) Ensure that the cable is fully located before adjusting
   (d) Grease the respective pivot joints during assembly
   (e) Adjust the handbrake to complete (see Section 3)

18 Brake pedal – adjustment

1   Although the free movement adjustment between the brake pedal pushrod and master cylinder piston is set during manufacture, further adjustment is possible should it be necessary.
2   The pedal free movement should be approximately 0·5 in (13 mm). This is measured from the pedal pad's highest point to the point where the piston pressure is felt.
3   To adjust loosen off the clevis rod locknut and screw the adjuster nut rod in or out of the clevis accordingly to get the required adjustment. Retighten the locknut to complete.
4   Should it be necessary to remove the pedal at any time refer to Chapter 5, Section 10.

19 Fault diagnosis – brakes

Symptom	Reason/s
Pedal travels a long way before the brakes operate	Brake shoes set too far from the drums Brake shoes/friction pads badly worn
Stopping ability poor, even though pedal pressure is firm	Linings, discs or drums badly worn or scored One or more wheel hydraulic cylinders seized, resulting in some brake shoes not pressing against the drums (or pads against discs) Brake linings contaminated with oil Wrong type of linings fitted (too hard) Brake shoes wrongly assembled
Car veers to one side when the brakes are applied	Brake pads or linings on one side are contaminated with oil Hydraulic wheel cylinder(s) on one side partially or fully seized A mixture of lining materials fitted between sides Brake discs not matched Unequal wear between sides caused by partially seized wheel cylinders
Pedal feels spongy when the brakes are applied	Air is present in the hydraulic system
Pedal feels springy when the brakes are applied	Brake linings not bedded into the drums (after fitting new ones) Master cylinder or brake backplate mounting bolts loose Severe wear in brake drums causing distortion when brakes are applied. Discs out of true
Pedal travels right down with little or no resistance and brakes are virtually non-operative	Leak in hydraulic system resulting in lack of pressure for operating wheel cylinders If no signs of leakage are apparent the master cylinder internal seals are failing to sustain pressure
Binding, juddering, overheating	One or a combination of reasons given in the foregoing Sections

The following list of defects in associate components may also give brake problems and should therefore be checked if necessary:

1. *Uneven and incorrect tyre pressures*
2. *Incorrect 'mix' of radial and crossply tyres*
3. *Wear in the steering mechanism*
4. *Defects in the suspension and dampers*
5. *Misalignment of the body frame*

Chapter 10 Electrical system

Contents

Batteries – removal and refitting	2	Instrument panel switches and gauges – removal and refitting	29
Battery charging	5	Number plate lights – bulb renewal	27
Battery electrolyte replenishment	4	Radios and tape players – fitting as accessories	35
Battery maintenance and inspection	3	Radios and tape players – suppression of interference	36
Dynamo – dismantling and inspection	9	Regulator and cut-out controls – maintenance	18
Dynamo – removal and refitting	8	Regulator control box – general information	17
Dynamo – repair and assembly	10	Starter motor – dismantling and reassembly	14
Dynamo – routine maintenance	6	Starter motor drive – general description	15
Dynamo – testing in position	7	Starter motor drive – removal and assembly	16
Fault diagnosis – electrical system	37	Starter motor – general description	11
Front side lights and indicator lights – bulb renewal	25	Starter motor – removal and refitting	13
Fuses – general	20	Starter motor – testing in position	12
General description	1	Tail and stop lights – bulb renewal	26
Headlights – adjustment	24	Voltage regulator – adjustment	19
Headlights – bulb renewal	22	Windscreen wiper arms and blades – removal and renewal	31
Headlights – sealed beam renewal	23	Windscreen wiper – fault diagnosis	32
Heater unit – general	34	Windscreen wiper mechanism – maintenance	30
Horns – fault tracing and rectification	21	Windscreen wiper motor, gearbox and wheelbox – removal and refitting	33
Instrument panel lights – bulb renewal	28		

Specifications

System type .... 12 volt – Positive earth (ground)

Battery type .... 6 volt (2 off)

Dynamo .... Lucas C39PV/2 early models, Lucas C40/1 later models

	C39PV/2	**C40/1**
Maximum output	19 amps	22 amps
No. of brushes	Two	Two
Minimum permissible brush length	0.34 in (8.7 mm)	0.28 in (7.1 mm)
Brush spring tension	22 to 25 oz (620 to 700 g)	30 to 33 oz (850 to 930 g)
Field resistance	6.0 ohms	6.0 ohms
Commutator – minimum undercut diameter	Not permissible	1.450 in (36.8 mm)
Commutator undercut dimensions:		
Width	—	0.040 in (1.016 mm)
Depth	—	0.020 to 0.035 in (0.508 to 0.889 mm)

Starter motor

Type .... Lucas M35G/1. 4 brush
Minimum permissible brush length .... $\frac{5}{16}$ in
Brush spring tension:
    Maximum .... 30 to 34 oz (850 to 960 g)
    Minimum .... 25 oz (700 g)

Regulator/control box

Type .... Lucas RB106/2 or modified RB106/2
Cut-in voltage .... 12.7 to 13.3 volts
Drop-off voltage .... 8.5 to 11.0 volts
Reverse current .... 3.0 to 5.0 amps (max)

Chapter 10 Electrical system

Voltage setting at 3000 rpm:
    Regulator RB 1 06/2 (modified) .... 10°C (50°F) 16.1 to16.7 amps
    20°C (68°F) 16.0 to 16.6 amps
    30°C (86°F) 15.9 to 16.5 amps
    40°C (104°F) 15.8 to 16.4 amps
    Regulator RB106/2 .... 10°C (50°F) 15.5 to 16.5 amps
    20°C (68°F) 15.4 to 16.4 amps
    30°C (86°F) 15.3 to 16.3 amps
    40°C (104°F) 15.2 to 16.2 amps

Windscreen wiper
Type .... Lucas DR. 3A single speed
Normal running current .... 2.7 to 3.4 amps
Drive to wheelbox .... Rack and cable
Armature end float .... 0.008 to 0.012 in (0.20 to 0.30 mm)
Armature resistance .... 0.28 to 0.35 ohms
Field resistance .... 8 to 9.5 ohms

Fuse unit
No. of fuses .... 2 by 35 amps
No. of spare fuses in holder .... 2 by 35 amps

Bulbs
    Watts
Headlamps 50/40
Headlamps (Europe except France-dip vertical) 45/40
Headlamps (Export LHD and USA – dip right) 50/40
Pilot with flashing direction indicator lamps 21/6
Rear flashing direction indicator lamps 21
Stop and tail lamps 21/6
Number plate lamp 6
Panel lights 2.2

1 General description

The electrical system is of the 12-volt type and the major components comprise: Two six-volt batteries wired in series with the positive terminal earthed; A voltage regulator and cut-out; A 12-volt two brush Lucas dynamo fitted to the front right-hand side of the engine and driven by the fan belt from the crankshaft pulley wheel; and a Lucas starter motor which is fitted to the end plate and gearbox bellhousing on the right-hand side. A standard Lucas wiring harness made up with the usual colour scheme is utilised. Feedwires are of one colour and wires from the switches contain a tracer colour.

The two six volt batteries supply a steady current of 12 volts for the ignition, lighting and other electrical circuits, and provide a reserve of electricity when the current consumed by the electrical equipment exceeds that being produced by the dynamo.

The dynamo is of the two brush type and works in conjunction with the voltage regulator and cut-out. The dynamo is cooled by a multi-bladed fan mounted behind the dynamo pulley, and blows air through cooling holes in the dynamo end brackets. The output from the dynamo is controlled by the voltage regulator which ensures a high output if the battery is in a low state of charge or the demands from the electrical equipment high, and a low output if the battery is fully charged and there is little demand from the electrical equipment.

2 Batteries – removal and refitting

1 The batteries are located in carriers directly under the hood stowage compartment floor at the rear of the seats. Remove/inspect as follows.
2 Hinge the seat backs forward and pivot the hood unit out of the compartment at the rear of the seats. Unclip and remove the floor panel for general access to the batteries.
3 Disconnect the respective positive (earth), then the negative leads from the batteries by slackening the clamp nuts and bolts, or by unscrewing the retaining screws if the lead clamps have been modified. It may be necessary to clean off the terminals where heavy corrosive build up has occurred. Chip the worst off with a screwdriver and then pour hot water over the terminal to remove the worst of the corrosion deposits.
4 Note the respective lead connections as they are disconnected.
5 Remove the respective battery clamps and lift each battery in turn out of its location. Hold the batteries vertical as they are removed to prevent spillage of electrolyte.
6 Refitting is a direct reversal of this procedure. Refit the negative lead before the earth (positive) lead and smear the terminals with petroleum jelly (vaseline) to prevent corrosion. *Never* use an ordinary grease as applied to other parts of the car.

3 Battery maintenance and inspection

1 Normal weekly battery maintenance consists of checking the electrolyte level of each cell to ensure that the separators are covered by 0.25 in (6 mm) of electrolyte. If the level has fallen top up the battery using distilled water only (photo). Do not overfill. If a battery is overfilled or any electrolyte spilled, immediately wipe away the excess as electrolyte attacks and corrodes any metal it comes into contact with very rapidly.
2 As well as keeping the terminals clean and covered with petroleum jelly, the top of the battery, and especially the top of the cells, should be kept clean and dry. This helps prevent corrosion and ensures that the battery does not become partially discharged by leakage through dampness and dirt.
3 Once every three months remove the battery and inspect the battery securing bolts, the battery clamp plate, tray, and battery leads for corrosion (white fluffy deposits on the metal which are brittle to touch). If any corrosion is found, clean off the deposits with ammonia and paint over the clean metal with an anti-rust/anti-acid paint.
4 At the same time inspect the battery case for cracks. If a crack is found, clean and plug it with one of the proprietary compounds made for this purpose. If leakage through the crack has been excessive then it will be necessary to refill the appropriate cell with fresh electrolyte as detailed later. Cracks are frequently caused to the top of the battery cases by pouring in distilled water in the middle of winter *after* instead of *before* a run. This gives the water no chance to mix with the electrolyte and so the former freezes and splits the battery case.
5 If topping-up the battery becomes excessive and the case has been inspected for cracks that could cause leakage, but none are found, the battery is being overcharged and the voltage regulator will have to be checked and reset.
6 With the battery on the bench at the three monthly interval check, measure its specific gravity with a hydrometer to determine the state of charge and condition of the electrolyte. There should be very little variation between the different cells and if a variation in excess of 0.025 is present it will be due to either:

(a) Loss of electrolyte from the battery at some time caused by spillage or a leak resulting in a drop in the specific gravity of the electrolyte, when the deficiency was replaced with distilled water instead of fresh electrolyte

(b) An internal short circuit caused by buckling of the plates or a similar malady pointing to the likelihood of total battery failure in the near future

7 The specific gravity of the electrolyte for fully charged conditions at the electrolyte temperature indicated, is listed in Table A. The specific gravity of a fully discharged battery at different temperatures of the electrolyte is given in Table B.

Table A
Specific Gravity – Battery Fully Charged
1.268 at 100°F or 38°C electrolyte temperature
1.272 at   90°F or 32°C electrolyte temperature
1.276 at   80°F or 27°C electrolyte temperature
1.280 at   70°F or 21°C electrolyte temperature
1.284 at   60°F or 16°C electrolyte temperature
1.288 at   50°F or 10°C electrolyte temperature
1.292 at   40°F or   4°C electrolyte temperature
1.296 at   30°C or -1.1°C electrolyte temperature

Table B
Specific Gravity – Battery Fully Discharged
1.098 at 100°F or 38°C electrolyte temperature
1.102 at   90°F or 32°C electrolyte temperature
1.106 at   80°F or 27°C electrolyte temperature
1.110 at   70°F or 21°C electrolyte temperature
1.114 at   60°F or 16°C electrolyte temperature
1.118 at   50°F or 10°C electrolyte temperature
1.122 at   40°F or   4°C electrolyte temperature
1.126 at   30°F or -1.1°C electrolyte temperature

4 Battery electrolyte replenishment

1 If the battery is in a fully charged state and one of the cells maintains a specific gravity reading which is 0.025 or more lower than the others, and a check of each cell has been made with a voltage meter to check for short circuits (a four to seven second test should give a steady reading of between 1.2 to 1.8 volts), then it is likely that electrolyte has been lost from the cell with the low reading at some time.
2 Top the cell up with a solution of 1 part sulphuric acid to 2.5 parts of water. If the cell is already fully topped up draw some electrolyte out of it with a pipette.
3 When mixing the sulphuric acid and water *never add water to sulphuric acid* – always pour the acid slowly onto the water in a glass container. *If water is added to sulphuric acid it will explode.*
4 Continue to top-up the cell with the freshly made electrolyte and then recharge the battery and check the hydrometer readings.

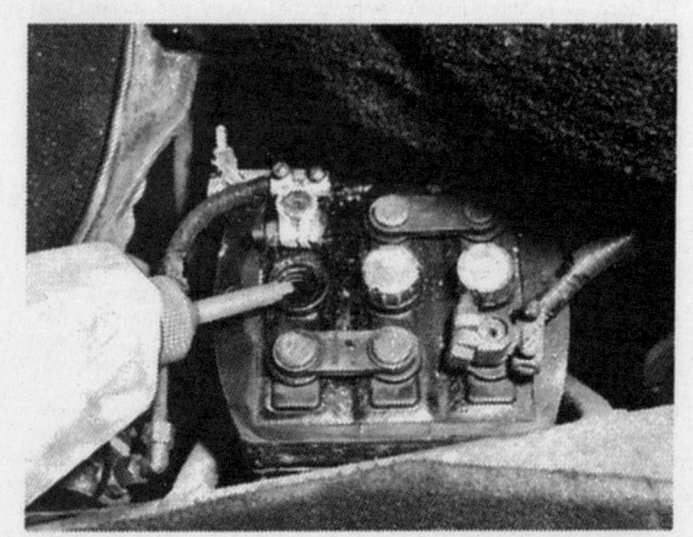

3.1 Top-up the battery cells when required – wipe any spillage dry

5 Battery charging

1 In winter time when heavy demand is placed upon the battery, such as when starting from cold, and much electrical equipment is continually in use, it is a good idea to occasionally have the batteries fully charged from an external source at the rate of 3.5 to 4 amps.
2 Continue to charge the battery at this rate until no further rise in specific gravity is noted over a four hour period.
3 Alternatively, a trickle charger charging at the rate of 1.5 amps can be safely used overnight.
4 Specially rapid 'boost' charges which are claimed to restore the power of the battery in 1 to 2 hours are most dangerous as they can cause serious damage to the battery plates through over-heating.
5 While charging the battery the temperature of the electrolyte should never exceed 37°C (100°F).

6 Dynamo – routine maintenance

1 Routine maintenance consists of checking the tension of the fan belt, and lubricating the dynamo rear bearing once every 6000 miles.
2 The fan belt should be tight enough to ensure no slip between the belt and the dynamo pulley. If a shrieking noise comes from the engine when the unit is accelerated rapidly, it is likely that it is the fan belt slipping. On the other hand, the belt must not be too taut or the bearings will wear rapidly and cause dynamo failure or bearing seizure. Ideally 0.5 in (13 mm) of total free movement should be available at the fan belt midway between the fan and the dynamo pulley.
3 Due to the close proximity of the radiator, accessibility to the dynamo mounting/adjusting bolts is not very good on the earlier models. Therefore to save a lot of frustration, it is recommended that the radiator be removed for greater access.
4 To adjust the fan belt tension slightly slacken the three dynamo retaining bolts, and swing the dynamo on the upper two bolts outwards to increase the tension, and inwards to lower it.
5 It is best to leave the bolts fairly tight so that considerable effort has to be used to move the dynamo; otherwise it is difficult to get the correct setting. If the dynamo is being moved outwards to increase the tension and the bolts have only been slackened a little, a long spanner acting as a lever placed behind the dynamo with the lower end resting against the block works very well in moving the dynamo outwards. Retighten the dynamo bolts and check that the dynamo pulley is correctly aligned with the fan belt.
6 Lubrication of the dynamo consists of inserting three drops of SAE 30 engine oil in the small oil hole in the centre of the commutator end bracket. This lubricates the rear bearing. The front bearing is prepacked with grease and requires no attention.

7 Dynamo – testing in position

1 If, with the engine running no charge comes from the dynamo, or the charge is very low, first check that the fan belt is in place and is not slipping. Then check that the leads from the control box to the dynamo are firmly attached and that one has not come loose from its terminal.
2 The lead from the 'D' terminal on the dynamo should be connected to the 'D' terminal on the control box, and similarly the 'F' terminals on the dynamo and control box should also be connected together. Check that this is so and that the leads have not been incorrectly fitted.
3 Make sure none of the electrical equipment (such as the lights or radio) is on and then pull the leads off the dynamo terminals marked 'D' and 'F', joining the terminals together with a short length of wire.
4 Attach to the centre of this length of wire the negative clip of a 0-20 volts voltmeter and run the other clip to earth on the dynamo yoke. Start the engine and allow it to idle at approximately 750 rpm. At this speed the dynamo should give a reading of about 15 volts on the voltmeter. There is no point in raising the engine speed above a fast idle as the reading will then be inaccurate.
5 If no reading is recorded then check the brushes and brush connections. If a very low reading of approximately 1 volt is observed then the field windings may be suspect.
6 If a reading of between 4 to 6 amps is recorded it is likely that the armature winding is at fault.
7 Remove the dynamo cover band and check the dynamo and brushes in position.

Chapter 10 Electrical system

8 If the voltmeter shows a good reading then with the temporary link still in position connect both leads from the control box to 'D' and 'F' on the dynamo ('D' to 'D' and 'F' to 'F'). Release the lead from the 'D' terminal at the control box and clip one lead from the voltmeter to the end of the cable, and the other lead to a good earth. With the engine running at the same speed as previously, an identical voltage to that recorded at the dynamo should be noted on the voltmeter. If no voltage is recorded then there is a break in the wire. If the voltage is the same as recorded at the dynamo then check the 'F' lead in a similar fashion. If both readings are the same as at the dynamo then it will be necessary to test the control box.

8 Dynamo – removal and refitting

1 Slacken the two dynamo retaining bolts, and the nut on the sliding link, and move the dynamo in towards the engine so that the fan belt can be removed.
2 Disconnect the two leads from the dynamo terminals.
3 Remove the nut from the sliding link bolt, and remove the two upper bolts. The dynamo is then free to be lifted away from the engine.
4 Refitting is a reversal of the removal procedure. Do not finally tighten the retaining bolts and the nut on the sliding link until the fan belt has been tensioned correctly. See Section 6 for details.

9 Dynamo – dismantling and inspection

1 Mount the dynamo in a vice and unscrew and remove the two through bolts from the commutator end bracket (photo).
2 Mark the commutator end bracket and the dynamo casing so the end bracket can be replaced in its original position. Pull the end bracket off the armature shaft. Some versions of the dynamo may have a raised pip on the end bracket which locates in a recess on the edge of the casing. If so, marking the end bracket and casing is not necessary. A pipe may also be found on the drive end bracket at the opposite end of the casing.
3 Lift the two brush springs and draw the brushes out of the brush holders (arrowed in photo).
4 Measure the brushes and if worn down to 0.28 in (7 mm) or less unscrew the screws holding the brush leads to the end bracket. Take off the brushes complete with leads.
5 If no locating pip can be found, mark the drive end bracket and the dynamo casing so the drive end bracket can be refitted in its original position. Pull the drive end bracket complete with armature out of the casing (photo).
6 Check the condition of the ball bearing in the drive end plate by firmly holding the plate and noting if there is visible side movement of the armature shaft in relation to the end plate. If play is present the armature assembly must be separated from the endplate. If the bearing is sound there is no need to carry out the work described in the following two paragraphs.
7 Hold the armature in one hand (mount it carefully in a soft jawed vice if preferred) and undo the nut holding the pulley wheel and fan in place. Pull off the pulley wheel and fan.
8 Next remove the woodruff key (arrowed in photo) from its slot in the armature shaft and also the bearing locating ring.
9 Place the drive end bracket across the open jaws of a vice with the armature downwards and gently tap the armature shaft from the bearing in the end plate with the aid of a suitable drift (photo).
10 Carefully inspect the armature and check it for open or short circuited windings. It is a good indication of an open circuit armature when the commutator segments are burnt. If the armature has short circuited the commutator segments will be very badly burnt, and the overheated armature windings badly discoloured. If open or short circuits are suspected then test by substituting the suspect armature for a new one.
11 Check the resistance of the field coils. To do this, connect an ohmmeter between the field terminal and the yoke and note the reading on the ohmmeter which should be about 6 ohms. If the ohmmeter reading is infinity this indicates an open circuit in the field winding. If the ohmmeter reading is below 5 ohms this indicates that one of the field coils is faulty and must be renewed.
12 Field coil renewal involves the use of a wheel operated screwdriver, a soldering iron, caulking and riveting and this operation is considered to be beyond the scope of most owners. Therefore, if the field coils are at fault either purchase a rebuilt dynamo, or take the casing to a Leyland dealer or electrical engineering works for new field coils to be fitted.
13 Next check the condition of the commutator (arrowed in photo). If it is dirty and blackened as shown clean it with a petrol damped rag. If the commutator is in good condition the surface will be smooth and quite free from pits or burnt areas, and the insulated segments clearly defined.
14 If, after the commutator has been cleaned pits and burnt spots are still present, wrap a strip of glass paper round the commutator taking great care to move the commutator $\frac{1}{4}$ of a turn every ten rubs till it is thoroughly clean (photo).
15 When badly worn, the commutator can be mounted in a lathe and with the lathe turning at high speed, a very fine cut may be taken off the commutator. Then polish the commutator with glass paper. If the commutator has worn so that the insulators betweens the segments are level with the top of the segments, then undercut the insulators to a depth of 0.03 in (8 mm). The best tool to use for this purpose is half a hacksaw blade ground to a thickness of the insulator, and with the handle end of the blade covered in insulating tape to make it comfortable to hold.
16 Check the bush bearing in the commutator end bracket for wear by noting if the armature spindle rocks when placed in it. If worn it must be renewed.
17 The bush bearing can be removed by a suitable extractor or by screwing a 0.63 in (16 mm) tap four or five times into the bush. The tap complete with bush is then pulled out of the end bracket.
18 Before fitting the new bush bearing that it is the porous bronze type, it is essential that it is allowed to stand in engine oil for at least 24 hours before fitment. In an emergency the bush can be immersed in hot oil (100°C) for 2 hours.
19 Carefully fit the new bush into the end plate, pressing it in until the end of the bearing is flush with the inner side of the end plate. If available press the bush in with a smooth shouldered mandrel the same diameter as the armature shaft.

10 Dynamo – repair and assembly

1 To renew the ball bearing fitted to the drive end bracket drill out the rivets which hold the bearing retainer plate to the end bracket and lift off the plate.
2 Press out the bearing from the end bracket and remove the corrugated and felt washers from the bearing housing.
3 Thoroughly clean the bearing housing, and the new bearing and pack with high melting point grease.
4 Place the felt washer and corrugated washer in that order in the end bracket bearing housing.
5 Fit the new bearing.
6 Gently tap the bearing into place with the aid of a suitable drift (photo).
7 Refit the bearing plate and fit three new rivets (photo).
8 Open up the rivets with the aid of a suitable centre punch.
9 Finally peen over the open end of the rivets with the aid of a ball hammer.
10 Refit the drive end bracket to the armature shaft. Do not try and force the bracket on but with the aid of a suitable socket abuting the bearing tap the bearing on gently, so pulling the end bracket down with it (photo).
11 Slide the spacer up the shaft and refit the Woodruff key (photo).
12 Refit the fan and pulley wheel and then fit the spring washer and

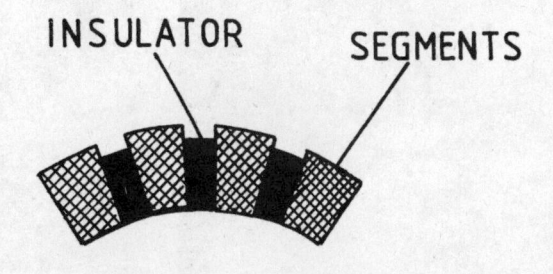

Fig. 10.1 How the dynamo commutator segments should look – end elevation (Sec 9)

9.1 Remove the end bracket with screws – note pip and notch for location (arrowed)

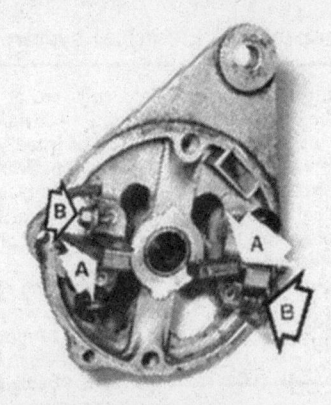

9.3 Withdraw the brushes from their holders (A) and if necessary detach leads from terminals (B)

9.5 Withdraw the drive end bracket and armature

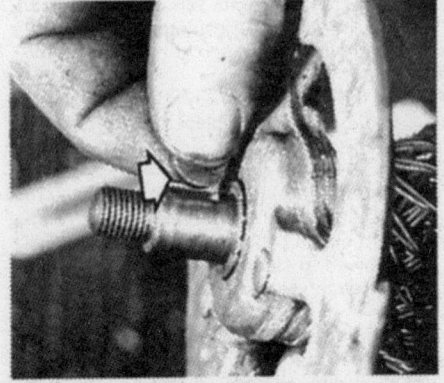

9.8 Extract the Woodruff key (arrowed)

9.9 Drive the shaft from the bearing

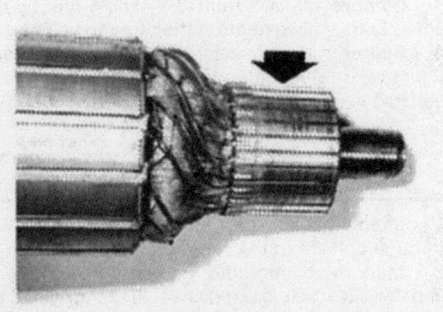

9.13 Check the commutator

9.14 Clean the commutator surface

10.6 Carefully insert the bearing

10.7 Refit the bearing plate with new rivets

10.10 Refit the end bracket

10.11 Fit spacer and key

10.12 The end bracket and armature reassembled

Chapter 10 Electrical system

10.15 Method of retaining brushes in position before fitting

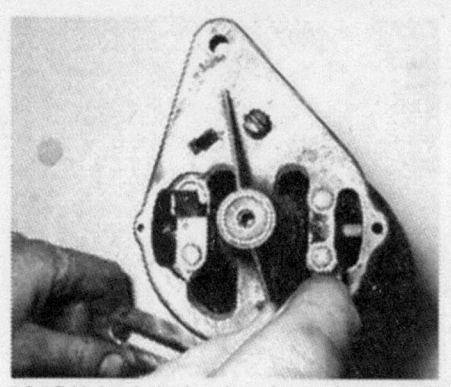

10.17 Unhook the brush springs using a small screwdriver inserted through the aperture each side as shown

12.4 The starter motor viewed from the top – note square section of armature – turn with spanner to ensure starter is not jammed

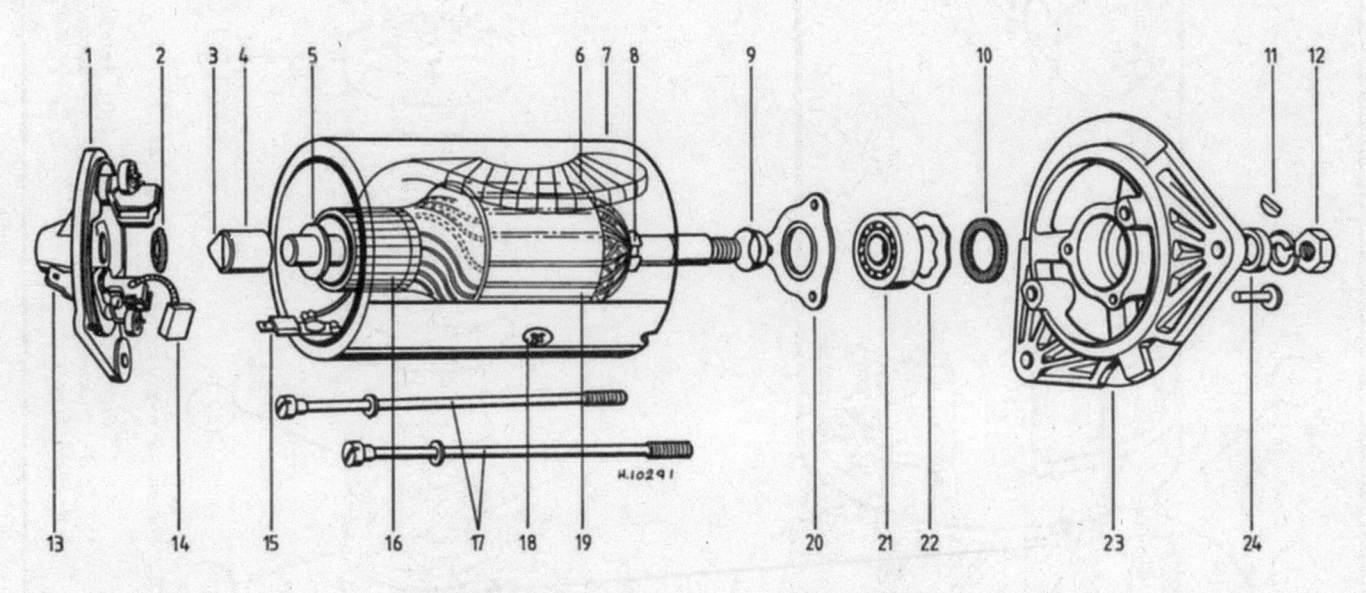

Fig. 10.2 The Lucas C40 dynamo components (Sec 10)

1 Commutator end bracket	7 Yoke	13 Output terminal 'D'	19 Armature
2 Felt ring	8 Shaft collar	14 Brushes	20 Bearing retaining plate
3 Felt ring retainer	9 Shaft collar retaining cup	15 Field terminal 'F'	21 Ball bearing
4 Bronze bush	10 Felt ring	16 Commutator	22 Corrugated washer
5 Thrust washer	11 Shaft key	17 Through-bolts	23 Driving end bracket
6 Field coils	12 Shaft nut	18 Pole-shoe securing screws	24 Pulley spacer

nut and tighten the latter. The drive bracket end of the dynamo is now fully assembled as shown (photo).

13 If the brushes are little worn and are to be used again then ensure that they are placed in the same holders from which they were removed. When refitting brushes, either new or old, check that they move freely in their holders. If either brush sticks, clean with a petrol moistened rag and if still stiff, lightly polish the sides of the brush with a very fine file until the brush moves quite freely in its holder.

14 Tighten the two retaining screws and washers which hold the wire leads to the brushes in place.

15 It is far easier to slip the end piece with brushes over the commutator if the brushes are raised in their holders as shown and held in this position by the pressure of the springs resting against their flanks (arrowed in photo).

16 Refit the armature to the casing and then the commutator end plate and screw up the two through bolts.

17 Finally, hook the ends of the two springs off the flanks of the brushes and onto their heads so the brushes are forced down into contact with the armature (photo).

11 Starter motor – general description

The starter motor is mounted on the right-hand lower side of the engine end plate, and is held in position by two bolts which also clamp the bellhousing flange. The motor is of the four field coil, four pole piece type, and utilises four spring-loaded commutator brushes. Two of these brushes are earthed, and the other two are insulated and attached to the field coil ends.

12 Starter motor – testing in position

1 If the starter motor fails to operate then check the condition of the battery by turning on the headlamps. If they glow brightly for several seconds and then gradually dim, the battery is in an uncharged condition.

2 If the headlamps glow brightly and it is obvious that the battery is in good condition then check the tightness of the battery wiring con-

Fig. 10.3 The starter motor components (Sec 14)

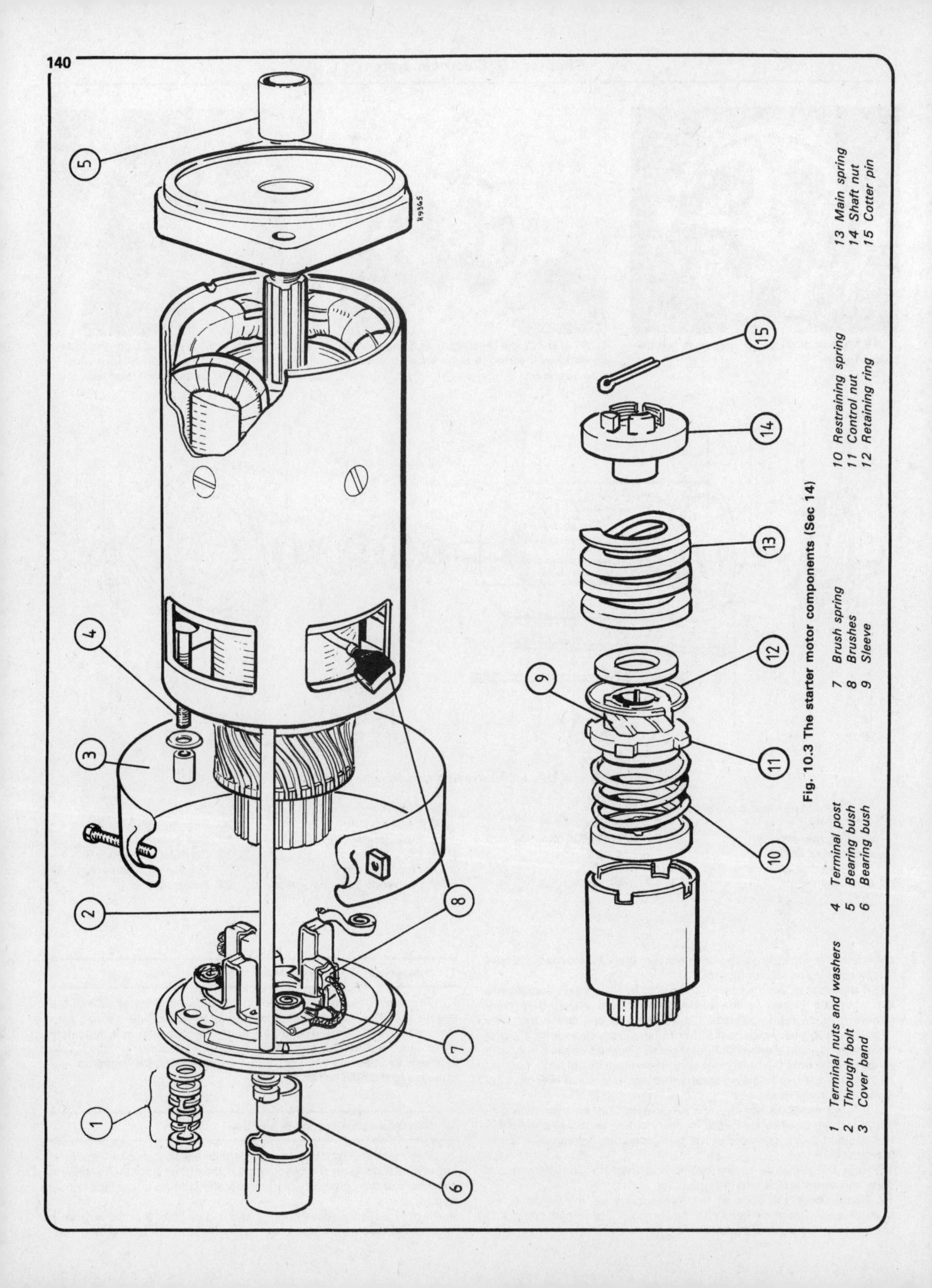

1 Terminal nuts and washers
2 Through bolt
3 Cover band
4 Terminal post
5 Bearing bush
6 Bearing bush
7 Brush spring
8 Brushes
9 Sleeve
10 Restraining spring
11 Control nut
12 Retaining ring
13 Main spring
14 Shaft nut
15 Cotter pin

Chapter 10 Electrical system

14.1a Detach the starter cover band and ...

14.1b ... pulling back the springs, withdraw the brushes

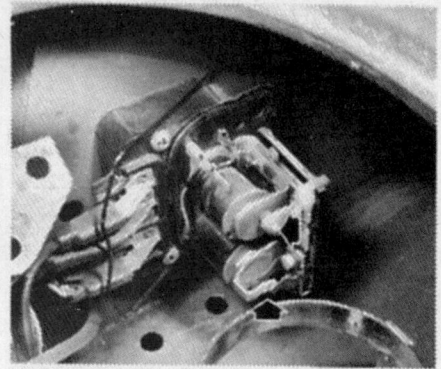

18.1 The regulator unit with cover removed – clean contact points arrowed

nections (and in particular the earth lead from the battery terminal to its connection on the bodyframe). Check the tightness of the connections at the relay switch and at the starter motor. Check the wiring with a voltmeter for breaks or shorts.

3 If the wiring is in order then check that the starter motor switch is operating. To do this press the rubber covered button in the centre of the relay switch under the bonnet. If it is working the starter motor will be heard to 'click' as it tries to rotate. Alternatively check it with a voltmeter.

4 If the battery is fully charged, the wiring in order, and the switch working and the starter motor fails to to operate then it will have to be removed from the car for examination. Before this is done, however, ensure that the starter pinion has not jammed in mesh with the flywheel. Check by turning the square end of armature shaft with a spanner. This will free the pinion if it is stuck in engagement with the flywheel teeth (photo).

13 Starter motor – removal and refitting

1 Disconnect the battery earth lead from the positive terminal.
2 Disconnect the starter motor cable from the terminal on the starter motor end plate.
3 Unscrew the two starter motor bolts.
4 Lift the starter motor out of engagement with the teeth on the flywheel ring and pull it forwards towards the radiator until it can be lifted clear.
5 Refitting is a straight reversal of the removal procedure.

14 Starter motor – dismantling and reassembly

1 With the starter motor on the bench, loosen the screw on the cover band and slip the cover band off. With a piece of wire bent into the shape of a hook, lift back each of the brush springs in turn and check the movement of the brushes in their holders by pulling on the flexible connectors (photos). If the brushes are so worn that their faces do not rest against the commutator, or if the end of the brush leads are exposed on their working face, they must be renewed.

2 If any of the brushes tend to stick in their holders then wash them with a petrol moistened cloth and, if necessary, lightly polish the sides of the brush with a very fine file, until the brushes move quite freely in their holders.

3 If the surface of the commutator is dirty or blackened, clean it with a petrol dampened rag. Secure the starter motor in a vice and check it by connecting a heavy gauge cable between the starter motor terminal and a 12-volt battery.

4 Connect the cable from the other battery terminal to earth in the starter motor body. If the motor turns at high speed it is in good order.

5 If the starter motor still fails to function or if it is wished to renew the brushes, then it is necessary to further dismantle the motor.

6 Lift the brush springs with the wire hook and lift all four brushes out of their holders one at a time.

7 Remove the terminal nuts and washers from the terminal post on the commutator end bracket.

8 Unscrew the two through bolts which hold the end plates together and pull off the commutator end bracket. Also remove the driving end bracket which will come away complete with the armature.

9 At this stage if the brushes are to be renewed, their flexible connectors must be unsoldered and the connectors of new brushes soldered in their place. Check that the new brushes move freely in their holders as detailed above. If cleaning the commutator with petrol fails to remove all the burnt areas and spots, then wrap a piece of glass paper round the commutator and rotate the armature.

10 If the commutator is very badly worn, remove the drive gear as detailed in the following section. Then mount the armature in a lathe and with the lathe turning at high speed, take a very fine cut out of the commutator and finish the surface by polishing with glass paper. *Do not undercut the mica insulators between the commutator segments.*

11 With the starter motor dismantled, test the four field coils for an open circuit. Connect a 12-volt battery with a 12-volt bulb in one of the leads between the field terminal post and the tapping point of the field coils to which the brushes are connected. An open circuit is proved by the bulb not lighting.

12 If the bulb lights, it does not necessarily mean that the field coils are in order, as there is a possibility that one of the coils will be earthing to the starter yoke or pole shoes. To check this, remove the lead from the brush connector and place it against a clean portion of the starter yoke. If the bulb lights the field coils are earthing. Renewal of the field coils calls for the use of a wheel operated screwdriver, a soldering iron, caulking and riveting operations and is beyond the scope of the majority of owners. The starter yoke should be taken to a reputable electrical engineering works for new field coils to be fitted. Alternatively, purchase an exchange Lucas starter motor.

13 If the armature is damaged this will be evident after visual inspection. Look for signs of burning, discolouration, and for conductors that have lifted away from the commutator.

14 With the starter motor stripped down check the condition of the bushes. They should be renewed when they are sufficiently worn to allow visible side movement of the armature shaft.

15 The old bushes are simply driven out with a suitable drift and the new bushes inserted by the same method. As the bearings are of the phosphor bronze type it is essential that they are allowed to stand in SAE 30 engine oil for at least 24 hours before fitment.

16 Reassembly is a straight reversal of the dismantling procedure.

15 Starter motor drive – general description

1 The starter motor drive is of the outboard type. When the starter motor is operated the pinion moves into contact with the flywheel gear ring by moving in towards the starter motor.

2 If the engine kicks back, or the pinion fails to engage with the flywheel ring gear when the starter motor is actuated no undue strain is placed on the armature shaft, as the pinion sleeve disengages from the pinion and turns independently.

16 Starter motor drive – removal and assembly

1 With the starter motor removed and held in a vice, extract the split pin from the shaft nut on the end of the starter drive.

Chapter 10 Electrical system

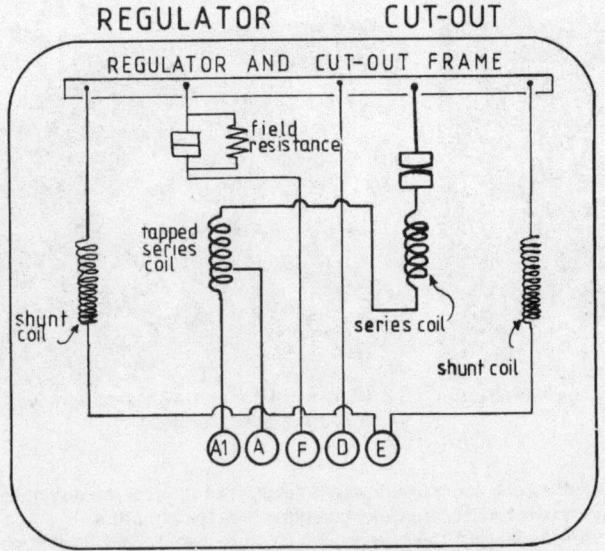

Fig. 10.4 The control box circuit diagram (Sec 17)

20.1 The fuse box with flasher unit alongside

2   Holding the squared end of the armature shaft at the commutator end bracket with a suitable spanner, unscrew the shaft nut which has a right-hand thread, and pull off the main-spring.
3   Slide the remaining parts with a rotary action off the armature shaft.
4   Reassembly is a straight reversal of the above procedure. Ensure that the split pin is refitted. **Note:** *It is most important that the drive gear is completely free from oil, grease and dirt. With the drive gear removed, clean all the parts thoroughly in paraffin. Under no circumstances oil the drive components. Lubrication of the drive components could easily cause the pinion to stick.*

17 Regulator control box – general description

1   The control box comprises the voltage regulator and the cut-out.
2   The voltage regulator controls the output from the dynamo depending on the state of the battery and the demands of the electrical equipment and ensures that the battery is not overcharged.
3   The cut-out is really an automatic switch and connects the dynamo to the battery when the dynamo is turning fast enough to produce a charge. Similarly it disconnects the battery from the dynamo when the engine is idling or stationary so that the battery does not discharge through the dynamo.
4   Both the regulator and cut-out are adjusted during manufacture and should not normally need further adjustment except for the reasons given in Section 19.

18 Regulator and cut-out contacts – maintenance

1   Every 12 000 miles (19 000 km) check the cut-out and regulator contacts. If they are dirty or rough or burnt, place a piece of fine glass paper *(do not use emery paper or carborundum paper)* between the cut-out contacts, close them naturally and draw the glass paper through several times (photo).
2   Clean the regulator contacts in exactly the same way, but use emery or carborundum paper and not glass paper. Carefully clean both sets of contacts from all traces of dust with a rag moistened in methylated spirits.

19 Voltage regulator – adjustment

1   If the battery is in sound condition, but is not holding its charge, or is being continually overcharged and the dynamo is in sound condition, then the voltage regulator in the control box must be adjusted.

Regulator adjustment

2   Check the regulator setting by removing and joining together the cables from the control box terminals A1 and A. Then connect the negative lead of a 20-volt voltmeter to the 'D' terminal on the dynamo and the positive lead to a good earth. Start the engine and increase its speed until the voltmeter needle flicks and then steadies. This should occur at about 2000 rpm. If the voltage at which the needle steadies is outside the limits listed below, then remove the control box cover and turn the adjusting screw, clockwise a quarter of a turn at a time to raise the setting and a similar amount, anti-clockwise, to lower it (Fig. 10.5).

Air temperature	Type RB 106/2 Open circuit voltage	Modified type RB106/2 Open circuit voltage
10°C or 50°F	16.1 to 16.7	15.9 to 16.5
20°C or 68°F	16.0 to 16.6	15.6 to 16.2
30°C or 86°F	15.9 to 16.5	15.4 to 16.0
40°C or 104°F	15.8 to 16.4	15.1 to 15.7

3   It is vital that the adjustments be completed within 30 seconds of starting the engine as otherwise the heat from the shunt coil will affect the readings.

Cut-out adjustment

4   Check the voltage required to operate the cut-out by connecting a voltmeter between the control box terminals 'D' and 'E'.
5   Remove the control box cover, start the engine and gradually increase its speed until the cut-out closes. This should occur when the reading is between 12·7 to 13·3 volts.
6   If the reading is outside these limits turn the cut-out adjusting screw in Fig. 10.5 a fraction at a time clockwise to raise the voltage, and anti-clockwise to lower it. To adjust the drop off voltage bend the fixed contact blade carefully. On early models shims are fitted at the rear of the fixed contact. The adjustment to the cut-out should be completed within 30 seconds of starting the engine as otherwise heat build-up from the shunt coil will affect the readings.
7   If the cut-out fails to work, clean the contacts, and, if there is still no response, renew the cut-out and regulator unit.

20 Fuses – general

1   Two fuses are fitted to a separate fuse holder positioned adjacent to the control box (photo). The fuse marked A1-A2 protects the electrical items such as the horn and lights, which function irrespective of whether the ignition is on or not.
2   The fuse marked A3-A4 protects the items which only operate when the ignition system is switched on, ie, the stop lights, fuel gauge, flasher unit, and windscreen wiper motor.
3   If either of these fuses blow due to a short circuit or similar trouble, trace and rectify the cause before renewing the fuse.

Chapter 10 Electrical system

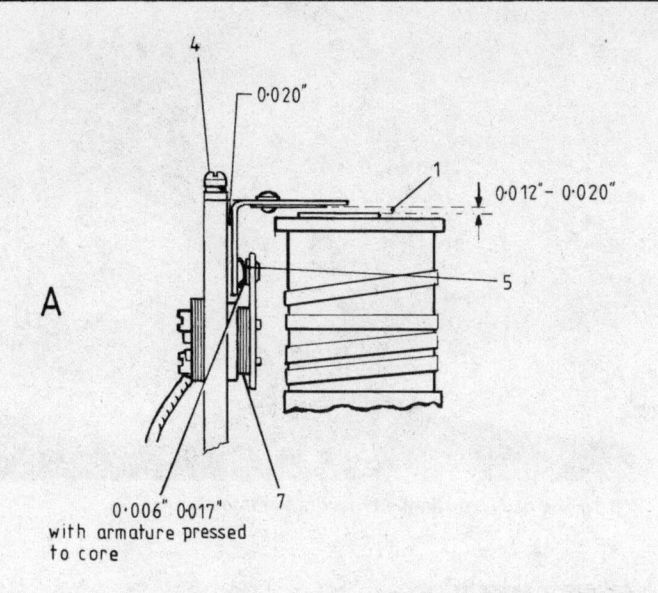

Fig. 10.5 Setting the regulator. Early type 'A'. Later type 'B' and cut-out 'C' (Sec 19)

1 Armature
2 Adjusting screw
3 Tension spring
4 Securing screw
5 Fixed contact blade
6 Fixed contact adjustment screw
7 Shims

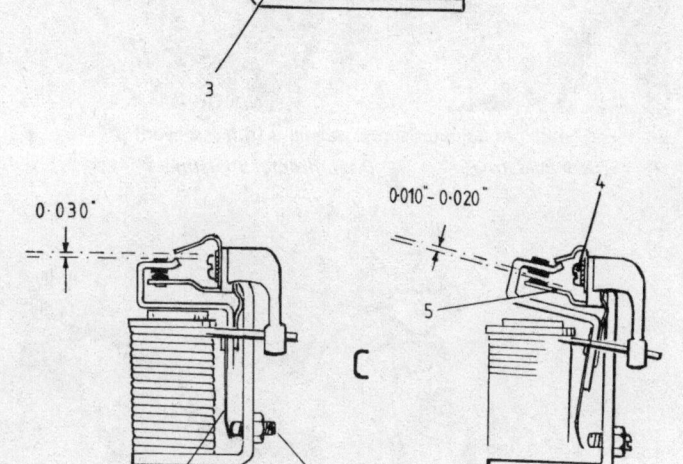

21 Horns – fault tracing and rectification

1 Should one or both of the horns operate poorly or possibly not at all, check the wiring to them for short circuits and loose connections.
2 Ensure that the horns are firmly secured and that there is nothing bearing against the horn body.
3 If the fault is not an external one remove the horn cover and check the leads inside the horn. If these are sound, check the contact breaker contacts. If these are burnt or dirty, clean them with a fine file and wipe all traces of dirt and dust away with a petrol moistened rag. Test the current consumption of the horn which should be between 3 and 3·5 amps.
4 The horns are not repairable and therefore should one become defective it must be renewed.

22 Headlights – bulb renewal

1 To remove the light unit to renew a bulb, unscrew the retaining screw at the bottom of the chromium plated rim, and gently prise the rim away from the rubber sealing ring.
2 Remove the rubber ring and press the light unit in onto the springs of the adjusting screws. Turn the light unit in an anti-clockwise direction until the heads of the screws come opposite the enlarged ends of the keyhole slots and withdraw the light unit.
3 The bulb holder is on the back of the light unit and is released by turning anti-clockwise.
4 Renew the defective bulb, making sure that the new bulb is properly seated in the holder.
5 Refitting of the bulb holder and light unit is a reversal of the removal procedure.

23 Headlights – sealed beam unit renewal

1 On later models sealed beam light units of Lucas manufacture are fitted. To remove this unit start by removing the rim fixing screw at the base of the rim and lift the rim off the locating lugs at the top of the headlight shell.
2 Remove the three cross-head screws holding the light unit rim, remove the rim and withdraw the light unit from its seating.
3 Disconnect the three pin socket from the light unit. Should a sealed beam fail, the whole unit will have to be renewed as owing to its sealed filaments no repairs are possible.
4 Refitting of a new unit is a direct reversal of the removal procedure.

24 Headlights – adjustment

1 On earlier cars without sealed beam units there are three adjusting screws, the screw at the top controls the vertical adjustment and the two side screws the horizontal adjustment (photo).
2 On models with sealed beam units there are only two adjusting screws. The top one being for vertical movement and the side one for horizontal movement.
3 Where possible adjustment should always be carried out using an optical-type beam setter or similar equipment. If this is not available the lights can be roughly aligned on a level piece of ground at night; checking both in the dipped and undipped position.

25 Front side lights and indicator lights – bulb renewal

1 On early models the side/indicator light lens and bulb are renewed as follows. To remove the lens simply push and twist it in an anti-clockwise direction. The bulb is then removed in a similar fashion (photos).
2 Refit in the reverse order and check light operation.
3 On later models the front side and indicator lights are as shown in Fig. 10.10. Individual bulbs were fitted instead of the twin filament type previously used. To remove the lens press and twist it clockwise. Remove the bulb/s in a similar fashion.

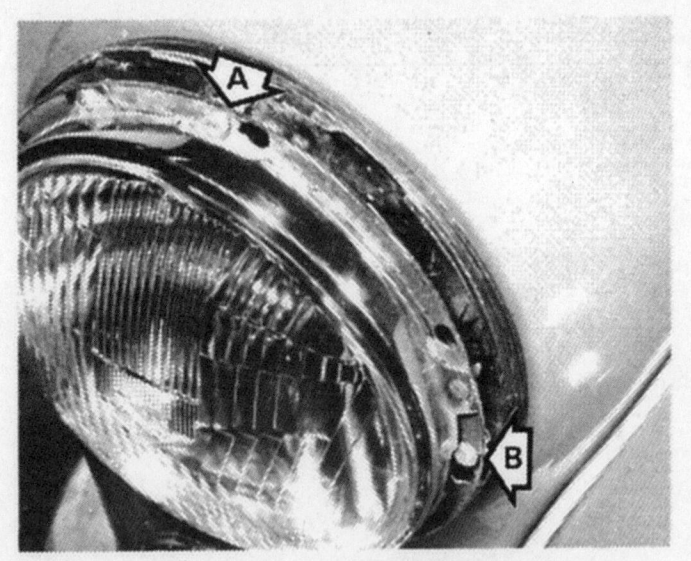

24.1 The headlight adjuster screw positions (rim removed)
A Vertical adjustment   B Horizontal adjustment

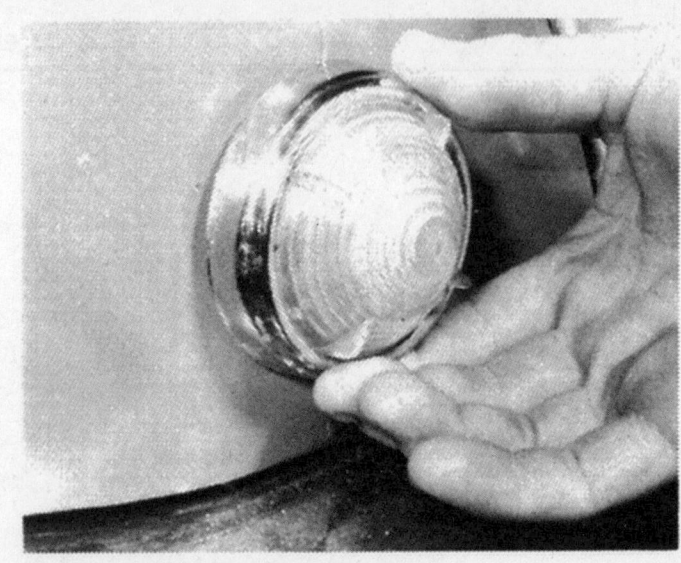

25.1a The early side light – twist rim to remove ...

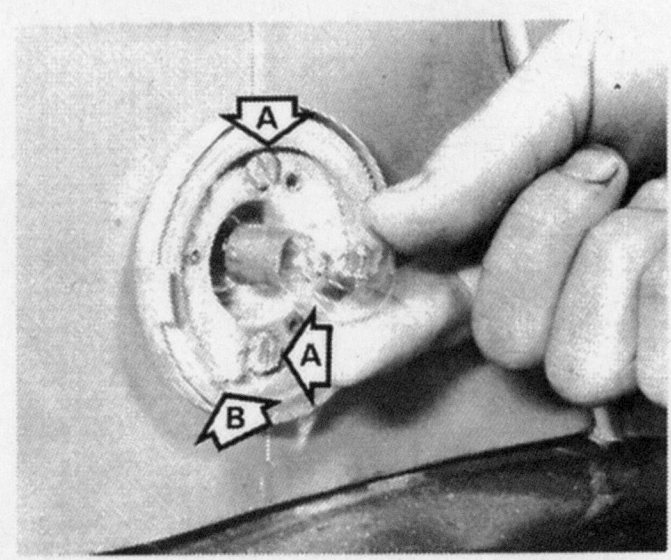

25.1b ... then extract bulb. Note unit retaining screws (A) and lens seal ring (B)

26.1a Remove lens retaining screws ...

26.1b ... and withdraw bulb from its holder

27.1 The number plate unit with lens removed

145

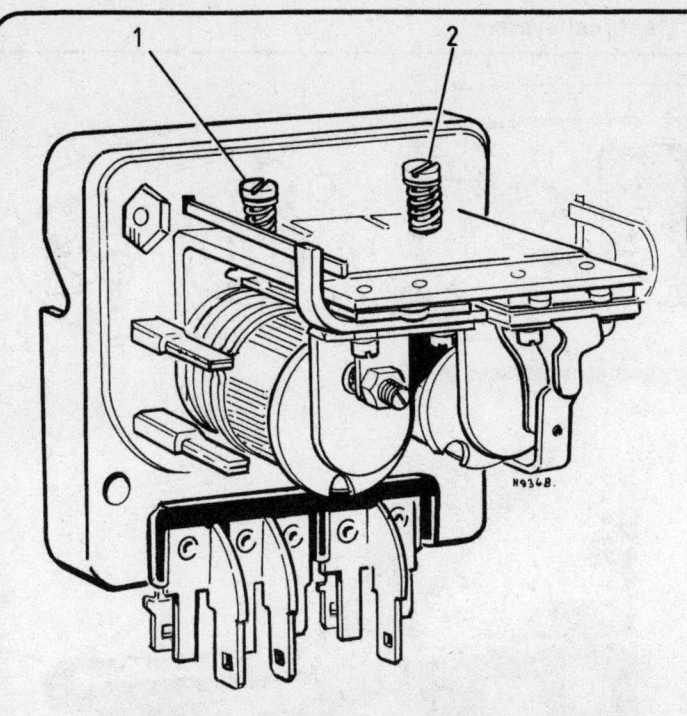

Fig. 10.6 The regulator and control box fitted to the later models showing the relevant spade connections and the regulator (1) and cut-out (2) adjustment screws (Sec 19)

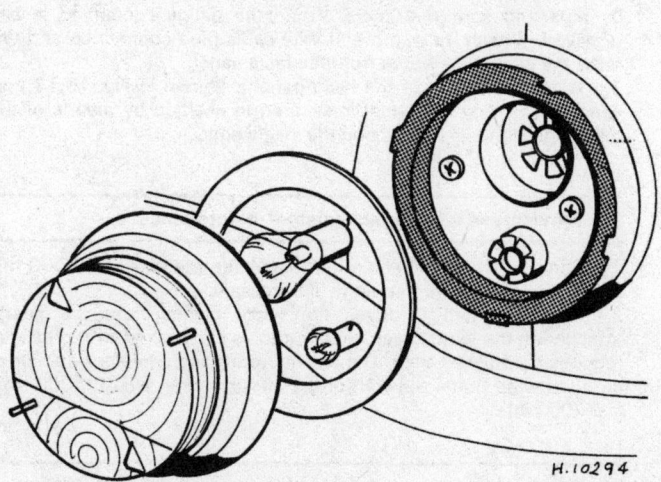

Fig. 10.7 Headlight unit – early models (Sec 22)

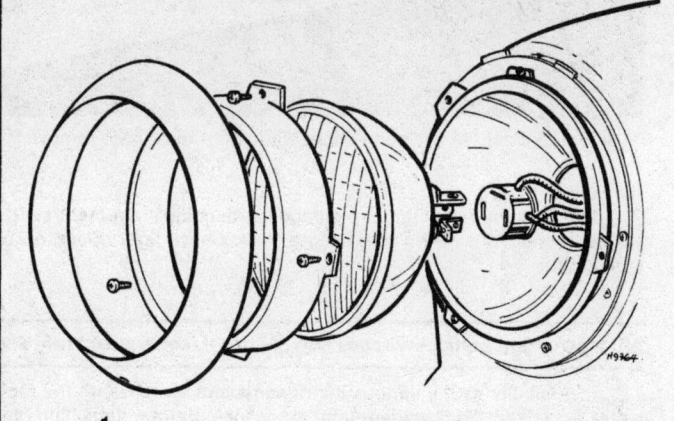

Fig. 10.8 Headlight unit – sealed beam type as fitted to later models (Sec 23)

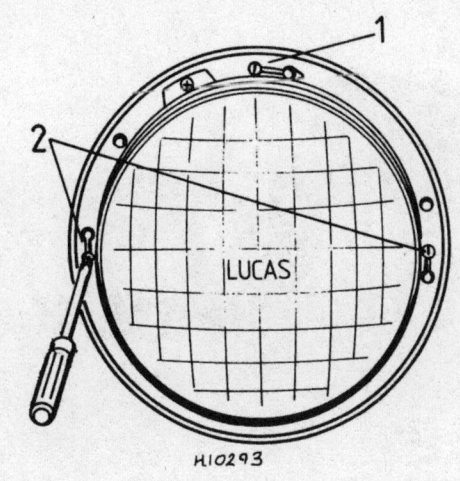

Fig. 10.9 Headlight beam adjustment screw positions (Sec 24)

1   Vertical adjuster screw   2   Horizontal adjuster screws

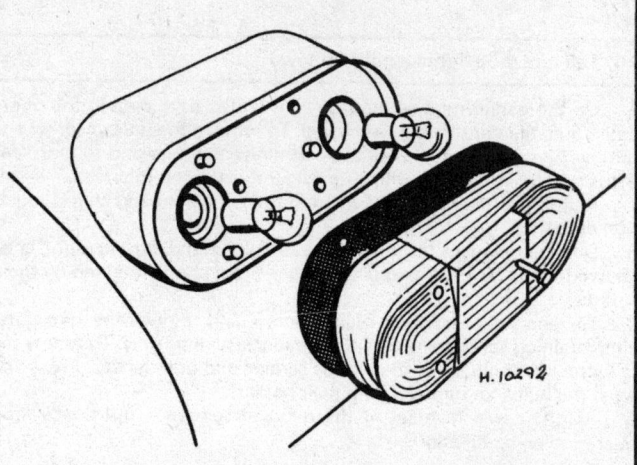

Fig. 10.11 The late type tail and stop lights (Sec 26)

◁ Fig. 10.10 The late type side/indicator light unit (Sec 25)

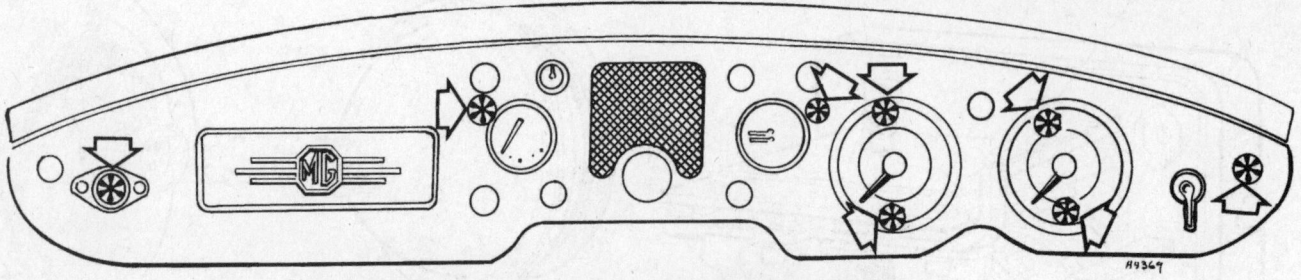

146　　　　　　　　　　　　　　　　　　　Chapter 10 Electrical system

Fig. 10.12 The instrument panel light locations (Sec 28)

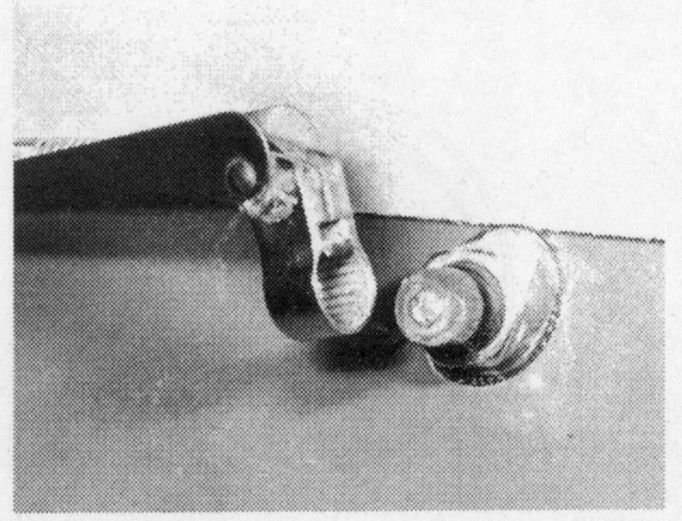

31.2 The wiper arm and pivot

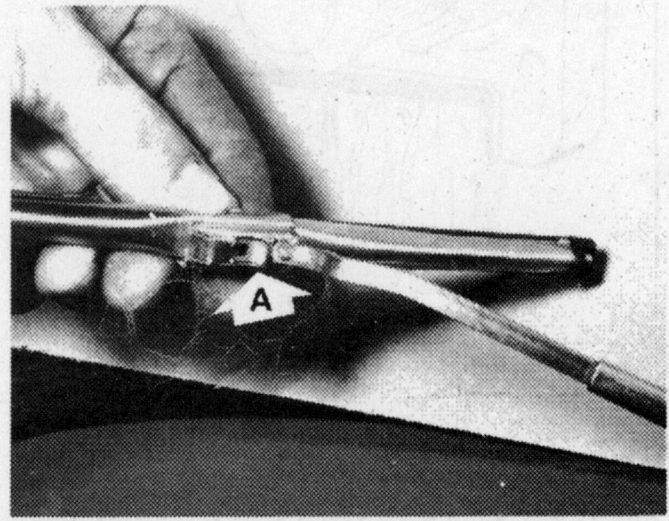

31.4 Pull retainer (A) and pivot wiper blade from the arm to remove

4　Refit in the reverse order but ensure that the lens seal is in good condition and check light operation on completion.

26　Tail and stop lights – bulb removal

1　On the earlier models the rear light unit is as shown in the photo and a dual filament bulb is employed. To remove the lens unscrew and remove the retaining screws and withdraw the lens and rubber seal. Press and twist the bulb within its holder to extract it (photos).
2　Refitting is the reverse of the removal sequence and check operation of light.
3　On later models the combined tail/brake and flasher light is as shown in Fig. 10.11. A two piece lens is fitted and is retained by three screws.
4　To renew the indicator bulb unscrew and remove the two outer lens retaining screws and remove the indicator lens only. To renew the tail/stop light bulb, remove all three screws and both lenses. Press and twist the bulbs for removal from their holders.
5　Refitting is a reversal of the removal sequence but check light operation on completion.

27　Number plate lights – bulb renewal

1　Unscrew the light cover retaining screw and detach the cover and lens. The bulbs can now be extracted from their holders by pressing and twisting them (photo).
2　Refitting is a reversal of the removal procedure but check light operation on completion.

28　Instrument panel lights – bulb renewal

1　The instrument panel bulb locations are indicated in Fig. 10.12. Access to the bulbs is obtainable from below the instrument panel on

the reverse face.
2　Care must be taken not to dislodge surrounding instrument/switch wiring connections when renewing a bulb. Check light operation on completion.

29　Instrument panel, switches and gauges – removal and refitting

1　Accessibility to the various instruments and switches on the facia panel is gained from underneath the panel. Before detaching any wiring it is advisable to disconnect the battery earth cable from its terminal. Make a note of the location of any of the wires on the switches before they are removed.
2　The gauges are secured in position by means of a clamp retained by nuts and spring washers. When the gauge concerned is being removed, detach its clamp and wire/cable pipe connection and withdraw the gauge rearwards from the facia panel.
3　A general layout of the facia panel is shown in Fig. 10.13 and it can be seen that the panel is secured in position by means of three main lugs along its top face on the inside edge.

30　Windscreen wiper mechanism – maintenance

1　Renew the windscreen wiper blades at intervals of 12 000 miles (19 000 km), or more frequently if necessary.
2　The cable which drives the wiper blades from the gearbox attached to the windscreen wiper motor is pre-packed with grease and requires no maintenance. The washer round the wheelbox spindle can be lubricated with several drops of glycerine every 6000 miles (10 000 km).

31　Windscreen wiper arms and blades – removal and refitting

1　Before removing a wiper arm, turn the windscreen wiper switch on

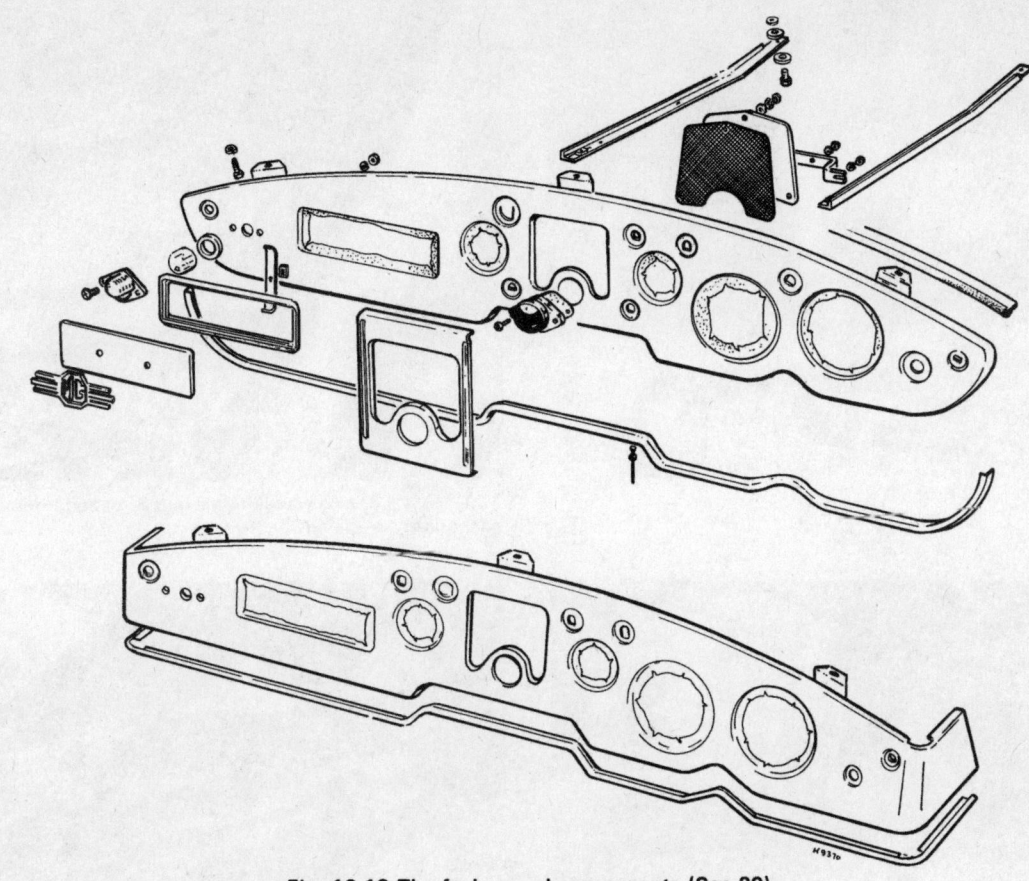

Fig. 10.13 The facia panel components (Sec 29)

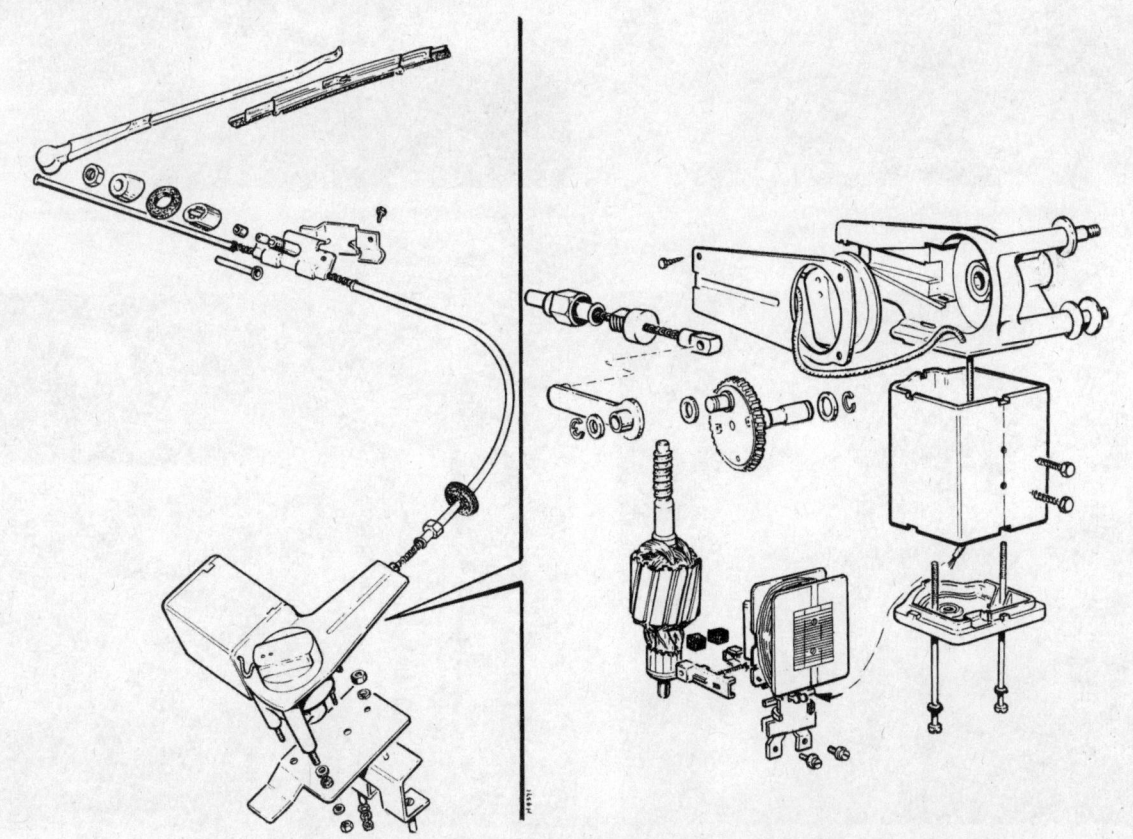

Fig. 10.14 The windscreen wiper motor and associate components layout (Sec 33)

33.2 The wiper motor

33.4 The wiper arm wheelbox viewed from underneath the dashboard

34.2a Check the pipes and connections for security

34.2b Lubricate the control cables and quadrants occasionally

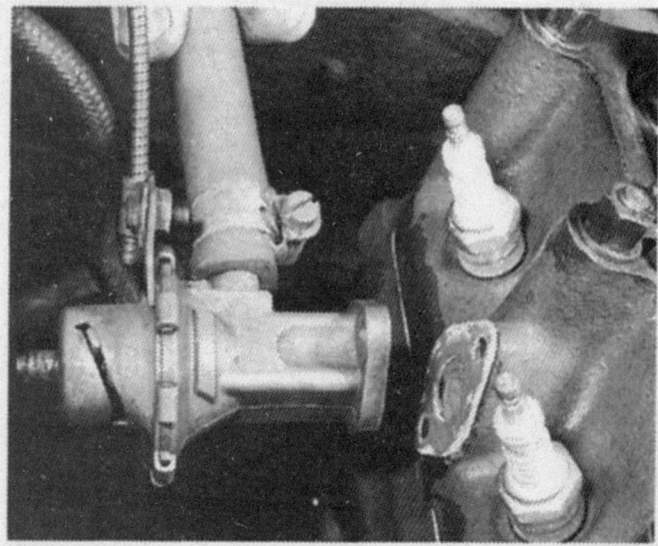

34.5 The heater control valve location on the 1500 engine – note new gasket

34.6 The flap valve control cable and clamp providing adjustment if necessary

Chapter 10 Electrical system

and off to ensure the arms are in their normal parked position parallel with the bottom of the windscreen.
2   To remove an arm, pivot the arm back and pull the wiper arm head off the splined drive (photo).
3   When refitting an arm position it so it is in the correct relative parked position and then press the arm head onto the splined drive till the retaining clip clicks into place.
4   The wiper blades can be removed and refitted without removing the arms. Spring the arm back from the screen and hinge the blade upwards (photo). Whenever a new rubber is being fitted extract the squeegee from the flexible carrier but be carefull not to lose any of the location pins.

32 Windscreen wiper – fault diagnosis

1   Should the windscreen wipers fail to park or park badly then check the limit switch on the gearbox cover (if a self parking motor is fitted). Loosen the four screws which retain the gearbox cover and place the projection close to the rim of the limit switch in line with the groove in the gearbox cover. Rotate the limit switch anti-clockwise 25° and tighten the four screws retaining the gearbox cover. If it is wished to park the windscreen wipers on the other side of the windscreen rotate the limit switch 180° clockwise.
2   Should the windscreen wipers fail, or work very slowly, then check the current the motor is taking by connecting up a 1-20 volt voltmeter in the circuit and turning on the wiper switch. Consumption should be between 2·3 to 3·1 amps.
3   If no current is passing through check the A3-A4 fuse. If the fuse has blown renew it after having checked the wiring of the motor and other electrical circuits serviced by this fuse for short circuits. If the fuse is in good condition check the wiper switch and the current operated thermostat (where fitted) by substitution.
4   If the wiper motor takes a very high current check the wiper blades for freedom of movement. If this is satisfactory check the gearbox cover and gear assembly for damage and measure the armature endfloat which should be between 0·008 to 0·012 in (0·20 to 0·30 mm). The endfloat is set by the adjusting screw. Check that excessive friction in the cable connecting tubes caused by too small a curvature is not the cause of the high current consumption.
5   If the motor takes a very low current ensure that the battery is fully charged. Check the brush gear after removing the commutator end bracket and ensure that the brushes are bearing on the commutator. If not, check the brushes for freedom of movement and if necessary renew the tension spring. Check the armature by substitution if this unit is suspected.

33 Windscreen wiper motor, gearbox and wheelbox – removal and refitting

1   Remove the windscreen wiper arms by lifting the blades, carefully raising the retaining clip and then pulling the arms off the splined drive shafts.
2   Disconnect the electrical cables from the wiper motor and release the outer cable from the gearbox housing (photo).
3   Unscrew and remove the nuts and spring washers which hold the wiper motor in position and lift off the motor unit.
4   The windscreen wiper arm wheelboxes are located immediately underneath the splined drive shafts over which the wiper arms fit. To remove these wheelboxes release the cable rack outer casings by slackening the wheelbox cover screws. Remove the external nut, bush, and washer from the base of the splines and pull out the wheelboxes from under the facia (photo).
5   Refitting is a straightforward reversal of the removal sequence but take care that the cable rack emerges properly and that the wheelboxes are correctly lined up.

34 Heater unit – general

1   A heater unit may be fitted as optional equipment to all models. The layout of the heater components is shown in Fig. 10.15 whilst the variations of control are shown in Fig. 10.16.
2   The heater unit requires very little maintenance apart from an occasional check to ensure that the coolant supply and return pipes are in good condition and securely located. The control cables will also need the occasional lubrication with a light oil (photos).
3   When a heater unit is fitted it is imperative that an antifreeze solution is used in the cooling circuit, since although the engine and radiator may be drained, coolant will be retained in the heater circuit where there is no drain plug.
4   The heater unit matrix (radiator) and electric fan motor are fitted in a common housing which is mounted on the bulkhead directly behind the engine. Access to either component is available after draining the cooling system, detaching the coolant supply and return pipes to the heater and disconnecting the motor wiring connections. Unclip and remove the housing front cover.
5   The heater control valve unit is shown in the accompanying photo and as can be seen, whenever it is disconnected a new gasket must be used to ensure a good seal.
6   If necessary the control cables can be adjusted or removed for renewal, being located by clamps (photo).

35 Radios and tape players – fitting as accessories

This Section describes the installation of in-car entertainment (ICE) equipment which was not fitted as standard or as an option by the car manufacturer during production of the car.
   A radio or tape player is an expensive item to buy; and will only give its best performance if fitted properly. It is useless to expect concert hall performance from a unit that is suspended from the dashpanel on string with its speaker resting on the floor. If you do not wish to do the installation yourself there are many in-car entertainment specialists who can do the fitting for you.
   Make sure the unit purchased is of the same polarity as the vehicle. Ensure that units with adjustable polarity are correctly set before commencing installation.
   It is difficult to give specific information with regard to fitting, as final positioning of the radio/tape player, speakers and aerial is entirely a matter of personal preference. However, the following paragraphs give guidelines to follow, which are relevant to all installations.

Radios
Most radios are a standardised size of 7 inches wide, by 2 inches deep – this ensures that they will fit into the radio aperture provided in most cars. If your car does not have such an aperture, then the radio must be fitted in a suitable position either in, or beneath, the dashpanel. Alternatively, a special console can be purchased which will fit between the dashpanel and the floor, or on the transmission tunnel. These consoles can also be used for additional switches and instrumentation if required. Where no radio aperture is provided, the following points should be borne in mind before deciding exactly where to fit the unit:

(a) The unit must be within easy reach of the driver wearing a seat belt
(b) The unit must not be mounted in close proximity to an electric tachometer, the ignition switch and its wiring, or the flasher unit and associated wiring
(c) The unit must be mounted within reach of the aerial leads, and in such a place that the aerial lead will not have to be routed near the components detailed in the preceding paragraph
(d) The unit should not be positioned in a place where it might cause injury to the car occupants in an accident; for instance, under the dashpanel above the driver's or passenger's legs
(e) The unit must be fitted really securely

Some radios will have mounting brackets provided together with instructions; others will need to be fitted using drilled and slotted metal strips, bent to form mounting brackets – these strips are available from most accessory stores. The unit must be properly earthed, by fitting a separate earth lead between the casing of the radio and the vehicle frame.
   Use the radio manufacturer's instructions when wiring the radio into the vehicle's electrical system. If no instructions are available refer to the relevant wiring diagram to find the location of the radio 'feed' connection in the vehicle's wiring circuit. A 1-2 amp 'in-line' fuse must be fitted in the radio's 'feed' wire – a choke may also be necessary (see next Section).
   The type of aerial used, and its fitted position, is a matter of

Fig. 10.15 The heater unit components (Sec 34)

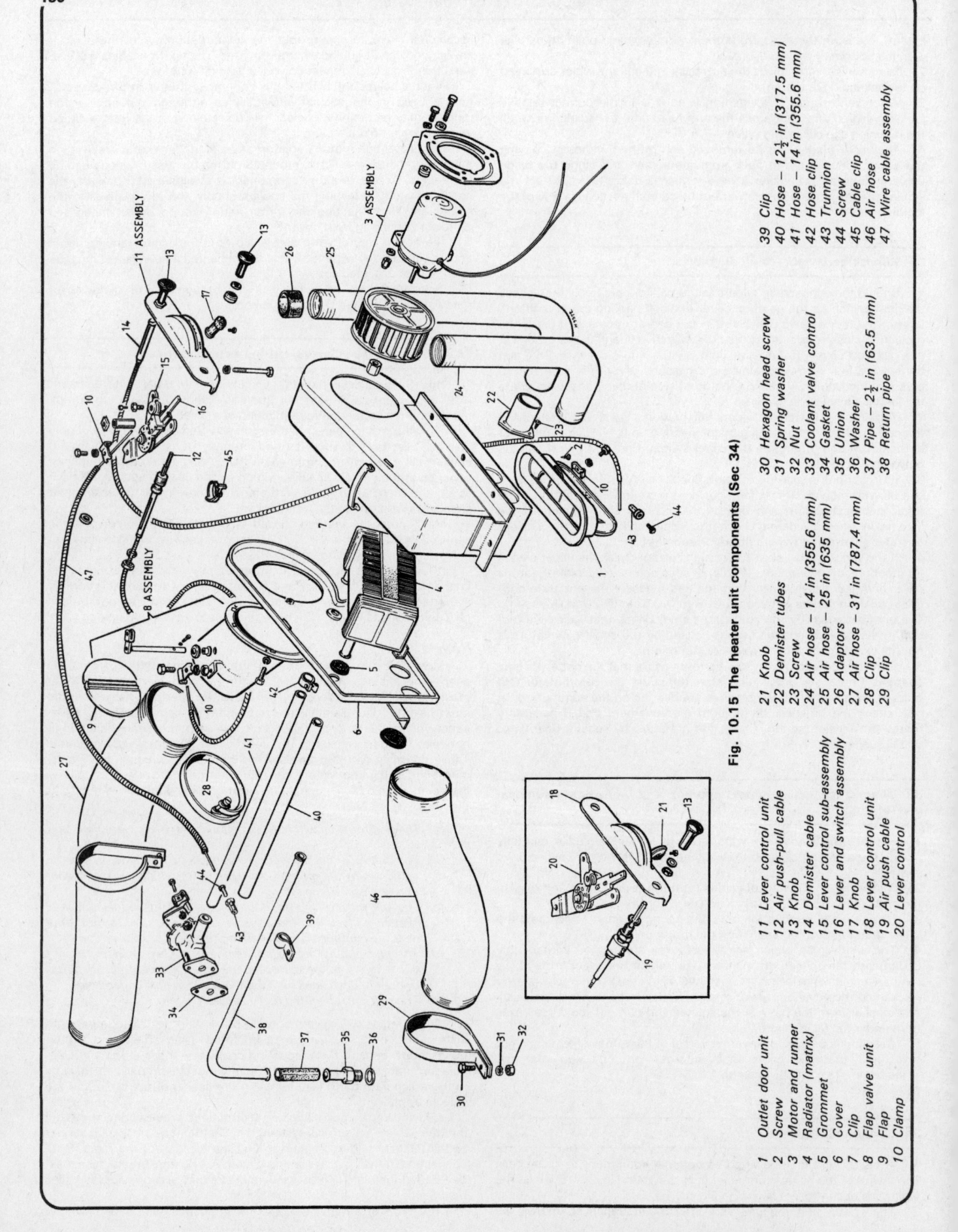

1 Outlet door unit
2 Screw
3 Motor and runner
4 Radiator (matrix)
5 Grommet
6 Cover
7 Clip
8 Flap valve unit
9 Flap
10 Clamp
11 Lever control unit
12 Air push-pull cable
13 Knob
14 Demister cable
15 Lever control sub-assembly
16 Lever and switch assembly
17 Knob
18 Lever control unit
19 Air push cable
20 Lever control
21 Knob
22 Demister tubes
23 Screw
24 Air hose – 14 in (355.6 mm)
25 Air hose – 25 in (635 mm)
26 Adaptors
27 Air hose – 31 in (787.4 mm)
28 Clip
29 Clip
30 Hexagon head screw
31 Spring washer
32 Nut
33 Coolant valve control
34 Gasket
35 Union
36 Washer
37 Pipe – 2½ in (63.5 mm)
38 Return pipe
39 Clip
40 Hose – 12½ in (317.5 mm)
41 Hose – 14 in (355.6 mm)
42 Hose clip
43 Trunnion
44 Screw
45 Cable clip
46 Air hose
47 Wire cable assembly

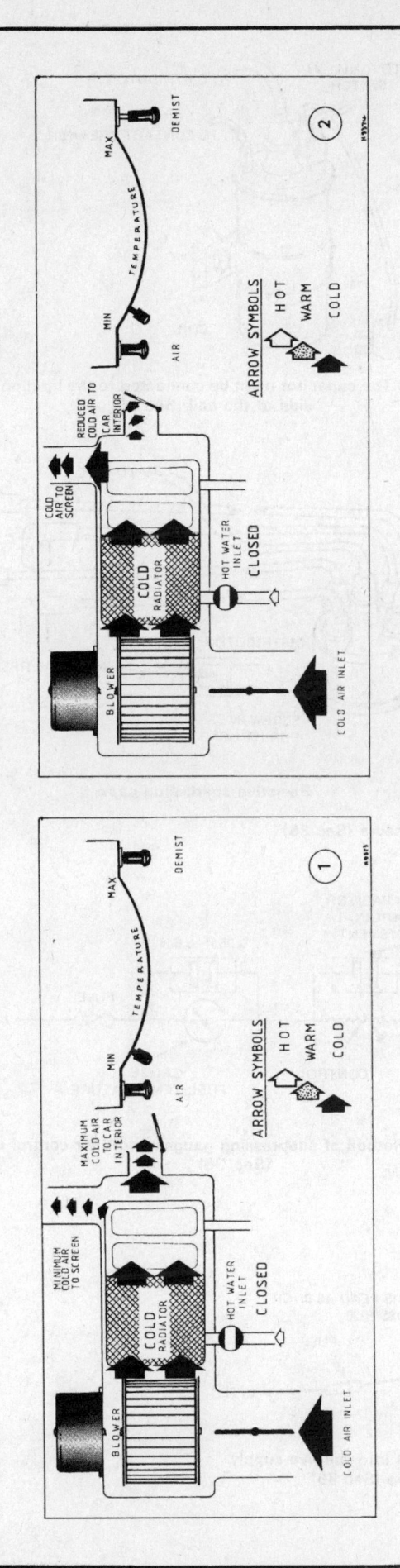

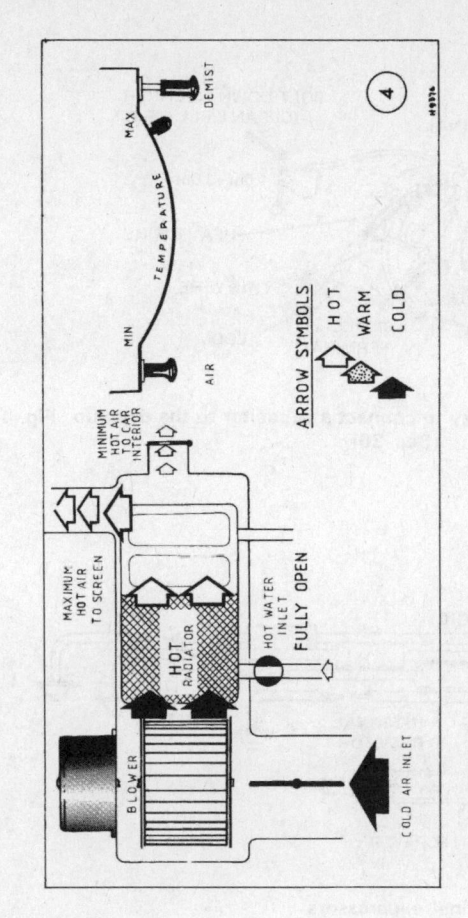

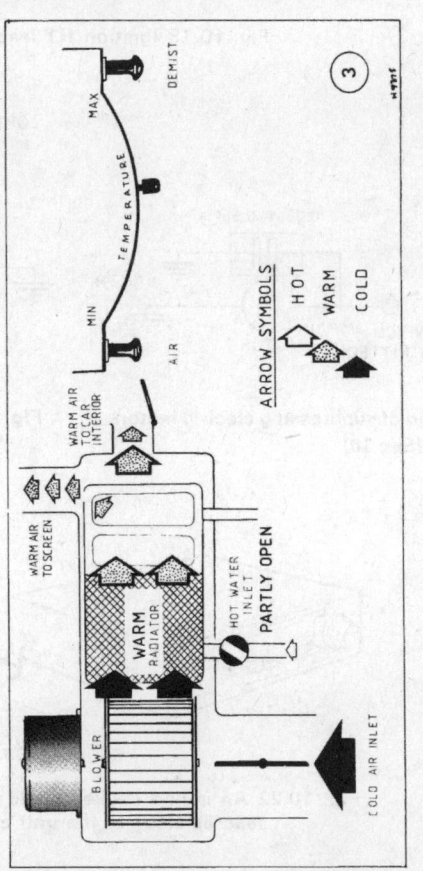

Fig. 10.16 The heater/demister control variations (Sec 34)

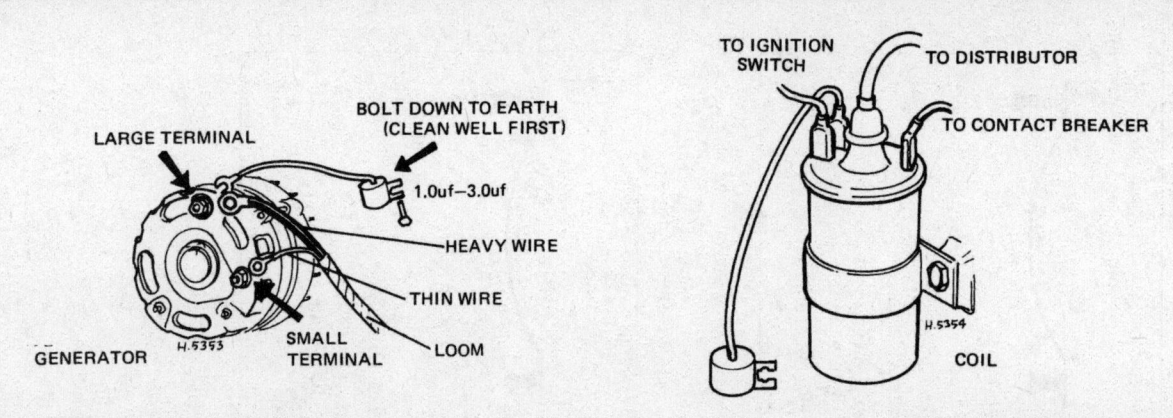

Fig. 10.17 The correct way to connect a capacitor to the dynamo (Sec 36)

Fig. 10.18 The capacitor must be connected to the ignition switch side of the coil (Sec 36)

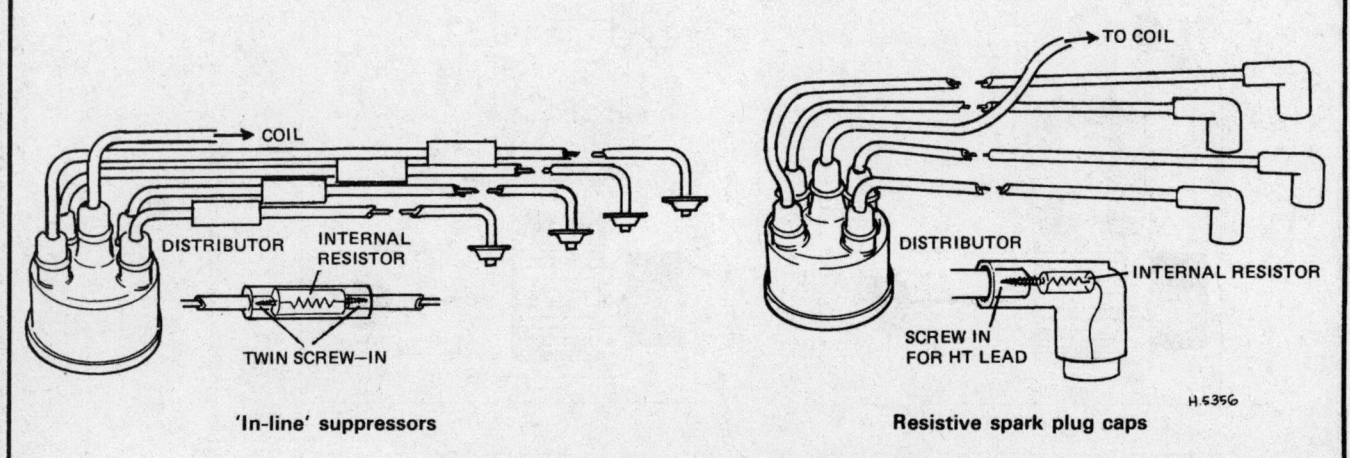

'In-line' suppressors

Resistive spark plug caps

Fig. 10.19 Ignition HT lead suppressors (Sec 36)

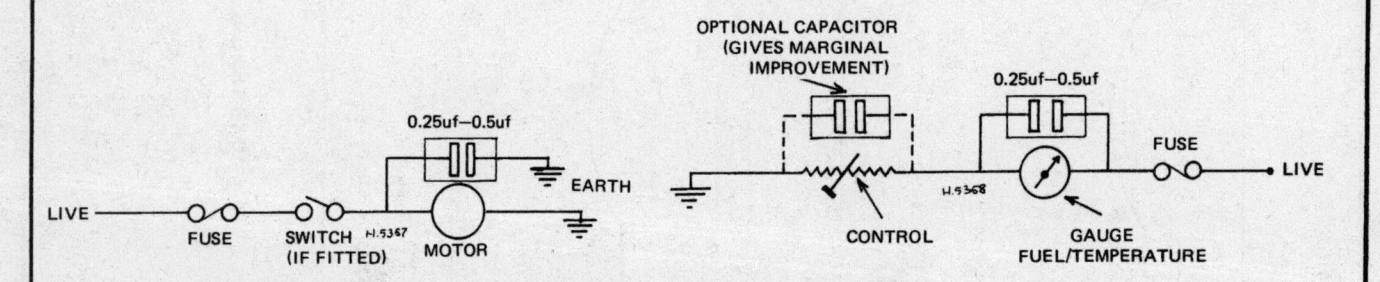

Fig. 10.20 Correct method of suppressing electric motors (Sec 36)

Fig. 10.21 Method of suppressing gauges and their control units (Sec 36)

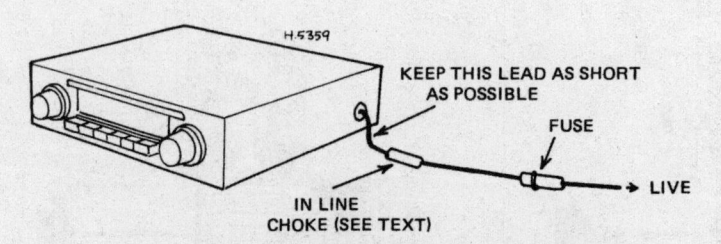

Fig. 10.22 An in-line choke should be fitted into the live supply lead as close to the unit as possible (Sec 36)

personal preference. In general the taller the aerial, the better the reception. It is best to fit a fully retractable aerial – especially, if a mechanical car-wash is used or if you live in an area where cars tend to be vandalised. In this respect electric aerials which are raised and lowered automatically when switching the radio on or off are convenient but are more likely to give trouble than the manual type.

When choosing a site for the aerial the following points should be considered:

(a) The aerial lead should be as short as possible – this means that the aerial should be mounted at the front of the vehicle
(b) The aerial must be mounted as far away from the distributor and HT leads as possible
(c) The part of the aerial which protrudes beneath the mounting point must not foul the roadwheels, or anything else
(d) If possible the aerial should be positioned so that the coaxial lead does not have to be routed through the engine compartment
(e) The plane of the panel on which the aerial is mounted should not be so steeply angled that the aerial cannot be mounted vertically (in relation to the 'end-on' aspect of the vehicle). Most aerials have a small amount of adjustment available

Having decided on a mounting position, a relatively large hole will have to be made in the panel. The exact size of the hole will depend upon the specific aerial being fitted, although, generally, the hole required is of ¾ inch (19 mm) diameter. On metal bodied cars, a 'tank-cutter' of the relevant diameter is the best tool to use for making the hole. This tool needs a small diameter pilot hole drilled through the panel, through which the tool clamping bolt is inserted. When the hole has been made the raw edges should be de-burred with a file and then painted, to prevent corrosion.

Fit the aerial according to the manufacturer's instructions. If the aerial is very tall, or if it protrudes beneath the mounting panel for a considerable distance, it is a good idea to fit a stay between the aerial and the vehicle frame. This stay can be manufactured from the slotted and drilled metal strips previously mentioned. The stay should be securely screwed or bolted in place. For best reception it is advisable to fit an earth lead between the aerial body and the vehicle frame.

It will probably be necessary to drill one or two holes through bodywork panels in order to feed the aerial lead into the interior of the car. Where this is the case ensure that the holes are fitted with rubber grommets to protect the cable, and to stop possible entry of water.

Positioning and fitting of the speaker depends mainly on its type. Generally, the speaker is designed to fit directly into the aperture already provided in the car (usually behind the seats, or in the top of the dashpanel). Where this is the case, fitting the speaker is just a matter of removing the protective grille from the aperture and screwing or bolting the speaker in place. Take great care not to damage the speaker diaphragm whilst doing this. It is a good idea to fit a 'gasket' between the speaker frame and the mounting panel in order to prevent vibration – some speakers will already have such a gasket fitted.

If a 'pod' type speaker was supplied with the radio, the best acoustic results will normally be obtained by mounting behind the seat. The pod can be secured to the mounting panel with self-tapping screws.

When connecting a rear mounted speaker to the radio, the wires should be routed through the vehicle beneath the carpets or floor mats – preferably through the middle, or along the side of the floorpan, where they will not be trodden on by passengers. Make the relevant connections as directed by the radio manufacturer.

By now you will have several yards of additional wiring in the car; use PVC tape to secure this wiring out of harm's way. Do not leave electrical leads dangling. Ensure that all new electrical connections are properly made (wires twisted together will not do) and completely secure.

The radio should now be working, but before you pack away your tools it will be necessary to 'trim' the radio to the aerial. Follow the radio manufacturer's instructions regarding this adjustment.

Tape players

Fitting instructions for both cartridge and cassette stereo tape players are the same and in general the same rules apply as when fitting a radio. Tape players are not usually prone to electrical interference like radios – although it can occur – so positioning is not so critical. If possible the player should be mounted on an 'even-keel'. Also, it must be possible for a driver wearing a seat belt to reach the unit in order to change, or turn over, tapes.

For the best results from speakers designed to be recessed into a panel, mount them so that the back of the speaker protrudes into an enclosed chamber within the vehicle (eg door interiors or the luggage boot cavity).

36 Radios and tape players – suppression of interference

To eliminate buzzes, and other unwanted noises, costs very little and is not as difficult as sometimes thought. With a modicum of common sense and patience and following the instructions in the following paragraphs, interference can be virtually eliminated.

The first cause for concern is the dynamo. The noise this makes over the radio is like an electric mixer and the noise speeds up when you rev up (if you wish to prove the point, you can remove the fan belt and try it). The remedy for this is simple, connect a 1·0 mf – 3·0 mf capacitor between earth, probably the bolt that holds down the generator base, and the *large* terminal on the dynamo. This is most important, for if you connect it to the small terminal, you will probably damage the dynamo permanently.

A second common cause of electrical interference is the ignition system. Here a 1·0 mf capacitor must be connected between earth and the SW terminal on the coil. This may stop the tick, tick, tick sound that comes over the speaker. Next comes the spark itself.

There are several ways of curing interference from the ignition system. One is to use carbon film high tension leads and the more successful method is to use resistive spark plug caps of about 10 000 ohm to 15 000 ohm resistance. If, due to lack of room, these cannot be used, an alternative is to use 'in-line' suppressors. If the interference is not too bad, you may get away with only one suppressor in the coil to distributor line. If the interference does continue (a 'clacking' noise) then 'doctor' all high tension leads.

At this stage it is advisable to check that the radio is well earthed, also the aerial, and to see that the aerial plug is pushed well into the set and that the radio is properly trimmed (see preceding Section). In addition, check that the wire which supplies the power to the set is as short as possible and does not wander all over the car. It is a good idea to check that the fuse is of the correct rating. For most sets this will be about 1 to 2 amps.

At this point the more usual causes of interference have been suppressed. If the problem still exists, a look at the causes of interference may help to pinpoint the component generating the stray electrical discharges.

The radio picks up electromagnetic waves in the air; now some are made by regular broadcasters, and some, which we do not want, are made by the car. The home made signals are produced by stray electrical discharges floating around the car. Common producers of these signals are electric motors, ie, the windscreen wipers, electric screen washers, electric window winders, heater fan or an electric aerial if fitted. Other sources of interference are electric fuel pumps, flashing turn signal and instruments. The remedy for these cases is shown for an electric motor whose interference is not too bad and for instrument suppression. Turn signals are not normally suppressed. In recent years, radio manufacturers have included in the line (live) of the radio, in addition to the fuse, an 'in-line' choke.

All the foregoing components are available from radio stores or accessory stores. If you have an electric clock fitted this should be suppressed by connecting a 0·5 mf capacity directly across it as shown.

If after all this, you are still experiencing radio interference, first assess how bad it is, for the human ear can filter out unobstrusive unwanted noises quite easily, but if you are still adamant about eradicating the noise, then continue.

As a first step, a few "experts" seem to favour a screen between the radio and the engine. This is OK as far as it goes – literally! – for the whole set is screened anyway and if interference can get past that then a small piece of aluminium is not going to stop it.

A more sensible way of screening is to discover if interference is coming down the wires. First, take the live lead; interference can get between the set and the choke (hence the reason for keeping the wires short). One remedy here is to screen the wire and this is done by buying screened wire and fitting that. The loudspeaker lead could be screened also to prevent "pickup" getting back to the radio – although this is unlikely.

Without doubt, the worst source of radio interference comes from

Chapter 10 Electrical system

the ignition HT leads, even if they have been suppressed. The ideal way of suppressing these is to slide screening tubes over the leads themselves. As this is impractical, we can place an aluminium shield over the majority of the lead areas. In a vee- or twin-cam engine this is relatively easy but for a straight engine, the results are not particularly good.

Now for the really impossible cases, here are a few tips to try out. Where metal comes into contact with metal, an electrical disturbance is caused which is why good clean connections are essential. To remove interference due to overlapping or butting panels you must bridge the join with a wide braided earth strap (like that from the frame to the engine/transmission). The most common moving parts that could create noise and should be strapped are, in order of importance:

(a) *Silencer to frame*
(b) *Exhaust pipe to engine block and frame*
(c) *Air cleaner to frame*
(d) *Front and rear bumpers to frame*
(e) *Steering column to frame*
(f) *Bonnet and boot lids to frame*

These faults are most pronounced when (1) the engine is idling, (2) labouring under load. Although the moving parts are already connected with nuts, bolts, etc, these do tend to rust and corrode, thus creating a high resistance interference source.

If you have a "ragged" sounding pulse when mobile, this could be wheel or tyre static. This can be cured by buying some anti-static powder and sprinkling it liberally inside the tyres.

If the interference takes the shape of a high pitched screeching noise that changes its note when the car is in motion and only comes now and then, this could be related to the aerial, especially if it is of the telescopic or whip type. This source can be cured quite simply by pushing a small rubber ball on top of the aerial (yes, really), as this breaks the electric field before it can form; but it would be much better to buy yourself a new aerial of a reputable brand. If, on the other hand, you are getting a loud rushing sound every time you brake, then this is brake static. This effect is most prominent on hot dry days and is cured only by fitting a special kit, which is quite expensive.

In conclusion, it is pointed out that it is relatively easy, and therefore cheap, to eliminate 95 per cent of all noise, but to eliminate the final 5 per cent is time and money consuming. It is up to the individual to decide if it is worth it. Please remember also, that you cannot get concert performance out of a cheap radio.

Chapter 10 Electrical system

37 Fault diagnosis – electrical system

Symptom	Reason/s
Starter motor fails to turn engine	Battery discharged Battery defective internally Battery terminal leads loose or ground lead not securely attached to body Loose or broken connections in starter motor circuit Starter motor switch faulty Starter motor pinion jammed in mesh with flywheel ring gear Starter brushes badly worn, sticking or brush wires loose Commutator dirty, worn or burnt Starter motor armature faulty Field coils grounded
Starter motor turns engine very slowly	Battery in discharged condition Starter brushes badly worn, sticking or brush wires loose Loose wires in starter motor circuit
Starter motor operates without turning engine	Pinion or flywheel gear teeth broken or worn
Starter motor noisy or engagement excessively rough	Pinion or flywheel teeth broken or worn Starter motor retaining bolts loose
Starter motor remains in operation after starter button released	Faulty starter button
Charging system indicator light on – engine speed above idling	Loose or broken drivebelt No output from dynamo
Charge indicator light not on when ignition switched on but engine not running	Burnt out bulb Lamp circuit open
Battery will not hold charge for more than a few days	Battery defective internally Electrolyte level too weak or too low Battery plates heavily sulphated
Horn will not operate or operates intermittently	Loose connections Defective switch Defective horn
Horn blows continually	Horn button stuck (earthed)
Lights do not come on	If engine not running, battery discharged Light bulb filament burnt out or bulbs broken Wire connections loose, disconnected or broken Light switch shorting or otherwise faulty
Lights come on but fade out	If engine not running battery discharged
Lights give very poor illumination	Lamp glasses dirty Lamps badly out of adjustment
Lights work erratically – flashing on and off, especially over bumps	Battery terminals or earth connection loose Light not earthing properly Contacts in light switch faulty
Wiper motor fails to work	Blown fuse Wire connections loose, disconnected, or broken Brushes badly worn Armature worn or faulty Field coils faulty
Wiper motor works very slowly and takes excessive current	Commutator dirty, greasy or burnt Armature bearings dirty or unaligned Armature badly worn or faulty
Wiper motor works slowly and takes little current	Brushes badly worn Commutator dirty, greasy or burnt Armature badly worn or faulty
Wiper motor works but wiper blades remain static	Wiper motor gearbox parts badly worn or teeth stripped

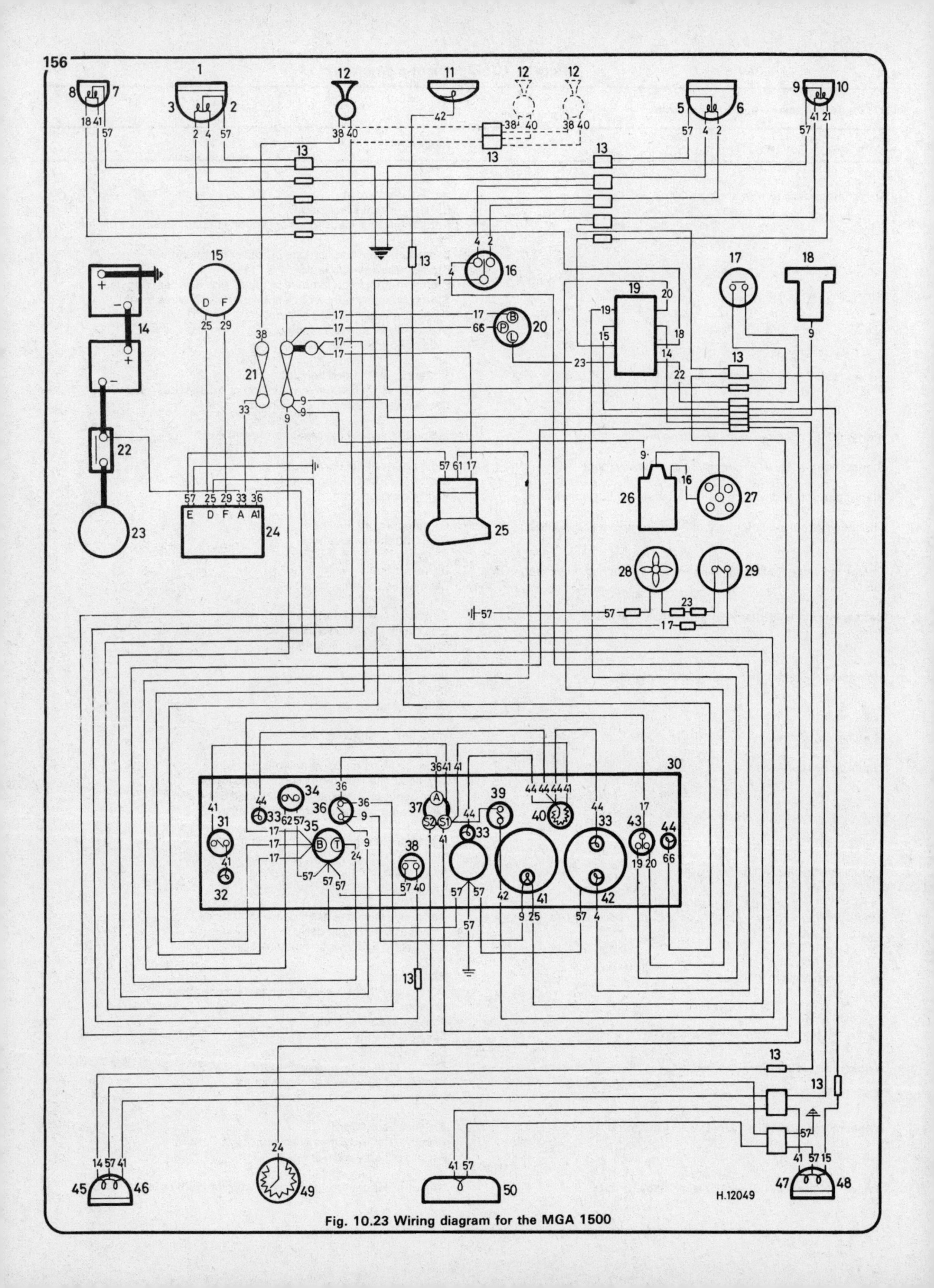

Fig. 10.23 Wiring diagram for the MGA 1500

Fig. 10.23 Key to wiring diagram for the MGA 1500

Key to cable colours

1	Blue	23	Green with Brown	45	Red with Green
2	Blue with Red	24	Green with Black	46	Red with Purple
3	Blue with Yellow	25	Yellow	47	Red with Brown
4	Blue with White	26	Yellow with Red	48	Red with Black
5	Blue with Green	27	Yellow with Blue	49	Purple
6	Blue with Purple	28	Yellow with White	50	Purple with Red
7	Blue with Brown	29	Yellow with Green	51	Purple with Yellow
8	Blue with Black	30	Yellow with Purple	52	Purple with Blue
9	White	31	Yellow with Brown	53	Purple with White
10	White with Red	32	Yellow with Black	54	Purple with Green
11	White with Yellow	33	Brown	55	Purple with Brown
12	White with Blue	34	Brown with Red	56	Purple with Black
13	White with Green	35	Brown with Yellow	57	Black
14	White with Purple	36	Brown with Blue	58	Black with Red
15	White with Brown	37	Brown with White	59	Black with Yellow
16	White with Black	38	Brown with Green	60	Black with Blue
17	Green	39	Brown with Purple	61	Black with White
18	Green with Red	40	Brown with Black	62	Black with Green
19	Green with Yellow	41	Red	63	Black with Purple
20	Green with Blue	42	Red with Yellow	64	Black with Brown
21	Green with White	43	Red with Blue	65	Dark Green
22	Green with Purple	44	Red with White	66	Light Green

Key to components

1	Headlamp Front LH	26	Coil
2	Main Beam	27	Distributor
3	Dip Beam	28	Heater Motor
4	Headlamp Front RH	29	Heater Motor Switch
5	Main Beam	30	Dashboard
6	Dip Beam	31	Map Lamp Switch
7	Sidelamp LH	32	Map Lamp
8	Direction Indicator Front LH	33	Panel Lamp
9	Sidelamp RH	34	Windscreen Wiper Switch
10	Direction Indicator Front RH	35	Petrol Gauge
11	Fog Lamp (when fitted)	36	Ignition Switch
12	Horn	37	Lighting Switch
13	Snap Connector(s)	38	Horn Push
14	Two 6v Batteries	39	Fog Lamp Switch
15	Generator	40	Panel Lamp Rheostat
16	Dip Switch	41	Ignition Warning Lamp
17	Stop Lamp switch	42	Main Beam Warning Lamp
18	Petrol Pump	43	Direction Indicator Switch
19	Direction Indicator Relay unit	44	Direction Indicator Warning Lamp
20	Direction Indicator Flasher Unit	45	Direction Indicator Rear LH
21	Fuse Box	46	Stop/tail Lamp LH
22	Starter Switch	47	Stop/tail Lamp RH
23	Starter	48	Direction Indicator Rear RH
24	Control Box	49	Petrol Tank Unit
25	Windscreen Wiper Motor	50	Number Plate Lamp

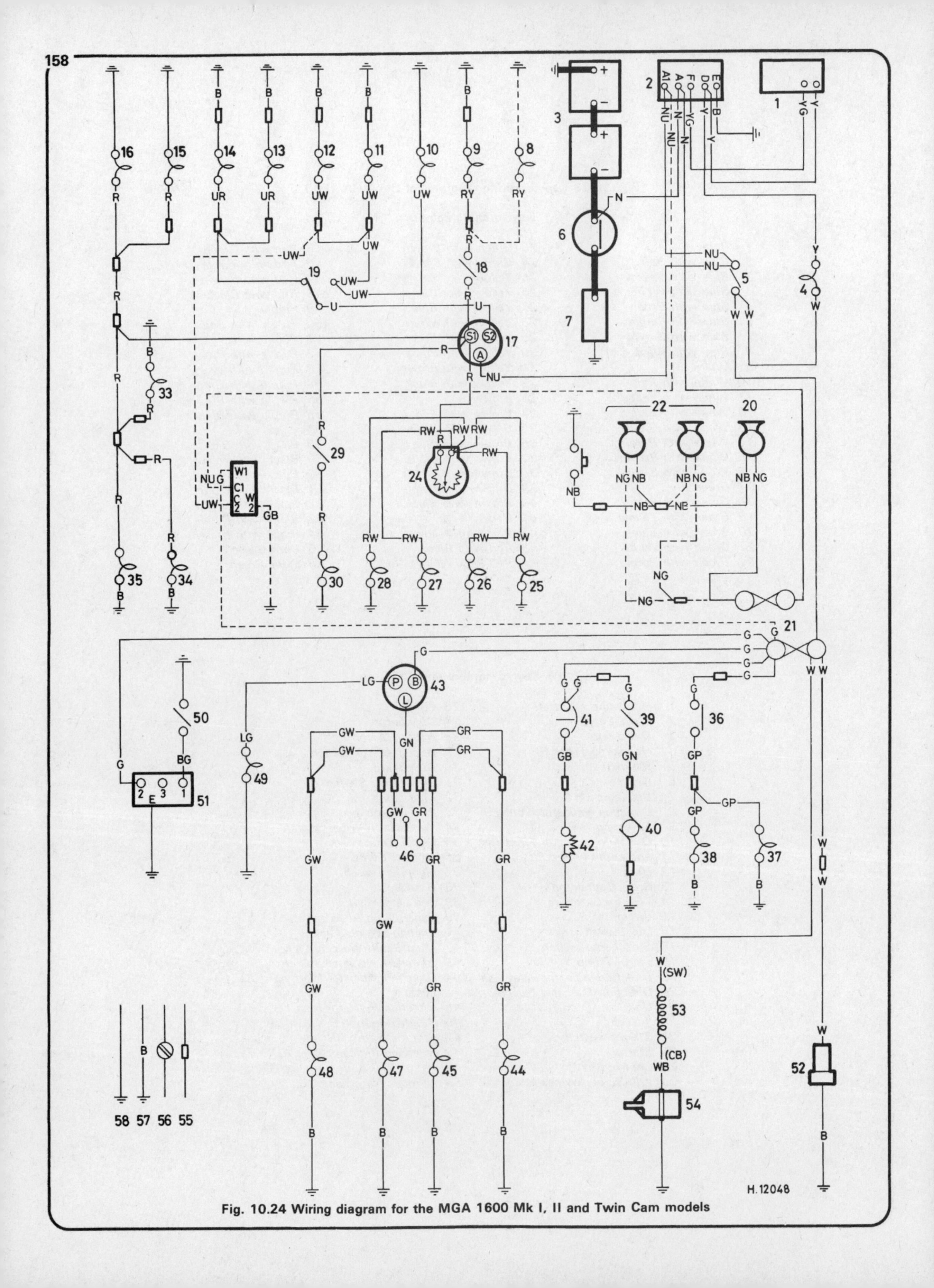

Fig. 10.24 Wiring diagram for the MGA 1600 Mk I, II and Twin Cam models

Fig. 10.24 Key to wiring diagram for the MGA 1600 Mk I, II and Twin Cam models

1	Dynamo	30	Map lamp
2	Control box	31	Headlamp flick relay
3	Two 6-volt batteries	32	Headlamp flick switch
4	Ignition warning light	33	LH tail lamp
5	Ignition switch	34	Number-plate lamp
6	Starter switch	35	RH tail lamp
7	Starter motor	36	Stop lamp switch
8	RH fog lamp (if fitted)	37	LH stop lamp
9	LH fog lamp	38	RH stop lamp
10	Main beam warning light	39	Heater switch (when fitted)
11	RH headlamp main beam	40	Heater motor
12	LH headlamp main beam	41	Fuel gauge
13	LH headlamp dip beam	42	Fuel tank unit
14	RH headlamp dip beam	43	Flasher unit
15	LH pilot lamp	44	LH rear flasher
16	RH pilot lamp	45	LH front flasher
17	Lighting switch	46	Flasher switch
18	Fog lamp switch	47	RH front flasher
19	Dipper switch	48	RH rear flasher
20	Horn	49	Flasher warning light
21	Fuse unit	50	Windshield wiper switch
22	Twin windtone horns (if fitted)	51	Windshield wiper motor
23	Horn push	52	Fuel pump
24	Panel lamp rheostat	53	Ignition coil
25	Panel lamp	54	Distributor
26	Panel lamp	55	Snap connectors
27	Panel lamp	56	Terminal blocks or junction box
28	Panel lamp	57	Earth connections made via cable
29	Map lamp switch	58	Earth connections made via fixing bolts

Cable colour code

B	Black	S	Slate
U	Blue	W	White
N	Brown	Y	Yellow
G	Green	L	Light
P	Purple	D	Dark
R	Red	M	Medium

Where two colour code letters are given, the first letter is the main colour whilst the second is the tracer colour

Chapter 11 Suspension and steering

Contents

Anti-roll bar – removal and refitting	3
Faults diagnosis – suspension and steering	23
Front coil springs – removal and refitting	4
Front shock absorbers – removal and refitting	5
Front hub bearings (Dunlop disc brakes) – adjustment	8
Front hub (disc brakes) – removal and refitting	7
Front hub (drum brakes) – removal and refitting	6
Front wheel alignment – checking and adjustment	18
General description	1
King pins and links – dismantling, inspection and assembly	12
King pins – removal and refitting	11
Rear hub unit – dismantling and overhaul	9
Rear shock absorbers – removal and refitting	20
Rear springs – removal and refitting	21
Rubber suspension bushes – renewal	10
Steering column – removal and refitting	14
Steering column universal joint – removal and refitting	15
Steering gearbox – dismantling and assembly	17
Steering gearbox – removal and refitting	16
Steering wheel – removal and refitting	13
Suspension, steering and shock absorbers – inspection for wear	2
Tie-rod outer balljoints – removal and refitting	19
Wheels and tyres – maintenance	22

Specifications

Front suspension
Type .... Independent-coil springs and wishbone

Spring free height
Overhead valve engine models up to Car No. 15151 .... 9.28 ± 0.06 in (234.9 ± 1.6 mm)
Overhead valve engine models from Car No. 15152 .... 8.88 ± 0.06 in (225.3 ± 1.6 mm)
Twin Cam engine models .... 9.09 ± 0.06 in (230.9 ± 1.6 mm)

Length of static spring (laden) .... 6.6 ± 0.03 in (167.6 ± 0.8 mm)

Rear suspension
Type .... Semi-elliptic

Spring leave width .... 1.750 in (44.45 mm)

Number of leaves 6

Working load .... 450 lb (203.7 kg)

Free camber .... 3.60 in (91.44 mm)

Steering
Type .... Rack and pinion

Toe-in .... Wheels parallel

King pin inclination .... 9° to 10.5° (on full bump)

Camber angle .... 1° positive to ½° negative (on full bump)

Castor angle .... 4°

Chapter 11 Suspension and steering

Track
MGA 1500 and 1600
    Front
    Rear
MGA 1600 and Twin Cam fitted with Dunlop disc brakes
    Front
    Rear

	Disc wheels	Wire wheels
Front (1500/1600)	47.5 in (1.203 m)	47.875 in (1.216 m)
Rear (1500/1600)	48.75 in (1.238 m)	48.75 in (1.238 m)
Front (Dunlop disc)	47.906 in (1.217 m)	47.906 in (1.217 m)
Rear (Dunlop disc)	48.875 in (1.242 m)	48.875 in (1.242 m)

Wheels and tyres

Wheel type .... Ventilated disc or wire type

Wheel size .... 4J x 15

Tyre size
Except models with Dunlop disc brakes .... 5.60 x 15
Models with Dunlop disc brakes .... 5.90 x 15

Tyre pressures

	Front	Rear
Normal motoring	17 lbf/in^2 (1.2 kgf/cm^2)	20 lbf/in^2 (1.4 kgf/cm^2)
Fast motoring	21 lbf/in^2 (1.48 kgf/cm^2)	24 lbf/in^2 (1.69 kgf/cm^2)
Competition/sustained high speed	23 lbf/in^2 (1.62 kgf/cm^2)	26 lbf/in^2 (1.83 kgf/cm^2)

1 General description

The front suspension unit on each side comprises a lower wishbone, a coil spring, double acting shock absorber, stub axle and king pin unit. The coil spring is located between the lower wishbone spring pan and the chassis directly below the damper unit.

The lower wishbone inner mountings are equipped with rubber bushes which eliminates the need for lubrication. Similar rubber bushes are used elsewhere in both the front and rear suspension systems to reduce the maintenance procedures.

Double acting lever-type hydraulic shock absorbers are fitted front and rear, the levers on the front shock absorbers acting as the upper links for the front suspension.

Rack and pinion steering is fitted to all models. The rear end of the helically toothed pinion protrudes from the rack housing and is splined and engages with the end of the steering column to which it is held by a clamp bolt.

Rotating the steering wheel turns the pinion which in turn moves the rack sideways in the required direction. The steering gear is adjustable for backlash and endfloat.

Tie-rods from each end of the steering gear housing operate the steering arms via balljoints. The steering arms are connected to the stub axle (steering knuckle) which pivots on the king pin. The king pin is located via the upper and lower links which are in turn attached to the upper and lower suspension link arms.

An anti-roll bar was fitted as an optional extra.

The rear suspension is by semi-elliptic leaf springs which are rubber mounted. The spring shackles make use of rubber bushes.

2 Suspension, steering and shock absorbers – inspection for wear

1 To check for wear in the outer balljoints of the tie-rods place the car over a pit, or lie on the ground looking at the balljoints, and get a friend to rock the steering wheel from side to side. Wear is present if there is play in the joints (photo).

2 To check for wear in the rubber and metal bushes, jack-up the front of the car until the wheels are clear of the ground. Hold each wheel in turn, at the top and bottom, and try to rock it. If the wheel rocks continue the movement at the same time inspecting the upper trunnion link rubber bushes, and the rubber bushes at the inner ends of the wishbone for play.

3 If the wheel rocks and there is no side movement in the rubber bushes then the kingpins and metal bushes will be worn. Alternatively, if the movement occurs between the wheel and the brake backplate, then the hub bearings require renewal.

4 The rubber bushes can be renewed by the owner but, if there is play between the lower end of the kingpin and the wishbone, then it will be necessary to renew the fulcrum pin.

5 Sideplay or vertical or horizontal movement of the upper link or shock absorber arms relative to the shock absorber body is best checked with the outer end of the shock absorber arms freed from the upper trunnion link. If play is present the shock absorber bearings are worn and a new shock absorber should be purchased.

6 How well the shock absorbers function can be checked by bouncing the car at each corner. After each bounce the car should return to its normal ride position within 1 to 1¼ up-and-down movements. If the car continues to move up-and-down in decreasing amounts it means that either the shock absorbers require topping up, or if they are already full, that the shock absorbers are worn and must be renewed.

7 The shock absorbers cannot be adjusted without special tools, and therefore must not be dismantled but exchanged with your local Leyland agent for new units. They must be renewed if they show signs of leakage.

8 Excessive play in the steering gear will lead to wheel wobble, and can be confirmed by checking if there is any lost movement between the end of the steering column and the rack. Rack and pinion steering is normally very accurate and lost motion in the steering gear indicates a considerable mileage or lack of lubrication.

9 The outer balljoints at either end of the tie-rods are the most likely items to wear first, followed by the rack balljoints at the inner end of the tie-rods.

3 Anti-roll bar – removal and refitting

1 Jack-up the front of the car and place support blocks under the wheels or run the front wheels up a pair of inspection ramps.

2 Refer to Chapter 12 and remove the front bumper and the front apron. Remove the four body retaining bolts of the front extension and the eight front extension to chassis bolts. Detach the extension.

3 Unscrew and remove the anti-roll bar right and left-hand link bolts.

4 Unscrew and remove the anti-roll bar clamp housing bolts and remove the anti-roll bar together with the clamp bushes.

5 To remove the left and right-hand link arms unscrew the balljoint nuts from the respective wishbone arms.

6 Refitting is a reversal of the removal procedure but ensure that new bushes are used. New Aerotight nuts should also be used to secure the link balljoints to the wishbone arms.

4 Front coil springs – removal and refitting

1 Removal of one of the front springs is not difficult but it requires the use of a good jack (preferably hydraulic) in the absence of a suitable spring compressor.

2 Loosen the front roadwheels nuts, jack-up the front of the car, place supports under each front side bodymember and remove the wheels. Where fitted remove the anti-roll bar as described in Section 3.

Chapter 11 Suspension and steering

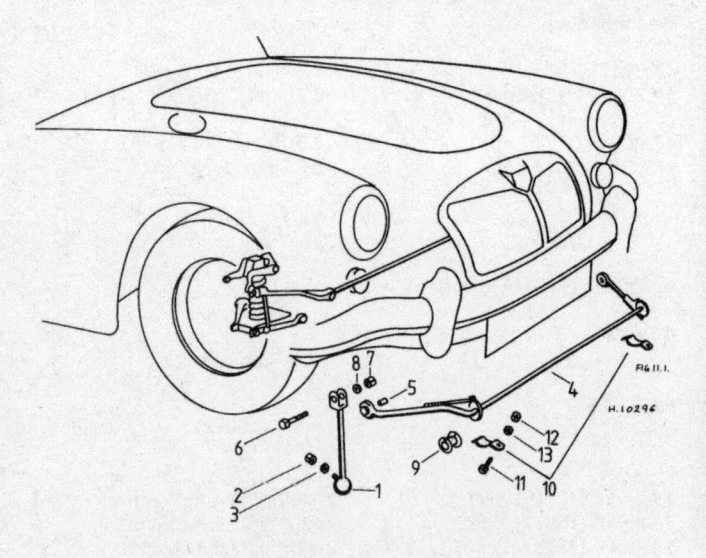

Fig. 11.1 The anti-roll bar components (Sec 3)

1. Link
2. Nut
3. Spring washer
4. Anti-roll bar
5. Bush
6. Bolt
7. Nut
8. Plain washer
9. Bush
10. Housing
11. Screw
12. Nut
13. Spring washer

2.1 Check the following front suspension/steering components

1. Shock absorber fluid level and shock absorber efficiency
2. Steering gaiter – check for security and signs of leakage
3. Steering rod joints for wear – lubricate at nipple
4. Suspension arm bushes
5. King pin bushes for wear – lubricate

3   Place a jack under the front suspension pan with a piece of wood interposed between the spring retaining pan and the head of the jack.
4   Raise the jack so that the shock absorber levers clear the rebound rubber.
5   Unscrew and remove the lower fulcrum bolt.
6   Pivot the hub unit upwards and support on a suitable wood block. Now slowly lower the jack under the spring pan and press down the lower wishbone unit to remove the spring.
7   Refitting is a reversal of the removal procedure but if fitting a new spring ensure that you have the correct type for your model as three types were employed according to car type (see Specifications). They are interchangeable but only as a pair.
8   When refitting the swivel pin to the lower wishbone ensure that the thrust washers, rubber seals and the retainers are fitted in the correct order as shown in Fig. 11.2.
9   Smear each end of the coil spring and the swivel pin with grease during assembly and when in position check that the upper end of the spring is securely located.

5   Front shock absorbers – removal and refitting

1   Loosen the roadwheel securing nuts, apply the handbrake and jack-up the front of the car, placing the jack under the wishbone spring pan. Remove the roadwheel from the side concerned.
2   Remove the split pin, unscrew and remove the nut from the swivel pin top pivot bolt, and withdraw the bolt (photo).
3   Pivot the hub out clear of the hub unit and support on a suitable block. Under no circumstances allow the weight of the hub unit to be taken by the brake hose.
4   Unscrew the four shock absorber unit to chassis retaining bolts and lift the shock absorber clear.
5   The shock absorber unit is not adjustable or repairable and must therefore be renewed if defective. To check this secure the shock absorber unit body in a vice and operate the lever by hand pressure. The pressure required to move the arm must be firm. Erratic or light pressure movement is indicative of a defective shock absorber unit. If however the lever arm cannot be moved under hand pressure their is an internal defect and the unit must be renewed.
6   Refitting is a direct reversal of the removal procedure. When topping up the fluid level in the damper unit ensure that no dirt enters the system. Use only Armstrong Super (Thin) Shock Absorber fluid No. 624 or a good quality SAE 20/20W mineral oil.

6   Front hub (drum brake models) – removal and refitting

1   Loosen the wheel nut/s on the wheel concerned, raise the front of the car so that the wheels are clear of the ground and remove the roadwheel. Ensure that the handbrake is fully applied and that 1st or reverse gear is selected and that the car is well supported.
2   Unscrew and remove the two countersunk screws that retain the brake drum in position. Chalk mark the drum and a wheel stud for relative position marking and withdraw the drum. It may be necessary to loosen off the brake adjustment to release the drum (see Chapter 9).
3   Prise free the grease cap from the hub using a suitable screwdriver as a lever. Wipe clean the grease from the hub nut and extract the split pin (photos).
4   Unscrew the hub nut (left-hand thread on left side, right-hand thread on right side), and detach it. The hub can now be withdrawn. If it will not pull free use a suitable hub puller (use Leyland special tool number 18G304 with adaptor bolts 18G304B if available).
5   The inner bearing can be withdrawn from the stub axle using a suitable puller, whilst the oil seal can be prised free and must always be renewed.
6   The outer bearing can be driven out of the hub housing for inspection.
7   Whenever the hub has been removed, the inner bearing must be refitted to the hub prior to assembly and not to the stub axle.
8   Pack the inner and outer bearings with clean grease and lubricate the oil seal lip to ease assembly of the hub onto the stub axle.
9   Refit the bearing spacer so that its chamfered face is towards the outer bearing (the smaller of the two). Support the hub and carefully press or drive the bearing into position. Insert the oil seal and the distance washer so that the seal metal face and the chamfered side of the washer are facing away from the bearing.
10   Carefully locate the assembled hub onto the stub axle and retain with the hub nut. Tighten it to the nearest split pin hole and insert a new split pin to secure. Smear some clean grease into the grease cap (do not fill it completely though) and tap it back into position in the hub. Check that the hub rotates freely and then refit the roadwheel.

163

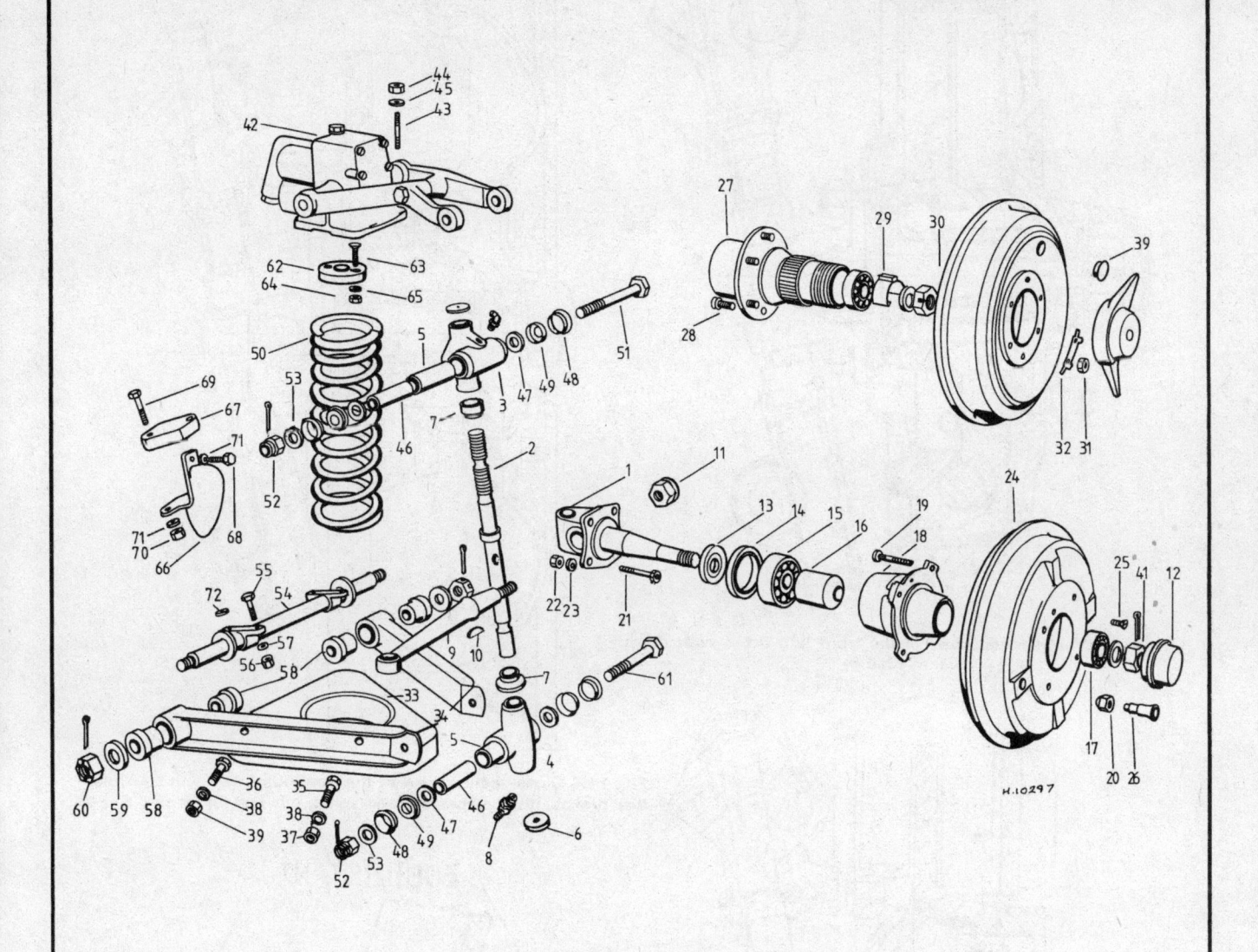

Fig. 11.2 The front suspension and hub components (Sec 4)

1 Steering knuckle – LH	19 Stud	37 Nut	55 Bolt
2 Swivel pin – LH	20 Nut	38 Washer	56 Nut
3 Link – swivel pin – upper LH	21 Bolt	39 Plug	57 Washer (spring)
4 Link – swivel pin – lower LH	22 Nut	40 Washer	58 Bush (bottom wishbone)
5 Bush	23 Washer	41 Nut (LH thread)	59 Washer
6 Plate	24 Brake drum	42 Hydraulic shock absorber	60 Nut (slotted)
7 Seal	25 Screw	43 Stud	61 Bolt
8 Grease nipple	26 Plug	44 Nut	62 Spigot
9 Steering lever – LH	27 Hub assembly	45 Washer (spring)	63 Screw
10 Woodruff key	28 Stud	46 Distance tube	64 Nut
11 Nut	29 Grease retainer	47 Thrust washer	65 Washer
12 Grease-retaining cup	30 Drum – brake wire wheel	48 Seal	66 Check rubber
13 Distance washer	31 Nut – drum to hub	49 Support	67 Distance piece
14 Oil seal	32 Locking tab – drum to hub	50 Coil spring	68 Screw
15 Bearing	33 Spring pan unit	51 Bolt	69 Bolt
16 Distance-piece	34 Bottom wishbone unit	52 Nut (castle)	70 Nut
17 Bearing	35 Screw	53 Washer (spring)	71 Washer
18 Hub assembly	36 Screw	54 Wishbone pivot	72 Washer

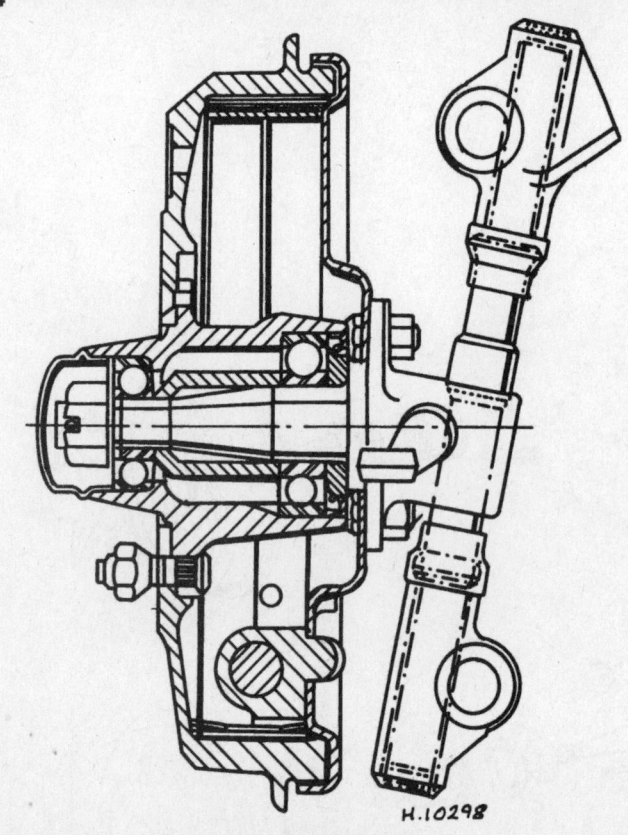

Fig. 11.3 Cross-section view of the front hub fitted with drum brakes (Sec 6)

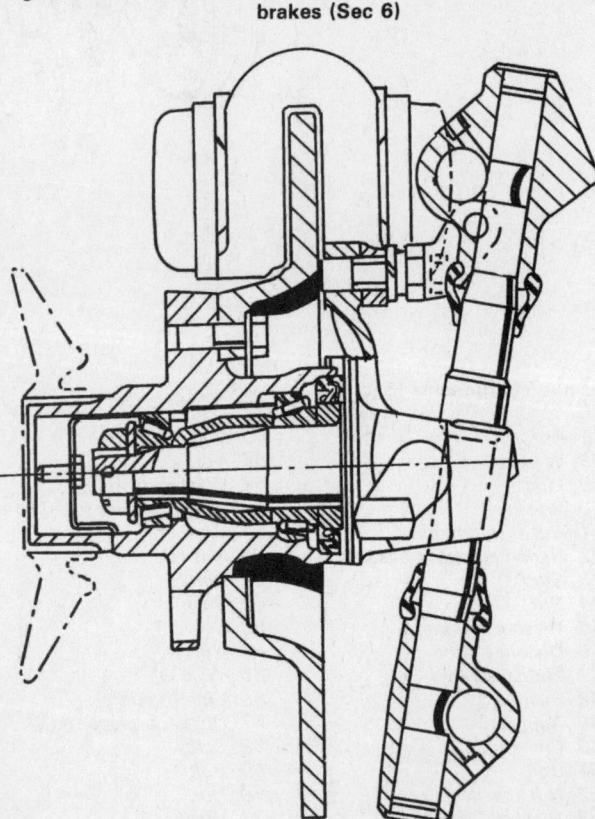

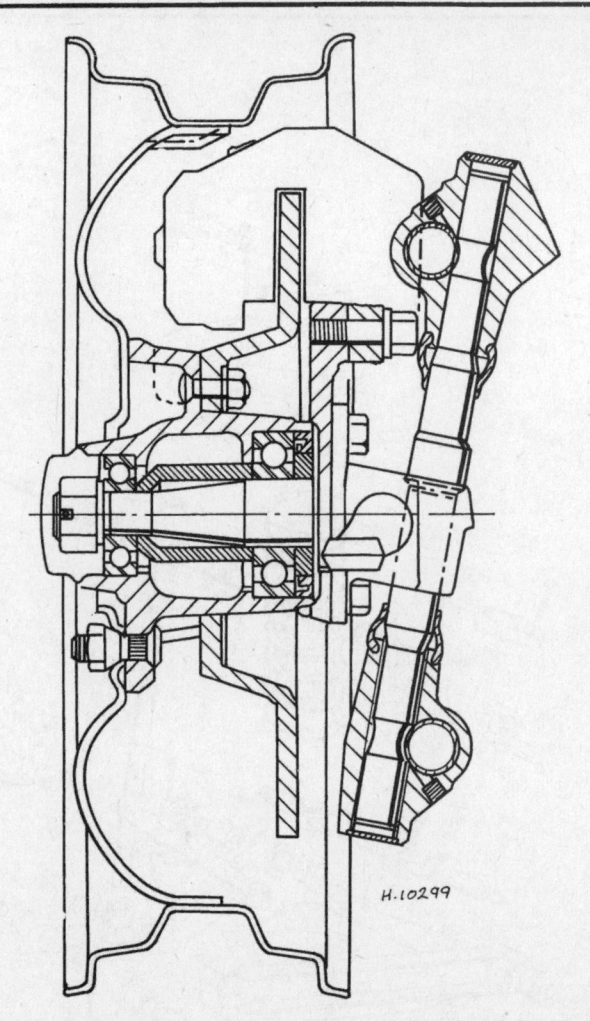

Fig. 11.4 Cross-section view of the front hub fitted with Lockheed disc brakes, (the calliper is drawn out of position for clarity) (Sec 7)

Fig. 11.5 Cross-section view of front hub fitted with Dunlop disc brakes (the calliper is shown out of position for clarity) (Sec 8)

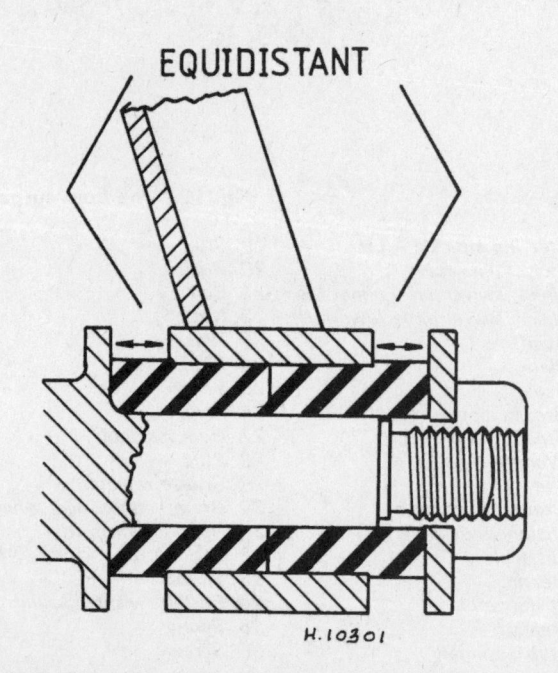

Fig. 11.6 The rubber bush location – lower suspension arm (Sec 10)

Chapter 11 Suspension and steering

5.2 The front shock absorber unit and upper link arms. Arrow indicates filler plug

6.3a Detach the grease cap and ...

6.3b ... extract the split pin

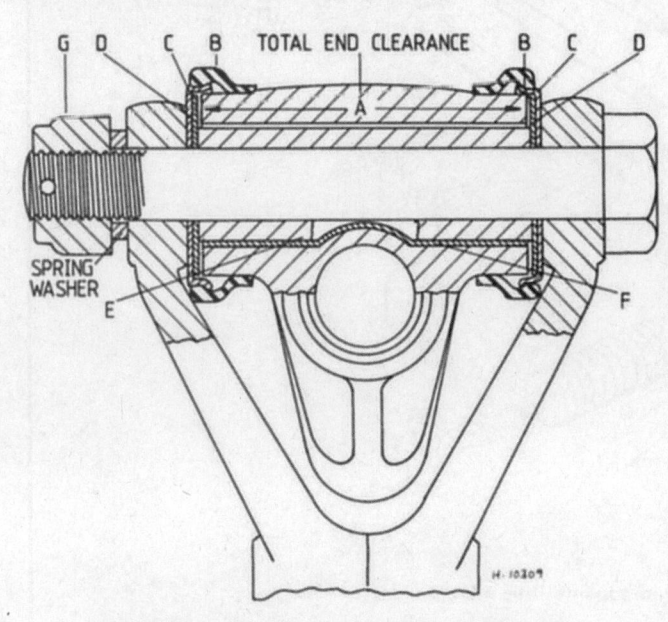

Fig. 11.7 The king pin swivel link unit (Sec 12)

A 0.008 to 0.013 in (0.2 to 0.33 mm)
B and C Dust seals/retainers
D Thrust washers
E Spacer tube
F Bush

7 Front hub (disc brakes) – removal and refitting

1 Loosen the wheel nut/s of the wheel concerned, raise the car at the front so that the wheels are clear of the ground and remove the roadwheel. Ensure that the handbrake is fully applied and engage 1st or reverse gear. Ensure that the car is well supported.
2 Refer to Chapter 9 and remove the brake calliper unit.
3 Prise free the grease cap from the hub and wipe the grease from the hub nut. Extract the split pin and unscrew the hub nut and washer, (left-hand thread on left side, right-hand thread on right side).
4 The hub and disc can now be withdrawn from the stub axle with the aid of a suitable puller or possibly even by prising from the rear using two screwdrivers diagonally opposed but take care if using this method not to damage the disc and/or adaptor plate.
5 Once removed the hub and disc can be separated by removing the four retaining nuts/bolts and spring washers.
6 Remove the distance washer from the stub axle (Dunlop system).
7 On the Lockheed type the small bearing may be removed from the hub using a suitable drift. Once the bearing is extracted, the spacer tube can be withdrawn and the large bearing and oil seal removed in a similar manner.
8 On the Dunlop type, extract the outer bearing centre together with the shims located between the bearing and distance piece. Prise free the oil seal and remove the inner bearing centre and distance piece. To remove the bearing outer tracks drive or press them out whilst supporting the hub.
9 Clean the respective parts and inspect for wear and/or damage. Renew any defective items. The oil seal should always be renewed as a matter of course.
10 Hub assembly is a reversal of the dismantling procedure. Ensure that all parts are perfectly clean prior to assembly and pack the bearings with grease.
11 On the Lockheed type assemble in the following order:

(a) Insert the outer bearing and its distance piece (chamfered edge to small bearing)
(b) Insert the inner bearing
(c) Carefully tap the oil seal into position with its metal face away from the bearing
(d) Fit the distance washer with the recessed side away from the bearing
(e) Refit the hub onto the stub axle and locate the stub axle nut and washer. Tighten the nut to the nearest split pin hole and insert a new split pin to secure. Check that the hub is free to rotate without excess play or tightness and then refit the grease cap. The cap should not be overfilled with grease

12 On the Dunlop type assemble in the following sequence:

(a) Press the inner and outer bearing outer races into position
(b) Locate the bearing distance piece and locate the inner bearing race
(c) Locate the oil seal and the distance washer. The steel face of the seal and washer chamfered face to be fitted away from the bearing
(d) Fit the hub assembly onto the stub axle and locate the adjuster shims and auto bearing race. Fit the stub axle nut and check the bearing endfloat as described in the next Section

8 Front hub bearings (Dunlop brakes) – adjustment

1 On models equipped with Dunlop disc brakes the front wheel hub bearings are of the taper roller type and the adjustment of which is made by shims. Adjustment is normally necessary to take up wear in the bearings or whenever the hub unit has been dismantled and new bearings fitted.
2 The car must be raised at the front and the roadwheel/s removed. Check that the handbrake is fully applied and that the car is well supported.
3 The correct endfloat is 0·002 to 0·004 in (0·051 to 0·102 mm) and this is best measured using a dial gauge if available. Excessive endfloat can be taken up by removing shims accordingly whilst insufficient endfloat is adjusted by adding shims as required.
4 To add or subtract shims, remove the hub nut and washer and extract the bearing race.
5 Add or remove the shim thicknesses as required and refit the bearing, the washer and hub nut. Tighten the nut to a torque wrench setting of between 40 and 70 lbf ft (5·3 to 9·6 kgf m) and insert a new split pin to secure.
6 Recheck the endfloat and ensure that the hub is free to rotate.

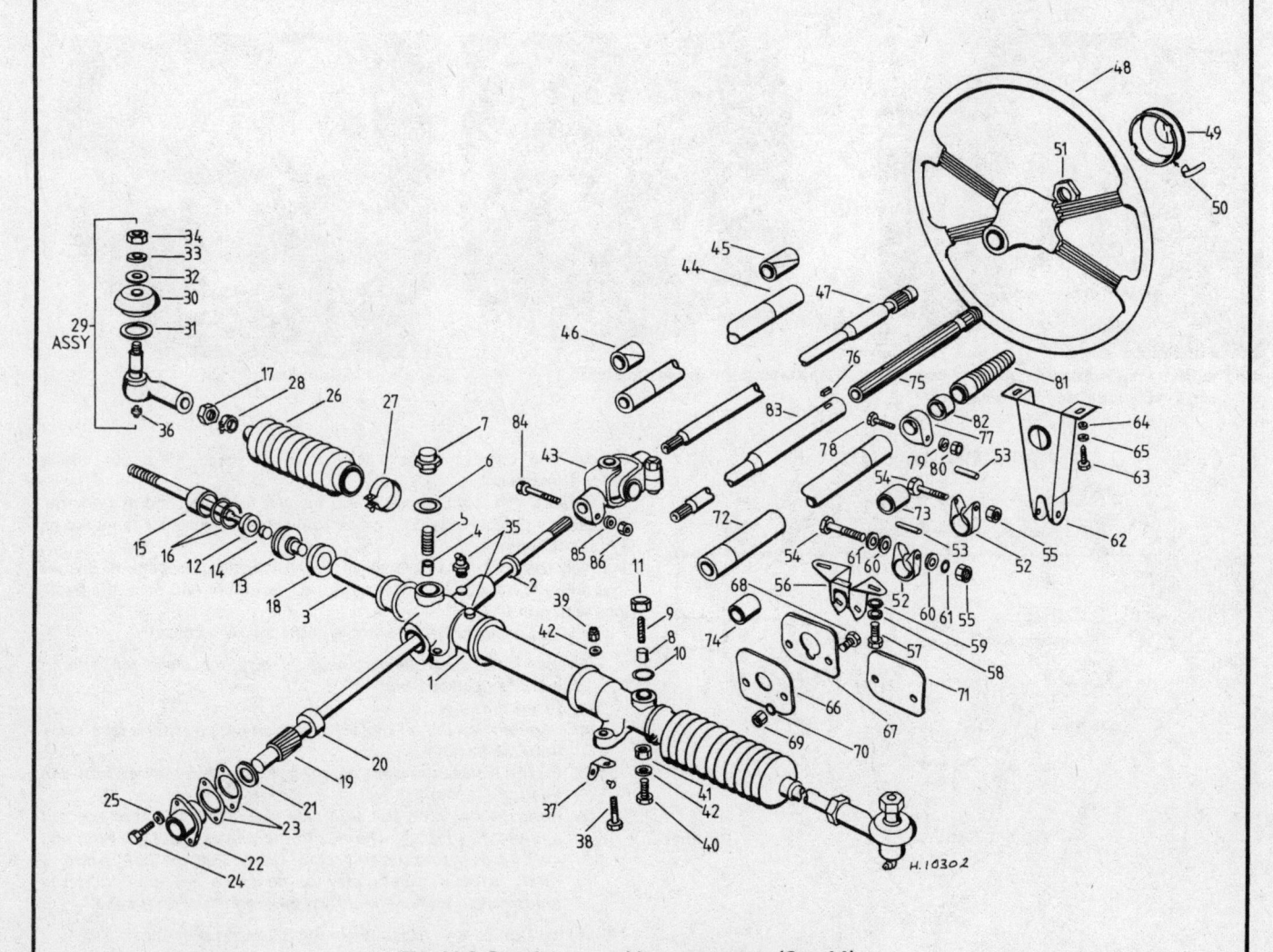

Fig. 11.8 Steering assembly components (Sec 14)

1 Rack housing RHD	23 Shim 0.005 in (0.13 mm)	45 Bush	67 Retainer
2 Seal	24 Screw	46 Bush	68 Screw
3 Steering rack	25 Washer	47 Tube assembly (inner)	69 Nut
4 Rack damper pad	26 Rack seal	48 Steering wheel	70 Washer
5 Rack damper spring	27 Clip	49 Steering wheel cover cap	71 Blanking plate
6 Pad housing shim	28 Clip	50 Spring clip	72 Tube*
7 Rack damper housing	29 Balljoint	51 Nut	73 Bush*
8 Pad	30 Rubber boot	52 Clamp	74 Bush*
9 Spring	31 Boot clip	53 Distance-piece	75 Top end* (adjustable)
10 Washer	32 Boot clip ring	54 Bolt	76 Key*
11 Housing	33 Ball socket washer	55 Nut	77 Clamp*
12 Tie-rod	34 Ball socket nut	56 Bracket	78 Bolt*
13 Male ball housing	35 Greaser	57 Screw	79 Washer* (spring)
14 Ball seat	36 Greaser	58 Washer	80 Nut*
15 Female ball housing	37 Shim	59 Washer	81 Spring cover*
16 Shim (ball housing) 0.003 in (0.07 mm)	38 Bolt	60 Washer	82 Cup*
	39 Nut	61 Washer	83 Tube assembly*
17 Locknut (tie rod)	40 Bolt	62 Bracket	84 Bolt*
18 Lockwasher (tie rod)	41 Nut	63 Screw	85 Washer*
19 Steering pinion	42 Washer	64 Washer	86 Nut*
20 Upper pinion thrust washer	43 Universal joint	65 Washer	
21 Lower pinion thrust washer	44 Tube (outer)	66 Seal	*Adjustable steering column
22 Pinion tail bearing			

Chapter 11 Suspension and steering

Refit the grease retainer.
7   Refit the wheel and lower the car.

9 Rear hub unit – dismantling and overhaul

Refer to Chapter 8, Section 5.

10 Rubber suspension bushes – renewal

1   Refer to Section 4 and remove the coil spring/s.
2   Unscrew and remove the four bolts that secure the spring pan to the levers.
3   Extract the split pins and unscrew the nuts and washers from the inner lower suspension arm pivot pin. Remove the levers and bushes.
4   The new bushes are a relatively loose fit into the levers but the free play will be taken up in the housing when the nut and washer are tightened. Take care during assembly to locate them centrally in order that they are expanded an equal amount when tightened.
5   When located each bush must protrude an equal amount, with the nut loosely fitted. Do not tighten the nut at this stage as it is important that the bushes are clamped up with the suspension levers parallel and must be left until the car is lowered.
6   Fit the spring pan between the levers with the bolt heads within the pan. Do not fully tighten the bolts yet, leave them half a turn loose.
7   Press down the lower wishbone unit and then locate the coil spring. Smear the ends of the spring prior to fitting with grease.
8   Raise the lower wishbone so that it is parallel to the ground and then pivot the hub unit down to enable the fulcrum bolt to be fitted together with the thrust washers, seals and retainers. Ensure that they are correctly fitted as shown in Fig. 11.7 and lubricate the fulcrum pin with grease.
9   Refit the roadwheel and lower the car. Now tighten the spring pan bolts and inner pivot nuts and fit new split pins to secure.
10 Apply grease to the fulcrum pin grease nipple to ensure full lubrication.

11 King pins – removal and refitting

1   Raise and support the front of the car with axle-stands or other suitable supports and remove the front roadwheels. Check that the handbrake is fully applied and engage a low gear.
2   Position a bottle jack under the spring pan on the side concerned and raise it so that the shock absorber arms are clear of the rebound rubbers.
3   The brake hose must now be detached from the wheel cylinder/caliper connection and to prevent leakage of fluid clamp the hose prior to disconnecting or plug it once detached.
4   Loosen off the steering tie-rod retaining nuts and with a suitable spanner engaged on the flats of the rods, unscrew them from the steering balljoints after marking their position. Alternatively detach the outer balljoint (see Section 19).
5   Extract the split pins from the respective outer suspension arm fulcrum bolts. Unscrew and remove the nuts and withdraw the bolts and swivel pin units complete noting the locations of the thrust washers, seals retainers and pins. Remove the hub and king pin assemblies complete.
6   For removal of the hub assembly refer to Sections 6 or 7 as applicable in this Chapter. The removal of the front brake assembly is described in Chapter 9.
7   The king pin units can be dismantled and overhauled as described in the following Section.
8   Refitting of the king pin and hub assemblies is basically a direct reversal of the removal procedure but note the following special points:

(a) When refitting the suspension arm swivel pins and bushes ensure that the bushes seals and thrust washers are correctly located. Each bush must be fitted so that it protrudes an equal amount each side. Tighten the retaining nuts to clamp up the bushes, insert new split pins to secure and then check that respective bush outer flanges are equal proportionally.
(b) The spring pan bolts must be left half a turn slack initially and finally tightened together with the inner bush nuts when the car is free standing with the jacks removed
(c) Lubricate the fulcrum pins during assembly and also on completion via the grease nipple
(d) The steering tie-rods must be screwed into the outer steering balljoint fully and then unscrewed by five full turns to give an approximate initial setting for the wheel alignment, (unless the previous position was marked). In any case the steering alignment settings should be checked and if necessary adjusted on completion.
(e) Reconnect the hydraulic brake hose and top-up and bleed the brakes as given in Chapter 9

12 King pins and links – dismantling, inspection and assembly

1   With the king pin units removed from the vehicle as described in the previous Section, clean them off and remove to a bench for dismantling.
2   Support the unit in a vice and unscrew the upper and lower links, noting that the left-hand side pin unit has a left-hand thread top and bottom.
3   To separate the stub axle from the king pin, it is necessary to detach the steering arm lever which engages with a cutaway section in the pin. Do not remove this lever unless it is absolutely necessary and do not separate the king pin from the stub axle unless absolutely necessary.
4   Clean the parts for inspection.
5   First inspect the top and bottom links. Check the measurement across the thrust faces which should be 2·327 in (59·11 mm).
6   If an appreciable amount of wear is present the link and bush must be renewed. Where only the bush is worn drive the old one out and press in a new one which must then be reamed and burnished to 0·750 in (19·05 mm). The bush hole must align with the threaded bore when fitted. This task is best left to an automotive machine shop unless of course you have the necessary tools and fitting experience.
7   Check the thrust washers, although case hardened, they may scored on their faces. They must be flat and the faces parallel to within a tolerance of 0·0005 in (0·01 mm).
8   The threaded bores of the swivel pin links will probably be worn but unless excessive they can be reused.
9   Inspect the fulcrum pin distance tubes for signs of excessive wear or scoring. They should be 2·337 in (59·36 mm) with a diameter of 0·748 in (19·00 mm). Renew if necessary.
10 Check the fulcrum pin thrust washers for signs of wear and or scoring. They should be 0·068 to 0·065 in (1·73 to 1·68 mm) thick, the inside bore diameter should be 0·510 to 0·505 in (12·95 to 12·83 mm) and the outside diameter must be 1·25 in (31·75 mm). Renew if worn beyond these dimensions or if they are not parallel to within 0·0005 in (0·01 mm) across the faces.
11 To assemble the king pins and linkages, screw the link onto the king pin to align the waisted section of the pin with the pivot bolt hole.
12 Insert the pivot bolt into the link and screw the link fully into position on the thread of the king pin (about three full turns), and then unscrew the link by about 1½ turns to allow a maximum pivot pin clearance in each direction.
13 Where the brake backplate has been removed, centralise the lower link in a similar manner prior to refitting the plate and king pin to the suspension arm
14 When the lower steering knuckle link is bolted in position check that the thrust washers and seals are correctly located and that the total end clearances of the links is 0·008 to 0·013 in (0·2 to 0·33 mm). This clearance is measured between the link end face and the thrust washer. The lower link must be fitted correctly prior to fitting of the brake backplate as it cannot be set afterwards.
15 Refit the grease nipples and pump some recommended grease into the nut/s. Check the king pin for satisfactory swivel action in the links.

13 Steering wheel – removal and refitting

1   Prise the cover from the centre of the steering wheel taking care not to damage it (photo).
2   Use a suitable box spanner and unscrew the steering wheel nut. Before withdrawing the wheel from the shaft, mark its relative position to ensure correct replacement.

168   Chapter 11 Suspension and steering

13.1 The steering wheel retaining nut with cover removed

14.1 Steering column universal joint

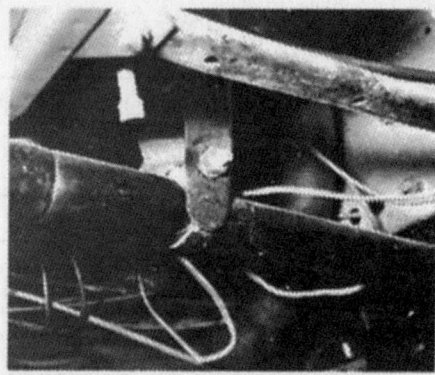

14.3 Steering column support bracket under dashboard

3   Pull the wheel from the shaft splines to remove. You may need the use of a steering wheel puller to achieve this.
4   Refitting is a reversal of the removal procedure but ensure that the wheel is aligned correctly and tighten the nut to a torque wrench setting of 41 lbf ft (5·75 kgf m).
5   On models equipped with the optional adjustable column the steering wheel and column extension can be removed as a combined unit if required as follows.
6   Unscrew and remove the clamp nut and bolt from the telescopic adjuster clamp. Extend the column to its fullest extent and contracting the plated helical sleeve and clamping collar in the direction of the steering wheel, withdraw the splined shaft engagement key. The wheel and column extension can then be removed.
7   Refitting the wheel and extension is a direct reversal of the removal procedure but ensure that the engagement key and clamp bolt are securely located on completion.

14 Steering column – removal and refitting

Non-adjustable column
1   Unscrew and remove the clamp bolt and nut from the universal joint to steering mast location (photo).
2   Unscrew the nuts and remove the clamp plate and draught excluder rubber from the column at the toe board.
3   Unscrew and remove the column clamp bolts and nuts with spring and flat washers from the column supports and withdraw the column complete (photo).
4   To renew the steering column bushes extract the main mast from the auto column and prise the old felt bushes free. Soak the new bushes in graphite oil prior to fitting.
5   Refitting is a reversal of the removal procedure but ensure that all fastenings are secure on completion.

Adjustable column
6   The procedure for removing the adjustable type column unit is identical to the fixed type except that the steering wheel and column extension are removed separately as detailed in the previous Section (paragraphs 5 and 6).

15 Steering column universal joint – removal and refitting

1   Unscrew and remove the universal joint clamp nuts and bolts.
2   Loosen the column clamp bolts beneath the dash panel.
3   Withdraw the column and mast assembly upwards sufficiently to disengage the universal joint.
4   If the universal joint unit is worn and in need of overhaul, the procedure for dismantling and reassembly is similar to that of the propeller shaft universal joints which is described in Chapter 7.

5   Refitting is a reversal of the removal procedure.

16 Steering gearbox – removal and refitting

1   Refer to Fig. 11.8 for details of the steering assembly components.
2   Unscrew and remove the steering rack damper and secondary damper units.
3   Unscrew and remove the pinion tail bearing retaining bolts and spring washers. Withdraw the pinion tail bearing and shims and the lower thrust washer. Catch any oil spillage from the rack.
4   Raise the front of the car, placing jacks under the lower suspension arm spring pans. Remove the wheels.
5   Extract the split pins from the tie-rod nuts, unscrew the nuts and using a balljoint separator (if available) detach the tie-rod joints from the steering arms.
6   On right-hand drive cars turn the steering to the left-hand lock whilst on left-hand drive cars turn the steering to the right-lock.
7   Unscrew and remove the steering pinion shaft universal joint clamp nut and bolt, disengage the joint and withdraw the pinion unit.
8   Unscrew and remove the steering rack to frame retaining bolts and nuts, noting that the nuts at the front side are self locking types. Note also any packing shims fitted between the rack and frame bracket (photo).
9   Now move the steering unit towards the middle of the car so that the tie-rod is clear of the front extension plate and carefully extract the unit downwards.
10 Refitting the steering box unit is a direct reversal of the removal procedure but note the following:
11 Align the cutaway section of the pinion and universal joint splines when reattaching the two.
12 Take special care to correctly align the steering column and box so that the universal joint has a 'free condition'. This condition is achieved by aligning the centres of the universal joint spiders, the steering rack pinion and the column (Fig. 11.9). An adjustment facility is provided via the slotted holes in the support bracket at the column lower end by packing shims inserted between the steering gearbox mounting bosses and the suspension member. The respective gearbox and column fastenings should only be tightened after the centralisation alignment has been made.
13 First tighten the universal joint clamp bolts, then locate the universal joint accordingly and tighten the column lower end support bracket clamps. Insert shims to take up the gap between the gearbox bosses and the mounting brackets, then tighten the retaining bolts. Rivets (0·125 in (3·2 mm) diameter) retain the shims to the chassis frame as shown in Fig. 11.10.
14 To ensure correct alignment loosen off and then retighten the lower steering column support bolt. Finally tighten the upper support bracket bolt.
15 When the steering tie-rods have been reconnected to the steering arms, check the steering alignment.

Chapter 11 Suspension and steering

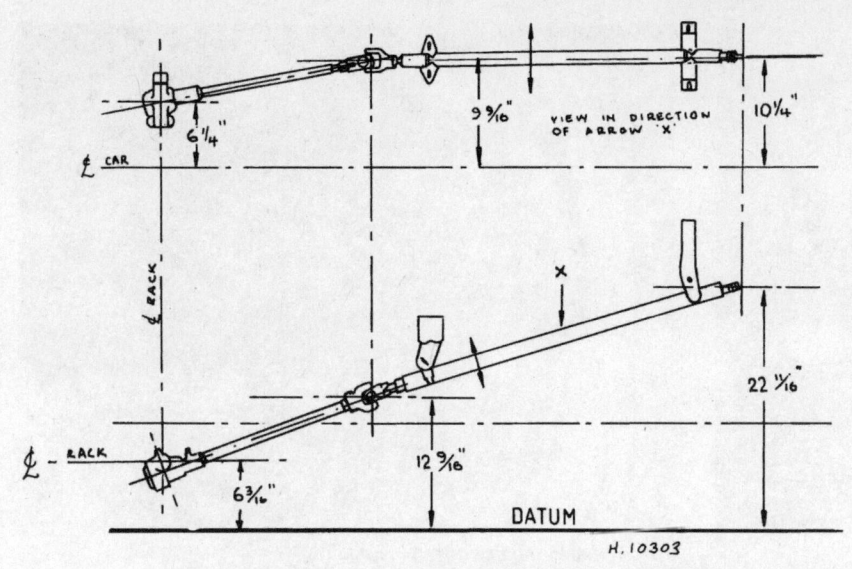

Fig. 11.9 Steering column alignment check (Sec 16)

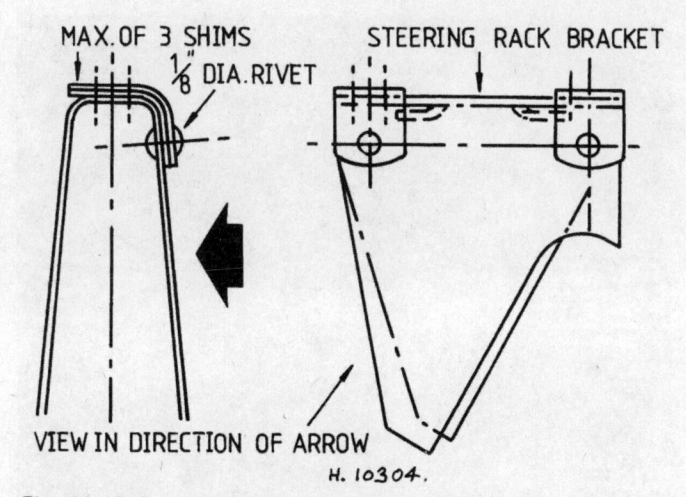

Fig. 11.10 Steering gearbox mounting bracket shim location to give correct alignment (Sec 16)

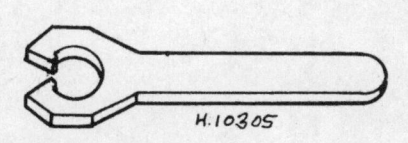

Fig. 11.11 Special tool No 18G313 – steering tie-rod C spanner (Sec 17)

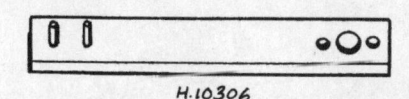

Fig. 11.12 Special tool number 18G312 – steering tie-rod pin spanner (Sec 17)

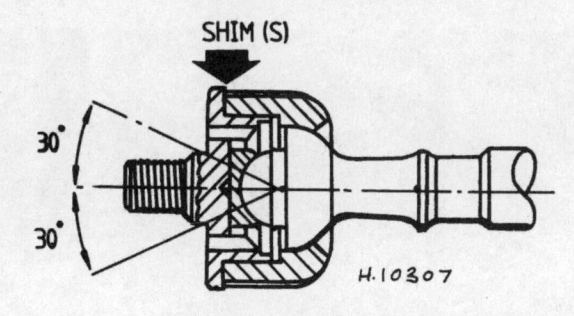

Fig. 11.13 Inner tie-rod balljoint cross-section view showing shim location (Sec 17)

17 Steering gearbox – dismantling and assembly

1 To remove the pinion unit, detach the damper housing, the spring, pad and shims from the top of the housing (Fig. 11.8).
2 Detach the secondary damper housing and extract the washer spring and damper pad.
3 Extract the pinion tail bearing and shims together with the bottom thrust washer (if not already removed). Catch oil spillage in a container. Remove the pinion.
4 Support the tie-rod balljoints and loosen the locking nuts. Detach the balljoints.
5 Unscrew and release the rubber gaiter seal retaining clips and slide the seal from the rod.
6 Support the rack housing in a vice and bend back the tie-rod ballhousing lockwashers, and unscrew the ball-housings using the special Leyland tool number 18G313 if available. Remove the lockwashers.
7 Now withdraw the steering rack from its housing. Remove the pinion top thrust washer.
8 Unscrew the ball seat housings from the caps using the previously mentioned special tool or suitable 'C' spanner, together with a tie-rod pin spanner (special Leyland tool 18G312).
9 Remove the respective shims and ball seats keeping them in order of removal.
10 The respective components can now be cleaned and inspected for wear and/or damage and renewed as necessary.
11 Before reassembly ensure that all components are perfectly clean.
12 Commence assembly by inserting the tie-rod ball end into the female housing, assemble the ball seat, the male seat housing and shims. The two housings are then tightened using the two special tools previously mentioned during dismantling. When assembled the ball must be a fairly tight sliding fit with no play detectable. Two thicknesses of shims are available (0·003 and 0·005 in (0·07 and 0·13 mm)) to make further adjustments should they be necessary.
13 Once adjusted a new locking washer can be fitted and the ballhousing tightened. Lock the housing in three places by bending over the flange of the lockwasher.
14 Locate the upper thrust washer into the pinion housing and ensure that the slotted side is facing away from the pinion. This washer is the thicker of the two.
15 Now reinsert the steering rack into the housing.
16 Assemble and adjust the opposing ballhousing in the same manner. Refit the rubber gaiters and clips.
17 Refit the ball end locking nuts and joints so that they are approximately in the same position as when removed.
18 Insert a new pinion shaft felt seal.
19 The steering rack unit can now be refitted to the mounting brackets and aligned with the column as detailed in Section 16.
20 With the steering box in position, insert the small thrust washer onto the plain end of the pinion shaft, refit the shims, the pinion tail bearing and secure them in position.
21 Check the pinion shaft endplay which should be within 0·002 to 0·005 in (0·05 to 0·13 mm). Add or subtract shims as required to achieve this tolerance of play.
22 Check the rack damper adjustment as follows:

  (a) *Refit the plunger into the cap and fit them less the spring or shims, screwing them in until it is just possible to turn the*

Chapter 11 Suspension and steering

16.8 Steering box to frame location

19.1 The steering tie-rod outer balljoint

20.1 The rear shock absorber location viewed from underneath

21.5 The rear spring U-bolt nuts, bracket and shock absorber arm location joint. Note also the check strap location

pinion shaft by drawing the rack through the housing. At this point use a feeler gauge to measure the clearance between the plunger cap hexagon and its seating to the rack housing. Add to this clearance 0.002 to 0.005 in (0.05 to 0.13 mm) and this is the thickness of shims required. Note that the shims are 0.003 in (0.08 mm) thick

(b) *Unscrew the damper cap and plunger and insert the required thickness of shims and spring. Retighten the damper cap and plunger.*

23 The secondary damper is fitted without shims.
24 To lubricate the completed assembly pump 0·5 pint (0·28 litre) of Hypoid oil into the rack housings via the nipple. As the oil is inserted move the rack backwards and forwards to ensure good initial distribution of the lubricant. Check for signs of leakage around the gaiters on completion.

18 Front wheel alignment – checking and adjustment

1 The front wheels are correctly aligned when they are exactly parallel.
2 Adjustment is effected by loosening the locknut on each tie-rod balljoint, and the clips on the gaiters, and turning both tie-rods equally until the adjustment is correct.
3 Accurate alignment requires the use of a base bar or an optical alignment device and this tank is therefore best entrusted to your local garage or Leyland dealer.
4 A wheel alignment check should always be made after dismantling or overhauling part of the steering equipment.
5 If the wheels are not aligned correctly, tyre wear will be heavy and uneven, and the steering will be stiff and unresponsive.

19 Tie-rod outer balljoints – removal and refitting

1 If the tie-rod outer balljoints are worn it be necessary to renew the whole balljoint assembly as they cannot be dismantled and repaired (photo).
2 To remove a balljoint, free the balljoint shank from the steering arm using a balljoint remover, after unscrewing the nut. Mark the position of the locknut on the tie-rod accurately to ensure near accurate toe-in on reassembly.
3 Slacken off the balljoint locknut, and holding the tie-rod by its flat with a spanner, to prevent it from turning, unscrew the complete ball assembly from the rod.
4 Refitting is a straightforward reversal of this process. Ensure that toe-in is correct.

Chapter 11 Suspension and steering

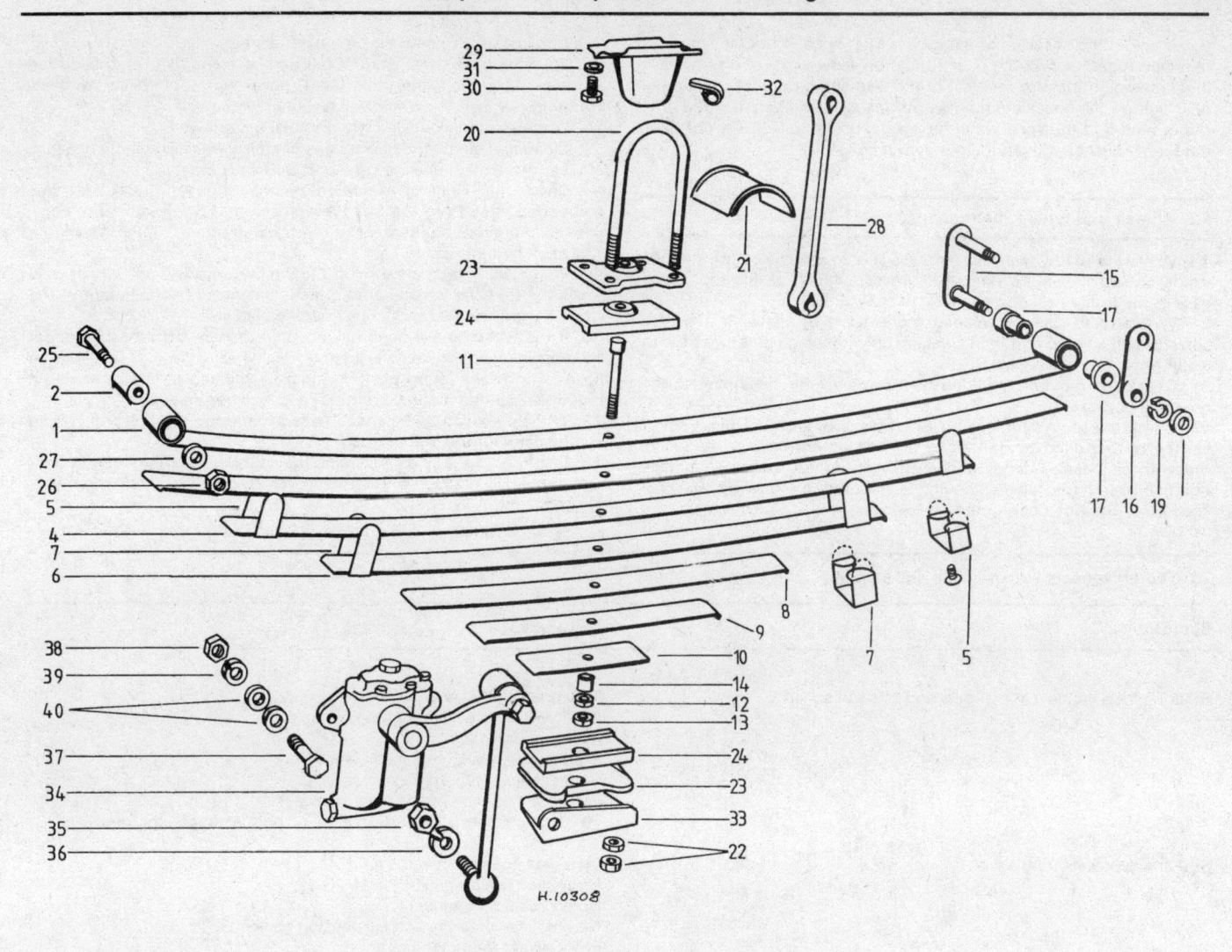

Fig. 11.14 The rear suspension components (Sec 20)

1 Main spring leaf
2 Bush
3 Leaf (second)
4 Leaf (third)
5 Clip
6 Leaf (fourth)
7 Clip
8 Leaf (fifth)
9 Leaf (sixth)
10 Bottom plate
11 Bolt
12 Nut
13 Locknut
14 Distance-piece
15 Shackle plate and pins
16 Shackle plate (inner)
17 Rubber bush
18 Nut
19 Washer (spring)
20 U-clip
21 Top U-clip plate
22 Nut
23 Plate
24 Pad
25 Bolt
26 Nut
27 Washer
28 Rebound strap
29 Bump rubber
30 Screw
31 Washer
32 Clip
33 Bracket
34 Shock absorber
35 Nut
36 Washer
37 Bolt
38 Nut
39 Washer
40 Washer

20 Rear shock absorbers – removal and refitting

It is not necessary to jack-up the rear of the car for removal of the rear shock absorbers if a pit or ramp is available. Otherwise jack-up, and firmly support the rear of the car.

1 To remove a shock absorber unscrew the nut and spring washer from the bolt which holds the shock absorber arm to the link arm; remove the two nuts and spring washers from the shock absorber securing bolts and remove the bolts (photo).
2 Keeping the shock absorber in the upright position remove it from the chassis. Whenever the shock absorber is removed or fitted keep it in the upright position to prevent the ingress of air into the operating chamber.
3 Refit the shock absorber unit in the reverse order ensuring that it is topped up with fluid and operate the lever a few times to expel any air that may possibly have entered the pressure chamber.

21 Rear springs – removal and refitting

1 Remove the wheel cap, loosen the wheel nuts, and jack-up the side of the car from which the spring is to be removed.
2 Unscrew the wheel nuts and lift away the wheel.
3 Place a suitable support under the rear cross-body member as close to the rear of the spring as possible.
4 Locate a bottle jack under the axle casing close to the spring so that the rear axle is well supported, but the spring not compressed.
5 Slacken off the U-bolt locknuts and remove the nuts (photo). Raise the U-bolts until the shock absorber link bracket can be pivoted clear of the springs. Remove the plate and rubber pad.
6 Unscrew the rear shackle nuts and remove the shackle pins and plates and rubber bush.
7 Unscrew the nut and washer from the anchor pin in the front eye of the spring, drive the pin out and remove the rubber bush. The spring can now be removed.

Chapter 11 Suspension and steering

8 If any of the shackles of the rubber bushes are worn they must be renewed together with the pins if they too show signs of wear. Refitting is a straightforward reversal of the dismantling procedure. Do not fully tighten the shackle pin nuts until the car has been lowered onto the ground and the spring is in its normal position. If this is not done the rubber bushes will require frequent renewal.

22 Wheels and tyres – maintenance

1 While the roadwheels are removed it is sound advice to clean the inside of each wheel, to remove the accumulation of dirt and, in the case of the front ones, disc pad dust (if applicable).
2 Wire wheels can be cleaned more easily by applying a grease solvent with a brush and then cleaning off with a high pressure hose or a stiff brush and clean water.
3 Check the general condition of the wheels for signs of rust and repaint if necessary.
4 Check the spokes for looseness, cracks or breakage. Loose spokes can be re-tensioned by tightening the adjustment nuts at the wheel rim with an open ended spanner. Only the loose spokes should be tightened, and the wheel should be checked for true by a wheel specialist. **Do not** overtighten the spokes, and if loose spokes are found to be badly rusted, they must be renewed.
5 Examine the wheel stud holes and, if elongated, or the dished recesses in which the nuts seat have worn, or become overcompressed, then the wheel will have to be renewed.
6 Likewise, badly buckled wheels must be renewed.
7 Clean and check the hub splines of spoke wheels. If showing signs of wear, have them checked and renewed if necessary.
8 Check the general condition of the tyres and pick out any embedded flints from the tread and check that the tread depth complies to the legal requirement. If the tread depth is 1 mm or less, the tyre must be renewed.
9 Periodical interchanging of the roadwheels is well worthwhile providing that the wheels are correctly balanced, (independent of the car). The spare wheel should be interchanged also.
10 If the wheels have been balanced on the car, then they must not be interchanged, as the balance of the wheel, tyre and hub will be upset. The exact fitting position must be marked before removing a roadwheel so that it can be refitted to its balanced position.
11 Wheels should be balanced halfway through the life of a tyre to compensate for the loss of tread.
12 Ensure that the tyres, including the spare, are kept inflated to their recommended pressures. Tyre pressures are best checked when tyres are cold.

23 Fault diagnosis – suspension and steering

Symptom	Reason/s
Steering feels vague, car wanders and floats at speed	Tyre pressures uneven Dampers worn or require topping up Spring clips broken Steering gear balljoints badly worn Suspension geometry incorrect Steering mechanism free play excessive Front suspension and rear axle pick-up points out of alignment
Stiff and heavy steering	Tyre pressures too low No grease in king pins No oil in steering gear No grease in steering and suspension balljoints Front wheel toe-in incorrect Suspension geometry incorrect Steering gear incorrectly adjusted too tightly Steering column misaligned
Wheel wobble and vibration	Wheel nuts loose Front wheels and tyres out of balance Steering balljoints badly worn Hub bearings badly worn Steering gear free play excessive Front springs loose, weak or broken

Chapter 12 Bodywork and fittings

Contents

Body – removal and refitting	17
Bonnet and boot lids – removal and refitting	14
Bumpers – removal and refitting	11
Doors – removal and refitting	15
Door trim and lock (Tourer) – removal and refitting	9
Door windows, window regulators and locks (Coupe models) – removal and refitting	16
Front wing panel – removal and refitting	12
General description	1
Maintenance – bodywork	2
Maintenance – hinges	6
Maintenance – upholstery and carpets	3
Major body damage – repair	5
Minor body damage – repair	4
Rear wing panel – removal and refitting	13
Soft-top – removal and refitting	10
Windscreen and frame (Tourer) – removal and refitting	7
Windscreen and rear window (Coupe) – removal and refitting	8

1 General description

Although the MGA body style was a complete breakaway from the traditional MG lines, it was still mounted on a chassis, which was of sturdy box type construction (Fig. 12.1). Whilst the main body frame is manufactured in steel, the doors, bonnet and boot are manufactured in aluminium and the 'cockpit' floor panels in wood.

Two basic body styles were produced being the soft-top 'Tourer' and the hardtop 'Coupe'. A fibre glass detachable hardtop was also available as an optional extra for fitting in place of the soft-top hood, which was stowed in its normal place at the rear of the seats. The hood frame pivot plates are used as attachment brackets for the hardtop when fitted. If the hood is removed from the car attachment brackets have to be fitted in place of the hood frame pivot plates.

Both front and rear wing panels are retained by bolts to the main body section and this makes for easier removal and repair when necessary by the DIY mechanic.

Whilst the plywood floor sections of the cockpit floor may not rust, they will after many years show signs of decay with the laminated layers starting to open up. New sections can be easily cut as replacements but make sure you use a Marine or exterior grade plywood of the correct thickness. Use the old panels as a template.

Most body panels are fortunately still available for the MGA if not from Leyland dealers, then from specialist firms.

2 Maintenance – bodywork and underframe

1 The general condition of a car's bodywork is one thing that significantly affects its value. Maintenance is easy but needs to be regular. Neglect, particularly after minor damage can lead quickly to further deterioration and costly repair bills. It is important also to keep watch on those parts of the car not immediately visible, for instance the underside, inside all the wheel arches and the lower part of the engine compartment.
2 The basic maintenance routine for the bodywork is washing – preferably with a lot of water, from a hose. This will remove all the loose solids which may have stuck to the car. It is important to flush these off in such a way as to prevent grit from scratching the finish. The wheel arches and underframe need washing in the same way to remove any accumulated mud which will retain moisture and tend to encourage rust. Paradoxically enough, the best time to clean the underframe and wheel arches is in wet weather when the mud is thoroughly wet and soft. In very wet weather the underframe is usually cleaned of large accumulations automatically and this is a good time for inspection.
3 Periodically, it is a good idea to have the whole of the underframe of the car steam cleaned, engine compartment included so that a thorough inspection can be carried out to see what minor repairs and renovations are necessary. Steam cleaning is available at many garages and is necessary for removal of the accumulation of oily grime which sometimes is allowed to cake thick in certain areas near the engine, gearbox and back axle. If steam cleaning facilities are not available, there are one or two excellent grease solvents available which can be brush applied. The dirt can then be simply hosed off.
4 After washing paintwork, wipe off with a chamois leather to give an unspotted clear finish. A coat of clear protective wax polish will give added protection against chemical pollutants in the air. If the paintwork sheen has dulled or oxidised, use a cleaner/polisher combination to restore the brilliance of the shine. This requires a little effort, but is usually caused because regular washing has been neglected. Always check that the door and ventilator opening drain holes and pipes are completely clear so that water can be drained out. Bright work should be treated the same way as paintwork. Windscreens and windows can be kept clear of the smeary film which often appears if a little ammonia is added to the water. If they are scratched, a good rub with a proprietary metal polish will often clear them. Never use any form of wax or other body or chromium polish on glass.

3 Maintenance – upholstery, carpets, soft-tops, side screens and tonneau covers

Remove the carpets and thoroughly vacuum clean the interior of the car every three months or more frequently if necessary.

Beat out the carpets and vacuum clean them if they are very dirty. If the headlining (Coupe) or upholstery is soiled apply an upholstery cleaner with a damp sponge and wipe off with a clean dry cloth. The original seats were leather covered. If you are fortunate enough to still have leather seats in your model clean them carefully using a leather upholstery cleaner. If not too damaged, the original leather can be cleaned and recoloured using a leather renovating kit available from various auto upholstery specialists.

When carpets are refitted make sure that they are aligned securely into position. Always renew defective carpet fastenings.

Under no circumstances try to clean the soft-top, side screws or tonneau cover with detergents, caustic soaps, or spirit cleaners. Plain soap and water is all that is required with a soft brush to clean dirt that

1. This photographic sequence shows the steps taken to repair the dent and paintwork damage shown above. In general, the procedure for repairing a hole will be similar; where there are substantial differences, the procedure is clearly described and shown in a separate photograph.

2. First remove any trim around the dent, then hammer out the dent where access is possible. This will minimise filling. Here, after the large dent has been hammered out, the damaged area is being made slightly concave.

3. Next, remove all paint from the damaged area by rubbing with course abrasive paper or using a power drill fitted with a wire brush or abrasive pad. 'Feather' the edge of the boundary with good paintwork using a finer grade of abrasive paper.

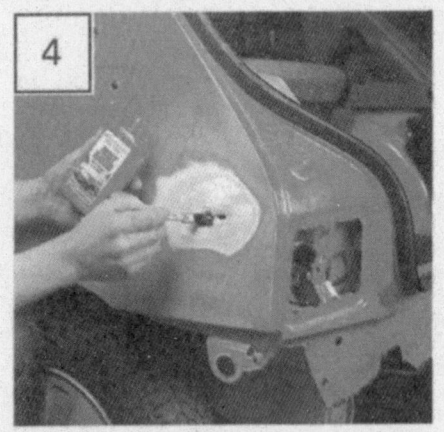

4. Where there are holes or other damage, the sheet metal should be cut away before proceeding further. The damaged area and any signs of rust should be treated with Turtle Wax Hi-Tech Rust Eater, which will also inhibit further rust formation.

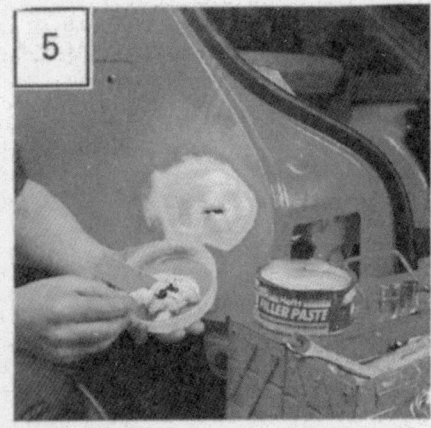

5. *For a large dent or hole* mix Holts Body Plus Resin and Hardener according to the manufacturer's instructions and apply around the edge of the repair. Press Glass Fibre Matting over the repair area and leave for 20-30 minutes to harden. Then ...

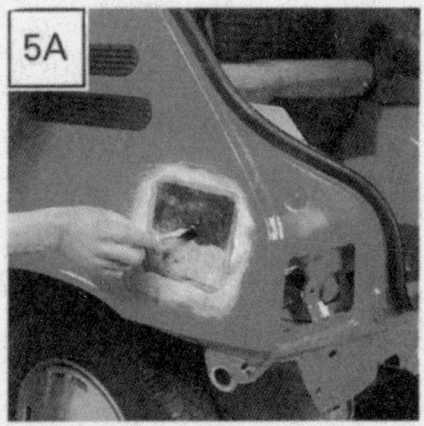

5A. ... brush more Holts Body Plus Resin and Hardener onto the matting and leave to harden. Repeat the sequence with two or three layers of matting, checking that the final layer is lower than the surrounding area. Apply Holts Body Plus Filler Paste as shown in Step 5B.

5B. *For a medium dent*, mix Holts Body Plus Filler Paste and Hardener according to the manufacturer's instructions and apply it with a flexible applicator. Apply thin layers of filler at 20-minute intervals, until the filler surface is slightly proud of the surrounding bodywork.

5C. *For small dents and scratches* use Holts No Mix Filler Paste straight from the tube. Apply it according to the instructions in thin layers, using the spatula provided. It will harden in minutes if applied outdoors and may then be used as its own knifing putting.

6. Use a plane or file for initial shaping. Then, using progressively finer grades of wet-and-dry paper, wrapped around a sanding block, and copious amounts of clean water, rub down the filler until glass smooth. 'Feather' the edges of adjoining paintwork.

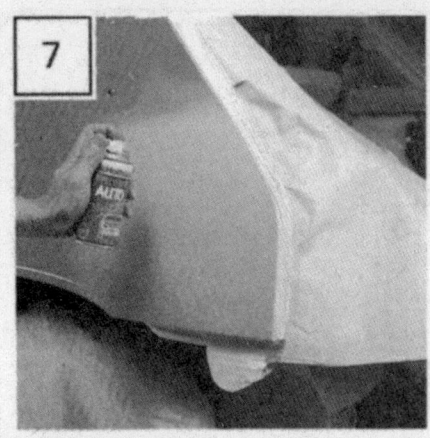

7. Protect adjoining areas before spraying the whole repair area and at least one inch of the surrounding sound paintwork with Holts Dupli-Color primer.

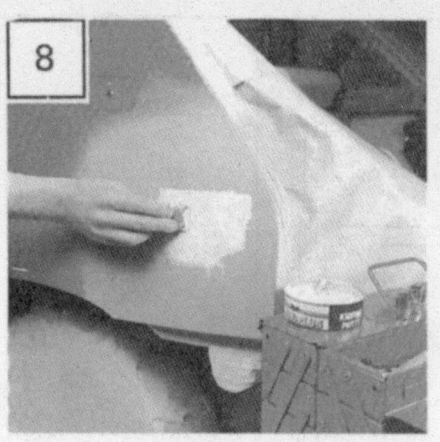

8. Fill any imperfections in the filler surface with a small amount of Holts Body Plus Knifing Putty. Using plenty of clean water, rub down the surface with a fine grade wet-and-dry paper - 400 grade is recommended - until it is really smooth.

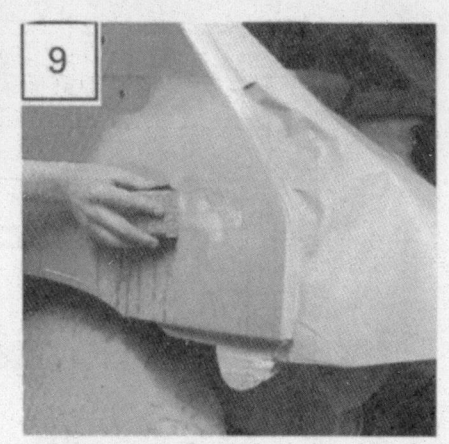

9. Carefully fill any remaining imperfections with knifing putty before applying the last coat of primer. Then rub down the surface with Holts Body Rubbing Compound to ensure a really smooth surface.

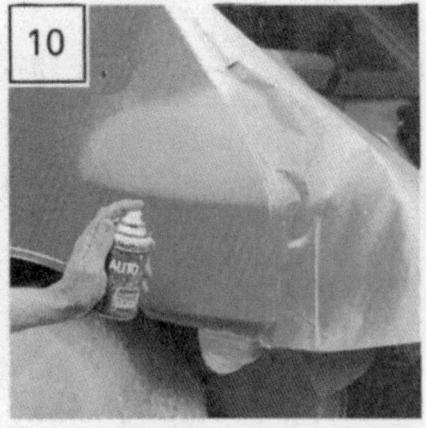

10. Protect surrounding areas from overspray before applying the topcoat in several thin layers. Agitate Holts Dupli-Color aerosol thoroughly. Start at the repair centre, spraying outwards with a side-to-side motion.

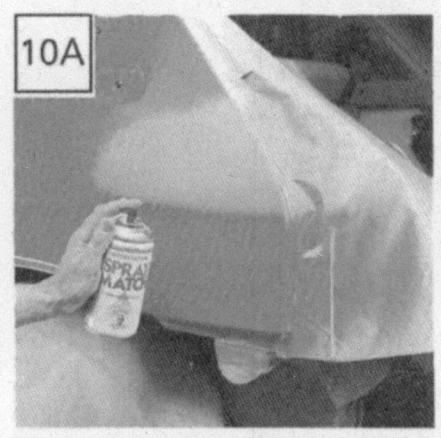

10A. If the exact colour is not available off the shelf, local Holts Professional Spraymatch Centres will custom fill an aerosol to match perfectly.

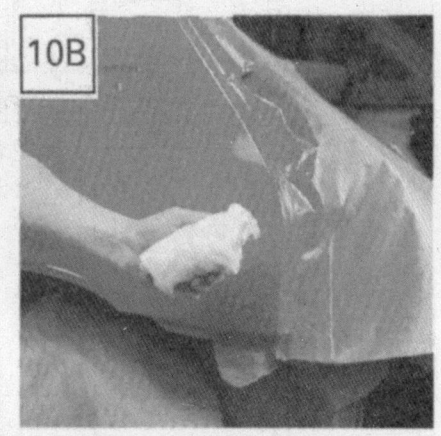

10B. To identify whether a lacquer finish is required, rub a painted unrepaired part of the body with wax and a clean cloth.

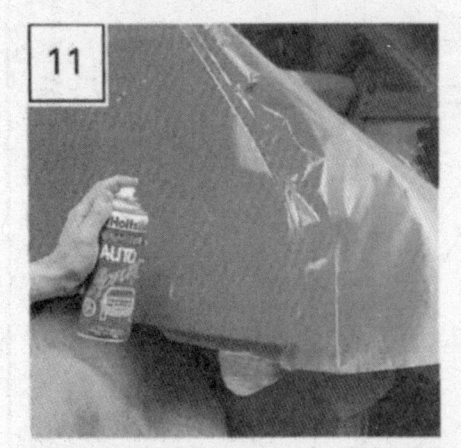

11. If *no* traces of paint appear on the cloth, spray Holts Dupli-Color clear lacquer over the repaired area to achieve the correct gloss level.

12. The paint will take about two weeks to harden fully. After this time it can be 'cut' with a mild cutting compound such as Turtle Wax Minute Cut prior to polishing with a final coating of Turtle Wax Extra.

14. When carrying out bodywork repairs, remember that the quality of the finished job is proportional to the time and effort expended.

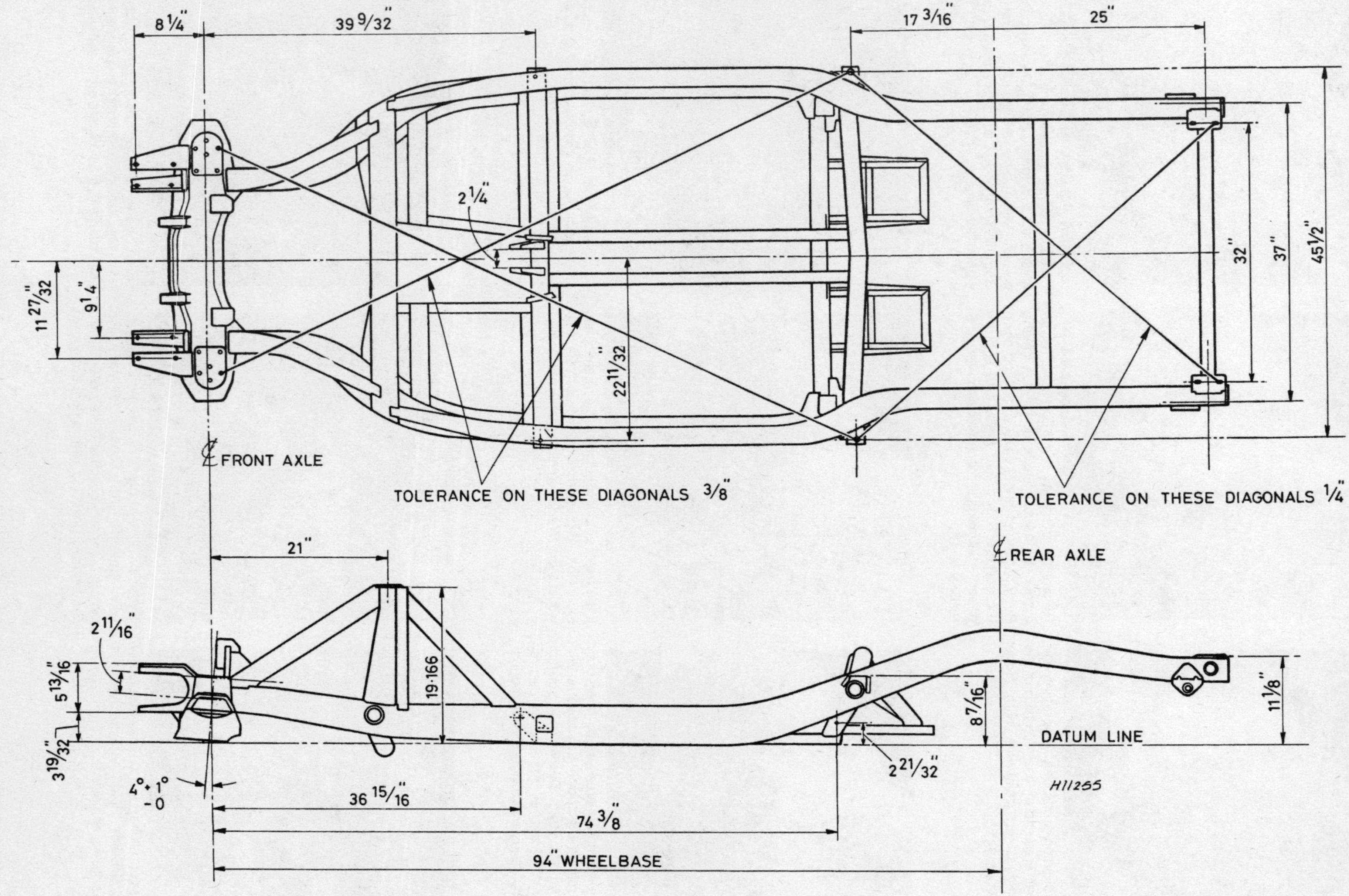

Fig. 12.1 The chassis frame, showing the dimensions and diagonal check points for misalignment (Sec 1)

may be ingrained. Wash the soft-top as frequently as the rest of the car.

The most common problem found with most soft-tops and side screens is that the windows become badly faded and scratched making vision distorted and blurred. Sadly once in this condition there is no easy remedy apart from renewing the window panel. This can only be successfully undertaken by specialist firms and will probably cost nearly as much as a new soft-top or side screen anyway! For this reason always fold the hood carefully when stowing and wash carefully to avoid scratching the surface. Minor marks may possibly be removed using a mild metal polish.

Lightly lubricate the pivot points of the soft-top frame and always check that the fasteners are secure when erected.

4 Minor body damage – repair

The photo sequences on pages 174 and 175 illustrate the operations detailed in the following sub-sections.

The following repair procedure is relevant to steel bodywork construction only, although it can be applied to the repair of aluminium alloy construction with the exception of the following points:

(a) *When removing paint from aluminium alloy panels, use paint remover and a wood or nylon scraper, ensuring the affected area is thoroughly rinsed down with clean, fresh water on completion of the job. Never use coarse abrasives (eg abrasive disc on power drill) as these will cause deep scoring of the aluminium alloy or in extreme cases, penetrate the thickness of the metal. It is advisable to wear protective gloves and eyeglasses when using paint remover*

(b) *Disregard the use of 'rust remover and inhibitor' when treating aluminium alloy panels for corrosion. Alternative products are available for this purpose*

(c) *If possible, use an etch-primer on untreated aluminium alloy-surfaces otherwise the primer may not key sufficiently and subsequently flake off*

Repair of minor scratches in the car's bodywork

If the scratch is very superficial, and does not penetrate to the metal of the bodywork, repair is very simple. Lightly rub the area of the scratch with a paintwork renovator, or a very fine cutting paste, to remove loose paint from the scratch and to clear the surrounding bodywork of wax polish. Rinse the area with clean water.

Apply touch-up paint to the scratch using a thin paint brush; continue to apply thin layers of paint until the surface of the paint in the scratch is level with the surrounding paintwork. Allow the new paint at least two weeks to harden: then blend it into the surrounding paintwork by rubbing the paintwork, in the scratch area, with a paintwork renovator or a very fine cutting paste. Finally, apply wax polish.

Where the scratch has penetrated right through to the metal of the bodywork, causing the metal to rust, a different repair technique is required. Remove any loose rust from the bottom of the scratch with a penknife, then apply rust inhibiting paint to prevent the formation of rust in the future. Using a rubber or nylon applicator fill the scratch with bodystopper paste. If required, this paste can be mixed with cellulose thinners to provide a very thin paste which is ideal for filling narrow scratches. Before the stopper-paste in the scratch hardens, wrap a piece of smooth cotton rag around the top of a finger. Dip the finger in cellulose thinners and then quickly sweep it across the surface of the stopper-paste in the scratch; this will ensure that the surface of the stopper-paste is slightly hollowed. The scratch can now be painted over as described earlier in this Section.

Repair of dents in the car's bodywork

When deep denting of the car's bodywork has taken place, the first task is to pull the dent out, until the affected bodywork almost attains its original shape. There is little point in trying to restore the original shape completely, as the metal in the damaged area will have stretched on impact and cannot be reshaped fully to its original contour. It is better to bring the level of the dent up to a point which is about $\frac{1}{8}$ in (3 mm) below the level of the surrounding bodywork. In cases where the dent is very shallow anyway, it is not worth trying to pull it out at all. If the underside of the dent is accessible, it can be hammered out gently from behind, using a mallet with a wooden or plastic head. Whilst doing this, hold a suitable block of wood firmly against the impact from the hammer blows and thus prevent a large area of the bodywork from being 'belled-out'.

Should the dent be in a section of the bodywork which has double skin or some other factor making it inaccessible from behind, a different technique is called for. Drill several small holes through the metal inside the area – particularly in the deeper section. Then screw long self-tapping screws into the holes just sufficiently for them to gain a good purchase in the metal. Now the dent can be pulled out by pulling on the protruding heads of the screws with a pair of pliers.

The next stage of the repair is the removal of the paint from the damaged area, and from an inch or so of the surrounding 'sound' bodywork. This is accomplished most easily by using a wire brush or abrasive pad on a power drill, although it can be done just as effectively by hand using sheets of abrasive paper. To complete the preparation for filling, score the surface of the bare metal with a screwdriver or the tang of a file, or alternatively, drill small holes in the affected area. This will provide a really good 'key' for the filler paste.

To complete the repair see the Section on filling and respraying.

Repair of rust holes or gashes in the car's bodywork

Remove all paint from the affected area and from an inch or so of the surrounding 'sound' bodywork, using an abrasive pad or a wire brush on a power drill. If these are not available a few sheets of abrasive paper will do the job just as effectively. With the paint removed you will be able to gauge the severity of the corrosion and therefore decide whether to renew the whole panel (if this is possible) or to repair the affected area. New body panels are not as expensive as most people think and it is often quicker and more satisfactory to fit a new panel than to attempt to repair large areas of corrosion.

Remove all fittings from the affected area except those which will act as a guide to the original shape of the damaged bodywork (eg headlamp shells etc). Then, using tin snips or a hacksaw blade, remove all loose metal and any other metal badly affected by corrosion. Hammer the edges of the hole inwards in order to create a slight depression for the filler paste.

Wire brush the affected area to remove the powdery rust from the surface of the remaining metal. Paint the affected area with rust inhibiting paint; if the back of the rusted area is accessible treat this also.

Before filling can take place it will be necessary to block the hole in some way. This can be achieved by the use of one of the following materials: Zinc gauze, Aluminium tape or Polyurethane foam.

Zinc gauze is probably the best material to use for a large hole. Cut a piece to the approximate size and shape of the hole to be filled, then position it in the hole so that its edges are below the level of the surrounding bodywork. It can be retained in position by several blobs of filler paste around its periphery.

Aluminium tape should be used for small or very narrow holes. Pull a piece off the roll and trim it to the approximate size and shape required, then pull off the backing paper (if used) and stick the tape over the hole; it can be overlapped if the thickness of one piece is insufficient. Burnish down the edges of the tape with the handle of a screwdriver or similar, to ensure that the tape is securely attached to the metal underneath.

Polyurethane foam is best used where the hole is situated in a section of bodywork of complex shape, backed by a small box section (eg where the sill panel meets the rear wheel arch on most cars). The usual mixing procedure for this foam is as follows: put equal amounts of fluid from each of the two cans provided in the kit, into one container. Stir until the mixture begins to thicken, then quickly pour this mixture into the hole, and hold a piece of cardboard over the larger apertures. Almost immediately the polyurethane will begin to expand, gushing out of any small holes left unblocked. When the foam hardens it can be cut back to just below the level of the surrounding bodywork with a hacksaw blade.

Bodywork repairs – filling and respraying

Before using this Section, see the Sections on dent, deep scratch, rust holes and gash repairs.

Many types of bodyfiller are available, but generally speaking those proprietary kits which contain a tin of filler paste and a tube of resin hardener are best for this type of repair. A wide, flexible plastic or nylon applicator will be found invaluable for imparting a smooth and well contoured finish to the surface of the filler.

Mix up a little filler on a clean piece of card or board – use the hardener sparingly (follow the maker's instructions on the pack) otherwise the filler will set too rapidly or too slowly.

Using the applicator apply the filler paste to the prepared area: draw the applicator across the surface of the filler to achieve the correct contour and to level the filler surface. As soon as a contour that approximates the correct one is achieved, stop working the paste – if you carry on too long the paste will become sticky and begin to 'pick up' on the applicator. Continue to add thin layers of filler paste at twenty-minute intervals until the level of the filler is just proud of the surrounding bodywork.

Once the filler has hardened, excess can be removed using a metal plane or file. From then on, progressively finer grades of abrasive paper should be used, starting with a 40 grade production paper and finishing with 400 grade wet-and-dry paper. Always wrap the abrasive paper around a flat rubber, cork, or wooden block – otherwise the surface of the filler will not be completely flat. During the smoothing of the filler surface the wet-and-dry paper should be periodically rinsed in water. This will ensure that a very smooth finish is imparted to the filler at the final stage.

At this stage the 'dent' should be surrounded by a ring of bare metal, which in turn should be encircled by the finely 'feathered' edge of the good paintwork. Rinse the repair area with clean water, until all of the dust produced by the rubbing-down operation has gone.

Spray the whole repair area with a light coat of primer – this will show up any imperfections in the surface of the filler. Repair these imperfections with fresh filler paste or bodystopper, and once more smooth the surface with abrasive paper. If bodystopper is used, it can be mixed with cellulose thinners to form a really thin paste which is ideal for filling small holes. Repeat this spray and repair procedure until you are satisfied that the surface of the filler, and the feathered edge of the paintwork are perfect. Clean the repair area with clean water and allow to dry fully.

The repair area is now ready for final spraying. Paint spraying must be carried out in a warm, dry, windless and dust free atmosphere. This condition can be created artificially if you have access to a large indoor working area, but if you are forced to work in the open, you will have to pick your day very carefully. If you are working indoors, dousing the floor in the work area with water will 'lay' the dust which would otherwise be in the atmosphere. If the repair area is confined to one body panel, mask off the surrounding panels; this will help to minimise the effects of a slight mis-match in paint colours. Bodywork fittings (eg chrome strips, door handles etc) will also need to be removed or masked off. Use genuine masking tape and several thicknesses of newspaper for the masking operations.

Before commencing to spray, agitate the aerosol can thoroughly, then spray a test area (an old tin, or similar) until the technique is mastered. Cover the repair area with a thick coat of primer; the thickness should be built up using several thin layers of paint rather than one thick one. Using 400 grade wet-and-dry paper, rub down the surface of the primer until it is really smooth. While doing this, the work area should be thoroughly doused with water, and the wet-and-dry paper periodically rinsed in water. Allow to dry before spraying on more paint.

Spray on the top coat, again building up the thickness by using several thin layers of paint. Start spraying in the centre of the repair area and then using a circular motion, work outwards until the whole repair area and about 2 inches of the surrounding original paintwork is covered. Remove all masking material 10 to 15 minutes after spraying on the final coat of paint.

Allow the new paint at least two weeks to harden, then, using a paintwork renovator or a very fine cutting paste, blend the edges of the paint into the existing paintwork. Finally, apply wax polish.

5 Major body damage – repair

Where serious damage has occurred or large areas need renewal due to neglect, it means certainly that completely new sections or panels will need welding in and this is best left to professionals. If the damage is due to impact it will also be necessary to completely check the alignment of the body shell structure. Due to the principle of construction the strength and shape of the whole car can be affected by damage to a part. In such instances the services of a workshop with specialist checking jigs are essential. If a body is left misaligned it is first of all dangerous as the car will not handle properly and secondly uneven stresses will be imposed on the steering, engine and transmission, causing abnormal wear or complete failure. Tyre wear may also be excessive.

6 Maintenance – hinges

Once every six months or 6000 miles (10 000 km) the door, bonnet, and boot hinges should be oiled with a few drops of engine oil from an oil can. The door striker plates can be given a thin smear of grease to reduce wear and ensure free movement.

7 Windscreen and frame (Tourer) – removal and refitting

1 The windscreen is removed complete with the frame. Commence by removing the interior trim panel forward of the doors each side (under the dash board). The panels are retained by four or six screws each side.
2 Prise free the sealing material which covers the windscreen retaining bolt holes. Unscrew and remove the bolts together with the plain and spring washers.
3 Unscrew and remove the three windscreen frame to hand grip screws each side and lift the windscreen and frame clear (photo). The glass can be removed by unscrewing the two screws at the top and bottom corners of the frame to angle bracket. Disconnect the frame sections and remove the glass and seal.
4 Refitting is a reversal of the removal procedure but engage all the bolts before tightening. Use a new glass seal if necessary, and fit the glass to the frame as follows:

(a) First make a check of the top and bottom frame rails against the curve of the glass and if necessary reset to suit, allowing a maximum tolerance margin of $\frac{1}{8}$ in (3·2 mm)
(b) To reset the rails, fit their rear face onto a soft wood block, and gripping by hand on each side (about 1 foot apart) carefully slide the rail to and fro whilst applying a gradual pressure to reshape the rail as necessary
(c) When the glass is inserted into the frame, ensure that the corners are correctly seated and aligned and then retighten the screws

8 Windscreen and rear window (Coupe) – removal and refitting

To remove the rear window follow paragraphs 6 onwards
1 Remove the rear view mirror which is secured by two screws.
2 Detach the windscreen wiper arms and blades.
3 Unscrew and remove the right and left-hand side filler retaining screws – seven each side – and detach the fillets.
4 Unscrew and remove the front windscreen fillet retaining screws

7.3 The windscreen support/grab handle

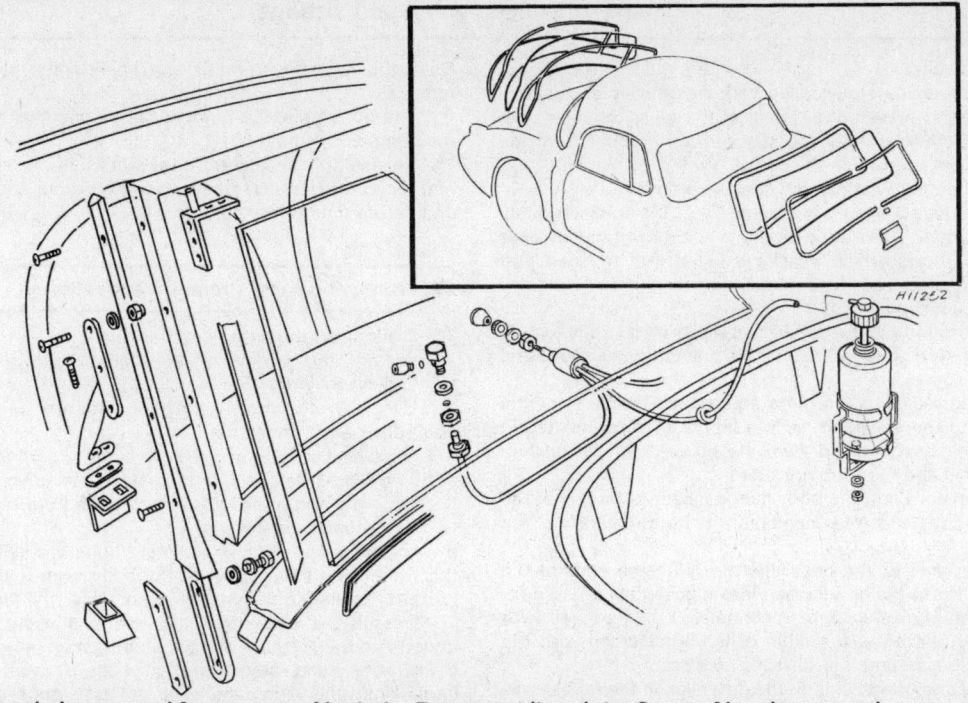

Fig. 12.2 The windscreen and frame parts of both the Tourer and (inset) the Coupe. Also shown are the components of the windscreen washer unit (Sec 7)

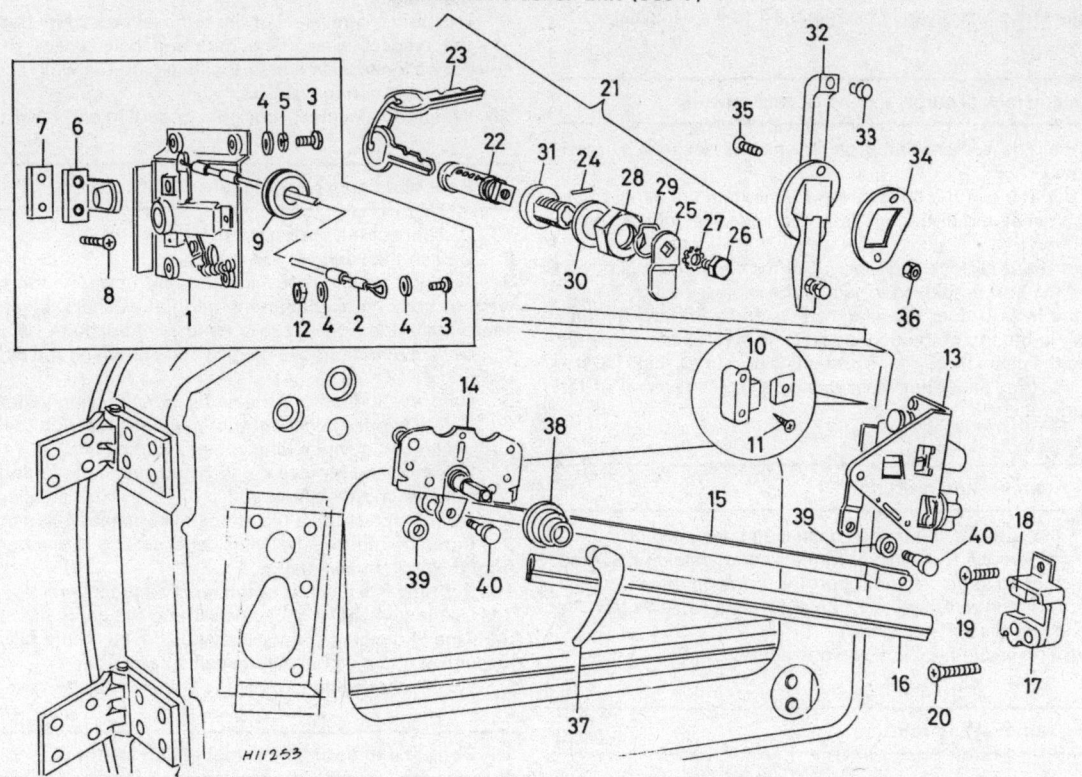

Fig. 12.3 The door catch and lock components of the Tourer (inset) and Coupe (Sec 9)

1 Lock assembly (RH)	12 Nut	21 Lock assembly	31 Lock housing
2 Cable	13 Lock (RH)	22 Lock cylinder	32 Handle
3 Screw	14 Remote-control mechanism	23 Key	33 Rubber insert
4 Washer	(RH)	24 Peg	34 Washer
5 Washer	15 Link	25 Latch	35 Screw
6 Striker plate	16 Sleeve	26 Bolt	36 Nut
7 Plate	17 Striker plate (RH)	27 Washer	37 Handle
8 Screw	18 Plate	28 Locknut	38 Escutcheon assembly
9 Grommet	19 Screw	29 Washer	39 Rubber washer
10 Buffer assembly	20 Screw	30 Washer	40 Rivet
11 Screw			

Chapter 12 Bodywork and fittings

(5 off) and detach the fillet.
5 The glass can now be carefully eased from the housing and seal.
6 From inside the car press out a corner of the glass together with the rubber surround and carefully pull the surround rubber from the metal edge of the glass aperture in the body.
7 The windscreen or rear window can now be removed.
8 If the front glass was broken it is essential that the demister ducts and tubing are separated from the heater box and blown out to clear the minute glass particles which will have fallen into the demister ducts. Also clear any pieces of glass from the channel in the surround rubber and renew it if it has been cut.
9 If the rubber surround has hardened or deteriorated in any way, it is best to fit a new strip. This will also help prevent leaks round the edge of the glass.
10 Fit the rubber surround to the glass and, where fitted, assemble the outer finishers to the surround using a length of cord inserted in the channel. As the cord is withdrawn, the finisher can be pushed firmly into the channel and the cappings fitted.
11 Insert a length of cord into the body flange locating channel of the rubber surround with the ends overlapping at the bottom centre of the windscreen.
12 Offer the windscreen to the body aperture with the ends of the cord inside the car. Press the windscreen into place while an assitant pulls each end of the cord; the rubber channel will then engage with the body flange. Tap all round the edge of the windscreen with the palm of the hand to ensure that it is correctly located.
13 Inject a sealing compound beneath the outer lips of the rubber surround, preferably using a dispenser to distribute the compound evenly. Remove any excess compound with a paraffin soaked rag.
14 Reverse the procedure given in paragraphs 1 to 4 as applicable.

9 Door trim and lock (Tourer) – removal and refitting

1 Remove the side screen clamp plate which is secured by three retaining screws.
2 Unscrew and remove the ten screws which retain the panel to the door, lower the panel and disengage from the lipped rail of the pocket lower edge.
3 Disconnect the door lock cable from the top forward bracket and make a note of the hole employed to secure the cable.
4 Remove the lock to door retaining screws and withdraw the lock via the opening in the top of the door pocket. As the lock and cable are extracted, feed the cable through the protective grommet, (Fig. 12.3).
5 Refitting the trim panel and door lock is a direct reversal of the removal procedure.

10 Soft-top – removal and refitting

1 To remove the soft-top unit it must be in the folded position.
2 Unscrew and remove the soft-top frame to body retaining screws on one side and get an assistant to support the frame on that side.
3 Now unscrew and remove the frame to body screws on the opposite side and lift the soft-top clear.
4 Refitting is a reversal of the removal procedure.

11 Bumpers – removal and refitting

Rear
1 Unscrew and remove the bumper retaining nuts to the frame each side. Wire brush then clean and apply some penetrating oil to ease removal and note the spring and plain washers.
2 Detach the number plate light wire and remove the bumper.
3 The overriders and support brackets can be unbolted from the bumper once removed.
4 Refitting is a reversal of the removal procedure but new spring washers should be fitted.

Front
5 The front bumper unit is retained by four mounting brackets which are attached to the front chassis extension. Unscrew and remove the four securing nuts with their spring and plain washers. Wire brush clean the nuts and threads and apply some penetrating oil to ease removal.
6 The overriders and bumper corner sections can be unbolted once the bumper is removed.
7 Reassembly and refitting the front bumper unit is a reversal of the removal procedure. Use new spring washers and locate the complete unit before tightening the nuts.

12 Front wing panel – removal and refitting

1 Disconnect the battery earth cable.
2 Detach the wiring at the connectors to the headlights and side/indicator lights.
3 Unscrew and remove the four nuts and bolts retaining the wing rear edge on the underside.
4 Unscrew and remove the six bolts and spring and plain washers securing the baffle panel to the body and remove the panel.
5 Unscrew and remove the three bolts from the front edge adjacent to the bumper outer section.
6 Unscrew and remove the nine bolts and spring and flat washers that retain the wing panel to the body from underneath and the two bolts at the rear corner working from under the bonnet.
7 Detach the side panel trim within the car (just forward of the doors) and then remove the two upper panel bolts.
8 Unscrew and remove the four bolts from the body side panel and carefully lift the wing panel clear. An assistant should support the wing during the removal of the final bolts to prevent it from falling off and being damaged.
9 Refitting is a reversal of the removal procedure but before tightening the respective securing nuts and bolts check that the panel is correctly aligned. Use a new seal between the wing and body and also renew the old spring washers.
10 When reconnected, check the operation of the lights.

13 Rear wing panel – removal and refitting

1 Disconnect the battery earth lead.
2 Detach the wiring to the rear lights.
3 Working underneath the rear wing unscrew and remove the five wing to body bolts with spring and flat washers. Clean the heads and soak in penetrating oil to ease removal of the bolts.
4 Unscrew and remove the five bolts retaining the baffle panel to the wing.
5 Unscrew and remove the baffle panel to wing flange bolt.
6 Carefully prise away the trim panel rear section (behind the seats), and unscrew the upper wing corner securing bolt.
7 Unscrew and remove the two nuts and bolts from the underside of the wing securing the front end.
8 Detach and remove the door striker panel screws to the wing.
9 Carefully remove the wing panel pulling it rearwards to detach it from the striker panel flange.
10 Refitting is a reversal of the removal procedure.
11 Use a new piping seal when fitting the wing and ensure that both the wing and piping are correctly positioned before fully tightening the respective retaining bolts, nuts and screws.
12 When reconnected, check the operation of the rear lights.

14 Bonnet and boot lid – removal and refitting

1 The removal of both the bonnet and boot lid are similar and are therefore both covered in this Section.
2 Raise the bonnet/boot lid and support it. Mark the outline around the hinge location using a soft lead pencil. This acts as a location guide for refitting.
3 Unscrew and remove the retaining nuts whilst an assistant supports the bonnet/boot lid and carefully lift it clear.
4 Refitting is the reverse of the removal procedure but align the bonnet/boot before fully tightening the retaining nuts.

15 Doors – removal and refitting

1 Mark an outline around the hinges with the door fully open to give

Chapter 12 Bodywork and fittings

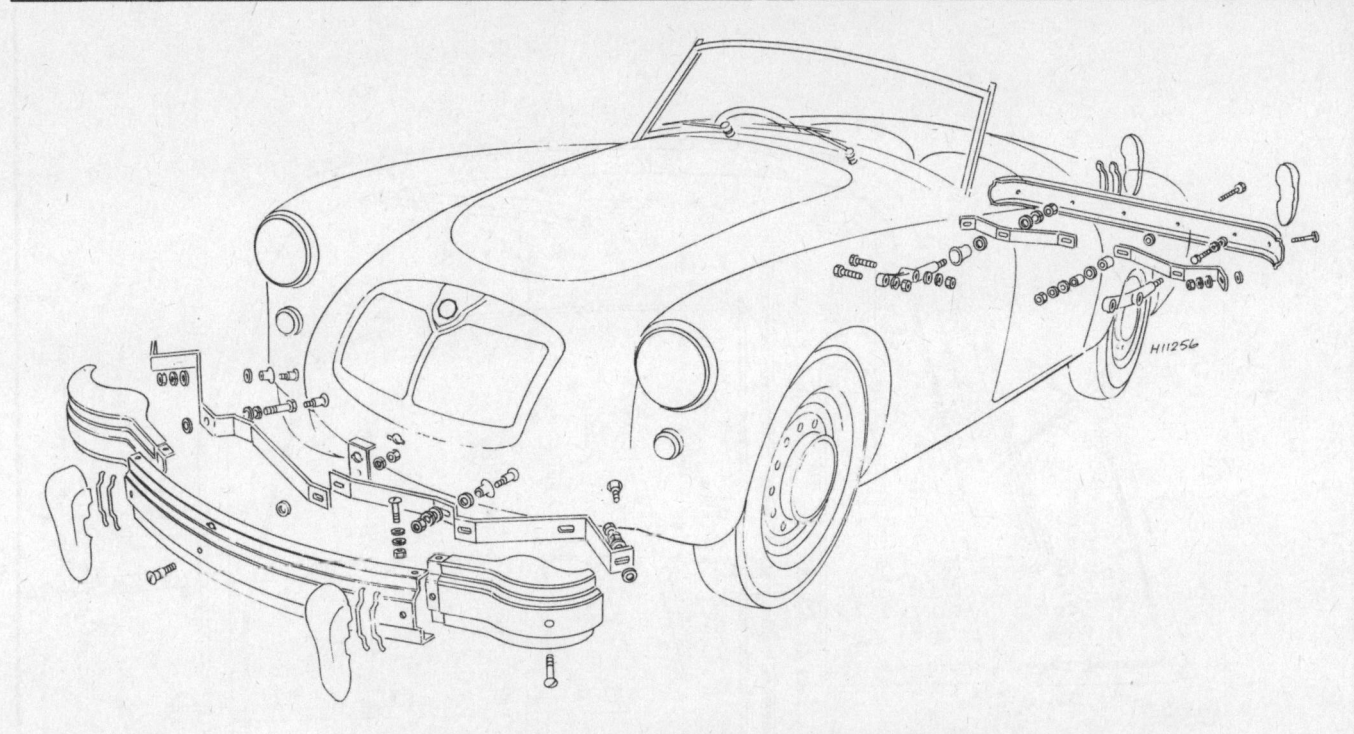

Fig. 12.4 The bumper assembly components front and rear (Sec 11)

an indication of the correct alignment position when refitting (photo).
2 Unscrew and remove the hinge to door pillar retaining screws on each hinge while an assistant supports the door. When the hinges are detached remove the door and note any packing behind the hinges.
3 Refitting is the reverse of the removal procedure but align the doors before fully tightening the retaining screws. Add or subtract packing washers between the hinges and the tapping plate as required (photo).

16 Door windows, window regulators and locks (Coupe model) – removal and refitting

Door windows
1 Remove the door top finisher panel which is retained by three screws.
2 Unscrew and remove the door pull and plate.
3 To remove the door lock and window winder handles, compress the escutcheon pieces so that the respective handle shanks are exposed and using a small punch or nail, push out the handle retaining pins. Withdraw the handles and escutcheon plates.
4 Detach the door trim panel which is retained in position by eight recessed screws and cup washers.
5 Detach the seal from the door aperture and then unscrew and remove the two screws retaining the window channel brackets at the top, (one each side). Extract the bottom channel felt and remove the bottom bracket screws.
6 Raise the window to the fully shut position and then remove the ventilator window self locking nut and tension spring through the aperture in the door. Lift the ventilator window clear.
7 Unscrew and remove the two barrel nuts retaining the window frame to the door, and the three waist rail finisher to door screws. The finisher can then be prised up and away from the door.
8 Detach the wooden glass stop attached to the door top rear inner face, lift the glass and extract the quadrant arm from the lifting channel and withdraw the glass. The frame and window assembly can then be lifted out.
9 Refitting is a reversal of the removal procedure. Renew the channel and seal if they are worn.

Window regulator
10 Unscrew and remove the six regulator-to-door inner panel retaining screws and disengage the regulator. Remove it through the aperture in the inner panel.
11 Refitting is a reversal of the removal procedure.

Door lock
12 Unscrew and remove the remote control unit-to-door retaining screws and also the four lock shut face screws. Withdraw the lock with remote control and link from the door.
13 Refitting is a reversal of the removal procedure.

17 Body – removal and refitting

If an extensive renovation is to be undertaken on the body and/or chassis and running gear, the body can be removed as a unit for improved access to the various components. Before rushing into this course of action, consideration must be given to certain important factors these being:

15.1 Mark an outline of the hinge position before removal

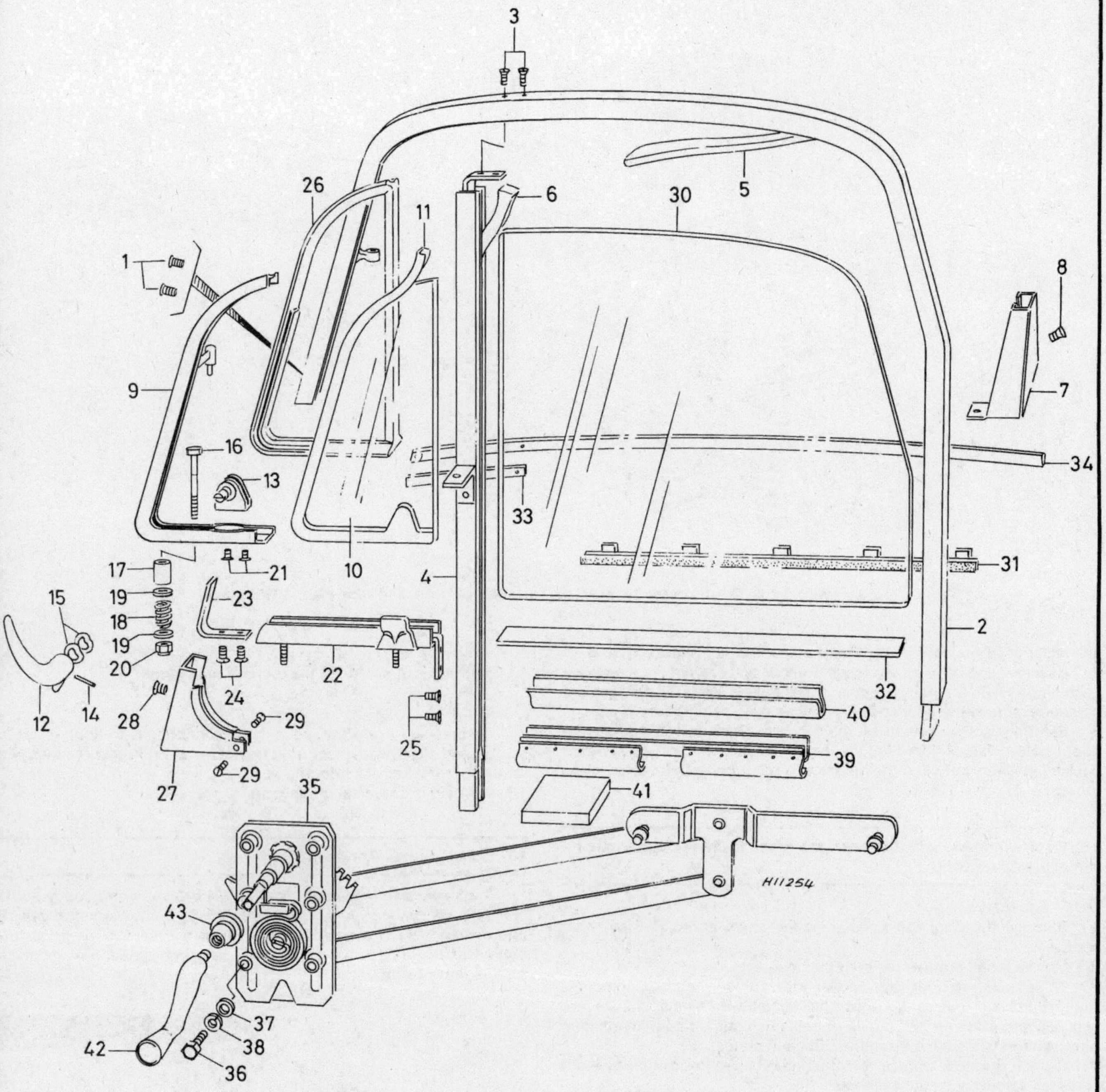

182

Fig. 12.5 The door window and regulator components of the Coupe (Sec 16)

1 Screws	12 Locking handle	23 Vent corner bracket	34 Finisher
2 Frame surround	13 Bracket	24 Screw	35 Regulator
3 Channel screws	14 Pin	25 Screw	36 Screw
4 Vertical channel	15 Washer	26 Vent surround (rubber)	37 Flat washer
5 Felt strip	16 Pivot bolt	27 Blending piece	38 Spring washer
6 Felt strip	17 Sleeve	28 Screw	39 Channel
7 Blending piece	18 Spring	29 Screw	40 Glazing strip
8 Screw	19 Flat washer	30 Glass	41 Buffer
9 Frame of vent	20 Nut	31 Weatherstrip	42 Regulator handle
10 Vent glass	21 Screw	32 Weatherstrip	43 Escutcheon
11 Glazing strip	22 Channel	33 Packing	

Chapter 12 Bodywork and fittings

(a) The reasons must warrant the effort
(b) Do you have somewhere to store and work on the body/chassis once separated?
(c) Do you have a comprehensive tool kit sufficient to undertake such a task?
(d) When the body is ready to be lifted clear you will need a suitable lifting hoist and sling. A prominant rusting point is around the body sills and central side members of the floor and therefore ensure that the unit is structurally sound enough in this critical area before lifting or you could well end up with two halves.
(e) Read through the instructions first to get an idea of what is involved and any possible requirements

1 Disconnect the following wiring

(a) Battery earth lead
(b) Starter motor low tension lead from the solenoid
(c) The wires to the dynamo
(d) The coil SW connection
(e) The horn wires
(f) Snap connectors located at rear of front wheel arches

2 Disconnect the oil gauge pipe from the flexible hose connection.
3 Disconnect the hydraulic brake connection to the three way connector on the chassis and drain the fluid into a container.
4 Disconnect the clutch hydraulic pipe from its flexible hose.
5 Unscrew and detach the tachometer drive cable from the engine and detach the speedometer drive cable clip on the bulkhead.
6 On Twin Cam models drain the cooling system and detach the header tank.
7 Disconnect the temperature gauge sender unit connection from the engine (overhead valve engine models) or from the thermostat housing (Twin Cam engine models).
8 Disconnect the choke cable from the carburettors, and remove the carburettor air cleaner. Remove the carburettors on Twin Cam models
9 Drain the cooling system and remove the radiator.
10 Detach and remove the bumpers front and rear, together with the support brackets.
11 Working underneath the car disconnect the speedometer drive cable from the gearbox.
12 Drain and remove the fuel tank.
13 Working inside the car disconnect the upper steering column clamp to body bracket.
14 Unscrew and remove the nine engine bulkhead bolts along its top forward edge.
15 Disconnect the brake and clutch pedal unit bracket from the bulkhead. These bolts are accessible from within the car each side of the pedals.
16 The body mounting fastenings can now be detached. In some cases where the bolts are severely rusted you may have to cut the bolts through with a hacksaw.
17 Unscrew and remove the small nut and bolt securing the baffle plate to the lower flange at the front of the front wing and the remaining baffle retaining bolts.
18 Remove the bolts retaining the body valances each side to the frame posts.
19 Working through the radiator grille the two nuts and bolts at the front on each side.
20 Detach the inner trim panels from the body sides immediately in front of the doors and lift free the loose trim cover from the body mounting bracket. Unscrew and remove the body bracket to chassis frame retaining bolts each side.
21 From underneath the car, remove the bolt immediately in front of the rear wheel arch in each side.
22 From within the boot unscrew and remove the two bolts from each side retaining the rear of the body to the chassis.
23 The body should now be ready for removal from the chassis frame. Check that all fastenings are detached before lifting.
24 Lift the body carefully and initially manoeuvre it forwards slightly to enable it to disengage from the protruding front mounting brackets. Once clear of the brackets, lift the body upwards and away from the chassis and running gear.
25 If the body is to be renovated its not a bad system to rest it on a suitable trolley frame giving it a nice working height. This can be fabricated using a wooden box frame allowing access within and around the body.
26 Refitting the body to the chassis is a reversal of the removal procedure but note the following:

(a) Renew the respective mounting bolts and also the laminated cork mountings. Ensure that the mountings are squarely located
(b) Renew the rubber strips fitted along the longitudinal chassis members, crossmember in front of the battery and the bulkhead crossmember
(c) Locate all of the main fastenings before finally tightening them

General repair procedures

Whenever servicing, repair or overhaul work is carried out on the car or its components, it is necessary to observe the following procedures and instructions. This will assist in carrying out the operation efficiently and to a professional standard of workmanship.

Joint mating faces and gaskets

Where a gasket is used between the mating faces of two components, ensure that it is renewed on reassembly, and fit it dry unless otherwise stated in the repair procedure. Make sure that the mating faces are clean and dry with all traces of old gasket removed. When cleaning a joint face, use a tool which is not likely to score or damage the face, and remove any burrs or nicks with an oilstone or fine file.

Make sure that tapped holes are cleaned with a pipe cleaner, and keep them free of jointing compound if this is being used unless specifically instructed otherwise.

Ensure that all orifices, channels or pipes are clear and blow through them, preferably using compressed air.

Oil seals

Whenever an oil seal is removed from its working location, either individually or as part of an assembly, it should be renewed.

The very fine sealing lip of the seal is easily damaged and will not seal if the surface it contacts is not completely clean and free from scratches, nicks or grooves. If the original sealing surface of the component cannot be restored, the component should be renewed.

Protect the lips of the seal from any surface which may damage them in the course of fitting. Use tape or a conical sleeve where possible. Lubricate the seal lips with oil before fitting and, on dual lipped seals, fill the space between the lips with grease.

Unless otherwise stated, oil seals must be fitted with their sealing lips toward the lubricant to be sealed.

Use a tubular drift or block of wood of the appropriate size to install the seal and, if the seal housing is shouldered, drive the seal down to the shoulder. If the seal housing is unshouldered, the seal should be fitted with its face flush with the housing top face.

Screw threads and fastenings

Always ensure that a blind tapped hole is completely free from oil, grease, water or other fluid before installing the bolt or stud. Failure to do this could cause the housing to crack due to the hydraulic action of the bolt or stud as it is screwed in.

When tightening a castellated nut to accept a split pin, tighten the nut to the specified torque, where applicable, and then tighten further to the next split pin hole. Never slacken the nut to align a split pin hole unless stated in the repair procedure.

When checking or retightening a nut or bolt to a specified torque setting, slacken the nut or bolt by a quarter of a turn, and then retighten to the specified setting.

Locknuts, locktabs and washers

Any fastening which will rotate against a component or housing in the course of tightening should always have a washer between it and the relevant component or housing.

Spring or split washers should always be renewed when they are used to lock a critical component such as a big-end bearing retaining nut or bolt.

Locktabs which are folded over to retain a nut or bolt should always be renewed.

Self-locking nuts can be reused in non-critical areas, providing resistance can be felt when the locking portion passes over the bolt or stud thread.

Split pins must always be replaced with new ones of the correct size for the hole.

Special tools

Some repair procedures in this manual entail the use of special tools such as a press, two or three-legged pullers, spring compressors etc. Wherever possible, suitable readily available alternatives to the manufacturer's special tools are described, and are shown in use. In some instances, where no alternative is possible, it has been necessary to resort to the use of a manufacturer's tool and this has been done for reasons of safety as well as the efficient completion of the repair operation. Unless you are highly skilled and have a thorough understanding of the procedure described, never attempt to bypass the use of any special tool when the procedure described specifies its use. Not only is there a very great risk of personal injury, but expensive damage could be caused to the components involved.

Conversion factors

Length (distance)
Inches (in)	X	25.4	= Millimetres (mm)	X	0.0394	= Inches (in)
Feet (ft)	X	0.305	= Metres (m)	X	3.281	= Feet (ft)
Miles	X	1.609	= Kilometres (km)	X	0.621	= Miles

Volume (capacity)
Cubic inches (cu in; in³)	X	16.387	= Cubic centimetres (cc; cm³)	X	0.061	= Cubic inches (cu in; in³)
Imperial pints (Imp pt)	X	0.568	= Litres (l)	X	1.76	= Imperial pints (Imp pt)
Imperial quarts (Imp qt)	X	1.137	= Litres (l)	X	0.88	= Imperial quarts (Imp qt)
Imperial quarts (Imp qt)	X	1.201	= US quarts (US qt)	X	0.833	= Imperial quarts (Imp qt)
US quarts (US qt)	X	0.946	= Litres (l)	X	1.057	= US quarts (US qt)
Imperial gallons (Imp gal)	X	4.546	= Litres (l)	X	0.22	= Imperial gallons (Imp gal)
Imperial gallons (Imp gal)	X	1.201	= US gallons (US gal)	X	0.833	= Imperial gallons (Imp gal)
US gallons (US gal)	X	3.785	= Litres (l)	X	0.264	= US gallons (US gal)

Mass (weight)
Ounces (oz)	X	28.35	= Grams (g)	X	0.035	= Ounces (oz)
Pounds (lb)	X	0.454	= Kilograms (kg)	X	2.205	= Pounds (lb)

Force
Ounces-force (ozf; oz)	X	0.278	= Newtons (N)	X	3.6	= Ounces-force (ozf; oz)
Pounds-force (lbf; lb)	X	4.448	= Newtons (N)	X	0.225	= Pounds-force (lbf; lb)
Newtons (N)	X	0.1	= Kilograms-force (kgf; kg)	X	9.81	= Newtons (N)

Pressure
Pounds-force per square inch (psi; lbf/in²; lb/in²)	X	0.070	= Kilograms-force per square centimetre (kgf/cm²; kg/cm²)	X	14.223	= Pounds-force per square inch (psi; lbf/in²; lb/in²)
Pounds-force per square inch (psi; lbf/in²; lb/in²)	X	0.068	= Atmospheres (atm)	X	14.696	= Pounds-force per square inch (psi; lbf/in²; lb/in²)
Pounds-force per square inch (psi; lbf/in²; lb/in²)	X	0.069	= Bars	X	14.5	= Pounds-force per square inch (psi; lbf/in²; lb/in²)
Pounds-force per square inch (psi; lbf/in²; lb/in²)	X	6.895	= Kilopascals (kPa)	X	0.145	= Pounds-force per square inch (psi; lbf/in²; lb/in²)
Kilopascals (kPa)	X	0.01	= Kilograms-force per square centimetre (kgf/cm²; kg/cm²)	X	98.1	= Kilopascals (kPa)
Millibar (mbar)	X	100	= Pascals (Pa)	X	0.01	= Millibar (mbar)
Millibar (mbar)	X	0.0145	= Pounds-force per square inch (psi; lbf/in²; lb/in²)	X	68.947	= Millibar (mbar)
Millibar (mbar)	X	0.75	= Millimetres of mercury (mmHg)	X	1.333	= Millibar (mbar)
Millibar (mbar)	X	0.401	= Inches of water (inH$_2$O)	X	2.491	= Millibar (mbar)
Millimetres of mercury (mmHg)	X	0.535	= Inches of water (inH$_2$O)	X	1.868	= Millimetres of mercury (mmHg)
Inches of water (inH$_2$O)	X	0.036	= Pounds-force per square inch (psi; lbf/in²; lb/in²)	X	27.68	= Inches of water (inH$_2$O)

Torque (moment of force)
Pounds-force inches (lbf in; lb in)	X	1.152	= Kilograms-force centimetre (kgf cm; kg cm)	X	0.868	= Pounds-force inches (lbf in; lb in)
Pounds-force inches (lbf in; lb in)	X	0.113	= Newton metres (Nm)	X	8.85	= Pounds-force inches (lbf in; lb in)
Pounds-force inches (lbf in; lb in)	X	0.083	= Pounds-force feet (lbf ft; lb ft)	X	12	= Pounds-force inches (lbf in; lb in)
Pounds-force feet (lbf ft; lb ft)	X	0.138	= Kilograms-force metres (kgf m; kg m)	X	7.233	= Pounds-force feet (lbf ft; lb ft)
Pounds-force feet (lbf ft; lb ft)	X	1.356	= Newton metres (Nm)	X	0.738	= Pounds-force feet (lbf ft; lb ft)
Newton metres (Nm)	X	0.102	= Kilograms-force metres (kgf m; kg m)	X	9.804	= Newton metres (Nm)

Power
Horsepower (hp)	X	745.7	= Watts (W)	X	0.0013	= Horsepower (hp)

Velocity (speed)
Miles per hour (miles/hr; mph)	X	1.609	= Kilometres per hour (km/hr; kph)	X	0.621	= Miles per hour (miles/hr; mph)

*Fuel consumption**
Miles per gallon, Imperial (mpg)	X	0.354	= Kilometres per litre (km/l)	X	2.825	= Miles per gallon, Imperial (mpg)
Miles per gallon, US (mpg)	X	0.425	= Kilometres per litre (km/l)	X	2.352	= Miles per gallon, US (mpg)

Temperature

Degrees Fahrenheit = (°C x 1.8) + 32   Degrees Celsius (Degrees Centigrade; °C) = (°F - 32) x 0.56

*It is common practice to convert from miles per gallon (mpg) to litres/100 kilometres (l/100km), where mpg (Imperial) x l/100 km = 282 and mpg (US) x l/100 km = 235

Index

A

Antifreeze mixture – 67

B

Battery
    charging – 136
    electrolyte replenishment – 136
    maintenance and inspection – 135
    removal and refitting – 135
Bodywork and fittings
    body
        removal and refitting – 181
    bonnet and boot lids
        removal and refitting – 180
    bumpers
        removal and refitting – 180
    doors
        removal and refitting – 180
    door trim and lock (Tourer)
        removal and refitting – 180
    door windows, window regulators and locks (Coupé models)
        removal and refitting – 181
    front wing panel
        removal and refitting – 180
    general description – 173
    maintenance
        bodywork and underframe – 173
        hinges – 178
        upholstery and carpets – 173
    major body damage repair – 178
    minor body damage repair – 177
    rear wing panel
        removal and refitting – 180
    soft top
        removal and refitting – 180
    windscreen and frame (Tourer)
        removal and refitting – 178
    windscreen and rear window (Coupé models)
        removal and refitting – 178

Bodywork repair sequence (colour) – 174, 175
Braking system
    bleeding the hydraulic system – 119
    brake master cylinder unit (Dunlop brakes)
        removal and refitting – 130
    brake pedal adjustment – 132
    disc brake pads
        inspection, removal and refitting – 119
    drum brake adjustment – 118
    drum brake shoes
        removal, inspection and refitting – 119
    Dunlop brake calliper
        dismantling and assembly – 126
    Dunlop disc and calliper nuts
        removal and refitting – 126
    fault diagnosis – 133
    general description – 118
    handbrake adjustment – 118
    handbrake cable
        removal and refitting – 132
    handbrake friction pads (Dunlop system)
        removal, inspection and refitting – 122
    hydraulic pipes and hoses
        inspection, removal and refitting – 127
    Lockheed brake calliper and disc units
        reassembly and refitting – 123
        removal and dismantling – 123
    Lockheed brake/clutch master cylinder
        removal and refitting – 130
    master cylinder
        dismantling and overhaul – 132
    specifications – 117
    wheel cylinder
        removal, overhaul and refitting – 127
Bulb renewal
    front side and indicator lights – 143
    headlights – 143
    instrument panel lights – 146
    number plate lights – 146
    tail and stop lights – 146
Buying spare parts – 7

Index

C

Carburettor
- dismantling – 73
- inspection and renovation – 73
- removal and refitting – 73
- synchronisation – 75

Clutch
- clutch and brake pedals
  - removal and refitting – 94
- clutch hydraulic system
  - bleeding – 90
- clutch master cylinder (dual type)
  - removal, dismantling, inspection, reassembly and refitting – 93
- clutch master cylinder (separate type)
  - removal, dismantling, inspection, reassembly and refitting – 92
- clutch release bearing unit – 94
- clutch slave cylinder
  - removal, dismantling, inspection, reassembly and refitting – 93
- clutch unit
  - dismantling and inspection – 91
  - removal and refitting – 90
- fault diagnosis – 94
- general description – 89
- maintenance and adjustment – 90
- reassembly – 92
- specifications – 89

Cooling system
- antifreeze mixture – 67
- draining – 62
- fanbelt
  - adjustment – 67
  - removal and refitting – 67
- fault diagnosis – 68
- filling – 62
- flushing – 62
- general description – 60
- header tank (Twin Cam engines)
  - dismantling and reassembly – 65
- radiator
  - removal and refitting – 62
- specifications – 60
- temperature gauge – 68
- thermostat
  - removal, testing and refitting – 63
- water pump
  - removal and refitting – 65
- water pump (overhead valve engines)
  - dismantling and reassembly – 65
- water pump (Twin Cam engines)
  - dismantling and reassembly – 65

E

Electrical system
- battery
  - charging – 136
  - electrolyte replenishment – 136
  - maintenance and inspection – 135
  - removal and refitting – 135
- bulb renewal
  - front, side and indicator lights – 143
  - headlights – 143
  - instrument panel lights – 146
  - number plate lights – 146
  - tail and stop lights – 146
- dynamo
  - dismantling and inspection – 137
  - removal and refitting – 137
  - repair and assembly – 137
  - routine maintenance – 136
  - testing in position – 136
- fault diagnosis – 155
- fuses general – 142
- general description – 135
- headlights
  - adjustment – 143
  - sealed beam renewal – 143
- heater unit – 149
- horns
  - fault tracing and rectification – 142
- instrument panel switches and gauges
  - removal and refitting – 146
- radios and tape players
  - fitting accessories – 149
  - suppression of interference – 153
- regulator and cut-out controls
  - maintenance – 142
- regulator control box
  - general information – 142
- specifications – 134
- starter motor
  - dismantling and reassembly – 141
  - general description – 139
  - removal and refitting – 141
  - testing in position – 139
- starter motor drive
  - general description – 141
  - removal and assembly – 141
- voltage regulator adjustment – 142
- windscreen wiper
  - arms and blades – 146
  - fault diagnosis – 149
  - mechanism maintenance – 146
- windscreen wiper motor, general and wheelbox
  - removal and refitting – 149

Engine (overhead valve engines)
- ancillary components – 26
- big-ends and main bearings
  - examination and renovation – 35
- camshaft and camshaft bearings
  - examination and renovation – 35
- camshaft engine frontplate – 40
- camshaft removal – 29
- components
  - examination and renovation – 34
- connecting rods, big-end bearings and pistons – 29
- connecting rods to crankshaft – 40
- crankcase cylinder bores and engine mountings
  - examination and renovation – 35
- crankshaft and main bearings
  - examination and renovation – 34
  - removal – 32
- crankshaft refitting – 38
- cylinder head
  - decarbonising and servicing – 36
  - refitting – 44
- cylinder head and rocker assembly – 26
- dismantling – 26
- distributor drive gear – 29
- distributor drive gear and distributor – 46
- engine and gearbox removal – 24
- engine without gearbox
  - removal – 26
- fault diagnosis – 47
- final assembly prior to refitting – 46
- flywheel and engine rear plate – 32
- flywheel and starter ring
  - examination and renovation – 38
- flywheel refitting – 40
- gauze strainer, oil pump and rear end plate – 40
- general description – 24
- initial start-up after major overhaul – 47
- lubrication system – 32
- major operations only possible with engine removed – 24
- major operations possible with engine fitted – 24
- oil filter renewal – 33
- oil pressure relief valve
  - removal and refitting – 34
- oil pump
  - examination and renovation – 37
  - reassembly and refitting – 40

pistons and connecting rods – 38
pistons and piston rings
    examination and renovation – 35
pistons, connecting rods and gudgeon pins
    dismantling – 29
pistons, piston rings, connecting rods and gudgeon pins
    reassembly – 38
piston rings – 32
reassembly – 38
refitting – 46
removal methods – 24
rocker armshaft assembly
    examination and renovation – 36
    dismantling – 27
    reassembly – 44
specifications – 19
sump
    examination and renovation – 37
    refitting – 40
sump, oil pump and strainer – 29
tappets
    examination and renovation – 36
tappets and tappet covers – 44
timing chain tensioner
    examination and renovation – 36
timing cover, sprockets and chain assembly – 27
timing gears and chain
    examination and renovation – 36
timing sprockets, chain, tensioner and cover – 40
valve
    removal – 27
valve clearance
    adjustment – 44
valve guides
    renewal – 27
valves and springs
    reassembly to cylinder head – 44
valves and valve seats
    examination and renovation – 37

Engine (Twin Cam engines)
ancillary components – 50
camshafts
    refitting – 56
    removal – 51
camshafts and camshaft bearings
    examination and renovation – 54
components
    examination and renovation – 87
connecting rods and big-end bearings
    examination and renovation – 54
crankcase and engine mounting
    examination and renovation – 54
crankshaft and main bearings
    examination and renovation – 54
    reassembly – 54
    removal – 53
cylinder bores
    examination and renovation – 54
cylinder head
    refitting – 55
    removal – 50
cylinder head, valves and valve seats
    decarbonisation and servicing – 54
dismantling – 50
distributor drivegear – 59
engine and gearbox – 50
engine front plate – 52
engine front plate and half-speed shaft – 55
engine without gearbox – 49
fault diagnosis – 59
final assembly – 59
flywheel – 55
flywheel and starter ring
    examination and renovation – 54
flywheel/starter ring – 53
general description – 49

gudgeon pins and connecting rod small-end bushes – 53
half-speed shaft – 53
initial start up after major overhaul – 59
lubrication system – 53
major operations possible with engine removed – 49
major operations possible with engine fitted – 49
oil filter renewal – 53
oil pressure relief valve
    removal, inspection and fitting – 53
oil pump and gauze strainer – 55
oil seals – 54
piston rings – 55
pistons and connecting rods
    reassembly – 55
    removal – 53
pistons and piston rings
    examination and renovation – 54
reassembly – 54
refitting – 59
specifications – 22
sump and oil pump assembly
    examination and renovation – 54
sump, oil pump and strainer – 52
tappet clearances
    checking and adjusting – 56
timing chain adjustment – 56
timing chain, sprockets and tensioner
    examination and renovation – 54
timing cover, sprockets and chain – 52
timing gears and half-speed shaft
    examination and renovation – 54
timing sprockets and chain – 56
valve guides – 52
valve timing – 57
valves – 51

F

Fuel and exhaust systems
air cleaners
    removal, maintenance and refitting – 70
carburettor jet
    adjustment and tuning – 74
    centralizing – 74
carburettors
    dismantling – 73
    inspection and renovation – 73
    removal and refitting – 73
    synchronisation – 75
exhaust system and manifolds – 79
fault diagnosis, fuel system – 80
float chamber unit
    removal, overhaul, fuel level adjustment and refitting – 72
fuel gauge sender unit – 79
fuel pump
    maintenance and fault checks – 75
    removal and refitting – 75
fuel tank
    cleaning – 79
    removal and refitting – 79
general description – 69
specifications – 69
SU carburettor
    general description – 70
    main faults and remedies – 70
SU electric fuel pump – 75

G

Gearbox
dismantling – 96
dismantling, general – 96
examination and renovation – 100
fault diagnosis – 105

Index

general description – 96
mainshaft and gearbox – 101
removal and installation – 96
specifications – 95
General dimensions – 5
General repair procedures – 184

I

Ignition system
condenser
removal, testing and refitting – 82
contact breaker points – 2
distributor
dismantling – 84
inspection and repair – 84
lubrication – 84
reassembly – 84
removal and refitting – 84
distributor contact breaker points – 82
fault diagnosis – 88
general description – 81
sparking plugs and leads – 86
specifications – 81
static ignition timing – 84

J

Jacking – 10

L

Lubrication charts – 11, 12

M

Metric conversion tables – 185

P

Propeller shaft
general description – 106
removal and refitting – 106
specifications – 106
universal joints
dismantling – 109
inspection and repair – 106
reassembly – 109

R

Rear axle
differential unit
dismantling and examination – 114
reassembly – 114
removal and refitting – 113
fault diagnosis – 116
general description – 110
half-shaft (drum brake models)
removal and refitting – 111
half-shaft (rear disc brake models)
removal and refitting – 111
pinion oil seal
removal and refitting – 111
rear axle unit
removal and refitting – 110
rear hub
removal and refitting – 111
specifications – 110
Routine maintenance – 14

S

Safety information – 13
Spark plug chart (colour) – 83
Starter motor
dismantling and reassembly – 141
general description – 139
removal and refitting – 141
testing in position – 139
Suspension and steering
anti-roll bar
removal and refitting – 161
fault diagnosis – 172
front coil springs
removal and refitting – 161
front shock absorbers
removal and refitting – 162
front hub (disc brakes)
removal and refitting – 165
front hub (drum brakes)
removal and refitting – 162
front hub bearings (Dunlop disc brakes)
adjustment – 165
front wheel alignment
checking and adjustment – 170
general description – 161
kingpins
removal and refitting – 167
kingpins and links
dismantling, inspection and assembly – 167
rear hub unit
dismantling and overhaul – 167
rear shock absorbers
removal and refitting – 171
rear springs
removal and refitting – 171
rubber suspension bushes – 167
specifications – 160
steering column
removal and refitting – 168
steering column universal joint
removal and refitting – 168
steering gearbox
dismantling and assembly – 169
removal and refitting – 168
steering wheel
removal and refitting – 167
suspension, steering and shock absorbers
inspection for wear – 161
tie-rod outer balljoints
removal and refitting – 170
wheels and tyres
maintenance – 172

T

Tools and working facilities – 8

U

Use of English – 6

V

Vehicle identification numbers – 7

W

Wheels and tyres – 172
Wiring diagrams – 156 to 159